Exponential Data Fitting and its Applications

Editors: V. Pereyra and G. Scherer

We dedicate this book to the memory of Gene H. Golub (1932-2007) and Herbert B. Keller (1925-2008), teachers, mentors, colleagues and dear friends. Gene and Herb with colleagues. Cumana, Venezuela, October 2007.

CONTENTS

CHAPTERS

Foreword

Exponential data fitting has a long history theoretically, algorithmically, and in its applications. Despite its widespread use and success there has been no unified presentation of the subject available. This book attempts to fill the gap. The problem and some of the most successful and proven algorithms for its solution are presented in detail. Then a number of experts in different fields describe their applications and specific models. This combination will alert many other researchers to what is out there and how their problems relate to various applications across disciplines. The editors have done a commendable job in assembling this material. They are experts in the field. We thank them for sharing their knowledge.

Michael Saunders
Stanford University

Preface

Exponential approximations are ubiquitous in scientific computing. There are many reasons for their success in modeling various phenomena. Processes that are modeled by linear differential equations with constant coefficients and Fourier expansions are just two such reasons. In particular, wave propagation problems in their many expressions are heavily represented because wave fronts in the far field are plane, and plane waves are described by complex exponentials.

In this volume we consider the least squares approximation of data by linear combinations of real or complex exponentials. In the first chapter, Pereyra and Scherer discuss the problem from a mathematical and numerical point of view, giving an historical perspective and detailed description of some of the most successful and frequently used methods. The Variable Projection (VP) method, introduced in 1973 by Golub and Pereyra, extending the initial contribution of Gutman, Pereyra and Scolnik, is carefully discussed as the nonlinear least squares method of choice. Prony's method and its more numerically stable variants are also discussed, as they are also frequently used in many applications. Some comparisons and discussion of advantages and shortcomings are included.

Various applications are then considered by experts in their respective fields. A common thread in these chapters is a fairly comprehensive presentation of the physical problem, then a discussion of the methods used by that particular community. Among these methods we find prominently the ones described in Chapter 1 and some of their variations.

In Chapter 2, Sima, Poullet and Van Huffel consider the problem of fitting Nuclear Magnetic Resonance (NMR) spectroscopic data from *in vivo* and *in vitro* biological specimens. They include a particularly detailed description of the NMR phenomenon and give important information on data preprocessing that experience through the years has indicated is necessary for handling the various sources of noise and complications inherent in this type of data.

The multi-disciplinary team of Paluzny, Lentini, M. Martin, R. Martin and Torres in Chapter 3 go into a different application of NMR, namely Imaging, as it pertains to brain tumor segmentation and identification.

Leaving Biology and Medicine we jump to High Energy Physics in Chapter 4, where Cohen, Fleming and Lin consider an application in Lattice Quantum Field Theory. Historically it is interesting to find that Fleming discovered some of the tools used in this approach from studying the NMR literature.

We then switch to a more generic algorithmic contribution in Chapter 5 by Kaufman, which extends the Variable Projection techniques to problems with multiple data sets, where a common set of nonlinear parameters is desired and where careful implementation can produce large savings in storage and computing time.

In Chapter 6, Mullen and van Stokkum consider in detail the problem of Time-Resolved Spectroscopy data. For multi-spectral data, tensor approximations are a natural tool and we find the type of problems considered by Kaufman in the previous chapter.

Hansen, Nielsen, Ankj{\ae}rgaard, & Jain in Chapter 7 attack the modeling of Optically Stimulated Luminescense by linear combinations of exponentials, sharing their experience and comparing two different models and two different techniques: VP and a Fredholm integral equation of the first kind approach.

In Chapter 8, Rust, O'Leary and Mullen study the modeling of Supernova Light curves using exponentials.

Finally, in Chapter 9, Srivastava, Suaya, Pereyra and Banerjee consider the application of exponential approximations to problems of electromagnetic wave propagation in modern chip design technology.

It is remarkable how in this apparently disparate ensemble of applications, rather few numerical algorithms have proven to be the tools of choice. Thus we hope that other practitioners will benefit from the insights given in this book and find that the same tools are useful in their own fields of application.

Taking advantage of the electronic nature of this book, some of the authors have added unconventional material that can be downloaded. Hyperlinks and brief descriptions are given in appendices to the chapters. This material includes computer programs, scripts, and data that will allow reproduction of some of the results. In general, colored boxes around some material indicate active links to Chapters, Sections, figures, cross-references, citations, external URL's or to the above mentioned additional materials.

We would like to thank all who have made it possible to complete this collaborative effort, and most specially Per Christian Hansen for his help in editing several of the chapters.

Victor Pereyra, Mountain View, CA
Godela Scherer, Reading, GB
September 2009

Contributors

Christina Ankjærgaard
Radiation Research Division, Riso National Laboratory for Sustainable Energy, Technical University of Denmark, DK-4000 Roskilde, Denmark; cank@risoe.dtu.dk

Kaustav Banerjee
Department of Electrical and Computer Engineering
University of California
Santa Barbara, CA 93106, USA
kaustav@ece.ucsb.edu

Saul D. Cohen
Thomas Jefferson National Accelerator Facility
Newport News, VA 23606, USA
sdcohen@jlab.org

George T. Fleming
Department of Physics, Yale University
New Haven, CT 06520, USA
George.Fleming@yale.edu

Per Christian Hansen
Department of Informatics and Mathematical Modelling
Technical University of Denmark, DK-2800 Kgs. Lyngby
Denmark; pch@imm.dtu.dk

Mayank Jain
Radiation Research Division, Riso National Laboratory for Sustainable Energy, Technical University of Denmark, DK-4000 Roskilde, Denmark
maja@risoe.dtu.dk

Linda Kaufman
Coach House, Room 213, Computer Science Dept., William Patterson University, Wayne, NJ 07470. kaufmanl@wpunj.edu

Marianela Lentini
Escuela de Matematicas
Universidad Nacional de Colombia
Sede Medellin; maclentingi@unal.edu.co

Huey-Wen Lin
Department of Physics
University of Washington
Seattle, WA 98195
hwlin@phys.washington.edu

Rafael Martín
Centro de Fisica Molecular y Medica
Escuela de Fisica, Facultad de Ciencias,
Universidad Central de Venezuela
Caracas, Venezuela; rmartinlandrove@yahoo.es

Miguel Martín-Landrove
Centro de Fisica Molecular y Medica, Escuela de Fisica
Facultad de Ciencias
Universidad Central de Venezuela y Centro de Diagnóstico Docente
Las Mercedes, Caracas, Venezuela; mmartin@fisica.ciens.ucv.ve

Katharine M. Mullen
Ceramics Division
National Institute of Standards and Technology (NIST)
100 Bureau Drive, M/S 8520
Gaithersburg, MD, 20899, USA
kmullen@nist.gov

Dianne P. O'Leary
Computer Science Department and Institute for Advanced Computer Studies
University of Maryland
College Park, MD 20742; and
National Institute of Standards and Technology
Gaithersburg, MD 20899-8910
oleary@cs.umd.edu

Hans Bruun Nielsen
Department of Informatics and Mathematical Modelling
Technical University of Denmark
DK-2800 Kgs. Lyngby, Denmark; hbn@imm.dtu.dk

Marco Paluszny
Escuela de Matematicas
Universidad Nacional de Colombia, Medellín; mpalusznyk@unal.edu.co

Victor Pereyra
Weidlinger Associates Inc. (retired), 399 W. El Camino Real, #200
Mountain View, CA 94040, USA.; and
Computational Sciences Research Institute
San Diego State University
San Diego, CA, USA
pereyra@wai.com

Jean-Baptiste Poullet
Formerly with Department of Electrical Engineering ESAT-SCD
Katholieke Universiteit Leuven, Kasteelpark Arenberg 10, 3001
Leuven-Heverlee, Belgium jeanbaptistepoullet@gmail.com

Bert W. Rust
Mathematical and Computational Sciences Division
National Institute of Standards and Technology (NIST)
100 Bureau Drive, MS 8910
Gaithersburg, MD 20899-8910, USA
bert.rust@nist.gov

Godela Scherer
Mathematics Department
University of Reading, UK.
A.Scherer@reading.ac.uk

Diana M. Sima
Department of Electrical Engineering ESAT-SCD
Katholieke Universiteit Leuven
Kasteelpark Arenberg 10, 3001
Leuven-Heverlee, Belgium
diana.sima@esat.kuleuven.be

Navin Srivastava
Mentor Graphics Corporation
8005 SW Boeckman Rd,
Wilsonville, Oregon 97070, USA
Navin_Srivastava@mentor.com

Roberto Suaya
Mentor Graphics Corporation
110 rue Blaise Pascal
38334 St Ismier Cedex, France
Roberto_Suaya@mentor.com

Wuilian Torres
Centro de Procesamiento Digital de Imagenes, Instituto de Ingenieria y
Laboratorio de Computacion Grafica y Geometria Aplicada
Escuela de Matematica
Facultad de Ciencias
Universidad Central de Venezuela
Caracas, Venezuela; wtorres@fii.org

Sabine Van Huffel
Department of Electrical Engineering ESAT-SCD
Katholieke Universiteit Leuven
Kasteelpark Arenberg 10, 3001
Leuven-Heverlee, Belgium.
Sabine.VanHuffel@esat.kuleuven.be

Ivo H. M. van Stokkum
Department of Physics and Astronomy
Faculty of Sciences,
Vrije Universiteit Amsterdam
de Boelelaan 1081, 1081 HV Amsterdam,
The Netherlands; ivo@nat.vu.nl

CHAPTER 1

Exponential data fitting

Victor Pereyra,
Computational Sciences Research Institute
San Diego State University
San Diego, CA, USA
vpereyra@yahoo.com

Godela Scherer
Mathematics Department
University of Reading, UK.
A.Scherer@reading.ac.uk

Abstract. In this initial chapter we consider some of the basic methods used in the fitting of data by real and complex linear combinations of exponentials. We have selected the classes of methods that are most frequently used in many different fields: variable projections for solving this separable nonlinear least squares problem, derivatives and variants of Prony's method, which rely on evenly sampled data and take special advantage of the particular form of the approximation and finally the matrix-pencil method. We also have implemented some of these techniques and compared them in a few examples to support some comments on their advantages and disadvantages and exemplify their performance in terms of computing time and robustness, specially considering that this is a notoriously ill-conditioned problem in many cases.

Keywords Exponential data fitting; separable nonlinear least squares; Prony's method

1.1. Introduction

Fitting data with linear combinations of real or complex exponentials is pervasive within many disciplines in Sciences and Engineering. Since Gaspard Riche de Prony invented a method in 1795 [**14**] to solve this problem for evenly spaced samples there have been many developments and applications. We will survey some of the more successful ones and then let leading experts from different fields describe their applications and experiences.

One obvious reason why these types of approximation functions are important is that combinations of exponentials are solutions of homogeneous linear ordinary differential equations and as such they naturally model many different physical processes. Thus, if we have measurements of a quantity that can be modelled by the solution of such an equation, fitting this data to a linear combination of exponentials can give valuable information on decay rates or other material properties of the physical system. Also, exponentials have good approximation properties on compact domains and, of course, complex exponentials lead to Fourier expansions.

If we know the exponents and are only interested in the coefficients of the linear combination and if we choose to minimize the l_2 norm of the residuals between observed and calculated values, then this fitting is a linear least squares problem. The interesting and more challenging case though, is when we want not only the weights but also the exponents, which leads to a nonlinear least squares problem. As indicated by Beylkin and Monzon [**5**], this is akin to Fourier series with adaptive exponents that can lead to more concise approximations as exemplified in a number of challenging examples.

It was observed (see [**17, 19, 21**]) that it is very useful to separate the treatment of the weights from that of the parameters appearing nonlinearly. Although the context of so-called separable problems is more general than fitting exponentials, the latter one turns out to have many successful applications.

Many algorithms have been developed for separable nonlinear least squares problems (**SNLS**). The *variable projections* algorithm designed and analyzed by G. Golub and V. Pereyra [**17**] uses nonlinear optimization techniques to compute the nonlinear parameters. A computer program (VARPRO was developed and put in the public domain). This program had great impact in many disciplines, as shown in the survey paper [**19**] and in several chapters of this book.

Another set of techniques, somewhat misnamed as "linear methods," are of importance because of their prevalence in the application fields. Among them are the Prony-type or polynomial methods, so called because the nonlinear parameters are obtained from the roots of a characteristic polynomial. The variants of this method differ in the way the coefficients of the polynomial are defined. An important variant is the *Modified Prony* method, originated by M. Osborne in [**37**]. It extends the "Prony method" for extracting sinusoidal or exponential signals from uniformly sampled time series data when there is no noise, to the case when the signal is imbedded in noise. The modified Prony method has been exhaustively analyzed [**39, 40**] for fitting with exponentials or other functions that satisfy a linear difference equation with constant coefficients, and a MATLAB program by G. K. Smyth, one of the coauthors, is available on the Internet [**56**]. In this approach, the coefficients of the polynomial are obtained by solving a generalized eigenproblem.

Another Prony-type method is the linear prediction algorithm presented in [**35, 51**]. It follows the general structure of the Prony method but uses a truncated singular value decomposition (TSVD) of a Hankel matrix defined by the noisy signal to solve for the polynomial coefficients. This allows one to determine the number of representative exponential terms of the fitting function that is appropriate for the noise level.

These algorithms use numerical linear algebra techniques, but generalized eigenvalues and zeros of polynomials are hardly linear problems, so that is the reason against cataloging them as "linear techniques".

A different approach that uses the separability of the approximating model is found in the subspace-based matrix-pencil methods. We outline below the HTLS/HSVD methods, extensively analysed and used by the Katholieke Universiteit Leuven group [**31, 51**]. (See also the chapter in this book by Sima, Poullet and Van Huffel.) They also start with a Hankel matrix of the data but define a multiple right-hand side linear least squares problem by comparing a Vandermonde and an SV decomposition. The nonlinear parameters are obtained by solving this problem.

Last but not least, alternatively to separation of linear and nonlinear variables, nonlinear optimization techniques can also be applied directly to the full functional problem. A prominent position in this approach is held by the secant type code NL2SOL [**13**], used for example in AMARES, a software for biomedical applications. It has the advantage of ease in incorporating *a priori* knowledge about the parameters.

A detailed survey of exponential fitting with many references and interesting discussions can be found in [**25**]. Some pitfalls on the indiscriminate use of the results of exponential fitting are discussed in [**54**]. See also [**61**] for an interesting discussion on the potential ill-conditioning of these problems that was already pointed out by Lanczos in 1956 [**30**]. In the following sections we will review some of these methods and compare them on several examples.

Acknowledgement

We would like to thank P. C. Hansen and M. Saunders for reading carefully this chapter and making many suggestions that considerably improved its presentation.

1.2. Solving separable nonlinear least squares problems with variable projections

A separable nonlinear least squares problem was defined in [**17**], as one for which the model used to approximate the data is a linear combination of nonlinear functions that can depend on multiple parameters. The ith component of the residual vector is written as

$$r_i(\mathbf{a}, \boldsymbol{\alpha}) = y_i - \sum_{j=1}^{n} a_j \phi_j(\boldsymbol{\alpha}; t_i), \ i = 1, \ldots, N, \qquad N > n + k. \tag{1.1}$$

Here the t_i are independent variables associated with the observations y_i, while the $\mathbf{a} = \{a_j\}$ and the components of the k-dimensional vector $\boldsymbol{\alpha}$ are the parameters to be determined by minimizing the functional $||\mathbf{r}(\mathbf{a}, \boldsymbol{\alpha})||_2^2$, where $|| \cdot ||_2$ stands for the l_2 vector norm, i.e., the functional to be minimized is the sum of squares of the residuals. We can write this functional using matrix notation as

$$r(\mathbf{a}, \boldsymbol{\alpha}) = \|r(\mathbf{a}, \boldsymbol{\alpha})\|_2^2 = \|\mathbf{y} - \boldsymbol{\Phi}(\boldsymbol{\alpha})\mathbf{a}\|_2^2, \tag{1.2}$$

where the columns of the matrix $\boldsymbol{\Phi}(\boldsymbol{\alpha})$ correspond to the nonlinear functions $\phi_j(\boldsymbol{\alpha};t_i)$ of the k parameters $\boldsymbol{\alpha}$ evaluated at all the t_i values, and the vectors $\mathbf{a}$ and $\mathbf{y}$ represent the linear parameters and the observations respectively. The minimization problem is then,

$$\min_{\mathbf{a}, \boldsymbol{\alpha}} \|r(\mathbf{a}, \boldsymbol{\alpha})\|_2^2. \tag{1.3}$$

Now it is easy to see that if we knew the nonlinear parameters $\boldsymbol{\alpha}$, then the linear parameters $\mathbf{a}$ could be obtained by solving the linear least squares problem:

$$\mathbf{a} = \boldsymbol{\Phi}(\boldsymbol{\alpha})^+ \mathbf{y}, \tag{1.4}$$

which stands for the minimum-norm solution of the linear least squares problem (1.2) for fixed $\boldsymbol{\alpha}$, where $\boldsymbol{\Phi}(\boldsymbol{\alpha})^+$ is the Moore-Penrose generalized inverse of

$\mathbf{\Phi}(\alpha)^1$(which can be ill-conditioned or even rank-deficient). Substituting this $\mathbf{a}$ into the original functional gives the problem

$$\min_{\alpha} \|(\mathbf{I} - \mathbf{\Phi}(\boldsymbol{\alpha})\mathbf{\Phi}(\boldsymbol{\alpha})^{+})\mathbf{y}\|_2^2, \tag{1.5}$$

where the linear parameters have been eliminated. Some good references for non-numeric persons further reading on these basic concepts are [**7, 20**].

We define,

$$\mathbf{r}_{VP}\ (\boldsymbol{\alpha}) = (\mathbf{I} - \mathbf{\Phi}(\boldsymbol{\alpha})\mathbf{\Phi}(\boldsymbol{\alpha})^{+})\mathbf{y}, \tag{1.6}$$

and call it the *Variable Projection (VP)* of $\mathbf{y}$. Its name stems from the fact that the matrix in parentheses is the projector onto the orthogonal complement of the column space of $\mathbf{\Phi}(\boldsymbol{\alpha})$, which we will denote in what follows by $\mathbf{P}^{\perp}_{\mathbf{\Phi}(\boldsymbol{\alpha})}$. We will also refer to $\|\mathbf{r}_{VP}\ (\boldsymbol{\alpha})\|_2^2$ as the *Variable Projection functional.*

This is a more powerful paradigm than the simple idea of alternating between minimization of the two sets of variables (such as the NIPALS algorithm of Wold and Lyttkens [**62**]), which can be proven theoretically and practically not to result, in general, in the same enhanced performance.

In summary, the Variable Projection algorithm consists of first minimizing (1.5) and then using the optimal value obtained for $\boldsymbol{\alpha}$ to solve for $\mathbf{a}$ in (1.4). One obvious advantage is that the iterative nonlinear algorithm used to solve the first minimization problem works in a space of smaller dimension and in consequence fewer initial guesses are necessary. However, the main payoff of this algorithm is the fact that, as the minima for the reduced functional are better defined than those for the full one, it always converges in fewer iterations than the minimization of the full functional, including convergence when the same minimization algorithm for the full functional diverges (see for instance [**27**]).

Therefore, a different reason to use the reduced functional is to observe from the above results that, since the linear parameters are determined by the nonlinear ones, then the full problem must be increasingly ill-conditioned as, and if, it converges to the optimal parameters. That is probably why the important problem of real or complex exponential fitting is so hard to solve directly. See for instance [**55**] for a theoretical discussion of this issue and an interesting application to the training of nonlinear neural networks [**49, 50, 43**].

It was also proven in the original paper [**17**] that the set of stationary points of the original and reduced functionals are the same. This theorem has been reassuring to many practitioners and has been used to derive other theoretical results in similar situations. Further comments on the basic results can also be found in the textbooks of Seber and Wild [**53**] and Björck [**7**].

1.3. Complex VARPRO

In this Section we consider the development of a Variable Projection type solver (VARPRO) for separable nonlinear least problems (SNLLSQ) [**17, 19**], for the case in which the model is a linear combination of complex exponentials.

We will discuss the essential elements of a modern VARPRO type implementation, without attempting to reproduce all the aspects of the compact original 1973 one, which was constrained by the computer capabilities of that time frame. We

[1] The generalized inverse plays a similar role for rectangular matrices as the inverse does for square ones. For a definition see [**7**].

can do a much simpler job now that memory is not an issue. Also the code can use reliable off-the-shelf open software as available.

Calculation of the VP functional and its derivative. There are two ways to calculate the necessary quantities and we explore them both: Singular Value Decomposition (SVD) or Linear Least Squares (LLSQ). The advantage of the first is that it gives good quantitative information about the condition of the problem and it facilitates its regularization if necessary.

The SVD of the complex matrix $\mathbf{\Phi} = \mathbf{UDV}^*$ always exist. $\boldsymbol{U}, \boldsymbol{V}$ are unitary and $\mathbf{D} = \mathrm{diag}(\sigma_j)$ is diagonal with the same rectangular shape of $\mathbf{\Phi}$, and the * stands for transposed conjugate. The diagonal contains the singular values of $\mathbf{\Phi}$, which are real and non-negative. As in the real case, the SVD is rank revealing: small singular values (relative to the largest) are a sign of ill-conditioning, while in the extreme case, zero singular values indicate rank deficiency. In all cases, truncating the small singular values regularizes the problem and gives the best approximation of that rank to the original matrix in the Frobenius norm.

If we calculate the SVD of the $m \times n$ matrix $\mathbf{\Phi} = \mathbf{UDV}^*$, then the Variable Projection functional can be written as

$$r_{VP}(\boldsymbol{\alpha}) = \left\| \mathbf{U} \begin{bmatrix} 0 & 0 \\ 0 & \mathbf{I}_{m-r} \end{bmatrix} \mathbf{U}^* \mathbf{y} \right\|_2^2 = \left\| \begin{bmatrix} 0 & 0 \\ 0 & \mathbf{I}_{m-r} \end{bmatrix} \mathbf{U}^* \mathbf{y} \right\|_2^2,$$

where r is the numerical rank of $\mathbf{\Phi}$ and we can eliminate the first $\mathbf{U}$ because it is a unitary matrix. Thus, if we call $\widetilde{\mathbf{y}} = \mathbf{U}^*\mathbf{y}$, we have

$$r_{VP}(\boldsymbol{\alpha}) = \sum_{i=r+1}^{m} \widetilde{y_i}^2.$$

Unfortunately most SVD codes compute only the "thin" matrix $\mathbf{U}$ ($m \times n$), which is not sufficient for this calculation. In that case we need to obtain $\mathbf{a}$ as indicated below in 1.9 and then calculate the residual directly as in 1.1.

Gradient. For the complex exponential case, since the gradient of the functional will be real, we need to be careful with how we compute it. First of all we observe that for any complex vector $\mathbf{f}(z)$,

$$D(\mathbf{f}^*\mathbf{f}) = D\mathbf{f}^*\mathbf{f} + \mathbf{f}^*D\mathbf{f} = D\mathbf{f}^*\mathbf{f} + (D\mathbf{f}^*\mathbf{f})^* = 2\Re(D\mathbf{f}^*\mathbf{f}).$$

Here D stands for the *Fréchet* derivative.

Therefore, for $\mathbf{f} = \mathbf{P}_{\mathbf{\Phi}}^{\perp}\mathbf{y}$, we will have

$$\frac{1}{2}\nabla r_{VP}(\boldsymbol{\alpha}) = \Re(\mathbf{y}^* D\mathbf{P}_{\mathbf{\Phi}}^{\perp *}\mathbf{P}_{\mathbf{\Phi}}^{\perp}\mathbf{y}) = -\Re(\mathbf{y}^*(\mathbf{P}_{\mathbf{\Phi}}^{\perp} D\mathbf{\Phi}\mathbf{\Phi}^+ + (\mathbf{P}_{\mathbf{\Phi}}^{\perp} D\mathbf{\Phi}\mathbf{\Phi}^+)^*)\mathbf{P}_{\mathbf{\Phi}}^{\perp}\mathbf{y}),$$

where the expanded expression comes from the derivative of the pseudoinverse as derived in [**17, 19**]. This is a 3-dimensional tensor consisting of the gradients with respect to the vector α of each component of $\mathbf{\Phi}$:

$$D\mathbf{\Phi} = \left\{ \frac{\partial \Phi_{i,j}}{\partial \alpha_l} \right\}.$$

The columns of $\mathbf{\Phi}$ are exponentials sampled at the data points and therefore $D\mathbf{\Phi}$ can be easily generated. But, because of the properties of the pseudoinverse,

$\mathbf{\Phi}^+\mathbf{P}_{\mathbf{\Phi}}^{\perp} = \mathbf{0}$, and therefore the first term in the formula above drops out, leaving

$$\frac{1}{2}\nabla r_{VP}(\boldsymbol{\alpha}) = -\Re(\mathbf{y}^*(\mathbf{P}_{\mathbf{\Phi}}^{\perp}D\mathbf{\Phi}\mathbf{\Phi}^+)^*\mathbf{P}_{\mathbf{\Phi}}^{\perp}\mathbf{y}) = -\Re(\mathbf{y}^*\mathbf{\Phi}^{+*}D\mathbf{\Phi}^*\mathbf{r}_{VP}). \tag{1.7}$$

Hessian. Levenberg-Marquardt's method for solving nonlinear least squares problems (as well as the Gauss-Newton method) uses a simplified Hessian that does not require second derivatives. This approximation is constructed with the Jacobian matrix of the vector residual:

$$\mathbf{H}(\boldsymbol{\alpha}) = \mathbf{J}^*\mathbf{J}, \tag{1.8}$$

where $\mathbf{J} = D\mathbf{P}_{\mathbf{\Phi}}^{\perp}\mathbf{y}$.

From **[17]** we know that

$$\mathbf{J} = -(\mathbf{P}_{\mathbf{\Phi}}^{\perp}D\mathbf{\Phi})\mathbf{\Phi}^+\mathbf{y} - ((\mathbf{P}_{\mathbf{\Phi}}^{\perp}D\mathbf{\Phi})\mathbf{\Phi}^+)^*\mathbf{y}.$$

Kaufman **[26]** has introduced a simplification that does not impair the efficiency of the iterative method and makes the cost of the iterations similar to that for the full functional. Kaufman's simplification consists of dropping the second term in the formula above. This is justified by observing that during calculation of the Hessian some of the terms cancel out. In summary, we can use in 1.8 the approximation:

$$\mathbf{J} = -(\mathbf{P}_{\mathbf{\Phi}}^{\perp}D\mathbf{\Phi})\mathbf{a}.$$

Ruano and his collaborators **[49, 50]** have introduced an interesting analysis that seems to indicate that from Kaufman's idea follows that there is actually a family of equally suitable Jacobians and they have introduced an even more simplified one that works well in their applications.

Alternative: no SVD's. Observing the formulas above we see that there are several multiplications by $\mathbf{\Phi}^+$. These multiplications can be interpreted as LLSQ solves, since

$$\mathbf{\Phi}^+\mathbf{y} = \mathbf{a} \qquad \Leftrightarrow \qquad \min_a \|\mathbf{\Phi}\mathbf{a} - \mathbf{y}\|_2^2.$$

$\mathbf{\Phi}^+\mathbf{y} = \mathbf{a}$ is an overdetermined system of linear equations and therefore a whole sub-space of $\mathbf{y}$'s gets mapped into the same $\mathbf{a}$. Thus, if we solve first these LLSQ problems (same matrix, multiple right-hand sides, a very economical proposition), then

$$\begin{aligned} r_{VP} &= \|\mathbf{y} - \mathbf{\Phi}\mathbf{a}\|_2^2, \\ \frac{1}{2}\nabla \mathbf{r}_{VP}(\boldsymbol{\alpha}) &= -\Re(\mathbf{a}^*D\mathbf{\Phi}^*\mathbf{r}_{\mathbf{VP}}), \\ \mathbf{J} &= -\mathbf{P}_{\mathbf{\Phi}}^{\perp}D\mathbf{\Phi}\mathbf{a}. \end{aligned}$$

Regularized VARPRO using PRAXIS. Sometimes is more expedient to use an optimization code that does not require derivatives to minimize $r_{VP}(\alpha)$. A good choice is the intelligent search method of R. Brent, implemented in the program PRAXIS **[8]**. Observe that by choosing the numerical rank of $\mathbf{\Phi}$ appropriately we will be regularizing the problem in case of severe ill-conditioning or actual rank deficiency (see **[22]** for detailed discussions on ill-conditioned problems). Finally we obtain $\mathbf{a}$ by using a regularized version of (1.4):

$$\mathbf{a} = \mathbf{\Phi}^+\mathbf{y} = \mathbf{V}\mathbf{D}_r^+\mathbf{U}^*\mathbf{y} = \mathbf{V}\mathbf{D}_r^+\widetilde{\mathbf{y}} = \sum_{j=1}^{r} v_{ij}\widetilde{y}_j/\sigma_j, \tag{1.9}$$

where we have assumed that the singular values are in descending order and that we have chosen to truncate the SVD after the first r components, so that $\sigma_{r+1}/\sigma_1 < \tau$, for a given threshold τ.

1.4. Prony-type or polynomial methods

In the next sections we consider the following simplified problem. Given N equally spaced samples of a signal (t_i, y_i), $i = 1, \cdots, N$, $t_i = i\Delta t$, $\Delta t = \frac{1}{N}$, use the model function

$$\mu(t) = \sum_{j=1}^{n} a_j \phi_j(\alpha_j) = \sum_{j=1}^{n} a_j e^{\alpha_j t}, \tag{1.10}$$

with N and n to be defined for each method, in order to interpolate or best fit the data in the least squares sense.

Prony's classical method interpolates a sequence of $N = 2n$ observations by a linear combination of n exponentials, separating the computation of the nonlinear and linear parameters. The method takes advantage of the fact that the $z_j \equiv e^{\alpha_j \Delta t}$ satisfy a linear difference equation that can be written as a recurrence equation,

$$\sum_{k=1}^{n+1} \delta_k E^{k-1}\, \mu(t) = 0, \tag{1.11}$$

where E is the translation operator, $E\,\mu(t) = \mu(t + \triangle t)$, and $\boldsymbol{\delta} = (\delta_1, \delta_2, \cdots, \delta_{n+1})$ are called the *Prony recurrence parameters.*

A more convenient matrix form for the recurrence equation is

$$\mathbf{X}_\delta^\top \boldsymbol{\mu} = \mathbf{0} \tag{1.12}$$

where $\boldsymbol{\mu} = (\mu(t_1), \mu(t_2), \cdots, \mu(t_N))$, and the $(N, N-n)$ matrix $\mathbf{X}_\delta$ is the rectangular Toeplitz matrix

$$\mathbf{X}_\delta = \begin{pmatrix} \delta_1 & & \\ \cdot & \cdot & \\ \cdot & & \cdot \;\; \delta_1 \\ \cdot & & \cdot \\ \delta_{n+1} & & \cdot \\ & & \cdot \\ & & \delta_{n+1} \end{pmatrix}.$$

Alternatively, if $\mathbf{y} = (y_1, y_2, \cdots, y_N)$ is the vector of data and $\mathbf{Y}(\mathbf{y})$ the $(N - n, n + 1)$ Hankel matrix defined using this vector,

$$\mathbf{Y}(\mathbf{y}) = \begin{pmatrix} y_1 & y_2 & \cdots & y_{n+1} \\ \cdot & \cdot & \cdot & \cdot \\ \cdot & & & \\ & & & \\ \cdot & \cdot & \cdot & \cdot \\ y_{N-n} & \cdot & \cdots & y_N \end{pmatrix},$$

then

$$\mathbf{X}_\delta^{\mathbf{T}} \mathbf{y} = \mathbf{Y}(\mathbf{y})\boldsymbol{\delta}.$$

Returning to equation (1.11), the z_j are the roots of the characteristic polynomial associated with $\boldsymbol{\delta}$

$$\delta_{n+1}z^n - \delta_n z^{n-1} - \cdots - \delta_1 = 0.$$

The unknown coefficients δ_k can be determined, assuming that there is no error in the observations, from the linear system of equations

$$\sum_{k=1}^{n+1} \delta_k E^{k-1} y_i = 0, \qquad i = 1, \cdots, n.$$

For the system to be determined, one unknown must be fixed and the Prony choice is $\delta_{n+1} = 1$.

There have been several attempts at adapting the Prony technique to the more general, *approximation* problem, i.e., a generalization to the overdetermined case, when $N \gg 2n$, leading to a least squares approximation to determine the δs. The structure of these Prony-type algorithms is: *Nonlinear stage:*

- Determine the Prony recurrence parameters from a least squares formulation.
- Determine the roots of the characteristic equation.
- Determine the nonlinear parameters α_j by taking $\ln(z_j)$.

Linear stage:

- Insert the α_j into the model and solve the resulting linear least squares problem in the a_j.

The algorithms differ in the techniques used to determine the Prony parameters. The current-day Prony's method and the Pisarenko or covariance method fail for large data sets (see [**40**]). We will describe in more detail the modified Prony method [**37, 38, 39, 40**] and the linear predictor method [**35, 51**]. The following table lists the best known algorithms.

Method	Technique
Classic Prony	Linear system $\mathbf{X}_\delta^\top \mathbf{y} = 0$
Prony	$\min_\delta \mathbf{y}^\top \mathbf{X}_\delta \mathbf{X}_\delta^\top \mathbf{y}, \quad \delta_{n+1} = 1$
Pisarenko	$\min_\delta \mathbf{y}^\top \mathbf{X}_\delta \mathbf{X}_\delta^\top \mathbf{y}, \quad \Vert\boldsymbol{\delta}\Vert_2 = 1$
Linear predictor	$\min_\delta \mathbf{y}^\top \mathbf{X}_\delta \mathbf{X}_\delta^\top \mathbf{y}, \quad \delta_K = 1, \ K > n$
Modified Prony	$\min_\delta \mathbf{y}^\top \mathbf{X}_\delta \mathbf{X}_\delta^+ \mathbf{y}, \quad \Vert\boldsymbol{\delta}\Vert_2 = 1$

The modified Prony method. The modified Prony method described in [**38**] estimates any function $\mu(t)$ that solves a linear homogeneous difference equation. This includes linear combinations of real and complex exponentials and damped/undamped sinusoids, without an *a priori* knowledge of how many terms fit best, but automatically adapting to the most appropriate number, and also, as in the other Prony-type methods, avoiding the evaluation of exponentials.

It will be assumed (see [**38**]) that the minimization problem (1.3) has a single isolated minimum for $\boldsymbol{\alpha}$ in an appropriate subset, and that $\Phi(\boldsymbol{\alpha})$ is continuously differentiable and has full rank there.

To set up a least squares formulation for the Prony parameters $\boldsymbol{\delta}$ we go back to the reduced minimization problem obtained in Section **??** for the nonlinear parameters α

$$r_{VP}(\boldsymbol{\alpha}) = \Vert\mathbf{r}_{VP}(\boldsymbol{\alpha})\Vert_2^2 = ||\mathbf{y} - \mathbf{P}_{\boldsymbol{\Phi}}\mathbf{y}||_2^2 = ||\mathbf{P}_{\boldsymbol{\Phi}}^{\perp}\mathbf{y}||_2^2. \tag{1.13}$$

Here, $\mathbf{P}_{\mathbf{\Phi}} = \mathbf{\Phi}(\boldsymbol{\alpha})\mathbf{\Phi}(\boldsymbol{\alpha})^+$ is the projection onto the column space of $\mathbf{\Phi}$ and $\mathbf{P}_{\mathbf{\Phi}}^{\perp}$ is therefore the projection onto its orthogonal complement. But, if we set $\boldsymbol{\mu} = \mathbf{\Phi}(\boldsymbol{\alpha})\mathbf{a}$, and use (1.12), then $\mathbf{P}_{\mathbf{\Phi}}^{\perp}$ is also the projection onto the column space of $\mathbf{X}_\delta$ and the reformulation as a minimization problem with respect to $\boldsymbol{\delta}$ uses the functional

$$r_{VP}(\boldsymbol{\delta}) = \mathbf{y}^{\mathrm{T}}\mathbf{P}_{X_\delta}\mathbf{y} = \mathbf{y}^{\mathrm{T}}\mathbf{X}_\delta(\mathbf{X}_\delta^{\mathrm{T}}\mathbf{X}_\delta)^{-1}\mathbf{X}_\delta^{\mathrm{T}}\mathbf{y}. \tag{1.14}$$

In this case $\mathbf{X}_\delta^+ = (\mathbf{X}_\delta^{\mathrm{T}}\mathbf{X}_\delta)^{-1}\mathbf{X}_\delta^{\mathrm{T}}$, because assuming that $\mathbf{\Phi}(\boldsymbol{\alpha})$ is a full-rank matrix implies that $\mathbf{X}_\delta$ has full column rank as well. When using the Prony parameters $\boldsymbol{\delta}$ there is one more variable to be determined than when using the minimisation in $\boldsymbol{\alpha}$ (the characteristic polynomial is not monic); thus an additional condition must be added, for example that $\boldsymbol{\delta}$ is normalized: $\boldsymbol{\delta}^T\boldsymbol{\delta} = 1$.

Including a constant term, i.e., choosing $\alpha_1 = 0$ so that

$$\mu(t) = a_1 + \sum_{i=2}^{n} a_i e^{\alpha_i t},$$

is equivalent to imposing a constraint $\sum_{j=1}^{n+1} \delta_j = 0 = \mathbf{g}^\top\boldsymbol{\delta} = 0$ on the parameters, with $\mathbf{e}^\top = (1, 1, \cdots, 1)^\top$.

The objective function to be minimized is then

$$F(\boldsymbol{\delta}, \lambda, \nu) = r_{VP}(\boldsymbol{\delta}) + \lambda(1 - \boldsymbol{\delta}^\top\boldsymbol{\delta}) + 2\nu \boldsymbol{e}^{\boldsymbol{T}}\boldsymbol{\delta}, \tag{1.15}$$

with λ, ν Lagrange multipliers.

Differentiating with respect to $\boldsymbol{\delta}$ and the Lagrange multipliers one obtains the necessary minimization conditions, which take the form of a generalized eigenproblem: Determine λ and $\mathbf{v}$ so that,

$$(\mathbf{A} - \lambda\mathbf{P})\mathbf{v} = 0, \tag{1.16}$$

$$\mathbf{v}^T\mathbf{P}\mathbf{v} = 1 \tag{1.17}$$

where

$$\mathbf{A} = \begin{pmatrix} \mathbf{B}_\delta & \mathbf{g} \\ \mathbf{g}^\top & \mathbf{0} \end{pmatrix}, \quad \mathbf{v} = \begin{pmatrix} \boldsymbol{\delta} \\ \nu \end{pmatrix}, \quad \mathbf{P} = \begin{pmatrix} \mathbf{I}_{n+1} & \mathbf{0} \\ \mathbf{0} & \mathbf{0} \end{pmatrix}.$$

The symmetric $(n+1) \times (n+1)$ matrix $\mathbf{B}_\delta(\boldsymbol{\delta})$ has elements:

$$\mathbf{B}_{\delta_{ij}} = \mathbf{y}^{\mathrm{T}}\mathbf{X}_{\delta_i}(\mathbf{X}_\delta^{\mathrm{T}}\mathbf{X}_\delta)^{-1}\mathbf{X}_{\delta_j}^{\mathrm{T}}\mathbf{y} - \mathbf{y}^{\mathrm{T}}\mathbf{X}_\delta(\mathbf{X}_\delta^{\mathrm{T}}\mathbf{X}_\delta)^{-1}\mathbf{X}_{\delta_i}^{\mathrm{T}}\mathbf{X}_{\delta_j}(\mathbf{X}_\delta^{\mathrm{T}}\mathbf{X}_\delta)^{-1}\mathbf{X}_\delta^{\mathrm{T}}\mathbf{y},$$

where $\mathbf{X}_{\delta_j} = \partial\mathbf{X}_\delta/\partial\delta_j$.

In the case of a model without constant terms, the matrices involved are reduced to $\mathbf{A} = \mathbf{B}_\delta, \quad \mathbf{v} = \boldsymbol{\delta}, \quad \mathbf{P} = \mathbf{I}$.

It can be shown [**38, 39**] that the Lagrange multiplier λ must be zero at a solution of the generalized eigenproblem. The similarity to an eigenproblem suggests the use of an iterative algorithm for linear eigenproblems, where at each step the eigenvalue nearest to zero is chosen as the new $\lambda^{(k+1)}$ and the corresponding vector as $\mathbf{v}^{(k+1)}$. Convergence is assumed when $\lambda^{(k+1)}$ is small compared to $\|\mathbf{B}_\delta\|_2$.

The detailed minimization algorithm is described in [**39**], and the simplifications for exponential fitting are sketched in [**40**]. See also [**38**] for some practical considerations, among them that the algorithm seems to be relatively insensitive to the starting values. The algorithm has been analyzed [**38**] as a nonlinear vector iteration in $\mathbf{v}$ and although it was not possible to obtain an estimate for the convergence rate it was asserted that the iteration will be successful if the functional at the minimum $r_{VP}(\boldsymbol{\delta}^*)$ is small; in data fitting problems this requires small experimental error and that the model be appropriate, i.e., the number of exponential terms must be the correct one.

After the Prony parameters $\boldsymbol{\delta}$ are estimated, the rate constants $z_j = e^{\alpha_j \Delta t}$ are recovered as the roots of the characteristic polynomial:

$$p(z) = \delta_{n+1} z^n + \delta_n z^{n-1} + ... + \delta_1 = 0.$$

Unfortunately, for large values of N, i.e., small Δt (remember $\Delta t = \frac{1}{N}$), this is an ill-conditioned problem because the roots will cluster around 1. Osborne **[41]** analyses this case showing favorable asymptotic results for the convergence of VARPRO type methods that use the Gauss-Newton minimization approach.

There remains the important question of the relation between the critical point sets for the problems $r_{VP}(\boldsymbol{\delta})$ and $\|\mathbf{r}(\mathbf{a}, \boldsymbol{\alpha})\|_2^2$. In fact, the two sets may be different:

$$\min_{\boldsymbol{\delta}} r_{VP}(\boldsymbol{\delta}) \leq \min_{\boldsymbol{\alpha}} r(\boldsymbol{a}, \boldsymbol{\alpha}).$$

The Prony parametrization is more general and may yield a larger set of solutions, including for example repeated roots of the characteristic polynomial. There is, however, a close relation between the two sets as the theorem in **[40]** proves:

"The Prony parametrization does in fact solve the exponential fitting problem in the sense that if $\boldsymbol{\alpha}$ is a minimizer of problem (1.13), then the corresponding elementary symmetric functions give Prony parameters that satisfy the necessary condition (1.16)."

Fast linear prediction method. As mentioned in the Introduction, the fitting technique suggested in **[35]** and **[51]** follows the general structure of the Prony method, but in the process also determines the appropriate number of exponential terms that best represent the data.

In general, even though one knows that the data $\mathbf{y} = (y_1, y_2, \cdots, y_N)$ can be modeled by $y_i \approx \mu(t_i)$, with $\mu(t) = \sum_{i=1}^{n} a_i e^{\alpha_i t}$, where α_1 may be zero, the correct number of terms is generally not known. The model satisfies a difference equation, stated in the digital signal processing literature as a forward linear predictor with coefficients $\mathbf{f} = (f_1, f_2, \cdots, f_K)$, for any $K \geq n$,

$$\mu(t_i) = \sum_{k=1}^{K} f_k \mu(t_{i-k}),$$

or recast in the recurrence equation format,

$$\sum_{k=1}^{K+1} \delta_k \mu(t_{i-k+1}) = 0, \quad i = K+1, ..., N. \tag{1.18}$$

Here $\delta_1 = 1$ and $\delta_{K+1} = f_K, \ k = 1, \cdots, K$.

We define now a $(N-K, K+1)$ Hankel matrix $\bar{\mathbf{Y}}(\boldsymbol{\mu})$ using the $\mu(t_i)$. If the model has n exponential terms, the Hankel matrix has rank n and that is independent of the choice of K. The rank can be computed from the SVD of the "exact" matrix $\bar{\mathbf{Y}}(\boldsymbol{\mu})$, where the singular values $\bar{\sigma}_i$ will be zero from $n+1$ onwards: $\bar{\sigma}_1 \geq \bar{\sigma}_2 \geq \cdots \geq \bar{\sigma}_n > \bar{\sigma}_{n+1} = \cdots = \bar{\sigma}_{K+1} = 0$.

Unfortunately one does not have the exact $\boldsymbol{\mu}$ but the noisy data $\mathbf{y}$. In this case, if one computes the SVD of the $(N-K, K+1)$ Hankel matrix $\mathbf{Y}(\mathbf{y}) = \mathbf{U\Sigma V}^\top$, then the singular values σ_i will all generally be different from zero. One can define n as the *numerical rank* with respect to a given tolerance τ **[20**, p. 261**]** if $\frac{\sigma_{n+1}}{\sigma_1} < \tau$.

This tolerance should be consistent with the data precision; for example, if the data have p correct decimal digits a good choice is $\tau = 10^{-p}$.

The matrix $\mathbf{Y}(\mathbf{y})$ can then be approximated by the truncated SVD (TSVD) expansion [**20**]:

$$\mathbf{Y}(\mathbf{y}) \approx \mathbf{U}_n \mathbf{\Sigma}_n \mathbf{V}_n^\top, \tag{1.19}$$

where $\mathbf{\Sigma}_n$ $(n \times n)$, contains the non-zero singular values of $\mathbf{Y}(\mathbf{y})$ and $\mathbf{U}_n$ $((N-K)\times n)$, $\mathbf{V}_n^\top$ $(n\times(K+1))$ are the corresponding sub-blocks of the unitary matrices involved in the SVD.

One could compute the Prony parameters $\boldsymbol{\delta}$ using the recurrence equation and the matrix $\bar{\mathbf{Y}}(\boldsymbol{\mu})$ if the signals were noiseless: $y_i = \mu(t_i)$,[2]

$$\bar{\mathbf{Y}}(\boldsymbol{\mu})_{:,1:K}\, \mathbf{f} = \bar{\mathbf{Y}}(\boldsymbol{\mu})_{:,K+1}. \tag{1.20}$$

However, this relation is only approximate for the $\mathbf{Y}(\mathbf{y})$ and

$$\mathbf{Y}(\mathbf{y})_{:,1:K}\, \mathbf{f} \approx \mathbf{Y}(\mathbf{y})_{:,K+1},$$

needs to be solved by linear least squares. Inserting the TSVD into (1.20) gives an under-determined system of equations for $\mathbf{f}$:

$$\min \|\mathbf{f}\|_2^2 \text{ such that } \mathbf{V}_{n\, 1:K,1:n}^\top\, \mathbf{f} = \mathbf{V}_{n\, K+1,1:n}{}^\top.$$

After this system is solved for the $K+1$ Prony parameters $\boldsymbol{\delta}$, the relevant roots $z_j = e^{\alpha_j \Delta t}$ of the characteristic equation corresponding to the recurrence (1.18) are computed. Note that there are n roots that should be separated from the other $K-n$ extraneous roots [**51**].

There remain several practical issues: one is the choice of K. In order to obtain a reliable value of n, K should be large - for some applications between $N/3$ and $N/2$. This implies costly computations of both the SVD of $\mathbf{Y}(\mathbf{y})$ and the roots of the characteristic polynomial. In [**35**] there are some pre-processing steps that might reduce these costs.

1.5. Subspace or matrix-pencil method HTLS/HSVD

A subspace-based method starts with the model $\mu(t_i)$ for $t_i = i\triangle t$, $i = 0, \cdots, N-1$, rewritten with the change of variable $e^{\alpha_j t_i} = e^{\alpha_j i \Delta t} = z_j^i$:

$$\mu(t_i) = \sum_{j=1}^{n} a_j z_j^i. \tag{1.21}$$

To describe the algorithm we will assume that the data are noiseless $y_i = \mu(t_i)$. The first step is to arrange the model values in an $L \times M$ Hankel matrix, with L and M greater than n and $L + M = N - 1$, the number of data samples:

$$\bar{\mathbf{Y}}(\boldsymbol{\mu}) = \begin{pmatrix} \mu(t_0) & \mu(t_1) & \dots & \dots & \mu(t_M) \\ \mu(t_1) & \mu(t_2) & \dots & \dots & \mu(t_{M+1}) \\ \cdot & \cdot & \cdot & \cdot & \cdot \\ \cdot & \cdot & \cdot & \cdot & \cdot \\ \mu(t_L) & \mu(t_{L+1}) & \cdot & \cdot & \mu(t_{N-1}) \end{pmatrix}.$$

[2]For convenience we use the *colon notation* for matrices (see [**20**], pp.7): if $\mathbf{A}_{m\times n}$, then $\mathbf{A}_{k,:}$ designates the whole kth-row, whereas $A_{k,i:j}$ denotes the positions between the ith and the jth columns. Similarly for columns.

The optimal values for L and M will be discussed later. It is easy to see that $\bar{\mathbf{Y}}$ can be expressed in terms of matrices where the a_j and z_j appear explicitly - the so-called Vandermode decomposition,

$$\bar{\mathbf{Y}}(\boldsymbol{\mu}) = \bar{\mathbf{S}}\bar{\mathbf{C}}\bar{\mathbf{T}}^\top.$$

Here $\bar{\mathbf{S}}_{(L+1)\times n}$ and $\bar{\mathbf{T}}_{(M+1)\times n}$ are Vandermonde matrices defined by the vector $\mathbf{z} = (z_1, z_2, \cdots, z_n)$, and $\bar{\mathbf{C}} = \mathrm{diag}(a_1, a_2, \cdots, a_n)$,

$$\bar{\mathbf{Y}}(\boldsymbol{\mu}) = \begin{pmatrix} 1 & 1 & \ldots & 1 \\ z_1 & z_2 & \ldots & z_n \\ \ldots & \ldots & \ldots & \ldots \\ z_1^L & z_2^L & \ldots & z_n^L \end{pmatrix} \begin{pmatrix} a_1 & & \\ & a_2 & \\ & & \\ & & a_n \end{pmatrix} \begin{pmatrix} 1 & 1 & \ldots & 1 \\ z_1 & z_2 & \ldots & z_n \\ \ldots & \ldots & \ldots & \ldots \\ z_1^M & z_2^M & \ldots & z_n^M \end{pmatrix}^\top.$$

An interesting property of the matrix $\bar{\mathbf{S}}$ is *shift-invariance.* If $\mathbf{Z} = \mathrm{diag}(\mathbf{z})$, it can easily be proved that

$$\bar{\mathbf{S}}_{2:L+1,:} = \bar{\mathbf{S}}_{1:L,:}\mathbf{Z},$$

where $\bar{\mathbf{S}}_{2:L+1,:}$, $\bar{\mathbf{S}}_{1:L,:}$ are derived by removing respectively the first or the last row from $\bar{\mathbf{S}}$.

On the other hand, the rank of $\bar{\mathbf{Y}}(\boldsymbol{\mu})$ is n. Therefore, in terms of the thin SVD [**20**, p. 72], $\bar{\mathbf{Y}}(\boldsymbol{\mu})$ can be written as $\bar{\mathbf{Y}} = \bar{\mathbf{U}}_n\bar{\mathbf{\Sigma}}_n\bar{\mathbf{V}}_n^\top$, where $\bar{\mathbf{\Sigma}}_n$ contains the non-zero singular values of $\bar{\mathbf{Y}}(\boldsymbol{\mu})$, and $\bar{\mathbf{U}}_n$ $((L+1)\times n)$, $\bar{\mathbf{V}}_{\mathbf{n}}^\top$ $(n \times (M+1))$ are the corresponding sub-blocks of the unitary matrices involved in the normal SVD.

Comparing this expression with the Vandermonde decomposition, one can see that the columns of $\bar{\mathbf{S}}$ and $\bar{\mathbf{U}}_n$ generate the same subspace and can therefore be obtained one from the other by a multiplication with a non-singular matrix $\bar{\mathbf{Q}}$:

$$\bar{\mathbf{U}}_n = \bar{\mathbf{S}}\bar{\mathbf{Q}}.$$

But then $\bar{\mathbf{U}}_n$ inherits the shift-invariance property of $\bar{\mathbf{S}}$:

$$\bar{\mathbf{U}}_{n\ 2:L+1,:} = \bar{\mathbf{U}}_{n\ 1:L,:}\bar{\mathbf{Q}}^{-1}\mathbf{Z}\bar{\mathbf{Q}}. \tag{1.22}$$

The matrix $\bar{\mathbf{Q}}^{-1}\mathbf{Z}\bar{\mathbf{Q}}$ that can be computed from this equation is similar to $\mathbf{Z}$. This implies that by calculating the eigenvalues of $\bar{\mathbf{Q}}^{-1}\mathbf{Z}\bar{\mathbf{Q}}$ one has the elements of the vector $\mathbf{z}$.

In the real case, with noisy data, if the noise-to-signal ratio is small enough, these calculations can be repeated "approximately" using the Hankel matrix $\mathbf{Y}(\mathbf{y})$ instead. Now, as in the previous section, one determines the numerical rank of $\mathbf{Y}(\mathbf{y})$ with respect to a given tolerance. Assuming that it is n, the matrix $\mathbf{Y}(\mathbf{y})$ can be approximated by the rank-n matrix obtained by the TSVD,

$$\mathbf{Y}(\mathbf{y}) \approx \mathbf{Y}_n = \mathbf{U}_n\mathbf{\Sigma}_n\mathbf{V}_n^\top,$$

where $\mathbf{\Sigma}_n = \mathrm{diag}(\sigma_1, \cdots, \sigma_n)$. The matrix $\mathbf{Y}(\mathbf{y})$ has no Vandermonde decomposition, so the shift-invariance equation (1.22) is only approximately valid and the next problem must be solved by least squares:

$$\mathbf{U}_{n\ 2:L+1,:} \approx \mathbf{U}_{n\ 1:L,:}\mathbf{Q}^{-1}\mathbf{Z}\mathbf{Q}. \tag{1.23}$$

One could use ordinary least squares, or the more adequate total least squares (in Magnetic Resonance Spectroscopy (MRS) applications these are known as the HSVD or the HTLS method, respectively), which has been found to be better for problems with noise-contaminated data. This is so, because the assumption used in TLS is that there are errors in both the matrix and the right-hand side and the idea is to minimize both. The application of TLS to the present problem is carefully

TABLE 1. Properties of various methods. FLP is the fast linear prediction method and M-P the HSVD matrix-pencil method.

Property	Mod. Prony	FLP	M-P	VARPRO
Non-uniform spacing	no	no	no	yes
Ill-conditioned $\mathbf{\Phi}(\boldsymbol{\alpha})$	no	yes	yes	yes
Equality constraints	no	no	no	yes
Complex models	yes	yes	yes	yes
Estimates "best" # of terms	no	yes	yes	no
Needs parameter initial guess	yes	no	no	yes

described in **[24]** for multimensional TLS problems. Both methods involve an SVD computation, either of $\mathbf{U}_{n\,1:L,:}$ for ordinary least squares, or of the augmented matrix $[\mathbf{U}_{n\,1:L};\ \mathbf{U}_{n\,2:L+1,:}]$ for HTLS.

The matrix $\mathbf{Y}(\mathbf{y})$ should be chosen as square as possible **[31**, p. 25**]**. The size of $\mathbf{Y}(\mathbf{y})$ will be decisive in whether an iterative Lanczos method with reorthogonalization (for larger sets) or the golub-Kahan QR based algorithm is more efficient for the computation of the SVD (see **[24**, Chapter 5**]** or **[20**, Chapter 9**]**).

Once the nonlinear parameters are known, in a second stage the linear ones are obtained, as in the Prony-type methods, by solving an appropriate linear least squares problem.

1.6. Numerical results

There are several codes based on variable projections in the public domain. A basic version can be found in Netlib **[64]** under the name of VARPRO. An extension for problems with multiple right-hand sides is VARP2, also in **[64]**. In the Port library, at the same site, there are careful implementations by Gay and Kaufman of versions for the case of constrained and unconstrained separable nonlinear problems. All these apply to linear combinations of real exponentials and many other basis functions.

We include in the Appendix an executable for a GUI based version of VARPRO using the Gay and Kaufman code as the computational engine. This program includes a pre-packaged catalogue of the most commonly used functions, such as sigmoids, Gaussians, etc., in addition to exponentials (see Documentation in the Appendix) and it is fairly straightforward to use. This code allows multiple input variables $\mathbf{t}$, which is quite useful for training Neural Networks **[43]** (Sigmoids or Radial functions) and other applications.

As mentioned in the introduction, the only available version of the modified Prony algorithm is the Matlab program by G. K. Smyth **[56]**. Although it is only implemented for models with no constant term, it can be easily modified to include this option and that is what we used in the numerical results below.

The matrix-pencil methods are straightforward to implement and there are a number of references in the specialized literature of programs tailored to specific problems in signal processing and high-resolution imaging **[31, 51]**. Again, we implemented a basic Matlab version, using ordinary least squares (HSVD) to solve problem (1.23). Table 1 summarizes some of the advantages and disadvantages of the different algorithms as described in the literature.

The variable projections implementation that we used permits initial guesses for the nonlinear parameters or provides a number of initial values at random and chooses the computations that give the best results. The modified Prony algorithm also has options, either to input suitable initial values or to compute them. For these two methods both approaches were tried.

Neither the fast linear prediction algorithm nor the matrix-pencil method require initial values. A drawback is then that they do not allow for a restriction on the possible parameter values, i.e., for the incorporation of some *a priori* information. On the other hand, when approximating data, these two subspace-based methods have as advantage that they automatically choose the most appropriate number of exponential terms. Of course, any of the methods can be run repeatedly with different number of terms and the best results (based on RMS, say) can be chosen, although there may be pitfalls associated with this approach..

All methods except VARPRO compute polynomial roots or eigenvalues of the form: $e^{\alpha_j \triangle t}$, which are therefore sensitive to the size of $\triangle t$. An additional difference, polynomial rootfinding, used in modified Prony and forward linear prediction, is an ill-conditioned problem, even more so for multiple, or clusters of roots, as is the case in some applications. On the other hand, the eigenvalue problem for a symmetric matrix, as is $\mathbf{Q}^{-1}\mathbf{ZQ}$ for the matrix-pencil methods HTLS/HSVD, is well-conditioned.

The conditioning or sensitivity of a nonlinear least squares problem to changes in the data, i.e., an estimate of how well the parameters can be determined, is given, to a first approximation, by the condition number[3] of the Jacobian $\mathbf{J}$ of $\mathbf{r}$: $\mathbf{J}_{ij} = \frac{\partial r_i}{\partial x_j}$, at the minimum $\mathbf{x}^* \equiv (\mathbf{a}, \boldsymbol{\alpha})$.

A necessary condition for a critical point to be a minimum is that the matrix $\mathbf{H}$ be positive definite, with $\mathbf{H} = \mathbf{J}^\top\mathbf{J} + \sum_{i=1}^{N} r_i \mathbf{G}_i$, where $\mathbf{G}_i$ is the Hessian of a component r_i: $\mathbf{G}_{i_{jk}} = \frac{\partial^2 r_i}{\partial x_j \partial x_k}$. In [**7**, Chapter 9] a more geometrical interpretation using the normal curvature matrix is given.

The data sets were chosen to test two data fitting applications, parameter estimation and data representation. We include timings as a reference, although the Matlab implementations are not optimal and cannot be directly compared with the VARPRO Fortran one. For the VARPRO runs with random initial guesses, the listed time is an average of the times for 40 trials. In the tables below, we list under (# l) and (# nl) the minimum number of correct decimals of the linear and nonlinear parameters computed by the programs. The tests were run under Windows with an Intel T9300, 2.5GHz, chip.

Simulated data problems. In the following two tests we try to recover the parameters of a linear combination of exponentials to which noise has been added. A measure of the sensitivity of the parameters to data perturbations can be derived if one assumes that $r(\mathbf{a}, \boldsymbol{\alpha})$ 1.2 is well approximated by a quadratic function in a neighbourhood of the point $\mathbf{x}^* \equiv (\mathbf{a}, \boldsymbol{\alpha})$,

$$\mathbf{H}\triangle\mathbf{x} = -\mathbf{J}^\top\mathbf{r}. \tag{1.24}$$

Here, $\triangle\mathbf{x}$ is the parameter's perturbation.

For more details see [**61**] and also the chapter "Two exponential models for optically stimulated luminiscence" in this volume.

---

[3]The Euclidean condition number of a rectangular matrix $\mathbf{A}$ is $\kappa_2(\mathbf{A}) = \|\mathbf{A}\|_2 \|\mathbf{A}^+\|_2$.

FIGURE 1.6.1. Norm of residual surface as function of the nonlinear parameters. The diagonal, where the parameters coincide and there is a discontinuity is plotted separately.

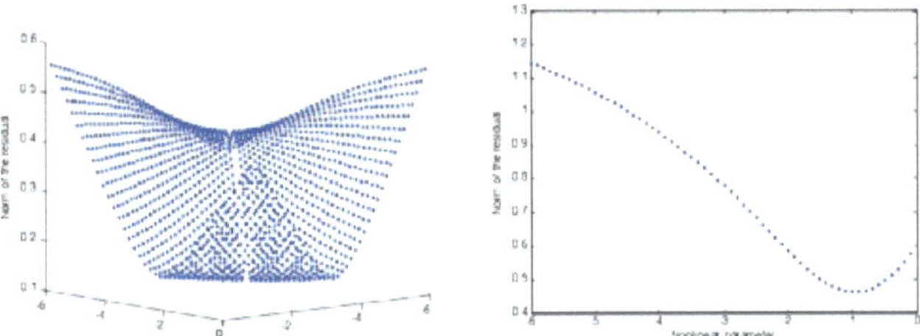

Test #1. This data set is taken from **[36]**. It has 46 data points (y_i, t_i), $i = 0, \cdots, 45$, with $t_i = 0.02i$ and $y_i \approx \mu(t_i) = 4e^{-4t_i} - 4e^{-5t_i}$, with noise added to the model so that the y_i have between one and two correct decimals (all the values of y_i are in the interval $[0, 0.35]$). The methods, VARPRO, modified Prony, and matrix-pencil (HSVD) were tested.

The relative bounds for the parameters established using equation (1.24) give a large uncertainty region that is consistent with the large errors in the data:

$$\frac{|\delta a_1|}{|a_1|} \leq 12.19, \quad \frac{|\delta a_2|}{|a_2|} \leq 12.18, \quad \frac{|\delta \alpha_1|}{|\alpha_1|} \leq 1.32, \quad \frac{|\delta \alpha_2|}{|\alpha_2|} \leq 1.44.$$

A plot of the surface $r(\mathbf{a}, \boldsymbol{\alpha})$ as a function of the nonlinear parameters $\boldsymbol{\alpha} \in [-6, 0] \times [-6, 0]$, assuming that the optimal linear parameters $\mathbf{a}$ are computed via linear least squares for each $\boldsymbol{\alpha}$, shows a mostly flat surface, convex near the nonlinear parameters $(-4, -5)$, and with a "saddle" close to the $(0, 0)$ corner. For confluent parameter values $\alpha = \alpha_1 = \alpha_2$, there is a discontinuity in the surface, (the model has only one term). The plot of the curve $r(a, \alpha)$ (where $a = a_1 = a_2$) has a well defined minimum at $\alpha = 1.27$. VARPRO converges to this $\boldsymbol{\alpha}$ when starting from randomly chosen initial values (see Table). However, a check of the eigenvalues of $\mathbf{H}$ proves that this cannot be a local minimum as the matrix is not positive definite.

For the HSVD, two options were tried: allow the algorithm to estimate the appropriate number of exponential terms, given the level of noise, or force it to use the (in this case known) 2-term approximation. In this last case, even though the RMS is small, the method failed to return an approximation of the parameter values. The reason is the assumption on which the method is based, namely that the shift-invariance property (1.22) for the model matrix $\bar{\mathbf{Y}}(\boldsymbol{\mu})$ case is approximately valid for the data matrix (1.23). For the present data set the noise is too large and this hypothesis does not hold. In fact, if instead of using the above data one decreases the noise level to 10^{-3} HSVD returns with 1-2 correct decimals, both, for the linear and the nonlinear parameters. RMS stands for Residual Mean Squares, i.e., the square root of the average sum of squares of residuals.

Test #2. This set **[35]** is obtained from a model with a constant term, $y_i \approx \mu(t_i) = 10^{-2} + 2e^{-0.5t_i} + 4e^{-t_i} + 8e^{-2t_i}$, where $t_i = 0.01i$ for $i = 0, \cdots, 999$. The y_i are derived from the model values by rounding to 6 decimal digits and adding noise of the order $O(10^{-3})$. Here, under method FLP, we list results from **[35]**.

TABLE 2. Results for Test #1

Method	Initial guess	# of terms	Max. rel. error	RMS	# digits	Time (sec.)
VARPRO	random	-	6.93e-1	5.33e-2	none	0.0018
"	$\alpha = (-1; -2)$	-	2.02e-1	1.49e-2	4l, 4nl	0.01
Mod. Prony	computed	-	2.38e-1	1.49e-2	2l, 3nl	0.46
"	$\alpha = (-1; -2)$	-	2.38e-1	1.49e-2	3l, 3nl	0.31
HSVD	-	2	2.35e-1	1.49e-2	none	0.06
"	-	estimated: 3	2.25e-1	1.48e-2	none	0.08

TABLE 3. Results for Test #2

Method	Initial guess	# of terms	Max. rel error	RMS	# digits	Time (sec.)
VARPRO	random	-	7.31e-4	3.14e-5	4l,4nl	0.05
Mod. Prony	computed	-	2.77e-1	1.89e-2	none	0.14
FLP	-	4	-	$\mathcal{O}(10^{-4})$	3l,3nl	-
HSVD	-	4	6.3e-4	3.14e-5	3l,3nl	1.92

TABLE 4. Parameter's uncertainty

parameter	bound
a_1	3×10^{-2}
a_2	3.16×10^{-2}
a_3	4.95×10^{-3}
a_4	7.47×10^{-3}
α_2	8.8×10^{-3}
α_3	1.31×10^{-2}
α_4	2.05×10^{-3}

The condition number of the Jacobian at the model parameters is $\kappa_2(\mathbf{J}) = 3.86 \times 10^3$, but the relative bounds for the parameters give a considerably smaller uncertainty region.

Here, the poor results of the modified Prony method can be explained because the roots of the characteristic polynomial $z_j = e^{\alpha_j \Delta t}$ are 0.9802, 0.9905 and 0.99501, i.e., they are close together, so that even a small perturbation in the coefficients $\boldsymbol{\delta}$ affects them.

Approximation of difficult functions with high accuracy. Next we present some results of exponential fitting for a couple of difficult functions mentioned in recent work by Beylkin, Monzon and Mohlenkamp [**4**, **3**]. The challenge is that high precision is required and the problems are very ill-conditioned.

Test #3. We use the algorithms to fit $1/x$ sampled uniformly over the interval $[0.01, 1]$ (100 samples) with a linear combination of exponentials. To have an estimate for the appropriate number of terms, the data were arranged in a 55×45 Hankel matrix and the numerical rank was computed, suggesting the use of 16 terms for the approximations. However, the numerical tests with the different algorithms show that it is not possible, or of any advantage to use this many terms, as one can

TABLE 5. Results for Test #3

Method	# terms	Max. rel error	RMS	Time (sec.)
VARPRO	10 + constant	3.51e-7	3.39e-7	0.28
"	12 + constant	3.65e-7	3.17e-7	0.22
Mod. Prony	10 + constant	9.93e-4	5.37e-4	0.08
"	12 + constant	too ill-cond	-	-

TABLE 6. Results for Test #4

Method	# terms	Max. rel error	RMS	Time (sec.)
VARPRO	21	1.68e-4	2.81e-7	1.4
"	28	1.66e-4	2.81e-7	1.64
Mod. Prony	10 with constant term	0.99	0.18	0.09
"	10	too ill-cond	-	-
HSVD	13	5.63e-5	9.04e-8	1.7
"	21	5.11e-11	6.04e-14	1.65
"	99	2.33e-11	2.9e-14	1.85

see from the table below. HSVD cannot be used for this example (at $t_0 = 0$ the data is not defined).

Test #4. Finally, we consider the approximation of the Bessel function J_0, a damped oscillating function in the range $[0,\ 20\pi]$, using 1000 equally spaced sample points. In VARPRO we take as basis functions the real part of a complex exponential with a complex weight. Since $\Re(\phi(x)) = \Re[(a+ib)e^{(c+id)x}] = a\ e^{cx}(\cos(dx) - b/a\ \sin(dx))$, we can consider the real basis functions $\psi(x) = e^{cx}(\cos(dx) - \lambda\ \sin(dx))$ with real weights as our approximants. As explained above the number of terms in HSVD are chosen automatically, depending on the level of noise in the data. We considered the data correct up to 6, 12 and 16 decimals, for the 13, 21 and 99 terms approximation. The non-VARPRO methods use complex exponential approximations. In 1.6.2 we show the fit (true and approximated are indistinguishable) and the absolute error for VARPRO using 20 terms.

These results are quite competitive with those obtained by Beylkin *et al* using quite different techniques. What is very interesting in their approach is that the approximation of $1/x$, which might seem an elementary example, is transformed into a powerful tool to obtain approximations to the Green function when x is interpreted as the Laplacian. Coming from a totally different direction, related results are obtained in the article by Srivastava, Suaya, Pereyra, Suaya and Banerjee in Chapter 9 of this book.

Numerical results for the complex case. We have implemented the simplest method of section 1.3. We used subroutine CGESVD from LAPACK to calculate the SVD of the complex matrix $\mathbf{\Phi}$. We have run a number of tests using randomly generated target values for the nonlinear parameters to create artificial data sets in order to validate the algorithm. The main observation is that, as we

FIGURE 1.6.2. Results for J_o

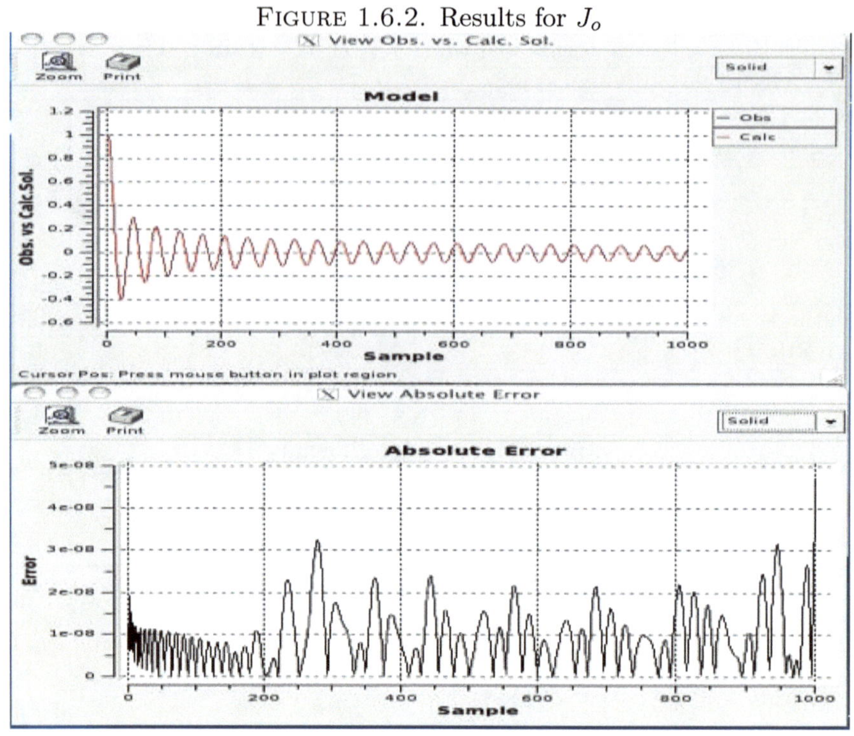

TABLE 7. Absolute errors on retrieved nonlinear parameters

$R(\alpha^* - \alpha)$	$I(\alpha^* - \alpha)$
−0.0072	−0.0045
0.12	0.19
−0.046	−0.073
0.0037	−0.015

have indicated before, it is wise to make several runs using different randomly chosen initial values and then select the best fit from them. For a particular case with 4 exponentials, we chose to make 10 runs and the 7th gave the smallest residual norm, namely 2.9 10^{-11}.

We consider now some typical real data for the problem discussed in Chapter 9 of this book by Srivastava, Suaya, Pereyra and Banerjee. The model for this problem is:

$$\mathbf{\Phi}(\lambda; \mathbf{a}, \boldsymbol{\alpha}) = \sum_{j=1}^{n} a_j e^{\alpha_j \lambda / z},$$

where $z = 2\pi 10^5(1+i)$, $i = \sqrt{(-1)}$ and λ is the independent variable. Thus, it can be writen as:

$$\mathbf{\Phi}(\lambda; \mathbf{a}, \boldsymbol{\alpha}) = \sum_{j=1}^{n} a_j e^{(1-i)\alpha_j \lambda / 4\pi 10^5},$$

FIGURE 1.6.3.

Data for fit by complex exponentials

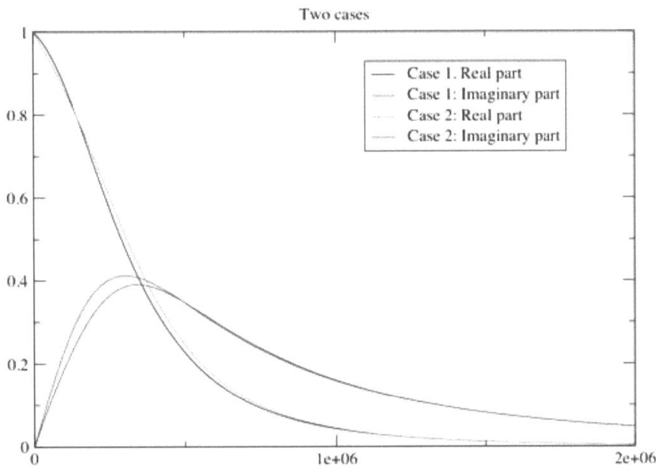

with α_j real and a_j complex. There are also some additional restrictions:

$$0 < \Re(a_j) < 1, \ \alpha_j \leq 0, \ \sum a_j = (1, \ 0).$$

The constraints on the nonlinear parameters α are introduced as a large penalty on the goal functional. However, for the VP algorithm there is no possibility of introducing constraints on the linear parameters, because they are eliminated from the problem and are recovered at the end as functions of the nonlinear ones. What happens is that through the definition of $\mathbf{a}$ (1.9), the constraints get translated into constraints on the nonlinear parameters.

In Table 8 we show some results of fitting the first data set with an increasing number of exponentials. We observe a consistent behavior, in the sense that an increasing number of exponentials improves the RMS. Two other good things seem to happen:

- The problems are not too ill-conditioned.
- The constraints on the linear parameters are satisfied automatically (to high precision!) - that is shown in column 3; recall that the a_i's are complex. This is altogether not very surprising if the model is a good approximation, because for small values of λ the data is essentially $(0, 1)$ and due to the small factor, the exponentials are essentially equal to 1 and therefore the model reduces to the sum of the linear parameters.

1.7. Some applications

A number of important applications of the above and other special methods are presented in the next chapters of this book. We survey here some additional applications related to classical and modern telecommunication and other problems, which can be cast as separable Nonlinear least squares **(SNLS)** problems of fitting

TABLE 8. Results for complex data. For cases 2, 4, 6, 8 we run only one trial; for case 10 we run 3 different randomly chosen initial values.

# exp.	RMS	Σa_i
2	0.025	(1.01,0.003)
4	0.0019	(0.9996,-2.7(-5))
6	0.00034	(0.99999, 5.2(-5))
8	0.000082	(0.9999998, -3.5(-6))
10	0.000031	(0.999989,-9.3(-6))

a linear combination of complex exponentials, where the linear coefficients represent amplitude while the nonlinear ones are the phases of the signals.

Roy and Kailath **[48]** describe in detail applications to practical signal processing problems. The objective there is to estimate from measurements a set of constant (time-independent) parameters upon which the received signal depends. Among these, high-resolution direction of arrival (DOA) estimation is important in many sensor systems such as radar, sonar, electronic surveillance, and seismic exploration. High-resolution frequency estimation is important in numerous applications, such as the design and control of robots and large flexible space structures. In such problems, the functional form of the underlying signals can often be assumed (e.g., narrow-band plane waves, cisoids). The quantities to be estimated are parameters in these functional descriptions, such as frequencies and directions of arrival for plane waves, or cisoid frequencies.

Several approaches have been developed through the years for solving these problems, including Capon's **[11]** maximum likelihood and Burg's **[9]** maximum entropy methods. These methods have significant limitations and Pisarenko was one of the first to consider the structure of the data model to estimate the parameters of cisoids in additive noise using a covariance approach. Schmidt **[52]** and Bienvenu **[6]** were the first to exploit correctly the measurement model in the case of a sensor array of arbitrary form. Schmidt's algorithm, MUSIC (MUltiple SIgnal Classification), which according to that author was inspired by the separation of variables technique, has been widely studied and was considered in an MIT study of that time as the most promising high-resolution algorithm. However, MUSIC's success came at a high computational cost that involved a search in parameter space and the storage of array calibration data.

Roy and Kailath developed a new algorithm, called ESPRIT, that dramatically reduced the computational cost and storage for sensor arrays that show what they call displacement invariance. These are arrays where the sensors come in matched pairs with identical displacement vectors.

Unfortunately, many of the earlier simplified algorithms are ineffective when some of the sources are coherent. This can stem from multipath effects or it can be introduced artificially to impede detection. Kumaresan and Shaw **[28]** and Cadzow **[10]** have studied in detail the application of separation of variables to this classical problem. More recently, a number of new algorithms have been developed to consider the more challenging problem of multiple broad-band source location. A variety of least squares modeling methods provide viable means for overcoming the difficulties of coherent sources.

Cadzow [**10**] presents a method that models the signal eigenvectors. These are linear combinations of steering vectors instead of the sensor signals, which introduces a smoothing effect and decreases the computational cost, while the use of the Variable Projection (**VP**) approach produces significant additional computational savings. As Roy and Kailath [**48**] indicate, **VP**-type algorithms were considered too expensive until fairly recently, thus justifying the use of the simplified **SVD** based ones. However, the increasing power of modern computers has rendered some of those arguments and simplified methods obsolete, especially in low signal-to-noise situations, where they do not work well.

Friedlander [**15**] has analyzed the sensitivity of the Maximum Likelihood method for the problem above. This is a separable problem and the sensitivity study involves the differentiation formulas of [**17**]. This analysis is valuable because the fast algorithms require a knowledge of the antenna array that is hard to come by in real situations, and thus have not been used as often as they deserve.

Talwar *et al.* [**58, 57**] have considered the problem of estimating co-channel digital signals using an antenna array when the spatial response of the array is unknown. Traditional techniques, such as MUSIC or ESPRIT, are dependent on the reliability of the array manifold. In the application the authors envision (mobile communications), the array manifold is poorly determined because of a highly variable propagation environment. They consider instead a block **SNLS** approach, which is both fast and reliable.

Rao and Arun [**46**] discuss the problem of estimating closely spaced frequencies of multiple, superimposed sinusoids from noisy measurements as a **SNLS** problem. This variant of the problem discussed earlier has wide applications in radio-astronomy, interference spectroscopy, seismic dataprocessing, and MR spectroscopy. Because of the cost of the computation, as compared to the simplified methods, **SNLS** is only advisable at low signal-to-noise ratios.

Zhou, Yip and Leung [**63**] consider the DOA problem for multiple moving targets by a passive array of sensors, a problem of great interest in communications, air traffic control, and tactical and strategic defense operations. In satellite and personal communication systems it is also advantageous to deploy sensor arrays to reject undesired signals. The classical techniques mentioned above deteriorate rapidly in the presence of moving targets, since they provide poor resolution because of the spread array spatial spectrum caused by the target motion. This deterioration increases with the number of sensors. Zhou *et al.* propose a maximum likelihood algorithm, where the target motion is assumed to be locally linear, which helps eliminate the spread spectrum effects and provides accurate target dynamical state estimates. Since they use the array signal model for an array of omnidirectional sensors, their approach leads to a separable problem that is solved by a **VP** method.

Lilleberg *et al.* from Nokia Mobile Phones [**32**] consider a near-far resistant iterative algorithm for multiuser signature sequence delay estimation. **VP** is used to separate the delay and data to be estimated, obtaining a so-called blind maximum likelihood estimator that does not require any knowledge of user amplitudes and data.

Heredia and Arce [**23**] have considered the splitting of a signal into a set of multilevel components as an **SNLS** problem. They use as a comparative example a system identification problem for wave propagation through a nonlinear multilayer channel, where they test the new concepts against Linear, Volterra, and Neural

Network alternatives. They show that the realization of piecewise linear filters with unknown thresholds leads to a **SNLS** problem. In the test problem they verify that the new approach can cope with the difficulties of the problem that trip the Volterra and Neural Network approaches.

Baum *et al.* [**1**] review the singularity expansion method (SEM) for quantifying the transient electromagnetic scattering from targets illuminated by pulsed EM radiation. The SEM theory suggests that the late-time scattered field of a target, interrogated by pulsed EM radiation, can be represented as a sum of natural-resonance modes. Since the excitation-independent natural frequencies depend upon the detailed size and shape of the target, the full complement of those frequencies is unique to a specified target and provides a potential basis for its identification. The first efforts to extract such natural frequencies from measured target pulse responses were based on Prony's method. However, in the practical low signal-to-noise environment in which this inverse problem occurs, only one or a few modes could be extracted reliably using that inherently unstable algorithm. Although several efforts have improved the reliability of Prony-based methods, realistic problems require a nonlinear approach, and since the problem is separable, **VP** has found another good application in the radar cross-section identification business.

In [**2**], Beece *et al.* use a **VP** algorithm in an exponential fitting problem associated with the effect of viscosity on the kinetics of the photochemical cycle of bacteriorhodopsin. Marque and Eisenstein [**34**] extend this work to consider pressure effects on the photocycle of purple membrane. By considering several kinetic data sets taken at the same temperature and pressure but with different monitoring wavelengths and an exponential model, they are able to use **VARP2** to separate the variables and efficiently solve a problem with multiple right-hand sides. The first to use this method in these type of problems was Richard Lozier [**33**], who motivated the development of the **VARP2** extension and became a champion in this field for many years (we thank Randy LeVeque for this insight).

A recent flurry of activity in using **VP** has occurred in the problem of super-resolution, i.e., the combination of multiple resolution signals that requires registration (alignment) [**12, 47, 60**].

1.8. Appendix

In this Appendix we collect additional material that might be useful to some readers. First of all, we offer an executable and corresponding documentation for the Gay-Kaufman VARPRO code (nsf) [**16**] with a GUI that, we hope, will facilitate considerably its use: VARPRO Documentation, VARPRO code.
We also include a number of data sets related to the problems used to compare codes in this chapter. For tests #1 to #4 in the Numerical results section, there are corresponding files with extension .dat:
Test_1_t_y.dat,
Test_2_t_y.dat,
Test_3_t_y.dat,
Test_4_t_y.dat.

The files contain N records, each with a data pair (y_i, t_i), as described in section 1.6.

Bibliography

[1] C. E. Baum, E. J. Rothwell, K-M. Chen and D. P. Nyquist, *The singularity expansion method and its application to target identification.* Proc. IEEE **79:**1481-1492 (1991).

[2] D.Beece, S. F. Bowne, J. Czege, L. Eisenstein, H. Frauenfelder, D. Good, M. C. Marden, J. Marque, P. Ormos, L. Reinisch and K. T. Yue, *The effect of viscosity on the photocycle of bacteriorhodopsin.* Photochem. Photobiol. **33**:517-522 (1981).

[3] G. Beylkin and M. Mohlenkamp, *Numerical operator calculus in higher dimensions* Proc. Nat. Acad. Sci. U.S.A. **99**:10246-10251 (2002).

[4] G. Beylkin and L. Monzon, *On generalized Gaussian quadratures for exponentials and their applications.* App. Comput. Harm. Anal., **12**:332-373 (2002).

[5] G. Beylkin and L. Monzon, *On approximation of functions by exponential sums.* Appl. Comput. Harmon. Anal. **19**:17-48 (2005).

[6] G. Bienvenu and L. Kopp, *Adaptivity to background noise spatial coherence for high resolution passive methods.* Proc. IEEE on Acoustics, Speech, and Signal Processing, **5**:307-310 (1980).

[7] Å. Björck, *Numerical Methods for Least Squares Problems.* SIAM Pub., Philadelphia, PA (1996).

[8] R. P. Brent, *Algorithms for Minimization Without Derivatives.* Prentice Hall, Englewood Cliffs, NJ (1973).

[9] J. P. Burg, *Maximum entropy spectral analysis.* Soc. Exp. Geophys. 37th Annual Meeting Extended Abstracts (1967).

[10] J. A. Cadzow, *Multiple source location–The signal subspace approach.* IEEE Trans. on Acoustics, Speech, and Signal Processing **38:**1110-1125 (1990).

[11] J. Capon, *High-resolution frequency-wavenumber spectrum analysis.* Proc. IEEE **57:**1408-1418 (1969).

[12] J. Chung, E. Haber and J. Nagy, *Numerical method for coupled super-resolution.* Inverse Prob. **22**:1261-1272 (2006).

[13] J. E. Dennis, D. M. Gay and R. W. Welsch, *NL2SOL-An adaptive nonlinear least squares algorithm.* ACM TOMS **7**:369-383 (1981).

[14] Baron Gaspard Riche de Prony, *Essai experimental et analytique: sur les lois de la dilatabilite de fluides elastique et sur celles de la force expansive de la vapeur de l'alkool, a differentes temperatures.* J. Ecole Polyt. **1**:24-76 (1795).

[15] B. Friedlander, *Sensitivity analysis of the maximum likelihood direction-finding algorithm.* IEEE Trans. Aerosp. Electron. Syst. **26:**953-968 (1990).

[16] D. Gay and L. Kaufman, *NSF, port library,* http://www.netlib.org/port/dnsf.f (last accessed: 9/2/2009).

[17] G. H. Golub and V. Pereyra, *The differentiation of pseudoinverses and nonlinear least squares problems whose variables separate.* SIAM J. Numer. Anal. **10**:413-432 (1973).

[18] G. H. Golub and R. LeVeque, *Extensions and uses of the variable projection algorithm for solving nonlinear least squares problems.* Proc. American Numerical Analysis and Computer Conference (1979).

[19] G. H. Golub and V. Pereyra, *Separable nonlinear least squares: the Variable Projection method and its applications.* Inverse Prob. **19**:R1-R26 (2003).

[20] G. H. Golub and C. F. Van Loan; *Matrix Computations,* 3rd. ed., John Hopkins Univ. Press, Baltimore (1996).

[21] I. Guttman, V. Pereyra and H. D. Scolnik, *Least squares estimation for a class of non-linear models.* Technometrics, **15**:209-218 (1973).

[22] P. C. Hansen, *Rank-Deficient and Discrete Ill-Posed Problems.* SIAM Pub., Philadelphia, PA (1998).

[23] E. A. Heredia and G. R. Arce, *Piecewise linear systems modeling based on a continuous threshold decomposition.* IEEE Trans. Signal Process. **44** (1996).
[24] S. Van Huffel and J. Vandewalle, *The Total Least Squares Problem*, SIAM Pub., Philadelphia, PA (1991).
[25] A. A. Istratov and O.F. Vyvenko, *Exponential analysis in physical phenomena.* Rev. Sc. Inst. **70**:1233-1257 (1999).
[26] L. Kaufman, *A variable projection method for solving separable non-linear least squares problems,* BIT **15**:49-57 (1975).
[27] F. T. Krogh, *Efficient implementation of a variable projection algorithm for nonlinear least squares problems.* Comm. ACM **17:**167-169 (1974).
[28] R. Kumaresan and A. K. Shaw, *Superresolution by structured matrix approximation.* IEEE Trans. Antennas Propag. **36:**34-44 (1988).
[29] S. Y. Kung, K. S. Arun and D. V. Bhaskar Rao, *State-space and singular value decomposition-based approximation methods for the harmonic retrieval problem*, J. Opt. Soc. Am. **73**: 1799-1811 (1983).
[30] C. Lanczos, *Applied Analysis.* Prentice-Hall, Englewood Cliffs, NJ (1956).
[31] T. Laudadio, *Subspace-Based Quantification of Magnetic Resonance Spectroscopy Data Using Biochemical Prior Knowledge*, Ph. D. Thesis, Faculty of Engineering, K. U. Leuven, Leuven, Belgium (2005).
[32] J. Lilleberg, E. Nieminen and M. Latva-aho, *Blind iterative multiuser delay estimator for CDMA.* Proc. IEEE Int. Symp. Personal Indoor and Mobile Radio Communications (PIMRC), pp. 565-568. Taipei, Taiwan (1996).
[33] R. H. Lozier, R. A. Bogomolni and W. Stoeckenius. *Bacteriorhodopsin: a light-driven proton pump in Halobacterium halobium.* Biophys. J. **15:**955-962 (1975).
[34] J. Marque and L. Eisenstein, *Pressure effects on the photocycle of purple membrane.* Biochem. **23**:5556-5563 (1984).
[35] H. B. Nielsen, *Multi-exponential fitting of low-field H NMR data*, Tecnical Report IMM-REP-2000-03, Dept. of Mathematical Modelling, Technical University of Denmark (2000).
[36] H. B. Nielsen, *UCTP test problems for unconstrained optimization*, Tecnical Report IMM-REP-2000-17, Dept. of Mathematical Modelling, Technical University of Denmark (2000).
[37] M. R. Osborne *A class of nonlinear regression problems*, in Data Representation, R. S. Anderssen and M. R. Osborne, eds., University of Queensland Press, St. Lucia, pp. 94-101 (1970).
[38] M. R. Osborne *Some special nonlinear least squares problems.* SIAM J. Numer. Anal. **12**:571-592 (1975).
[39] M. R. Osborne and G. K. Smyth, *A modified Prony algorithm for fitting functions defined by difference equations.* SIAM J. Sci. Comp. 12:362-382 (1991).
[40] M. R. Osborne and G. K. Smyth, *A modified Prony algorithm for exponential function fitting.* SIAM J. Sci. Comp. **16**:119-138 (1995).
[41] M. R. Osborne, *Separable least squares, variable projections, and the Gauss-Newton algorithm.* ETNA 28:1-15 (2007).
[42] J. M. Papy, L. De Lathauwer and S. Van Huffel, *Exponential data fitting using multilinear algebra: The single-channel and multi-channel case.* Numer. Lin. Alg. Appl. **12**:809-826 (2005).
[43] V. Pereyra, G. Scherer and F. Wong, *Variable projections neural network training.* Mathematics and Computers in Simulation **73**:231-243 (2006).
[44] V. Pereyra, *Fast computation of equispaced Pareto manifolds and Pareto fronts for multiobjective optimization problems.* Math. Comput. Simul. **79**:1935-1947 (2009).
[45] V. Pereyra, M. Saunders and J. Castillo, *Equispaced Pareto front construction for constrained multiobjective optimization.* CSRC, Tecn. Rep., San Diego State Univ. (2009).
[46] B. D. Rao, and K. S. Arun, *Model based processing of signals: a state space approach.* Proc. IEEE **80:**283-309 (1992).
[47] D. Robinson, F. Farsiu and P. Milanfar, *Optimal registration of aliased images using variable projection with applications to super-resolution.* Comp. J. (2007).
[48] R. Roy and T. Kailath, *ESPRIT-estimation of signal parameters via rotational invariance techniques.* IEEE Trans. Acoust. Speech Signal Process. **37:**984-995 (1989).
[49] Antonio E. Ruano, Pedro M. Ferreira, C. Cabrita and S. Matos, *Training neural networks and neuro-fuzzy systems: an unified view.* Proc. IFAC 15th Triennial World Congress (2002).

[50] Antonio E. Ruano, P. J. Fleming and D. I. Jones, *Connectionist approach to PID autotuning.* Cont. Th. Appl. IEEE Proc. D **139**:279-285 (2002).

[51] T. K. Sarkar and O. Pereira, *Using the matrix pencil method to estimate the parameters of a sum of complex exponentials*, IEEE Antennas Propag. **37**: 48-55 (1995).

[52] R. O. Schmidt, *Multiple emitter location and signal parameter estimation.* Proc. RADC Spectrum Estimation Workshop (1979).

[53] G. A. F. Seber and C. J. Wild, *Nonlinear Regression.* Wiley Interscience, New York (2003).

[54] R. I. Shrager and R. W. Hendler, *Some pitfalls in curve-fitting and how to avoid them: A case in point.* J. Biochem. Biophys. 36:157-173 (1998).

[55] J. Sjöberg, and M. Viberg, *Separable non-linear least squares minimization – possible improvements for neural net fitting.* IEEE Workshop in Neural Networks for Signal Processing. Amelia Island Plantation, FL (1997).

[56] G. Smyth, http://www.statsci.org/other/prony.html, 30 June 2009.

[57] S. Talwar, *Blind Space-Time Algorithms for Wireless Communication Systems.* Ph. D. Thesis, SCCM, Stanford University (1996).

[58] S. Talwar, M. Viberg and A. Paulraj, *Blind estimation of multiple co-channel digital signals arriving at an antenna array.* IEEE SP Letters **1**:29-31 (1994).

[59] M. L. Van Blaricum and R. Mittra, *Problems and solutions associated with Prony's method for processing transient data*, IEEE Trans. Antennas Propag. **AP-26**:174-182 (1978).

[60] P. Vandenwalle, *Super-Resolution From Unregistered Aliased Images.* Master Thesis in E. E., Katholieke Univ. Leuven, Belgium (2006).

[61] J. M. Varah, *On fitting exponentials by nonlinear least squares.* SIAM J. Sci. Stat. Comput. **6**:30-44 (1985).

[62] H. Wold and E. Lyttkens, *Nonlinear iterative partial least squares (NIPALS) estimation procedures.* Bull. ISI **43:**29-51 (1969).

[63] Y. Zhou, P. C. Yip and H. Leung, textitTracking the direction-of-arrival of multiple moving targets by passive arrays: algorithm. IEEE Trans. Signal Proc. **47:**2655-2666 (1999).

[64] http://www.netlib.org, 30 June 2009.

CHAPTER 2

Computational aspects of exponential data fitting in Magnetic Resonance Spectroscopy

Diana M. Sima
Department of Electrical Engineering ESAT-SCD
Katholieke Universiteit Leuven
Kasteelpark Arenberg 10, 3001
Leuven-Heverlee, Belgium
diana.sima@esat.kuleuven.be

Jean-Baptiste Poullet
Formerly with Department of Electrical Engineering ESAT-SCD
Katholieke Universiteit Leuven, Kasteelpark Arenberg 10, 3001
Leuven-Heverlee, Belgium jeanbaptistepoullet@gmail.com

Sabine Van Huffel
Department of Electrical Engineering ESAT-SCD
Katholieke Universiteit Leuven
Kasteelpark Arenberg 10, 3001
Leuven-Heverlee, Belgium.
Sabine.VanHuffel@esat.kuleuven.be

Victor Pereyra & Godela Scherer (Eds)

ABSTRACT. Magnetic Resonance Spectroscopy (MRS) is one of the practical biomedical applications where exponential data fitting is an essential tool. An MRS signal is a complex-valued time-domain signal that satisfies in theory a model expressed as a sum of complex damped exponentials. The model parameters provide useful information about metabolites, *i.e.*, about the chemical content of the sample or tissue under study. *In vivo* MRS signals are characterized by the presence of noise and by deviations from the theoretical model. Along the years many fitting methods have been employed for the so-called "metabolite quantification" problem. These are, to mention just a few, subspace-based methods such as HSVD, or optimization-based methods such as VARPRO. In recent years more focus has been placed upon methods that incorporate prior knowledge into the model. Initially, prior knowledge has been included in the form of simple relationships between parameters of the exponential model (for instance, linear relations between the parameters of individual exponential components, when it is known that these components originate from the same metabolite). More advanced methods are able to include much more prior knowledge by combining whole metabolite profiles into the model; these metabolite profiles are quantum-mechanically simulated or *in vitro* measured MRS signals. Other interesting computational issues related to MRS quantification include preprocessing techniques (such as filtering out some unwanted spectral components) aimed at modifying the measured data without loss of essential information, in order to match the assumed exponential model. This chapter reviews time-domain MRS quantification methods and related preprocessing techniques, it emphasizes the computational aspects such as the use of variable projection in the optimization-based methods, and it hints towards some of the features of existing software packages for MRS.

Keywords: Magnetic Resonance Spectroscopy (MRS), metabolite quantification, Hankel Singular Value Decomposition, nonlinear least squares, variable projection

2.1. Introduction

2.1.1. Basics of the NMR phenomenon. [1]

Nuclear Magnetic Resonance (NMR) is a quantum mechanical phenomenon observed when a population of atomic nuclei is placed into an external magnetic field B_0. Nuclei such as ^1H—hydrogen (also referred to simply as proton), ^{13}C—carbon, or ^{31}P—phosphorus possess an inherent angular momentum called *spin*, capable of two equivalent states. When the nucleus is immersed in an external magnetic field, the two spin states are no longer equivalent and can be visualized as states of precession of the spin around the magnetic field direction (low energy) and around the direction opposite the field (high energy). The spin precesses about the external field axis with an angular frequency ω_0 (called Larmor frequency) equal to the product between the gyromagnetic ratio γ characteristic for the nucleus (*e.g.*, γ=42.58, 10.71, and 17.25 MHz/T, for ^{1}H, ^{13}C, and ^{31}P, respectively) and the magnetic field strength B_0:

$$\omega_0 = \gamma B_0. \tag{2.1}$$

[1]The material in this section is more extensively discussed in Chapter 1 of **[10]**. Interesting resources on the basics of NMR can also be found online; see, *e.g.*, the Wikipedia pages, or the "Virtual Textbook of Organic Chemistry".

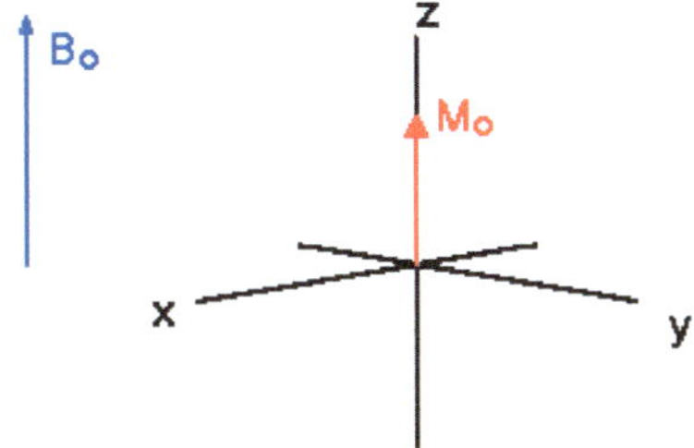

FIGURE 2.1.1. At equilibrium, the net magnetization M_0 of a large population of nuclei is aligned with the external field B_0. The explanation is that an excess of nuclei is found in the low energy state, thus these spins sum up to a nonzero vector with positive magnitude in the z-direction, $M_z = M_0$, but with zero magnitude in the x or y directions, $M_{xy} = 0$, for which the spins show no preference; *i.e.*, there is no phase coherence in the precession of the spins in the xy-plane.

Due to its two states, the nucleus can be seen as a little magnet that tends to align with the magnetic field in order to reach the state of minimum magnetic potential energy. The analogy with classical physics is limited by the fact that in quantum mechanics the energy difference between high and low energy states is quantized; this is given by

$$\Delta E = \gamma \hbar B_0 = \hbar \omega_0, \ \hbar = h/(2\pi), \tag{2.2}$$

where h is Planck's constant (6.626×10^{-34} J s), which means that only a photon whose frequency matches exactly the Larmor frequency ω_0 is able to be absorbed/emitted by the nucleus in order for it to jump between the two energy states.

When a population of the same nuclei is considered to be immersed into a static magnetic field B_0, its equilibrium state gives a total magnetization vector (as the sum of directions of all individual spins) that points in the direction of the magnetic field (see Figure 2.1.1). In thermal equilibrium, the ratio between the number $n-$ and $n+$ of nuclei in the high and low energy states is given by

$$n - /n+ = e^{-\Delta E/kT}, \tag{2.3}$$

where k is the Boltzman constant (1.381×10^{-23} J/K), T is the temperature in Kelvin and ΔE is the energy difference between the states as given in (2.2). The ratio $n - /n+$ is very close to 1 in normal circumstances, resulting in a tiny excess of nuclei in the low state (this excess is about four in a million in clinical NMR scanners with $B_0 = 1.5$ Tesla), but this is enough to allow sufficient signal strength.

The equilibrium state is non-informative and has to be perturbed in order to obtain a measurable effect. To this end, a second oscillating magnetic field B_1, created by a radio-frequency (RF) electric field in a coil of wire and oscillating at the Larmor frequency of interest in a plane perpendicular to the direction of B_0, is used to perturb the static magnetic field. The RF photons are absorbed by some of the nuclei to flip their spin from aligned to the magnetic field to anti-aligned, reducing thus the magnitude of the magnetization vector in the direction of B_0.

(M_z becomes smaller than M_0, and it may reach zero magnitude in the so-called 90° RF pulses, or even $-M_0$ in the so-called 180° RF pulses). At the same time, the spins also start to process about the second magnetic field B_1, yielding a tilt of the magnetization vector M to the plane perpendicular onto B_0, making the M_{xy} component non-zero. After the RF pulse is turned off, the spins tend to return to their low energy state, with the effect that the magnetization vector M precesses about B_0 in a spiral until it reaches the equilibrium state. This "relaxation" of the magnetization induces a current in a detector coil, which in turn is captured as an NMR signal (a free induction decay (FID) signal), see Figure 2.1.2. The time dependence of the return to equilibrium is governed by *Bloch's equations* [**5**], which are first-order differential equations describing the motion of the magnetization vector M as a function of time.

The time T_1, called the spin-lattice relaxation time, is the time to reduce the difference between the longitudinal magnetization after the RF pulse and its equilibrium value (see Figure 2.1.1) by a factor of e,

$$M_z(t) = M_0(1 - e^{\frac{-t}{T_1}}) \tag{2.4}$$

where $M_z(t)$ is the longitudinal magnetization at time t.

The time constant which describes the return to equilibrium of the transverse magnetization, M_{xy}, is called the spin-spin relaxation time, T_2, and is defined such that

$$M_{xy}(t) = M_0 e^{\frac{-t}{T_2}}. \tag{2.5}$$

T_1 and T_2 depend on the chemical compound, but T_2 is always less than or equal to T_1. Note that the coils which acquire the signal are located along the x- and y-axes. This explains why T_2 is more important than T_1 in MRS. Due to Bloch's laws [**5**], the induced signal has the shape of a complex exponentially decaying sinusoid in the time domain. The amount of energy emitted by the nuclei, and thus the signal intensity (*i.e.*, its amplitude), is proportional to the number of nuclei that contribute to it, thus to the population difference between the two energy states at every given moment. Equations (2.2)-(2.3) show that a higher intensity is obtained for higher B_0 and lower temperature. For *in vivo* experiments, the temperature is fixed at body temperature and one can only vary B_0 within a secure range to prevent tissue heating.

Note. In order to increase the inherently low signal-to-noise ratio (SNR), several data acquisitions are performed consecutively and the final signal is the average of all measured signals.

Note. In an idealized nuclear magnetic resonance experiment, the FID decays approximately exponentially with a time constant T_2, but, in practice, small differences in the static magnetic field at different spatial locations, also called inhomogeneities, cause the Larmor frequency to vary across the body creating destructive interference which shortens the FID. The time constant for the observed decay of the FID is called T_2* ("T 2 star") relaxation time, and is always shorter than T_2.

2.1.2. Magnetic resonance spectroscopy. From the idealized description in the previous section it might seem that every type of nucleus gives rise to a single exponentially decaying sinusoid at its Larmor frequency. However this is not the case due to the influence of the electrons that are present in the atoms, which perturb the static magnetic field B_0 with their own magnetic environment.

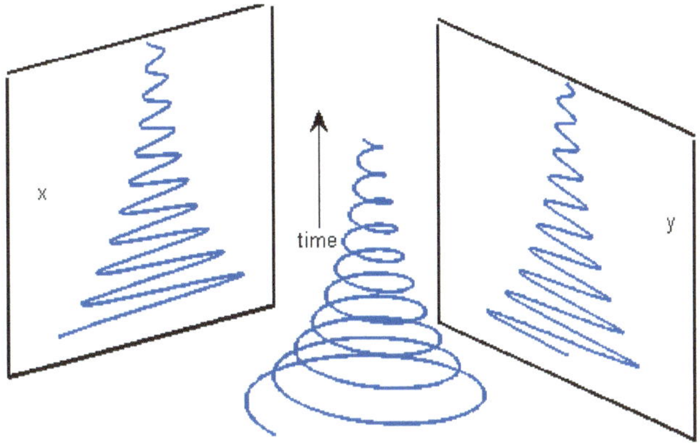

a

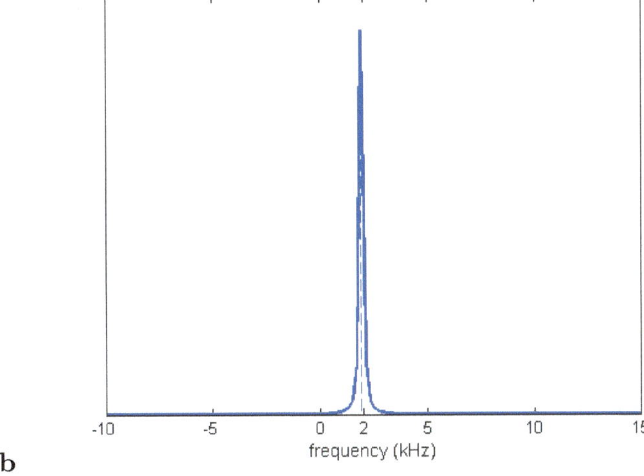

b

FIGURE 2.1.2. **a.** Relaxation of the net magnetization M when the field B_1 is turned off can be measured as an exponentially decaying complex valued signal in the time domain. **b.** Real part of the Fourier transform of the exponential decay in **a.** exhibits a single Lorentzian peak. The area under this peak is equal to the amplitude of the time-domain signal, thus it is proportional to the concentration of the spin population.

This is called a shielding effect and it is essential in separating the chemically and magnetically nonequivalent nuclei of the same isotope. For example, a hydrogen bonded to an oxygen will be shielded differently from a hydrogen bonded to a carbon atom. The electrons are responsible for a small magnetic field at the nucleus, which opposes the externally applied field. The amount of shielding experienced

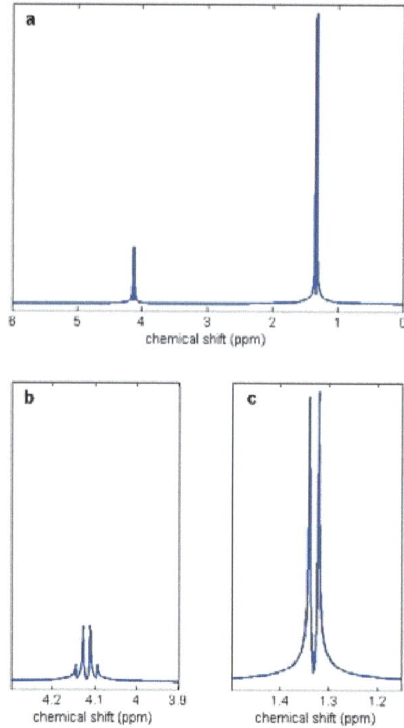

FIGURE 2.1.3. **a.** ^{1}H NMR spectrum of lactate, $CH_3CH(OH)COO$ simulated for a 400MHz spectrometer frequency. The methine proton (*i.e.*, the H in CH) resonates as a quartet at 4.11 ppm (**b**), while the three methyl protons (*i.e.*, the H in CH_3) resonate as a doublet at 1.33 ppm (**c**).

by a nucleus depends on the exact local environment, *i.e.*, on the bonding pattern between atoms in a molecule, and determines the effective magnetic field,

$$B_{\text{eff}} = B_0(1 - \sigma') \tag{2.6}$$

where σ' is the shielding constant, a dimensionless unit that depends on the electrical environment of a nucleus. The effective field at each nucleus will vary. This is called the *chemical shift* phenomenon and it is essential in Magnetic Resonance Spectroscopy because it allows to spectrally distinguish between different chemical compounds.

In addition to the effect of electrons, nuclei which are close to each other exert an influence on each other's effective magnetic field. This effect shows up in the MRS signal when the nuclei are nonequivalent, *i.e.*, have different chemical shifts. If the distance between nonequivalent nuclei is less than or equal to three bond lengths, the effect called *spin-spin coupling* or *J-coupling* is observable. When a nucleus is coupled to n equivalent nuclei, its signal splits into an $n+1$ multiplet with amplitude ratios following Pascal's triangle: Singlet 1; Doublet 1:1; Triplet 1:2:1; Quartet 1:3:3:1; Quintet 1:4:6:4:1; etc. Coupling to additional spins will lead to further splittings of each component of the multiplet, with the possibility to obtain, e.g., a doublet of doublets. Besides the chemical shift, J-coupling is contributing to the specific pattern of the NMR spectrum of a chemical compound, providing thus an important feature for identifying it. This spectral *prior knowledge* (*i.e.*, the shape of an MRS signal given the chemical formula of a compound) can be used to quantum mechanically simulate *metabolite signals*, which can further be used to improve the analysis of *in vivo* measured signals, as illustrated further in Section 2.3.

Note. MRS signals are measured in the time domain as complex-valued decaying signals. For visualization and analysis purposes they are usually Fourier transformed to the frequency domain, yielding MR spectra.

Note. In MRS, the frequency axis is given in part per million (ppm) in order to be independent from the spectrometer frequency (that is, the RF field frequency) in the sense that, if a nucleus resonates at a certain ppm-value for a spectrometer frequency of 63.8 MHz, it will resonate at the same ppm-value for a spectrometer frequency of 500 MHz. The ppm-value of a resonance is defined by

$$\mathrm{ppm}_M = \frac{f_{\mathrm{Hz}} 10^6}{f_S} + \mathrm{ppm}_{\mathrm{Ref}} \tag{2.7}$$

where f_{Hz} is the resonance frequency in Hz, f_S the spectrometer frequency in Hz and $\mathrm{ppm}_{\mathrm{Ref}}$ the ppm-value of a certain reference resonance.

2.1.3. Biomedical applications of ^{1}H NMR. The hydrogen proton (^{1}H) is the most sensitive nucleus in what concerns NMR measurements, and moreover it is abundant in *in vivo* samples. In particular, water is the largest component of the human body. For this reason the water resonance is about 10^5 times more intense compared to other resonances. One of the most widely used ^{1}H NMR techniques is Magnetic Resonance Imaging (MRI), where signals from hydrogen protons from the water molecules are used to form anatomic images that emphasize differences in tissue types. Complementary to MRI, the technique of Magnetic Resonance Spectroscopy has a much higher *spectral resolution* at the expense of lower spatial resolution compared to MRI. This information is used to determine the concentration of brain *metabolites* (*i.e.*, specific chemical compounds) such as N-acetyl aspartate (NAA), choline (Cho), creatine (Cr) and lactate (Lac) in a tissue. Specific patterns of metabolites can be helpful in the diagnosis of certain central nervous system disorders [**6**] such as Alzheimer's disease or epilepsy [**18, 17**], and in the differentiation of high grade from low grade brain tumors [**12**]. *Single-voxel* MRS measures one signal from a voxel (spatial volume element), while *multi-voxel* spectroscopy or MRSI (*MRS imaging*) is designed to combine spatial techniques from MRI with MRS, yielding a compromise between spatial and spectral resolution.

2.1.4. Metabolite quantification. The main computational problem associated with the analysis of MRS signals is called *metabolite quantification (or quantitation)*. This problem aims at determining the concentration of each metabolite in the voxel under investigation, by fitting an appropriate model to the measured signal and computing concentration values from the retrieved parameters. Recall that the concentration of the nucleus under investigation can be computed from the amplitude of the corresponding spectral components.

The rest of this Chapter focuses on computational techniques that perform metabolite quantification in the time domain (the data acquisition domain), although there are some popular methods that solve this problem in the frequency domain (after applying Fourier transform to the original signal). The frequency domain methods range from very simple *peak integration*, where metabolite concentrations are estimated from the area under the peaks obtained via numerical integration of the real or absolute value of the spectrum (see Figure 2.1.2**b.**), or complex model-based optimization algorithms, such as the regularized nonlinear least squares method implemented in the widely-used commercial package LCModel [**34, 35**].

Metabolite quantification methods assume a certain model for the signals. Most certainly, *in vivo* signals do not satisfy all model assumptions, and for this reason various *preprocessing methods* have been designed with the goal of modifying the measured signals such that they better approach the desired model [**31**]. (As a simple example, phase correction is necessary if peak integration is used on the real part of a spectrum, such that all peaks point upwards.)

Although this Chapter focuses on quantification (also referred to simply as *processing*), it also illustrates a number of time-domain preprocessing techniques and explains various artifacts appearing in the signals.

2.2. The classical exponential model for MRS signals

Traditionally, the function used to model an MRS signal is the sum of exponentially damped complex sinusoids:

$$y(t) = \widehat{y}(t) + \varepsilon_t := \sum_{k=1}^{K} \alpha_k \, \zeta_k^t + \varepsilon_t, \quad t = t_0, \ldots, t_{m-1}, \; t_\ell = t_0 + \ell\,\Delta t, \tag{2.8}$$

where K is the number of exponential components, α_k is the complex amplitude of the kth component, which can also be written as

$$\alpha_k = a_k \exp(j\phi_k), \tag{2.9}$$

with a_k the positive real amplitude, ϕ_k the phase, and ζ_k is the signal pole of the kth component, which can be written as

$$\zeta_k = \exp(-d_k + j2\pi f_k), \tag{2.10}$$

with $d_k > 0$ the damping factor, f_k the frequency, and $j = \sqrt{-1}$.

The model $\widehat{y}$ can be seen as the discretized solution of a linear time-invariant (LTI) system. The theory of LTI system identification opens a wide range of possible methods for going from data to a model and then to a particular parametrization. In the MRS community, state-space and linear prediction methods have become popular as black-box identification methods [**2**]. However, optimization methods based on the nonlinear least squares fit of the measured y with the model $\widehat{y}$ are even more appreciated due to the easy incorporation of extra parameter constraints coming from biochemical prior knowledge and to the possibility of modifying the model function to account for various distortions.

2.2.1. Subspace-based methods. HSVD (Hankel singular value decomposition) [**27**] is among the most well-known subspace-based methods applied to the exponential data fitting problem in the MRS application. It is very popular due to its full automation (no essential user interaction is required), but it has also some potential drawbacks. In particular, deviations of the data from the assumed model may lead to bad parameter estimates. Moreover, the original HSVD gives full freedom to the model parameters, while MRS quantification might benefit from imposing some prior knowledge. As further described in Section 2.4, HSVD is most successfully used as a black-box modeling technique in the preprocessing step of *removal of the water component.*

HSVD requires computing the truncated singular value decomposition (SVD) of a Hankel matrix H, containing the noisy signal in its first column and row. If the signal is a sum of K complex damped exponentials (giving K Lorentzian peaks, when the signal is Fourier transformed to the frequency domain), then the data matrix H has rank exactly equal to K. Noise in the signal or a signal not satisfying the exponentially decaying model yields a full rank matrix H. By truncating the SVD to lower rank, one can approximately model the signal as a sum of complex damped exponentials. A recent review of the basic derivation of HSVD and numerical implementation issues (such as the application of the Lanczos method in the computation of a truncated SVD, with a partial reorthogonalization procedure for accuracy improvement **[23]**) can be found in **[22]**. See also the discussion in the first chapter of this book. Moreover, HSVD can be improved by considering a total least squares solution (yielding the HTLS method **[49]**) instead of a least squares solution in approximately solving an incompatible linear system. Special developments allowing to impose prior knowledge include:

- frequencies and damping factors of some exponentials are known **[8, 9]**;
- frequencies and phases of some exponentials are known **[7]**;
- frequencies, dampings and phases of some exponentials are known **[7]**;
- phases of some exponentials are known **[7]**;
- equal phases, equal dampings, linearly related amplitudes are imposed, and frequency shifts are known in signals with multiplet structure **[24]**.

These methods can be more computationally demanding compared to the original HSVD. Furthermore, they require user interaction for choosing the correct prior knowledge or for selecting the type and the frequency region of a multiplet structure.

2.2.2. Optimization-based methods: VARPRO and AMARES. These methods explicitly minimize the function $\|\mathbf{y} - \widehat{\mathbf{y}}\|^2$ (where $\mathbf{y}$, $\widehat{\mathbf{y}}$ stand for vectors obtained from the signals $y(t)$, $\widehat{y}(t)$ at time instants $t = t_0, \ldots, t_{m-1}$) over the model parameters a_k, d_k, f_k, ϕ_k. The variable projection (VARPRO) **[14]** method has been used since the 1980's **[48]** in the context of MRS quantification. The reason of this success story is that the sum of complex damped exponential model suits the separability condition of VARPRO, since its variables can be split into linear—the complex amplitudes α_k, and nonlinear—the complex signal poles ζ_k. Let Φ_k denote the column vector $[(\zeta_k)^{t_0}, \ldots, (\zeta_k)^{t_{m-1}}]^T$ and $\Phi(\zeta)$ the matrix $[\Phi_1, \ldots, \Phi_K]$. With this notation, the model (2.8) can be written as $\widehat{\mathbf{y}} = \Phi(\boldsymbol{\zeta})\boldsymbol{\alpha}$. Then for each fixed instance of the nonlinear parameter vector $\boldsymbol{\zeta} = [\zeta_1, \ldots, \zeta_K]$, the linear variables $\boldsymbol{\alpha} = [\alpha_1, \ldots, \alpha_K]$ can be computed in the least squares sense as $\boldsymbol{\alpha}(\boldsymbol{\zeta}) = \Phi(\boldsymbol{\zeta})^{\dagger}\mathbf{y}$, and the nonlinear least squares objective becomes $\|\mathbf{y} - \Phi(\boldsymbol{\zeta})\Phi(\boldsymbol{\zeta})^{\dagger}\mathbf{y}\|$. The advantage of this formulation is that no starting values are needed for the linear parameters, and that the number of parameters is halved. Moreover, it is well known and proven by theory **[39]** and practice that variable projection always converges with less iterations than the full functional approach. This includes convergence in cases when the full functional approach diverges. A historical note on the application of VARPRO to MRS data quantification can be read in Section 17 of the review paper **[15]**.

In [**48, 47**] imposing prior knowledge about the model parameters is also discussed. The main advantage that can be used is eliminating redundant parameters from a multiplet structure. For example, consider a simple doublet (*e.g.*, the Lactate doublet in Figure 2.1.3**c.**). For this doublet we know that

$$a_1 = a_2, \quad \phi_1 = \phi_2, \quad d_1 = d_2, \quad f_1 = f_2 + \delta f, \quad \delta f \text{ known}.$$

Thus the number of variables can be effectively halved and the VARPRO method can still be used. The admissible prior knowledge (linear relations between amplitudes, equal phases, equal dampings, constant frequency shifts) should be in such a way that a common factor can be extracted from a group of multiplet peaks.

Extensive comparisons between minimization of the full and the variable projection functional based upon the software implementations for nonlinear optimization available at the time have been presented for this MRS model in [**50, 52**] (see also the comments related to this comparison in Section 17 of the review paper [**15**]). In general, the two approaches are equally efficient, but for some of the optimization algorithms the implementation used for VARPRO was less robust, *i.e.*, it had a slightly larger number of convergence failures. The tested implementations differ, however, in some other respects that could have in fact led to this conclusion. For instance, ensuring positivity of the damping factors d_k was done in the VARPRO implementation by using the square of d_k as optimization variable, while the inequality bound $d_k > 0$ was explicitly imposed in the minimization of the full functional. Moreover, the tested VARPRO implementation did not include Kaufman's simplification for Jacobian evaluation [**20**]. However, the main reason for recommending the minimization of the full functional as implemented in AMARES (advanced method for accurate, robust and efficient spectral fitting) [**52**] is the possibility of allowing more flexibility to the prior knowledge (*e.g.*, equal dampings between 2 peaks, but different amplitudes and phases). The implementation of AMARES into jMRUI [**26**] allows for an interactive peak-picking procedure where the user identifies the peaks of the spectrum by mouse-clicking, and starting values for the nonlinear model parameters d_k and f_k are thus computed. The linear parameters are initialized to the linear least squares solution when these nonlinear parameter values are fixed, thus improving considerably the efficiency and robustness of the method.

Note. Optimization-based methods allow for more variation of the model function, by considering other lineshapes apart from the Lorentzian function. Gaussian or Voigt lineshapes (the latter being a combination of Lorentzian and Gaussian functions) are often used. In this case

$$\widehat{y}(t) := \sum_{k=1}^{K} \alpha_k \, (\zeta_k)^t (\eta_k)^{t^2}, \quad t = t_0, \ldots, t_{m-1}, \tag{2.11}$$

where

$$\begin{aligned} \alpha_k &= a_k \exp(j\phi_k), \\ \zeta_k &= \begin{cases} \exp(-d_k + j2\pi f_k), & \text{for Lorentzian and Voigt lineshapes} \\ \exp(j2\pi f_k), & \text{for Gaussian lineshapes} \end{cases} \\ \eta_k &= \begin{cases} \exp(j2\pi e_k), & \text{for Lorentzian lineshapes} \\ \exp(-g_k + j2\pi e_k), & \text{for Gaussian and Voigt lineshapes} \end{cases} \end{aligned} \tag{2.12}$$

where a_k are the real amplitudes, ϕ_k are the phases, d_k are Lorentzian dampings, f_k are frequencies, g_k are Gaussian dampings, and e_k are eddy current correction terms.

2.3. The model for short echo time MRS signals

The model and methods described in the previous section are appropriate for fitting the so-called long echo-time MRS signals. Nowadays, the nuclear magnetic resonance scanners record short echo-time signals that are richer in information because they display the responses of significantly more metabolites. As we saw in Section 2.1, due to chemical shift and J-coupling, the response of each metabolite can be spread out over the whole spectrum. The methods described above might break down if peaks that are in the same frequency region but are unwanted (nuisance peaks) have large amplitudes or are close, in frequency, to the peaks of interest [**38, 51**]. Although methods such as AMARES have been applied quite successfully to short echo time MR spectra [**19**], the nuisance peaks and the more intensive user interaction tend to encourage methods based on the use of *metabolite profiles*, where more prior knowledge can be implicitly included in the model, especially information related to experimental conditions of acquisition.

During an *in vivo* NMR experiment, the measured time-domain signal consists of responses from all metabolites (including macromolecules), noise and (partially suppressed or unsuppressed) water. Spectra of metabolites that are visible during *in vivo* spectroscopy can be measured *in vitro* or they can also be simulated using quantum mechanical knowledge [**16, 45**], and these signals can be grouped in a basis set of metabolite profiles. As discussed in the Introduction, an *in vivo* time-domain signal has, in theory, the shape of a sum of complex damped exponentials. Instead of modeling these individual components, the *in vivo* short echo time MRS signal can be modeled using the profiles in the basis set, such that the prior knowledge that relates individual peaks in the *in vivo* spectrum is implicitly imposed. The quantities of interest, the metabolite *concentrations*, can be estimated from the weighting coefficients (amplitudes) of the linearly combined *in vitro* profiles. The linear combination should allow small corrections in spectral parameters like frequency shifts, damping corrections and phase shifts, since these parameters may vary from measurement to measurement [**37**], *e.g.*, from *in vitro*, to *in vivo*.

We consider that we are given a "metabolite basis set" as a set $\{v_k, \text{ for } k = 1, \ldots, K\}$ of complex-valued time series of length N, representing *in vitro* measured NMR responses. Examples of *in vitro* metabolite spectra are given in Figure 2.3.1.

When lineshape distortions are ignored, we assume that an *in vivo* measured MRS signal y satisfies the model

$$y(t) = \widehat{y}(t) + \varepsilon_t, \quad t = t_0, \ldots, t_{m-1}, \qquad \text{with} \tag{2.13}$$

$$\widehat{y}(t) = \sum_{k=1}^{K} \alpha_k (\zeta_k)^t v_k(t) + b(t) + w(t), \tag{2.14}$$

where $\alpha_k, \zeta_k \in \mathbb{C}$ are unknown parameters that account for amplitudes of the metabolites in the basis set and for the necessary corrections of the basis set signals. The complex amplitudes α_k and the complex values ζ_k can be expanded as in (2.9-2.10), or Gaussian/Voigt correction terms can be considered as in (2.12). In (2.13), the term ε_t denotes an unknown noise perturbation with zero mean, and in (2.14), $b(t)$ denotes the "macromolecular baseline", and $w(t)$ denotes the water component.

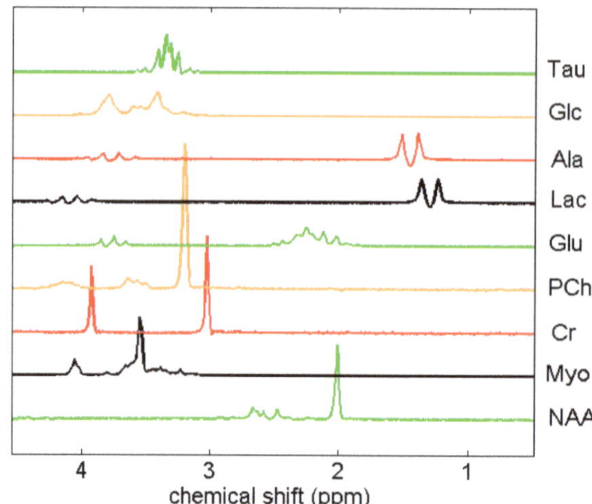

FIGURE 2.3.1. Examples of *in vitro* metabolite spectra (NAA, Myo, Cr, Pch, Glu, Lac, Ala, Glc, Tau) acquired on a 1.5 T Philips NT Gyroscan using a PRESS sequence. They can be used for fitting *in vivo* signals acquired under the same conditions.

The identification of complex amplitudes α_k and complex correction factors ζ_k, for $k = 1, \ldots, K$, can be accomplished by minimizing the least squares criterion: $\sum_{t=t_0,\ldots,t_{m-1}} |y(t) - \widehat{y}(t)|^2$. We ignore for the moment the nuisance signals of water $w(t)$ and macromolecular baseline $b(t)$, which will be dealt with in Section 2.4. This nonlinear least squares problem formulation constitutes the kernel of the algorithms and software implementations such as QUEST [**37**] (included in jMRUI) and AQSES [**30**] (included in the Java interface AqsesGUI [**11**] and in the Matlab package SPID [**28**]). This problem is a separable problem, where linear parameters α_k can be projected out of the least squares problem in closed-form expression. An iterative minimization algorithm of the Levenberg-Marquardt type [**25**] can be used for the numerical minimization of the variable projection functional. The solution of this local optimization method depends on the starting values. In AQSES, for instance, we set initial values to zero, which means that we start the optimization with no spectral corrections to the signals in the basis set, which is appropriate for reasonably frequency-aligned signals. Moreover, we use linear bounds on each nonlinear parameter (soft constraints), since, for instance, frequency shifts should be restricted only to small variations in order to remain relevant.

As explained in [**41**], a variable projection approach [**14**] with approximate Jacobian evaluation is used in AQSES, modified in order to include simple box constraints on the linear and nonlinear variables. According to the authors' experience, this is more robust than optimizing the nonlinear least squares problem directly over all linear and nonlinear parameters without separation, and more computationally efficient, especially in the case when a baseline is also modeled (see Section 2.4 and the Appendix). More importantly, in the variable projection method nearly zero amplitudes a_k do not yield a rank-deficient Jacobian, as it is the case with the full functional. The trust region or Levenberg-Marquardt methods used with either of the functionals are naturally guarded against rank-deficient Jacobians, but it seems preferable to avoid reaching this situation altogether.

Note. Handling (nearly) zero amplitudes without damaging the method's convergence is very important in the fitting of the metabolite-based model. The reason is that we can include more metabolite profiles in the basis set than what is actually present in the *in vivo* signal. Recall that some metabolites are present or not depending of the tissue type, *e.g.*, normal versus tumor. Obtaining nearly zero amplitudes plays the role of "de-selecting" the metabolites that are not contained in the signal.

2.4. Model distortions and preprocessing methods

The aim of the preprocessing steps is to remove irrelevant information, while enhancing the key features (*i.e.*, the metabolic components of interest in the MRS signal) in order to extract parameters (*e.g.*, concentrations) more accurately. MRS signals are affected by the presence of artifacts, instrumental errors, noise and other unwanted components. The spectral quality can be considerably improved by appropriate manipulation of the data. Typical preprocessing steps are enumerated and illustrated below, in their logical sequential order.

Frequency alignment. Frequency alignment is needed when a batch of signals need to be automatically processed, as is the case for MRSI data (*i.e.*, signals in a 2D or 3D grid of voxels). The reason why signals might be spectrally misaligned is the fact that the resonating frequencies are proportional to the static magnetic field B_0, and any spatial inhomogeneities of B_0 are directly translated in frequency misalignment between signals from different regions. This step is performed before other preprocessing steps since most of the subsequent methods require correctly aligned spectra. For the task of aligning two signals, a frequency shift Δf has to be estimated, and the signals have to be shifted by point-wise multiplication in the time-domain with $\exp(2\pi\Delta ft)$. In *in vivo* MR data at 1.5T, large peaks such as NAA, Cho or Cr are generally used as reference for alignment. Alternatively, the spectra can be manually shifted in the frequency domain (for instance, jMRUI offers a drag-and-drop utility for this task) and transformed back into the time domain by the inverse Fourier transformation. For *in vitro* signals, a substance such as TSPS (3-trimethylsilyl-1-propane-sulfonic acid) can be added to each sample and later be used as reference for frequency alignment (see Figure 2.4.1).

Phase and lineshape correction. The zero-order phase is the overall phase of the signal, *i.e.*, the common phase of all spectral components at time 0. The signal can be trivially corrected if an estimate of the phase at time 0 is available. First-order or higher-order phase distortions, which are due to hardware imperfections or timing errors, may depend upon the frequency, thus their correction is more challenging. Time-domain quantification methods account for higher-order phase distortions by incorporating different phases ϕ_k for each spectral component into the model.

Lineshape distortions in the MRS signals are usually caused by eddy currents and magnetic field inhomogeneities. Eddy currents are in turn appearing when a conductor encounters a varying magnetic field, which is the case for the coils of the NMR scanner. Good hardware techniques are nowadays available for compensating against eddy current effects [**46**], but signal processing can also provide an effective

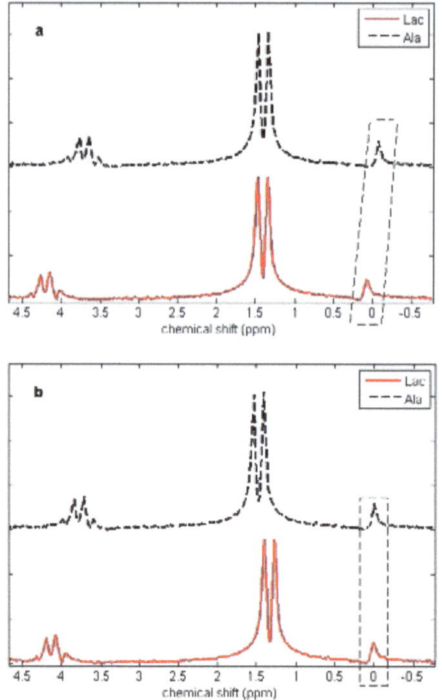

FIGURE 2.4.1. Frequency alignment is essential for these two similarly looking metabolite spectra measured *in vitro*, Alanine and Lactate. **a**) The two signals are not aligned according to the reference peak of TSPS at 0 ppm, thus the doublets at around 1.4 ppm are indistinguishable from each other. **b**) The two signals are aligned according to the reference peak at 0 ppm, making the doublets and quartets of Alanine and Lactate more easily distinguishable.

solution. For instance, in the case a water-unsuppressed signal is available together with the water-suppressed signal, Klose's method [**21**] can be carried out for phase and eddy current correction. This corrects for eddy currents by dividing the water-suppressed signal to the phase term of the water-unsuppressed signal. (See Figure 2.4.2.) Lineshape correction methods like QUALITY [**10**] and QUECC [**4**] can also correct for distortions in the magnitude of the signal, while other phase artifacts are dealt with by phase filtering in [**53**]. The goal of these methods is to transform the original signal such that it follows a Lorentzian model (*i.e.*, sum of complex damped exponentials), which is often used in quantification methods.

Water filtering. As mentioned before, the water component in ^{1}H MRS signals is several orders of magnitude higher than the other metabolite contributions. For this reason many efforts have been put into hardware-based suppression techniques of the water signal through the design of special pulse sequences [**33, 43, 44**]. It is nowadays common practice to acquire so-called "water-suppressed" signals besides/instead of the "water-unsuppressed" signals that are normally obtained by

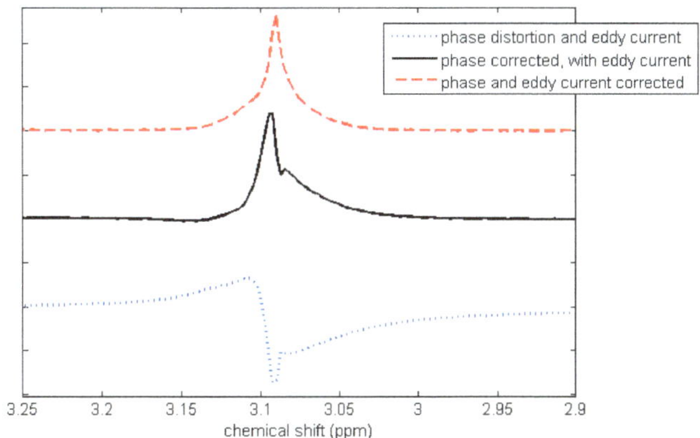

FIGURE 2.4.2. Phase and eddy current correction (illustrated here on a singlet) can be accomplished in the scanner or by Klose's method.

MRS. However, these signals still contain water resonances higher than the metabolite signals. Signal processing methods must and can in fact deal with these two types of water signals, in order to extract only the metabolite information. Frequency selective filtering is the key tool, since the metabolites of interest and the water components are resonating at sufficiently distant frequencies.

Residual water removal can be performed by a black-box modeling approach such as HSVD [**3**], based on the idea of first fitting the whole signal as a sum of complex damped exponentials and then subtracting all the components whose frequencies were estimated in the frequency region of the water resonance. In Figure 2.4.3**a.** we illustrate this procedure using the HLSVD-PRO implementation [**23**]. Wavelets and the Gabor transform [**1**] have also been successful for this task. Finally, pass-band filtering can also be performed by FIR filtering, after appropriate filter design. Here we cite the MP-FIR (maximum-phase finite impulse response filter) [**51**] and its recent improvement MP-FIR0 [**29**]. These methods are based on finding the coefficients of an FIR filter that will be convolved with the MRS signal. The filters are optimized to suppress the resonances that are outside the frequency region of interest and to keep the region of interest (where the metabolites are visible) with minimal distortions [**28**]. (See Figure 2.4.3**b.**)

Note. AQSES [**30**] does not use MP-FIR in a preprocessing step, but includes it *during* the nonlinear least squares optimization. Therefore, the quantification algorithm fits a filtered model based on metabolite profiles to a filtered *in vivo* signal. This approach leaves model parameters (in particular, the amplitudes) intact, since the FIR filtering is a linear operation, *i.e.*, it can be expressed as a matrix-vector product. Results in [**32**] indicate that this approach is superior in terms of accuracy of estimated amplitudes compared to quantifying preprocessed signals by water filtering with HLSVD-PRO.

Baseline correction. Baselines in the NMR spectra are caused by distortion of the first few data points in the time domain signal. Two different phenomena may contribute to this distortion: 1) the amplitudes of the initial data points are

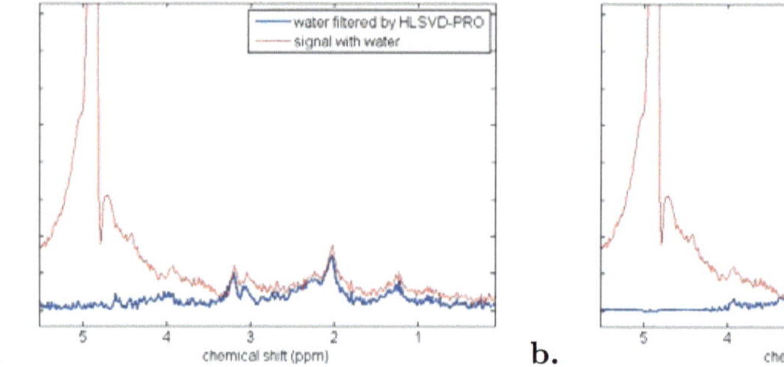

a. **b.**

FIGURE 2.4.3. Filtering water components at around 4.7 ppm from a realistically simulated noisy MRS signal. **a.** HLSVD-PRO [**23**], **b.** MP-FIR0 [**29**].

distorted due to instrumental imperfections (baseline distortion), 2) actual resonances of weakly mobile *macromolecules* are present in the signal (macromolecular background). Macromolecular signals, coming from the macromolecules present in the tissue under investigation, are characterized by broad spectral lines (short T_2), which often overlap in the frequency domain with metabolite components. Short echo time ^{1}H-MR spectra of human brain contain a significant macromolecular background that complicates drastically the quantification process.

We illustrate in Figure 2.4.4 a realistically simulated signal (using 8 metabolites from the basis set in Figure 2.3.1 at relative amplitudes corresponding to values found in healthy human brain), and we artificially add a simulated macromolecular baseline (created by adding 5 Gaussian components as suggested in [**40**]).

There exist several types of baseline correction methods.

- Multiplication of the FID by an exponentially decaying function. The baseline is fitted as the product of the original FID and an exponentially decreasing *apodization* function $\exp(-d_0 t)$ [**42**], which requires only the decay as parameter to be selected. As the baseline consists of broad fast decaying components, their main contribution is in the first part of the FID. After multiplication with a decaying function, the resulting function will mainly contain the broad baseline components. As illustrated in Figure 2.4.5 for a range of decay parameters d_0, the obtained baseline also takes a significant part of the metabolite components and strongly overestimates the baseline contribution.
- Truncation of the initial points in the FID proposed by Ratiney *et al.* [**36**] in the method QUEST. The baseline, being a broad component in the spectrum, decays very rapidly (T_2-value of the macromolecules is small compared to the T_2 of the metabolites of interest). Hence, removing the initial part of the FID should suppress the baseline components. However, this operation also suppresses part of the metabolite contributions and might reduce the accuracy of the estimates since the SNR is decreased. QUEST fits a basis set of truncated metabolite signals to the truncated signal, then extrapolates the model backwards to time 0, and subtracts it from the original signal. What is obtained is a (noisy) estimation of the baseline. Figure 2.4.6 illustrates several baseline estimates obtained

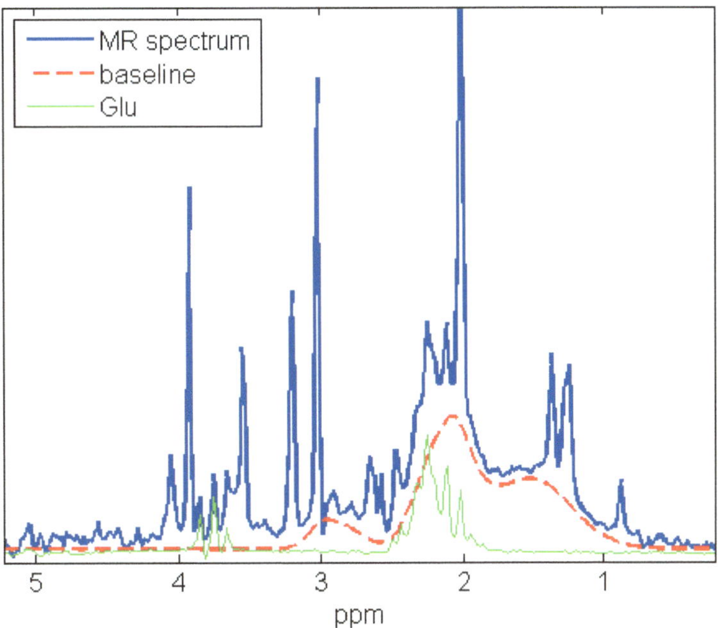

FIGURE 2.4.4. Real part of a realistically simulated MRS signal (thick blue line) with an added macromolecular baseline (interrupted red line). The metabolite Glutamate (Glu), highly overlapping with the simulated baseline, is also shown as a thin green line.

for different number of truncation points and denoised using smoothing spline.

- Nonparametric modeling of the baseline, characterized by a smooth function in the frequency domain, by penalized splines [**13**] in AQSES [**30, 41**]. In order to fit the model and the smooth baseline at the same time, a regularized nonlinear least squares criterion is considered

$$\min \|\mathbf{y} - \widehat{\mathbf{y}}\|^2 + \lambda \|D\mathbf{c}\|^2, \tag{2.15}$$

where $\widehat{\mathbf{y}}$ is given in (2.14), but with the baseline b replaced by the formula $b = \mathcal{A} \cdot \mathbf{c}$, which is the inverse Fourier transformation of the frequency-domain baseline linearly modeled as a sum of spline functions, $A \cdot \mathbf{c}$. In (2.15), the whole term $\lambda\|D\mathbf{c}\|^2$ is responsible for ensuring a certain degree of smoothness to the baseline b. The regularization matrix D is a (combination of) discrete derivative operator(s) [**13**]. The regularization parameter λ is a positive scalar that controls the degree of smoothness. Figure 2.4.7 illustrates the baseline fit obtained for the same example as above; here the regularization parameter was modified to vary the degree of smoothness.

None of the methods above is perfect, partly because the main assumption made is only about the smoothness of the baseline in the frequency domain (equivalent

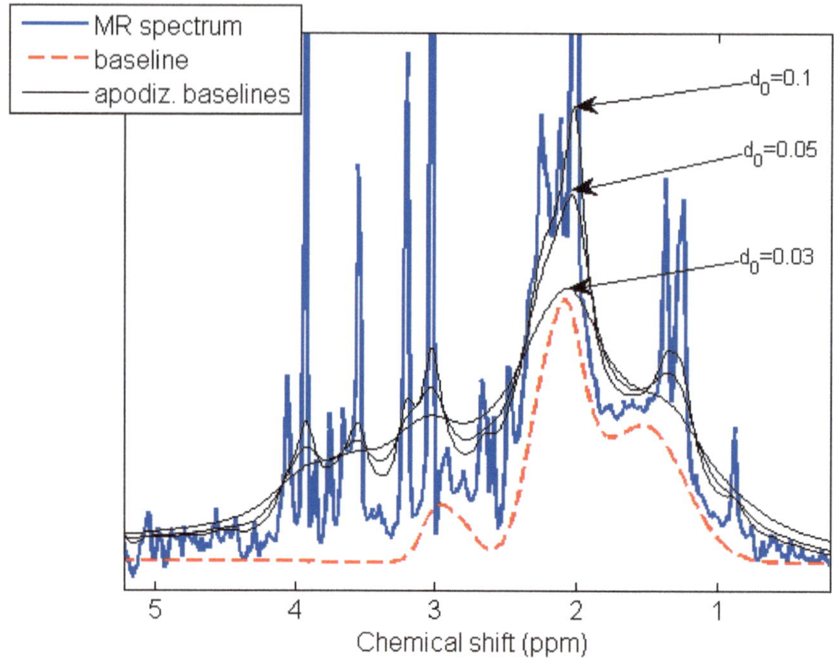

FIGURE 2.4.5. Real part of a simulated MRS signal with added macromolecular baseline, and three baseline estimates obtained by apodization with decay parameters $d_0 = 0.1, 0.05, 0.03$. For this example, the baseline is systematically overestimated.

to saying that the time-domain counterpart decays in the first few time points), and this smoothness has to be controlled through tuning certain hyper-parameters. However, there are other limitations not taken into account, as for example the fact that the baseline is highly overlapping to some metabolites of interest, thus their contributions to the whole signal cannot always be disentagled. We illustrate this fact in Figure 2.4.8, where the metabolite error (*i.e.,* the difference between simulated and reconstructed signals based only on the metabolite profiles) is shown together with the simulated baseline, a reconstructed baseline (with splines in AQSES), as well as the baseline residual fit. The estimated amplitudes of all metabolites are overestimated by around 7% compared to the true values, while the baseline is underestimated. The high spectral overlap between metabolites and the baseline thus leads to systematic bias in the estimation.

Note. When a baseline is modeled nonparametrically with splines, a large number of additional linear variables (the spline coefficients) need also to be estimated. In this case it is essential to make use of the variable projection approach, as illustrated in the appendix.

2.5. Conclusions

In this Chapter we discussed Magnetic Resonance Spectroscopy from basic theoretical concepts to typical signal analysis techniques. The concepts of chemical shift and J-coupling have been instrumental for the definition of biochemical prior

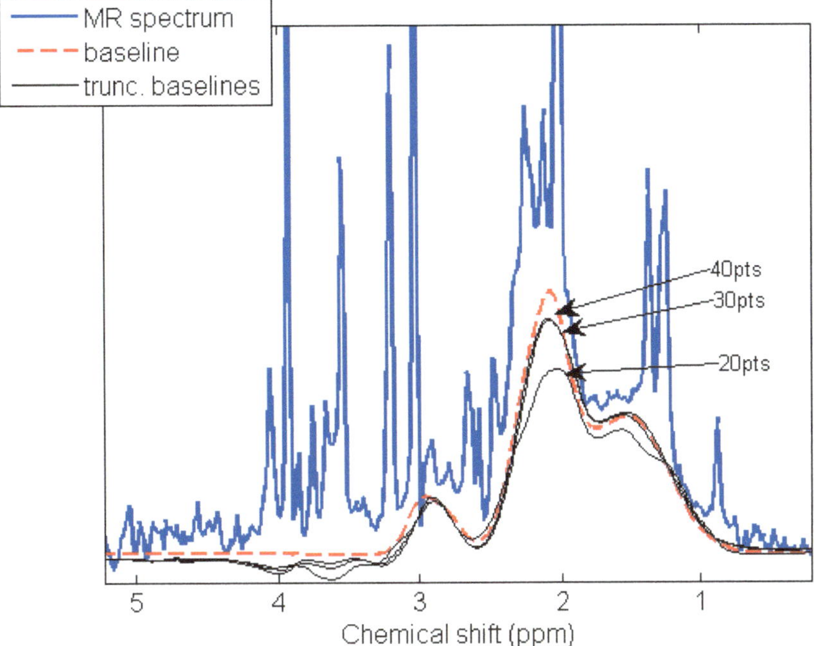

FIGURE 2.4.6. Real part of a simulated MRS signal with added macromolecular baseline, and three baseline estimates obtained by truncation, back-extrapolation, subtraction and denoising—a QUEST-like procedure—with number of truncation points equal to 20, 30, and 40. For this example, the baseline is systematically underestimated.

knowledge, which makes it possible to differentiate between different metabolites present in the voxel under investigation. The problem of metabolite quantification can be formulated mathematically as a nonlinear least squares fit between the data and a model. Traditional models based on a sum of complex damped exponential, although very successful for signals with few spectral components and no artifacts, have given way in more recent years to methods that can incorporate more prior knowledge, *e.g.*, models based on a weighted sum of metabolite signals. The numerical methods used for metabolite quantification range from black-box subspace-based methods that can only incorporate very limited prior knowledge to optimization-based methods that are allowing more flexibility to the model. The separation of the model parameters into linear and nonlinear motivates the applicability of the variable projection technique in a number of MRS models.

MRS signals measured in the human brain may contain nuisance components originating from inhomogeneous magnetic field, patient movement, interference from the skull, etc, which must be removed during preprocessing or taken into account at the modeling stage. Although water suppression or eddy current corrections are well studied at both hardware and signal processing stages, other problems with artifacts are still under study, such as the best model for the macromolecular background, or the automatic estimation of non-Lorentzian lineshape models.

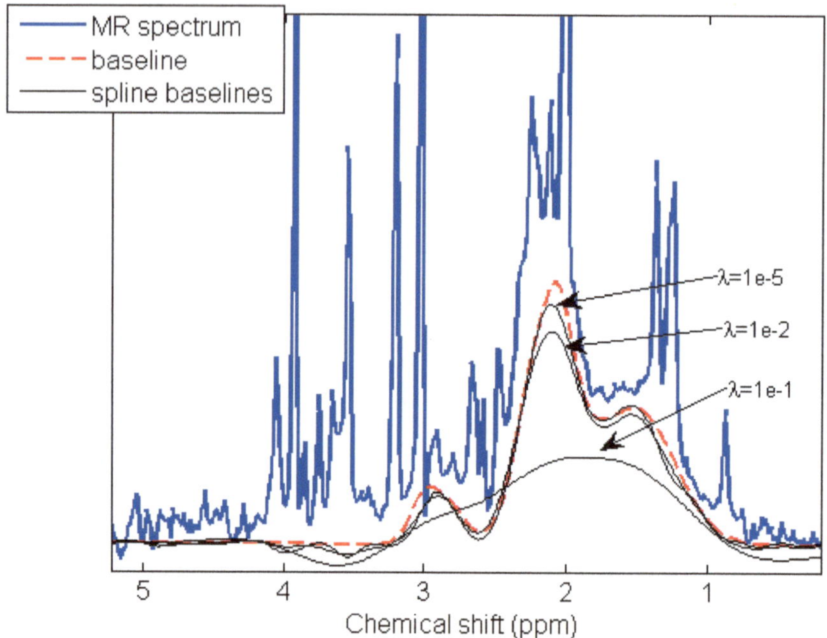

FIGURE 2.4.7. Real part of a simulated MRS signal with added macromolecular baseline, and three baseline estimates obtained by simultaneous fitting the metabolites and the spline baseline in the time-domain—the AQSES procedure—with regularization parameters λ equal to 1e−5, 1e−2, and 1e−1. For this example, the baseline is systematically underestimated.

Appendix

In this appendix we illustrate the convergence of the quantification method based on a metabolite basis set (AQSES [**30**]) in the cases when is implemented or not in the nonlinear least squares objective, and when a baseline modeled with splines is used into the model or not. Results are obtained in Matlab® (The Mathworks) using the Optimization Toolbox. For the variable projection version we use the AQSES implementation in SPID, while the minimization of the full functional is available in an older AQSES version.

The considered example is a noise-free signal of length 1024 containing 8 metabolite profiles, each perturbed by a frequency shift and a damping variation, but without other artifacts. Note that this zero-residual example is not typical, as there are always artifacts and noise in MRS signals, but these would impair the illustrative effect of this example, since convergence would not be so easily visualized.

When no baseline is estimated, the model has an equal number of linear and nonlinear variables (*i.e.*, 16 (non)linear variables for the 8 metabolites). In this case, the evaluation of the projected functional and Jacobian (with Kaufman's simplification [**20**]) is more expensive than of the full functional. The number of iterations needed for convergence is similar for the two approaches because good

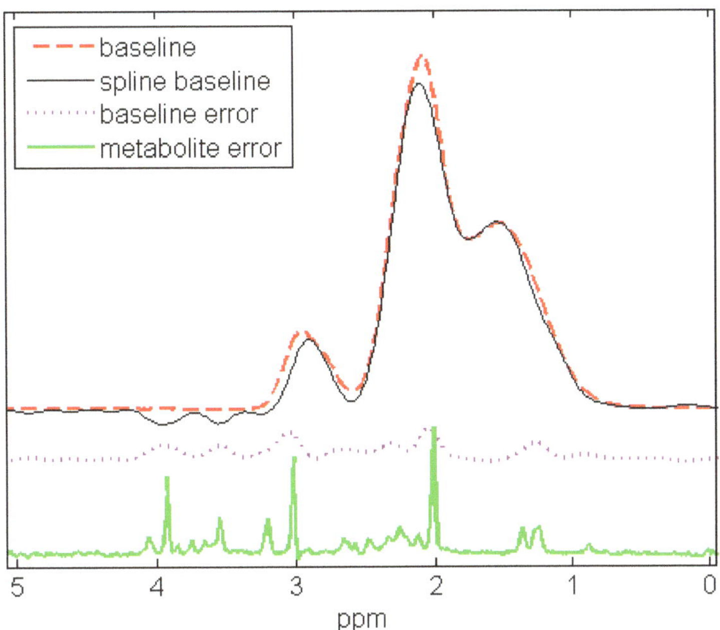

FIGURE 2.4.8. Real part of a simulated MRS macromolecular baseline (interrupted red line), and a spline baseline estimate (thin black line). The error in the estimation of the metabolites, *i.e.*, an overestimation of about 7% compared to the true values, is shown as a thick green line. This error is highly correlated with the baseline estimation error (dotted magenta line).

starting values for the linear parameters are provided in the minimization of the full functional by a linear least squares fit with fixed initial nonlinear parameters values, which makes the variable projection slower for this example (9 versus 4 seconds on a 2.4GHz processor; without counting plotting time, the effective time becomes 4.7s versus 0.7s). (See Figure 2.5.1 **a.-b.** and the corresponding videos.)

We also illustrate the case when a baseline is considered in the model, which is nonparametrically fitted with splines. In this case there are additional linear parameters (the spline coefficients, where we considered a spline function per 10% of the data points, leading to 102 additional linear parameters). Without doubt, the variable projection is faster and more stable in this case. The number of iterations needed for convergence is lower for the variable projection approach, which makes the variable projection faster for this example (28 versus 113 seconds on a 2.4GHz processor; without counting plotting time, the effective time becomes 24s versus 109s). (See Figure 2.5.1 **c.-d.** and the corresponding videos.)

Acknowledgments

Dr. Diana M. Sima is a postdoctoral fellow of the Fund for Scientific Research-Flanders. Dr. Sabine Van Huffel is a full professor at the Katholieke Universiteit Leuven, Belgium. Research supported by

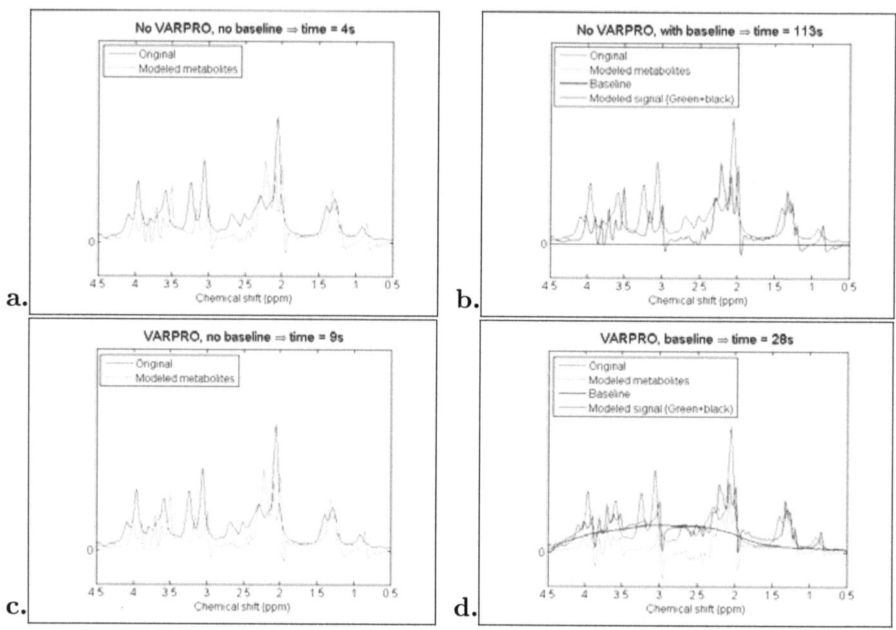

FIGURE 2.5.1. Real part of a simulated MRS signal (blue) and the initial fit with a combination of 8 metabolite signals (green in **a.** and **c.**, red in **b.** and **d.**, where a spline baseline in black is also added). Recall that the initialization is set to no corrections in the metabolite profiles. **a.** Convergence occurs in 12 iterations and takes 4 seconds when the full functional is used and no baseline is included. **b.** Convergence occurs in 17 iterations and takes 113 seconds when the full functional is used and baseline is included. **c.** Convergence occurs in 15 iterations and takes 9 seconds when variable projection is used and no baseline is included. **d.** Convergence occurs in 12 iterations and takes 28 seconds when variable projection is used and baseline is included.

- Research Council KUL: GOA-MANET, GOA-AMBioRICS, CoE EF/05/006 Optimization in Engineering (OPTEC), IDO 05/010 EEG-fMRI, IOF-KP06/11, several PhD/postdoc and fellow grants;
- Flemish Government:
  - FWO: PhD/postdoc grants, projects, G.0407.02 (support vector machines), G.0360.05 (EEG, Epileptic), G.0519.06 (Noninvasive brain oxygenation), FWO-G.0321.06 (Tensors/Spectral Analysis), G.0302.07 (SVM), G.0341.07 (Data fusion), research communities (ICCoS, ANMMM);
  - IWT: PhD Grants;
- Belgian Federal Science Policy Office IUAP P6/04 (DYSCO, 'Dynamical systems, control and optimization', 2007-2011);
- EU: BIOPATTERN (FP6-2002-IST 508803), ETUMOUR (FP6-2002-LIFESCIHEALTH 503094), Healthagents (IST-2004-27214), FAST (FP6-MC-RTN-035801)
- ESA: Cardiovascular Control (Prodex-8 C90242)

Bibliography

1. J. P. Antoine, A. Coron, and J. M. Dereppe, *Water peak suppression: time-frequency vs time-scale approach*, J. Magn. Reson. **144**, no. 2, 189–194 (2000).
2. H. Barkhuijsen, R. de Beer, W. M. Bovee, J. H. Creyghton, and D. van Ormondt, *Application of linear prediction and singular value decomposition (LPSVD) to determine NMR frequencies and intensities from the FID*, Magn. Reson. Med. **2**, no. 1, 86–9 (1985).
3. H. Barkhuijsen, R. de Beer, and D. van Ormondt, *Improved algorithm for noniterative time-domain model fitting to exponentially damped magnetic resonance signals*, J. Magn. Reson. **73**, no. 3, 553–57 (1987).
4. R. Bartha, D. J. Drost, R. S. Menon, and P. C. Williamson, *Spectroscopic lineshape correction by QUECC: combined QUALITY deconvolution and eddy current correction*, Magn. Reson. Med. **44**, no. 4, 641–5 (2000).
5. F. Bloch, *Nuclear induction*, Physics Review **70**:460–473 (1946).
6. I.M. Burtscher and S. Holtøas, *Proton MR spectroscopy in clinical routine*, J. Magn. Reson. Imaging **13**, no. 3, 560–567 (2001).
7. H. Chen, S. Van Huffel, A. van den Boom, and P. van den Bosch, *Subspace-based parameter estimation of exponentially damped sinusoids using prior knowledge of frequency and phase*, Signal Process. **59**, no. 1, 129–36 (1997).
8. H. Chen, S. Van Huffel, D. van Ormondt, and R. de Beer, *Parameter estimation with prior knowledge of known signal poles for the quantification of NMR spectroscopy data in the time domain*, J. Magn. Reson. A **119**, no. 2, 225–34 (1996).
9. H. Chen, S. Van Huffel, and J. Vandewalle, *Improved methods for exponential parameter estimation in the presence of known poles and noise*, IEEE T. Signal Proces. **45**, no. 5, 1390–1393 (1997).
10. A. A. de Graaf, *QUALITY: quantification improvement by converting lineshapes to the Lorentzian type*, Magn. Reson. Med. **13**:343–57 (1990).
11. B. De Neuter, J. Luts, L. Vanhamme, P. Lemmerling, and S. Van Huffel, *Java-based framework for processing and displaying short-echo-time magnetic resonance spectroscopy signals*, Comp. Meth. Prog. Biom. **85**:129–137 (2007).
12. A. Devos, L. Lukas, J. A. K. Suykens, L. Vanhamme, A. R. Tate, F. A. Howe, C. Majos, A. Moreno Torres, C. van der Graaf, M. Arus, and S. Van Huffel, *Classification of brain tumours using short echo time* ^1H *MR spectra*, J. Magn. Reson. **170**, no. 1, 164–75 (2004).
13. P. H. C. Eilers and B. D. Marx, *Flexible smoothing with B-splines and penalties*, Stat. Sci. **11**:89–121 (1997).
14. G. H. Golub and V. Pereyra, *The differentiation of pseudo-inverses and nonlinear least squares problems whose variables separate*, SIAM J. Numer. Anal. **10**:413–32 (1973).
15. G. H. Golub and V. Pereyra, *Separable nonlinear least squares: the variable projection method and its applications*, Inverse Probl. **19**, no. 2, 1–26 (2003).
16. D. Graveron Demilly, A. Diop, A. Briguet, and B. Fenet, *Product-operator algebra for strongly coupled spin systems*, J. Magn. Reson. A **101**, no. 3, 233–39 (1993).
17. Y.Y. Hsu, A.T. Du, N Schuff, and Weiner M.W., *Magnetic resonance imaging and magnetic resonance spectroscopy in dementias*, J. Geriatr. Psychiatry Neurol. **14**, no. 3, 145–166 (2001).
18. W. Huang, G. E. Alexander, L. Chang, H. U. Shetty, J. S. Krasuski, S. I. Rapoport, and M. B. Schapiro, *Brain metabolite concentration and dementia severity in Alzheimer's disease: a* ^1H *MRS study.*, Neurology **57**, no. 4, 626–632 (2001).
19. M. Kanowski, J. Kaufmann, J. Braun, J. Bernarding, and C. Tempelmann, *Quantitation of simulated short echo time* ^1H *human brain spectra by LCModel and AMARES*, Magn. Reson. Med. **51**, no. 5, 904–912 (2004).

20. L. Kaufman, *A variable projection method for solving separable nonlinear least squares problems*, BIT **15**:49–57 (1975).
21. U. Klose, *In vivo proton spectroscopy in presence of eddy currents*, Magn. Reson. Med. **14**:26–30 (1990).
22. T. Laudadio, *Subspace-based quantification of magnetic resonance spectroscopy data using biochemical prior knowledge*, Ph.D. thesis, Faculty of Engineering, K.U.Leuven, Leuven, Belgium (2005).
23. T. Laudadio, N. Mastronardi, L. Vanhamme, P. Van Hecke, and S. Van Huffel, *Improved Lanczos algorithms for blackbox MRS data quantitation*, J. Magn. Reson. **157**, no. 2, 292–7 (2002).
24. T. Laudadio, Y. Selën, L. Vanhamme, P. Stoica, P. Van Hecke, and S. Van Huffel, *Subspace-based MRS data quantitation of multiplets using prior knowledge*, J. Magn. Reson. **168**, no. 1, 53–65 (2004).
25. J. J. Moré, *The Levenberg-Marquardt algorithm: Implementation and theory*, Numerical Analysis: Proceedings of the Biennial Conference held at Dundee, June 28-July 1, 1977 (Lecture Notes in Mathematics #630), 104–16 (1978).
26. A. Naressi, C. Couturier, I. Castang, R. de Beer, and D. Graveron-Demilly, *Java-based graphical user interface for MRUI , a software package for quantitation of in vivo/medical magnetic resonance spectroscopy signals.*, Comput Biol Med **31**, no. 4, 269–286 (2001).
27. W. W. F. Pijnappel, A. van den Boogaart, R. de Beer, and D. van Ormondt, *SVD-based quantification of magnetic resonance signals*, J. Magn. Reson. **97**, no. 1, 122–34 (1992).
28. J. Poullet, *Quantification and Classification of Magnetic Resonance Spectroscopic Data for Brain Tumor Diagnosis*, Ph.D. thesis, Faculty of Engineering, K.U.Leuven, Leuven, Belgium (2008).
29. J. Poullet, R. Pintelon, and S. Van Huffel, *A new fir filter technique for solvent suppression in mrs signals*, J. Magn. Reson. **196**:61–73 (2009).
30. J. Poullet, D. M. Sima, A. W. Simonetti, B. De Neuter, L. Vanhamme, P. Lemmerling, and S. Van Huffel, *An automated quantitation of short echo time MRS spectra in an open source software environment: AQSES*, NMR Biomed. **20**, no. 5, 493–504 (2007).
31. J. Poullet, D. M. Sima, and S. Van Huffel, *MRS signal quantitation: a review of time- and frequency-domain methods*, J. Magn. Reson. **195**:134–144 (2008).
32. J. Poullet, D. M. Sima, S. Van Huffel, and P. Van Hecke, *Frequency-selective quantitation of short-echo time ^1H magnetic resonance spectra*, J. Magn. Reson. **186**, no. 2, 293–304 (2007).
33. E. Prost, P. Sizun, M. Piotto, and J. M. Nuzillard, *A simple scheme for the design of solvent-suppression pulses*, J. Magn. Reson. **159**, no. 1, 76–81 (2002).
34. S. W. Provencher, *Estimation of metabolite concentrations from localized in vivo proton NMR spectra*, Magn. Reson. Med. **30**, no. 6, 672–79 (1993).
35. S. W. Provencher, *Automatic quantitation of localized in vivo ^1H spectra with LCModel*, NMR Biomed. **14**, no. 4, 260–4 (2001).
36. H. Ratiney, Y. Coenradie, S. Cavassila, D. van Ormondt, and D. Graveron-Demilly, *Time-domain quantitation of ^1H short echo-time signals: background accommodation*, MAGMA **16**, no. 6, 284–96 (2004).
37. H. Ratiney, M. Sdika, Y. Coenradie, S. Cavassila, D. van Ormondt, and D. Graveron-Demilly, *Time-domain semi-parametric estimation based on a metabolite basis set*, NMR Biomed. **18**, no. 1, 1–13 (2005).
38. R. Romano, A. Motta, S. Camassa, C. Pagano, M. T. Santini, and P. L. Indovina, *A new time-domain frequency-selective quantification algorithm*, J. Magn. Reson. **155**, no. 2, 226–35 (2002).
39. A. Ruhe and P.A. Wedin, *Algorithms for separable nonlinear least squares problems*, SIAM Rev. **22**, no. 3, 318–37 (1980).
40. U. Seeger and U. Klose, *Parameterized evaluation of macromolecules and lipids in proton MR spectroscopy of brain diseases*, Magn. Reson. Med. **49**:19–28 (2003).
41. D. M. Sima and S. Van Huffel, *Regularized semiparametric model identification with application to NMR signal quantification with unknown macromolecular baseline*, J. Royal Stat. Soc. B **68**, no. 3, 383–409 (2006).
42. A. W. Simonetti, W. Melsen, M. van der Graaf, G. Postma, A. Heerschap, and L. M. C. Buydens, *A chemometric approach for brain tumor classsification using magnetic resonance imaging and spectroscopy*, Anal. Chem. **75(20)**, 29–36 (2003).

43. A. J. Simpson and S. A. Brown, *Purge NMR: effective and easy solvent suppression*, J. Magn. Reson. **175**, no. 2, 340–6 (2005).
44. M. A. Smith, J. Gillen, M. T. McMahon, P. B. Barker, and X. Golay, *Simultaneous water and lipid suppression for in vivo brain spectroscopy in humans*, Magn. Reson. Med. **54**, no. 3, 691–6 (2005).
45. S. A. Smith, T. O. Levante, B. H. Meier, and R. R. Ernst, *Computer simulations in magnetic resonance. An object-oriented programming approach*, J. Magn. Reson. A **106**, no. 1, 75–105 (1994).
46. M. Terpstra, P. M. Andersen, and R. Gruetter, *Localized eddy current compensation using quantitative field mapping.*, J. Magn. Reson. **131**, no. 1, 139–143 (1998).
47. A. van den Boogaart, F. A. Howe, L. M. Rodrigues, M. Stubbs, and J. R. Griffiths, *In vivo ^{31}P MRS: absolute concentrations, signal-to-noise and prior knowledge*, NMR Biomed. **8**, no. 2, 87–93 (1995).
48. J. W. van der Veen, R. de Beer, P. R. Luyten, and D. van Ormondt, *Accurate quantification of in vivo ^{31}P NMR signals using the variable projection method and prior knowledge*, Magn. Reson. Med. **6**, no. 1, 92–8 (1988).
49. S. Van Huffel, H. Chen, C. Decanniere, and P. Van Hecke, *Algorithm for time-domain NMR data fitting based on total least squares*, J. Magn. Reson. A **110**:228–237 (1994).
50. L. Vanhamme, S. Van Huffel, P. Van Hecke, and D. van Ormondt, *Time-domain quantification of series of biomedical magnetic resonance spectroscopy signals.*, J. Magn. Reson. **140**, no. 1, 120–130 (1999).
51. L. Vanhamme, T. Sundin, P. Van Hecke, S. Van Huffel, and R. Pintelon, *Frequency-selective quantification of biomedical magnetic resonance spectroscopy data.*, J. Magn. Reson. **143**, no. 1, 1–16 (2000).
52. L. Vanhamme, A. van den Boogaart, and S. Van Huffel, *Improved method for accurate and efficient quantification of MRS data with use of prior knowledge*, J. Magn. Reson. **129**:35–43 (1997).
53. J. M. Wild, *Artifacts introduced by zero order phase correction in proton NMR spectroscopy and a method of elimination by phase filtering*, J. Magn. Reson. **137**:430–436 (1999).

CHAPTER 3

Recovery of relaxation rates in MRI T_2–weighted brain images via exponential fitting

Marco Paluszny, Marianela Lentini,
Escuela de Matematicas
Universidad Nacional de Colombia, Medellin
mpalusznyk@unal.edu.co

Miguel Martin-Landrove
Centro de Fisica Molecular y Medica, Escuela de Fisica, Facultad de Ciencias
Universidad Central de Venezuela y Centro de Diagnostico Docente
Las Mercedes, Caracas, Venezuela
mmartin@fisica.ciens.ucv.ve

Wuilian Torres
Centro de Procesamiento Digital de Imagenes, Instituto de Ingenieria y
Laboratorio de Computacion Grafica y Geometria Aplicada
Escuela de Matematica, Facultad de Ciencias
Universidad Central de Venezuela
Caracas, Venezuela
wtorres@fii.org

Rafael Martin
Centro de Fisica Molecular y Medica
Escuela de Fisica, Facultad de Ciencias
Universidad Central de Venezuela
Caracas, Venezuela
rmartinlandrove@yahoo.es

Victor Pereyra & Godela Scherer (Eds)

ABSTRACT. We consider synthetic magnetic resonance images of a brain slice generated with the BrainWeb resource. They correspond to measurements taken at various times and record the intensity of the response signal of the probed tissue to a magnetic pulse. The specific property measured, which is considered in this chapter, is transverse magnetization. The transverse magnetization decay technique can be used to obtain several images for a given axial slice of tissue. Namely, for each pixel the time uniform sequence of transverse magnetization measurements yields information about the tissues at that pixel and for a given time the responses of all the pixels form an image of the slice. In clinical studies this data is acquired using the magnetic resonance procedure. Mathematically this decay is described as a linear combination of decaying exponentials and it strongly correlates to the tissue type at each pixel. We consider several approaches to extract the exponents and estimates of the fractions of each tissue type for every pixel in a region of interest. The main thrust is on separation of variables techniques, by looking at Prony's method, some special Vandermonde systems and linear regression. We consider comparisons of a Prony technique and the classical separable nonlinear least squares method.

Keywords: Magnetic Resonance Imaging (MRI), Prony method, Separable Nonlinear Least Squares, T_2-weighted, Transverse Magnetization Decay

3.1. Introduction

Living tissues are complex and heterogeneous systems and nuclear magnetic resonance probes are very powerful tools in the study of these systems from an anatomical point of view as well as from a functional point of view. In proton relaxation studies the T_2-weighted transverse magnetization decay[1] is not governed by a single relaxation rate but by a superposition of different relaxation rates, each one corresponding to a different environment and to different dynamics which are probed by the interplay of external and local magnetic fields and their interaction with local nuclear spins. In this sense a particular relaxation rate is a signature of a particular kind of tissue and then it opens the possibility for image segmentation, which is the classification of pixels (in two dimensions) or voxels (in three dimensions) based on the kind of tissue found in them. From the clinical point of view this classification is of paramount importance in diagnosis and treatment planning for different pathological conditions.

In order to proceed with a classification scheme we have to look for a mathematical object which contains all the required information for the completion of such a task. In practical terms, this means that there is a probability distribution function for relaxation rates. Given a pixel the probability distribution function for relaxation rate is the normalized frequency histogram which is constructed as follows.

---

[1] Transverse magnetization is the measurable response to the radio frequency (RF) pulse in the transversal directions to the applied magnetic field. This response corresponds to the spin precession induced by the RF pulse. The transverse magnetization decay is the set of such measurements of the transverse magnetization taken at various time intervals as the spin precession returns to equilibrium. The term T_2-weighted transverse magnetization decay refers to the fact that the response of each tissue decays at an exponential rate that is described by the constant T_2.

For each decay exponent λ, let $C(\lambda)$ be the fraction of the pixel's intensity (i.e., the measured T_2-weighted transverse magnetization response) that corresponds to λ, then to construct the frequency histogram add up $C(\lambda)$ over the pixels of the region of interest in the slice. This probability density is useful because abnormalities in the content of the various tissues in the region of interest show up as abnormal peaks in the density graph.

From the physical point of view the analysis is more convenient and transparent in the domain of the relaxation rates λ rather than in the time domain t. Therefore, in general transverse magnetization decay the problem is written as a Laplace transform for the probability distribution function, to obtain the Fredholm integral equation of the first kind

$$M(t) = \int_0^\infty e^{-\lambda t}\, C(\lambda)\, d\lambda \tag{3.1}$$

In equation (3.1), t is the time at which the measurement is taken, λ is the decay exponent that is characteristic of the tissue type, $e^{-\lambda t}$ is the measured response at time t; the model allows for a continuous range of tissue variation, so λ could take any positive real value. $C(\lambda)$ is the fraction of the response corresponding to the tissue characterized by λ and $M(t)$ is the total response at time t of all the tissues.

In **[2]** Abate and Valko point out that there are more than one hundred algorithms for the inversion of the Laplace transform. The book of A. Cohen **[3]** describes and compares the methods and has an excellent Survey Results chapter that analyses the most important review papers. Similarly, B. Davis in chapter 19 of his book **[4]** has also a very nice review that gives the flavor of the numerical considerations: most of the effort is directed to controlling round-off errors because the process is unstable, i.e., as the user tries to increase accuracy there is a point where round-off error propagation causes the computational error to increase dramatically.

The algorithms fall into four categories depending upon the basic approach of the method as follows:

- Fourier series expansion
- Laguerre functional expansion
- Combination of Gaver functionals
- Deformation of the Bromwich contour.

The most popular approach is the Fourier series expansion[2]; there are about 15 different algorithms based on Fourier expansion. The review paper by Abate and Whitt **[5]** has a good discussion about the early work; since then the articles by D'Amore *et al* **[6]** and Sakurai **[7]** seem to be of particular interest.

The Laguerre functional expansion method is second in popularity and there about 15 methods based on Laguerre expansion; the 1996 survey paper by Abate *et al* **[8]** discusses the algorithms and their references. More recently Weideman **[9]** made an important contribution to the Laguerre method, see also **[10]**.

[2]Fourier methods require the knowledge of $M(t)$ along the imaginary axis of the complex plane, which is very difficult to obtain; in the literature there are analytical continuation procedures to get this information, but they provide an additional source of uncertainty. In fact, magnitude images are most common in MRI because they avoid the problem of phase artifacts by deliberately discarding the phase information, (see **[1]**) and also perform better in maximizing the signal-to-noise ratio (see http://www.revisemri.com/blog/2007/mri-image-types/).

In the third and fourth categories are the methods originally developed by Garver [**11**] and Talbot [**12**]. These were the methods considered by Abate and Valko [**2**] to obtain multi-precision algorithms.

A different approach is to consider equation (3.1) as a particular case of an integral equation and to use the methods developed to approximate its solution. In this category falls the program CONTIN [**14**], [**15**] that has been used extensively in applications including MRI calculations. CONTIN is a general-purpose constrained regularization program for inverting noisy linear algebraic and integral equations. However, as stated in [**16**], the analysis of a single picture element (pixel) in a series of MRI images using CONTIN may take more than a minute on a sequential machine. Thus, the predicted time for a typical 512×512 pixel series of magnetic resonance images on the same machine is 21 weeks! This is clearly too long for effective use as a diagnostic tool. Two of us also worked on a computational tool for the inversion of the Laplace transform trying to balance out the accuracy of the inversion process with the computation time, see [**17**].

In this chapter we compare two methods on a pixel to pixel basis, the classical separable nonlinear least squares technique and a method of Prony. See also the introductory chapter of this book for a nice survey of several methods for exponential fitting.

Our case study problem consists in looking at a brain slice of which nine gray level images are given. Each image records a measurement at a specific time; the gray level at each pixel corresponds to the intensity of the response to the magnetic field at this time. Figure 3.6.1 shows three images of a given slice, the darkening of the images illustrates the weakening of the measured response signal in time. It is costumary to refer to the image corresponding to a given time as an echo. We are interested in the problem of inferring information of the tissue types in a region of interest (see Figure 3.3.1) from the measured echoes.

It is useful to assume that in T_2-weighted brain magnetic resonance images there are up to four types of tissues, each one corresponding to a different relaxation rate[3].

We will consider datasets consisting of nine measurements at uniformly prescribed times $k\Delta$, for $k = 1, \ldots, 9$. The main issue is that at each pixel there are contributions of an unknown number of tissues chosen from a set of four. To introduce the problem assume that we know the decay rates λ_1, λ_2, λ_3 and λ_4 associated to each tissue type and the fraction C_i of each type at a given pixel. Then we can compute the nine given echoes as follows:

$$\begin{aligned} p_1 &= C_1e^{-\lambda_1\Delta} + C_2e^{-\lambda_2\Delta} + C_3e^{-\lambda_3\Delta} + C_4e^{-\lambda_4\Delta} \\ p_2 &= C_1e^{-\lambda_1 2\Delta} + C_2e^{-\lambda_2 2\Delta} + C_3e^{-\lambda_3 2\Delta} + C_4e^{-\lambda_4 2\Delta} \\ &\vdots \\ p_9 &= C_1e^{-\lambda_1 9\Delta} + C_2e^{-\lambda_2 9\Delta} + C_3e^{-\lambda_3 9\Delta} + C_4e^{-\lambda_4 9\Delta} \end{aligned}$$

The knowledge of this information at all the points of the slice would allow us to construct nine gray level images similar to those in the Appendix. Our goal is to solve the inverse problem: given the echoes to retrieve the exponents and the fractions C_i. Hence, given nine measurements at uniformly spaced times we need to approximate them with a linear combination of a baseline plus up to four

[3]The relaxation rate at a given pixel with a fixed tissue type is a positive exponent lambda such that $e^{-\lambda t}$ is the least squares fit for the measurements $M(t_i)$ at times t_i.

decaying exponentials and these can be obtained by solving the following set of nine equations that involve exponentials

$$\begin{aligned} p_1 &= b + C_1 e^{-\lambda_1 \Delta} + C_2 e^{-\lambda_2 \Delta} + C_3 e^{-\lambda_3 \Delta} + C_4 e^{-\lambda_4 \Delta} \\ p_2 &= b + C_1 e^{-\lambda_1 2\Delta} + C_2 e^{-\lambda_2 2\Delta} + C_3 e^{-\lambda_3 2\Delta} + C_4 e^{-\lambda_4 2\Delta} \\ &\vdots \\ p_9 &= b + C_1 e^{-\lambda_1 9\Delta} + C_2 e^{-\lambda_2 9\Delta} + C_3 e^{-\lambda_3 9\Delta} + C_4 e^{-\lambda_4 9\Delta}. \end{aligned} \tag{3.2}$$

The unknown b in equation (3.2) accounts for the background noise in the images and it is usually referred to as the baseline.

The noise comes from two sources: the Gaussian distribution of each of the exponents λ_i and the Rice noise [4] associated with the measuring instrument (see **[1]**, freely available at http://www.ncbi.nlm.nih.gov/pmc/articles/PMC2254141). Both components are lumped together into the unknown b. Choosing b to be the same for each one of the measurements is a simplifying assumption.

In our case study we consider nine measurements that is the minimum to determine up to four tissues, as the nonlinear system (3.4) contains nine variables for $k = 4$. This choice for the number of measurements agrees reasonably well with those available from MRI equipment in use presently. The two methods described in the chapter will work for any number of tissues k provided that there are at least $2k + 1$ measurements, to guarantee that the system to be solved is not underdetermined.

Both methods work on one pixel at a time basis, so that the computation time is linear in the number of pixels. In sections 3.2 and 3.3 two methods will be considered: the Prony method and the separable least squares method introduced by Victor Pereyra and Gene Golub **[18]**. These methods are developed to allow up to four relaxation rates per pixel and in each case the best model is chosen. Section 3.4 discusses the numerical results and section 3.5 summarizes the chapter. Section 3.6 provides some images that illustrate the datasets.

3.2. The Prony method

Following **[19]**[5] we convert the above nine equations into a polynomial system

$$\begin{aligned} p_1 &= b + C_1 x_1 + C_2 x_2 + C_3 x_3 + C_4 x_4 \\ p_2 &= b + C_1 x_1^2 + C_2 x_2^2 + C_3 x_3^2 + C_4 x_4^2 \\ &\vdots \\ p_9 &= b + C_1 x_1^9 + C_2 x_2^9 + C_3 x_3^9 + C_4 x_4^9, \end{aligned}$$

which is a special case of a separable nonlinear problem as presented in **[18]**. In **[20]** a similar system is considered for seven variables: $x_1, x_2, x_3, b, C_1, C_2, C_3$ and seven measurements. A solution is produced performing a sequence of nonlinear changes of variables that transform the above polynomial system into a linear system in some new variables and finding the roots of a cubic polynomial in a single variable.

---

[4] We refer to a random variable whose probability density function has a Rice distribution as Rice noise, a good reference to Rice distribution and probability density is *http : //en.wikipedia.org*.

[5] See also the introductory chapter of this book for another view of the Prony method.

Using the same idea the above polynomial system can be reduced to a linear system of four equations and finding the roots of a quartic polynomial.

In practice the gray level of each pixel in the image corresponds to a blend of up to four tissues, hence one is really interested in the augmented problem of determining the number of tissues at each pixel, besides the tissue types, their fractions and the baseline. So, we consider the polynomial system (3.3) for $k = 1, 2, 3$ and 4, find a solution for each k and among them pick the best solution. For $k < 4$ this turns the above nonlinear problem into an approximation problem, so called a separable nonlinear least square problem in **[18]**. We sketch briefly how the nonlinear system

$$\begin{aligned} p_1 &= b + C_1 x_1 + \cdots + C_k x_k \\ p_2 &= b + C_1 x_1^2 + \cdots + C_k x_k^2 \\ &\vdots \\ p_9 &= b + C_1 x_1^9 + \cdots + C_k x_k^9 \end{aligned} \tag{3.3}$$

can be solved using only linear regression and finding roots, for $k = 1, 2, 3$ and 4. In (3.3) introduce the new variables

$$q_j = p_j - p_{j+1} \text{ and } u_i = C_i(1 - x_i)$$

to get

$$\begin{aligned} q_1 &= u_1 x_1 + \cdots + u_k x_k \\ q_2 &= u_1 x_1^2 + \cdots + u_k x_k^2 \\ &\vdots \\ q_8 &= u_1 x_1^8 + \cdots + u_k x_k^8. \end{aligned}$$

Combining the equations: $q_{j+1} - q_j x_1$ and performing the additional change of variables $v_i = u_i(x_i - x_1)$ transforms the previous system of eight equations of degree eight into a system of seven equations of degree seven:

$$\begin{aligned} q_2 &= q_1 x_1 + v_2 x_2 \cdots + v_k x_k \\ q_3 &= q_2 x_1 + v_2 x_2^2 \cdots + v_k x_k^2 \\ &\vdots \\ q_8 &= q_7 x_1 + v_2 x_2^7 \cdots + v_k x_k^7. \end{aligned} \tag{3.4}$$

This process is iterated to get a linear least squares problem in the symmetric functions of $x_1, x_2, \cdots, x_k$. We complete the explanation after the next example, which clarifies the process.

To provide an example, we write down the case $k = 3$. Consider

$$\begin{aligned} q_2 - q_1 x_1 &= u_1 x_1^2 + u_2 x_2^2 + u_3 x_3^2 - (u_1 x_1 + u_2 x_2 + u_3 x_3) x_1 \\ &= u_2 x_2 (x_2 - x_1) + u_3 x_3 (x_3 - x_1) \end{aligned}$$

and introducing new variables $v_2 = x_2 u_2 (x_2 - x_1)$ and $v_3 = x_3 u_3 (x_3 - x_1)$ we get

$$q_2 = q_1 x_1 + v_2 x_2 + v_3 x_3.$$

Similarly

$$\begin{aligned} q_3 - q_2 x_1 &= u_1 x_1^3 + u_2 x_2^3 + u_3 x_3^3 - (u_1 x_1^2 + u_2 x_2^2 + u_3 x_3^2) x_1 \\ &= u_2 x_2^2 (x_2 - x_1) + u_3 x_3^2 (x_3 - x_1) \end{aligned}$$

so, working analogously with q_4, q_5, q_6, q_7 and q_8 we obtain seven nonlinear equations in the variables x_1, x_2, x_3:

$$\begin{aligned} q_2 &= q_1 x_1 + v_2 x_2 + v_3 x_3 \\ q_3 &= q_2 x_1 + v_2 x_2^2 + v_3 x_3^2 \\ &\vdots \\ q_8 &= q_7 x_1 + v_2 x_2^7 + v_3 x_3^7 \end{aligned}$$

This is equation (3.4) in the case $k = 3$. This system can be reduced further by introducing another change of variables: $w_3 = v_3(x_3 - x_2)$ and considering

$$\begin{aligned} q_3 - q_2 x_2 &= q_2 x_1 + v_2 x_2^2 + v_3 x_3^2 - x_2(q_1 x_1 + v_2 x_2 + v_3 x_3) \\ q_4 - q_3 x_2 &= q_3 x_1 + v_2 x_2^3 + v_3 x_3^3 - x_2(q_2 x_1 + v_2 x_2^2 + v_3 x_3^2) \\ &\vdots \\ q_8 - q_7 x_2 &= q_7 x_1 + v_2 x_2^7 + v_3 x_3^7 - x_2(q_6 x_1 + v_2 x_2^6 + v_3 x_3^6) \end{aligned}$$

we obtain

$$\begin{aligned} q_3 &= q_2(x_1 + x_2) - q_1 x_1 x_2 + w_3 x_3 \\ q_4 &= q_3(x_1 + x_2) - q_2 x_1 x_2 + w_3 x_3^2 \\ &\vdots \\ q_8 &= q_7(x_1 + x_2) - q_6 x_1 x_2 + w_3 x_3^6. \end{aligned}$$

Finally, the variable w_3 is eliminated and we get

$$\begin{aligned} q_4 &= q_3(x_1 + x_2 + x_3) - q_2(x_1 x_2 + x_2 x_3 + x_3 x_1) + q_1 x_1 x_2 x_3 \\ q_5 &= q_4(x_1 + x_2 + x_3) - q_3(x_1 x_2 + x_2 x_3 + x_3 x_1) + q_2 x_1 x_2 x_3 \\ q_6 &= q_5(x_1 + x_2 + x_3) - q_4(x_1 x_2 + x_2 x_3 + x_3 x_1) + q_3 x_1 x_2 x_3 \\ q_7 &= q_6(x_1 + x_2 + x_3) - q_5(x_1 x_2 + x_2 x_3 + x_3 x_1) + q_4 x_1 x_2 x_3 \\ q_8 &= q_7(x_1 + x_2 + x_3) - q_6(x_1 x_2 + x_2 x_3 + x_3 x_1) + q_5 x_1 x_2 x_3, \end{aligned}$$

a linear equation in the symmetric functions of x_1, x_2, x_3.

Going back to the case of arbitrary k and iterating the process starting from equation (3.3) we get

$$Q = MZ$$

where the components of Z are the symmetric functions in $x_1, \cdots, x_k$, M is an alternating Toeplitz matrix[6] and

$$Q = \begin{bmatrix} q_{k+1} \\ q_{k+2} \\ \vdots \\ q_8 \end{bmatrix}.$$

[6]An alternating Toeplitz matrix is a Toeplitz matrix times diag(1,-1,1,-1,...).

More precisely, for $k = 4, 3, 2, 1$ (i.e. we solve for four, three, two and one tissue, respectively) the matrix M is:

$$\begin{bmatrix} q_4 & -q_3 & q_2 & -q_1 \\ q_5 & -q_4 & q_3 & -q_2 \\ q_6 & -q_5 & q_4 & -q_3 \\ q_7 & -q_6 & q_5 & -q_4 \end{bmatrix}, \begin{bmatrix} q_3 & -q_2 & q_1 \\ q_4 & -q_3 & q_2 \\ q_5 & -q_4 & q_3 \\ q_6 & -q_5 & q_4 \\ q_7 & -q_6 & q_5 \end{bmatrix}, \begin{bmatrix} q_2 & -q_1 \\ q_3 & -q_2 \\ q_4 & -q_3 \\ q_5 & -q_4 \\ q_6 & -q_5 \\ q_7 & -q_6 \end{bmatrix} \text{and} \begin{bmatrix} q_1 \\ q_2 \\ q_3 \\ q_4 \\ q_5 \\ q_6 \\ q_7 \end{bmatrix},$$

respectively.

The polynomial variables (and hence the exponents that characterize the tissue types) can be retrieved from the components of Z by solving a quartic, cubic, quadratic or an affine linear equation. For example in the case of $k = 3$ as above, the knowledge of $Z = (Z_1, Z_2, Z_3)$ where

$$\begin{aligned} Z_1 &= x_1 + x_2 + x_3 \\ Z_2 &= x_1x_2 + x_2x_3 + x_3x_1 \\ Z_3 &= x_1x_2x_3 \end{aligned}$$

allows us to compute the x_i's by finding the roots of the cubic polynomial $z^3 - Z_1z^2 + Z_2z - Z_3 = 0$.

Finally the baseline and the fractions C_i are obtained by solving a linear least squares problem. The size of the system is $9 \times (k + 1)$ where k is the number of tissues.

The strategy is to solve for each pixel assuming that there are four, three, two and one tissue. In each case we get Z, if it leads to nonphysical solutions (i.e., polynomial variables outside the $(0, 1)$ range, negative values for the C_i and/or the baseline) they are discarded and the best is chosen among the physically meaningful solutions. For each pixel the chosen solution is the one that best approximates the given nine data points and we refer to it as the optimal Prony solution.

3.3. The separable nonlinear least squares approach

Separable least squares is a general technique that works for a wide family of minimization problems. It can be employed to find the solutions of (3.2) for any number of exponentials.

As stated in the introduction, our goal is to approximate nine measurements with a linear combination of up to four exponentials plus a constant term, the baseline. The exponents correspond to distinct tissues that will vary from pixel to pixel but should cluster around 2, 10, 12 and 20: these are the expected values of the relaxation rates in actual clinical data corresponding to cerebrospinal fluid, gray matter, white matter and connective tissue.

The baseline also varies from pixel to pixel and this variation is associated to Rice noise in the data. The baseline, fractions and exponents can be obtained by solving the nonlinear least squares problem:

$$\min_{b, C_k, \lambda_k} \left(\sum_i (p_i - b - \sum_k C_k e^{-\lambda_k \Delta_i})^2 \right) \tag{3.5}$$

where $\Delta_i = i\Delta$ and $i = 1, 2, ..., 9$. The number of summands in (3.5) coincides with the number of tissues.

Following **[18]** and assuming that the number of tissues is four, we can rewrite equation (3.5) using matrix notation as follows, let

$$\Theta(\widehat{x}) = \begin{bmatrix} 1 & x_1 & x_2 & x_3 & x_4 \\ 1 & x_1^2 & x_2^2 & x_3^2 & x_4^2 \\ \vdots & \vdots & \vdots & \vdots & \vdots \\ 1 & x_1^9 & x_2^9 & x_3^9 & x_4^9 \end{bmatrix}, \widehat{C} = \begin{bmatrix} b \\ C_1 \\ C_2 \\ C_3 \\ C_4 \end{bmatrix} \text{ and } \widehat{p} = \begin{bmatrix} p_1 \\ p_2 \\ \vdots \\ p_9 \end{bmatrix}$$

where $\widehat{x} = (x_1, x_2, x_3, x_4)^t$ and $x_k = e^{-\lambda_k \Delta}$ for $k = 1, 2, 3, 4$. Finally, equation (3.5) gets transformed into

$$\min_{\widehat{x}, \widehat{C}} \|\widehat{p} - \Theta(\widehat{x})\widehat{C}\|_2^2 \tag{3.6}$$

As in **[18]**, we assume that the matrix Θ has constant rank in a neighborhood of the desired solution; then the variables of the problem can be separated in the following way: Let the variable projection functional be

$$r_2(\widehat{x}) = \|\widehat{p} - \Theta(\widehat{x}) \left[\Theta(\widehat{x})\right]^+ \widehat{p}\|_2^2$$

where $[\Theta(\widehat{x})]^+$ is the pseudo-inverse of $\Theta(\widehat{x})$, then we consider the reduced nonlinear least squares problem

$$\min_{\widehat{x}} r_2(\widehat{x}). \tag{3.7}$$

Once the solution $\widehat{x}^*$ of equation (3.7) is obtained, the fractions $\widehat{C}^*$ are computed as the solution of the resulting linear least squares problem:

$$\widehat{C}^* = \Theta(\widehat{x})^+ \widehat{p}. \tag{3.8}$$

Golub and Pereyra showed in **[18]** that, under the above hypothesis on the rank of $\Theta(\widehat{x})$, if $\widehat{x}^*$ is a critical point (global minimizer) of (3.7) then $(\widehat{x}^*, \widehat{C}^*)$ is a critical point (global minimizer) of (3.6).

With the appropriate modifications in the length of $\widehat{C}$ and the dimensions of $\Theta(\widehat{x})$ the above process might also be performed assuming that there are three, two or one tissue per pixel.

For the numerical computations we use the Matlab program *lsqnonlin* to solve the reduced nonlinear least squares problem (3.7) for the variable projection functional and to get the exponents and equation (3.8) for the computation of the baseline and the fractions.

Since we do not know a priori the number of tissues in a particular pixel, we repeat the computation for one, two, three and four exponentials for the whole region of interest (see Figure 3.3.1), discard the solutions that do not have physical meaning and take for each pixel the model that gives the smallest residual.

3.4. Numerical results

We consider synthetically generated data using the Simulated Brain Data: BrainWeb resource **[21]**. We focus on axial slices for which a nine echo magnetization decay is acquired. The axial slice is defined starting with four relaxation exponents: 2, 10, 12 and 20 and for each pixel, four values of $C_i, i = 1, 2, 3, 4$, between 0 and 255 that add up to 255. The relaxation exponents are associated to

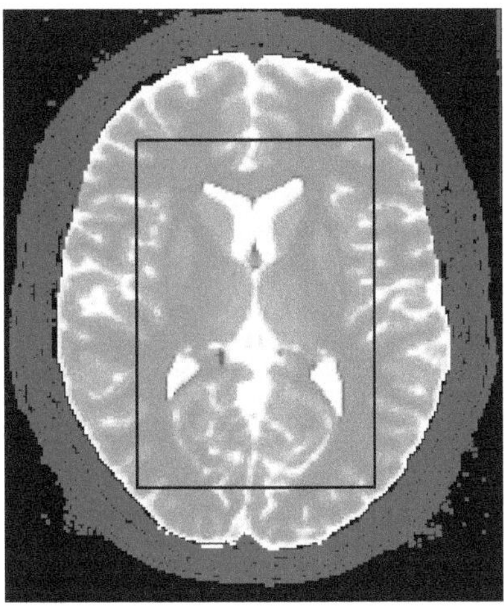

FIGURE 3.3.1. The region of interest.

tissue types and the C_i's to the actual fraction of each tissue at every pixel. This corresponds to the partial volume problem as reported in [**22**] and [**?**].
A noiseless data set is given by

$$p_i = \sum_k C_k e^{-\lambda_k t_i}$$

for $i = 1, \ldots, 9$, $0 \leq C_k \leq 255$, $t_i = 44i/1000$ and $\lambda_k = 2, 10, 12, 20$.
We will work with the region of interest (RoI) as depicted in Figure 3.3.1.

Noisy datasets are constructed by choosing the exponents with Gaussian distribution of standard deviation 0.5 about the tissue characterizing exponents 2, 10, 12 and 20. The corresponding measurements are perturbed with Rice noise with parameters $\sigma = \nu = 0.0001$ and $\sigma = \nu = 5$. We refer to these datasets as IM0-0001-0-5 and IM5-0-5, respectively. We also consider two additional noisy datasets, both with standard deviation 2 and the same Rice noise levels as above, namely IM0-0001-2 and IM5-2.

The decay rates, i.e., the exponents λ and the fractions $C(\lambda)$ are computed as explained above. For each pixel we pick the solution with the smallest residual. Exceptionally there are pixels with no optimal solution because the method, either Prony and/or separable nonlinear least squares (NLLS), is not able to compute any physically meaningful solutions for them. In this case we set all the fractions and the baseline equal to zero. In the Tables 1–4 we show the percentages of pixels with zero, one, two, three and four tissues as computed by the two methods and compared with the information of each dataset.

For each dataset and each of the two methods we calculate the frequency diagram as follows. We partition the interval [0,25] into 1000 bins of equal length and for each pixel add the fractions of the solution to the bins prescribed by its exponents. Each frequency diagram is normalized to a probability density, and in the Figures below these are compared for various noise levels.

TABLE 1. Percentage of pixels with zero, one, two, three and four tissues.

Dataset IM0-0001-0-5					
Method	zero	one	two	three	four
Data	0.002	50.95	47.74	1.23	0.09
Prony	0.002	50.99	48.00	1.00	0.0
NLLS	0.0	53.14	44.56	2.23	0.068

TABLE 2. Percentage of pixels with zero, one, two, three and four tissues.

Dataset IM0-0001-2					
Method	zero	one	two	three	four
Data	0.002	50.95	47.74	1.23	0.09
Prony	1.179	53.68	44.37	0.77	0.002
NLLS	1.156	56.03	40.52	2.21	0.088

TABLE 3. Percentage of pixels with zero, one, two, three and four tissues.

Dataset IM5-0-5					
Method	zero	one	two	three	four
Data	0.002	50.95	47.74	1.23	0.09
Prony	0.276	99.61	0.117	0.0	0.0
NLLS	3.60	91.2	5.43	0.19	0.0

TABLE 4. Percentage of pixels with zero, one, two, three and four tissues.

Dataset IM5-2					
Method	zero	one	two	three	four
Data	0.002	50.95	47.74	1.23	0.09
Prony	2.86	97.05	0.11	0.0	0.0
NLLS	4.12	91.23	4.43	0.21	0.011

Figures 3.4.1-3.4.4 illustrate numerical experiments run on various datasets generated with the BrainWeb resource ([**21**]). In each case the green probability density curve corresponds to the actual original distribution, i.e., the zero Rice noise itself and not the result of applying the Prony or separable nonlinear least squares procedure to these data. Figure 3.4.1 shows the reconstructed probability density of the images with Gaussian standard deviation 0.5 and Rice noise levels: $\sigma = \nu = 0.0001$ and $\sigma = \nu = 5$ in the case of the Prony solutions. Note that for low Rice noise level the Prony method produces an excellent match. In fact the green and red curves, which represent the exact and the low Rice noise probability densities, almost coincide; hence the green is not very noticeable since it was drawn first.

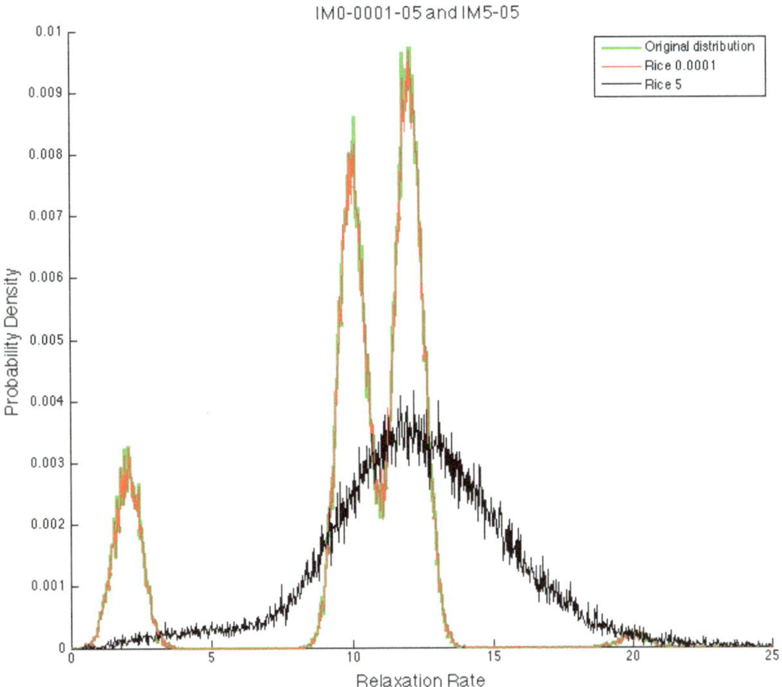

FIGURE 3.4.1. The actual original distribution is green, the red and black correspond to the datasets with standard deviation 0.5 and Rice noise 0.0001 and 5, respectively. The solutions were computed with the Prony method. The low Rice noise density almost coincides with the original noiseless data.

Figure 3.4.2 depicts the same probability density computed with the technique of separable nonlinear least squares. Again, for low Rice noise the match is very good and for higher Rice noise this method is still capable of resolving the peak near 2. Moreover, for higher Rice noise separable least squares picks up a larger number of pixels in the $10 - 12$ range than Prony.

Figure 3.4.3 shows the probability densities computed with the Prony method for Gauss standard deviation equal to 2 and Rice noise with parameters $\sigma = \nu = 0.0001$ and $\sigma = \nu = 5$. The data sets are IM0-0001-2 and IM5-2, respectively. Here again, Prony reproduces faithfully the probability densities for large standard deviation and low Rice noise.

Figure 3.4.4 illustrates resulting densities as in Figure 3.4.3, using separable nonlinear least squares. They are of similar quality to those of the Prony method in Figure 3.4.3. Neither of the two methods is capable of resolving the 2 peak for high Rice noise.

All computations have been made on a Mac Book Pro with 4 Gb of RAM memory with a 2.5 GHz Intel Core 2 Duo processor. Table 5 lists the CPU times for Prony and NLLS for the four datasets.

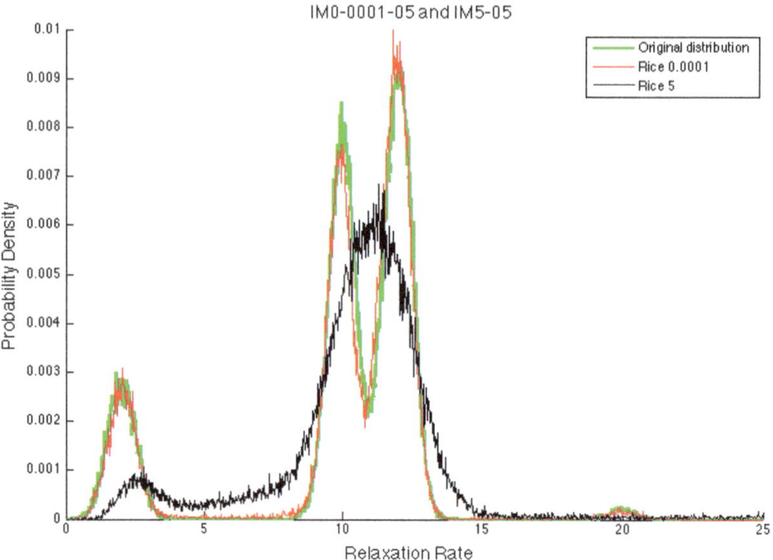

FIGURE 3.4.2. Separable nonlinear least squares probability densities. Gauss standard deviation and noise as in Figure 3.4.1.

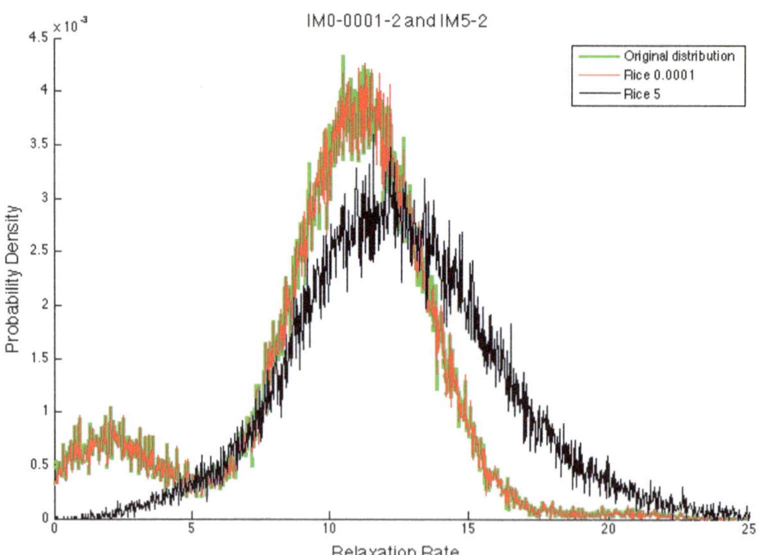

FIGURE 3.4.3. The original distribution with standard deviation 2 is green, the noisy data sets are IM0-0001-2 and IM5-2 are red and black, respectively. The computation was performed with Prony.

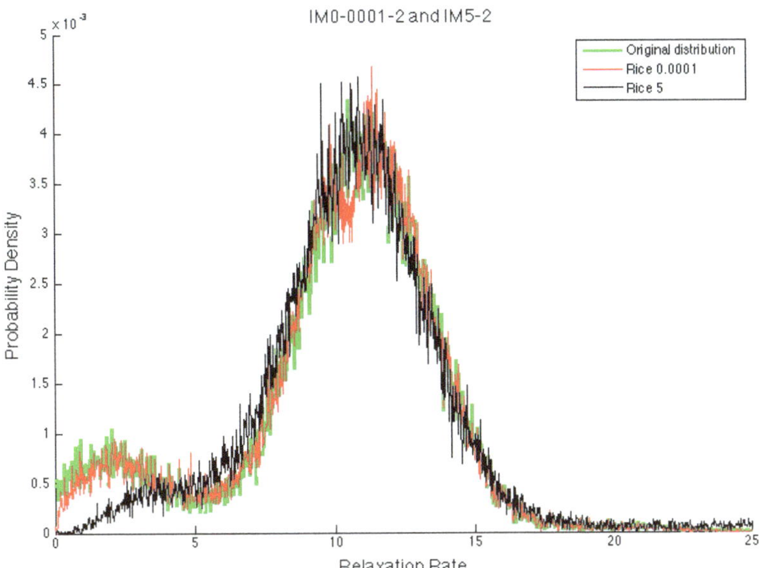

FIGURE 3.4.4. Probability densities of the data sets IM0-0001-2 and IM5-2 computed with separable nonlinear least squares.

TABLE 5. Computation times in seconds for Prony and NLLS.

	Data sets			
Method	IM0.0001-0.5	IM0.0001-2	IM5-0.5	IM5-2
Prony	72.68	71.60	62.66	62.0
NLLS	2712.75	2729.53	7474.01	8193.27

3.5. Conclusions and final remarks

Figures 3.4.1 and 3.4.2 illustrate graphically that both methods reproduce very closely the original data in the case of small standard deviation and small Rice noise.

Figures 3.4.3 and 3.4.4 illustrate the fact that both methods also produce excellent results for large standard deviation and small Rice noise.

The situation deteriorates when the Rice noise is increased substantially, as illustrated by the black curves in Figures 3.4.1, 3.4.2, 3.4.3 and 3.4.4, although the separable nonlinear least squares seems to fare better: it is capable of resolving the 2 and $10 - 12$ peaks. The Prony method is consistently much faster than the separable nonlinear least squares technique. For high Rice noise none of the methods is capable of resolving the four peaks. See the black graphs of Figures 3.4.1 and 3.4.2, which correspond to datasets with Rice noise with $\sigma = \nu = 5$

For the implementation of the separable nonlinear least squares method we used standard Matlab procedures so most probably the computation times could be brought down. One way to procede might be to adapt the VARPRO interface to our specific MRI problem.

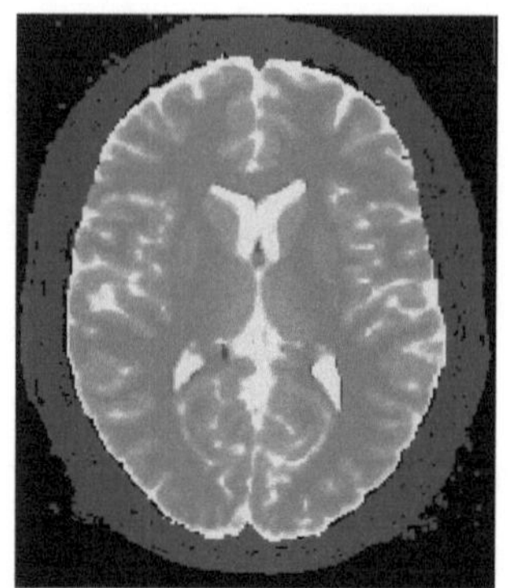

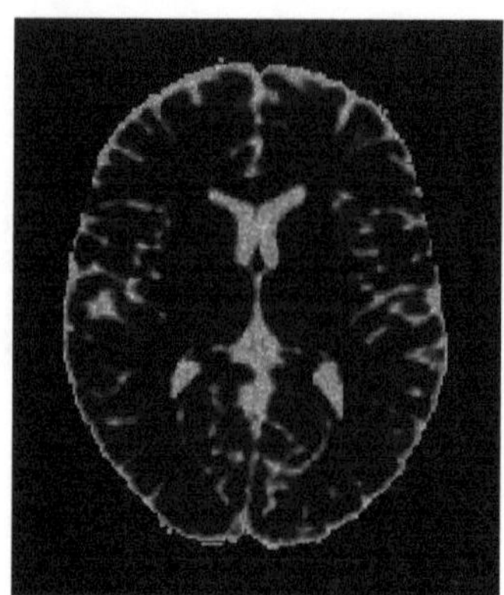

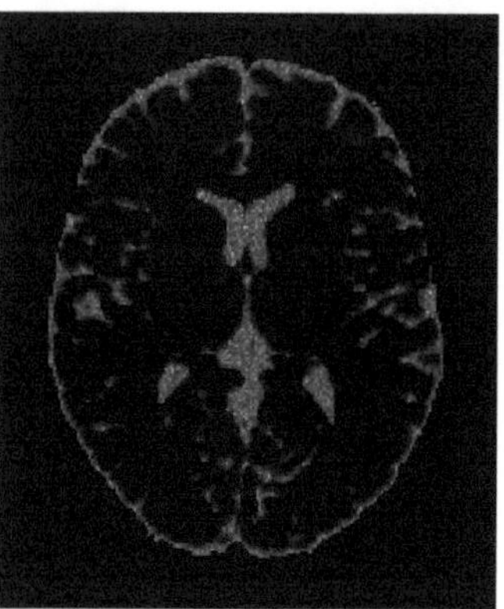

FIGURE 3.6.1. First, fifth and ninth echoes corresponding to the axial slice with standard deviation 0.5 and Rice noise 0.0001.

On the other hand the accuracy of the Prony method is tied up with the numerical dependence of the roots on the coefficients of the polynomials as exemplified in section 3.2 in the case of 3 tissues. One approach to improve the accuracy of the Prony method is to study in more detail the resulting polynomials. The authors are now engaged in this investigation.

A more general approach that might enhance the effectivity of both methods is to do some filtering of the data. This approach has been explored in **[24]** and **[25]**.

3.6. Appendix

Figure 3.6.1 illustrates three (namely the first, fifth and ninth echoes) of the nine images corresponding to an axial slice with standard deviation 0.5 and Rice noise 0.0001. Figure 3.6.2 illustrates the same images for standard deviation 2 and Rice noise 5.

Figures 3.6.3 and 3.6.4 illustrate the polygonal decay of the nine echoes for a cluster of about 40 pixels within the RoI; for each pixel there are nine measurements

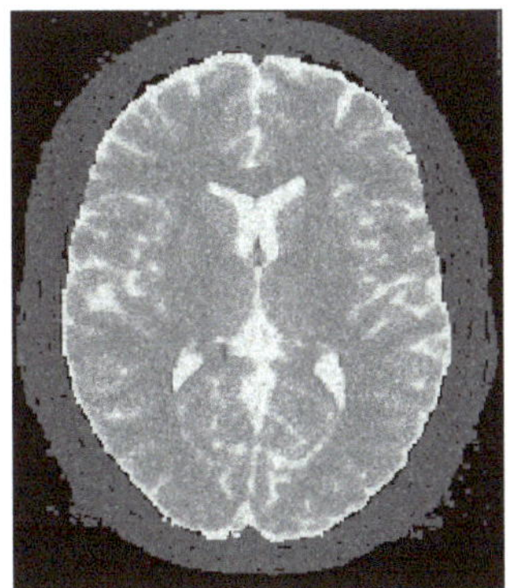

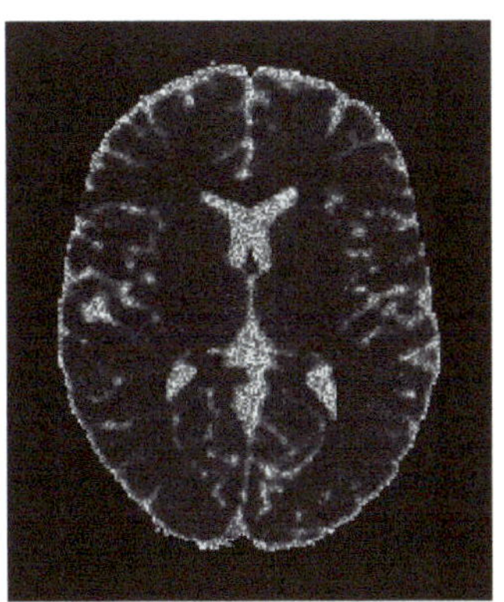

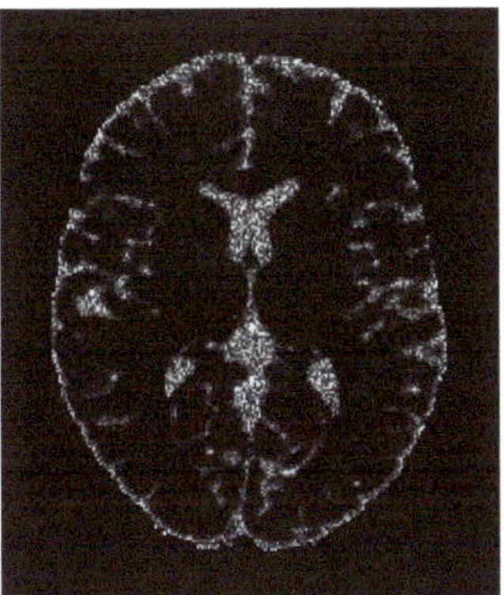

FIGURE 3.6.2. First, fifth and ninth echoes corresponding to the axial slice with standard deviation 2 and Rice noise 5.

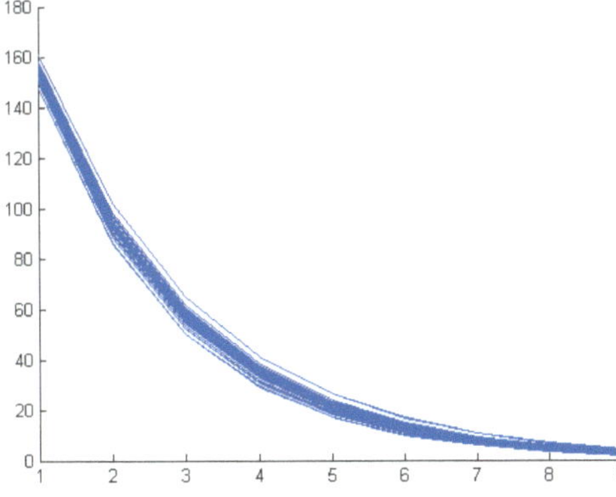

FIGURE 3.6.3. Decay polygonals corresponding to a cluster of pixels of the data with standard deviation 0.5 and Rice noise 0.0001.

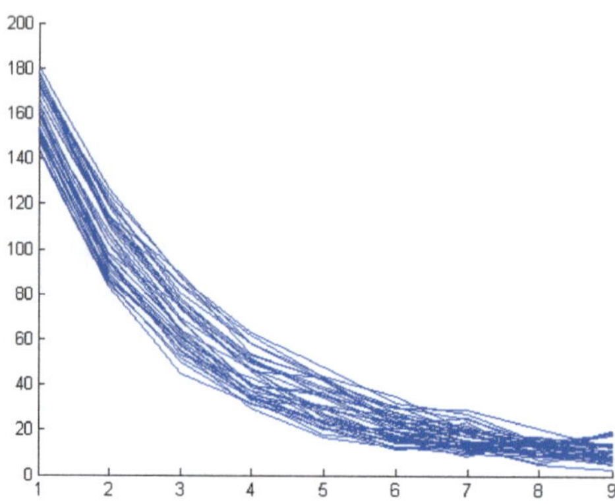

FIGURE 3.6.4. Decay polygonals corresponding to a cluster of pixels of the data with standard deviation 2 and Rice noise 5.

taken at uniformly distributed times. The polygonal decays are their graphs. There are 40 polygonal lines because we are illustrating a cluster of 40 pixels. The widest span in Figure 3.6.4 is due to the larger standard deviation and Rice noise in the data.

3.7. Acknowledgements

The authors wish to thank the anonymous referees for their valuable suggestions that lead to important improvements in this contribution.

M. Paluszny thanks financial support of Universidad Nacional de Colombia, through the Grant DIME 200101007733.

Bibliography

1. H. Gudbjartson and S. Patz, *The Rician distribution of of noisy MRI data*, Magnetic Resonance in Medicine, vol. 34, no. 6, 910–914 (1995).
2. J. Abate and P. P. Valko, *Multi-precision Laplace tranforms inversion*, International Journal for Numerical Methods in Engineering, vol. 60, 979–993 (2004).
3. A. Cohen, *Numerical Methods for Laplace Transform Inversion*, Springer (2007).
4. B. Davis, *Integral Transforms and their Applications*, (3rd. edition), Springer (2002).
5. J. Abate and W. Whitt, *The Fourier-series method for inverting transforms of probability distributions*, Queueing Systems, vol. 10, 5–88 (1992).
6. L. D'Amore, G. Lacetti and A. Murli, *An implementation of a Fourier-series method for the numerical inversion of the Laplace transform*, ACM Transactions on Mathematical Software, vol. 25, 279–305 (1999).
7. T. Sakurai, *Numerical inversion of the Laplace transform of functions with discontinuities*, Advances in Applied Probability, vol. 36 Nr. 2, 616–642 (2004).
8. J. Abate, G. Choudhury and W. Whitt, *On the Laguerre-method for numerically inverting the Laplace transform*, INFORMS, Journal of Computing, vol. 8, 413–427 (1996).
9. J.A.C. Weideman, *Algorithms for parameter selection in the Weeks method for inverting the Laplace transform*, SIAM Journal of Scientific Computing, vol. 21, 111–128 (1999).
10. S. Cuomo, L. D'Amore, A. Murli and M.R. Rizzardi, *Computation of the inverse Laplace transform based on a collocation method which uses only real values*, Journal of Computational and Applied Mathematics, vol. 198 Nr. 1 (2007).
11. D.P. Garver Jr, , *Algorithms observing stochastic processes and approximate transform inversion*, Operations Research, vol. 14, 444–459 (1966).
12. A. Talbot, *The accurate numerical inversion of Laplace transforms*, Journal of the Institute of Mathematics and its Applications, vol. 23, 97–120 (1979).
13. B. Davies and B. Martin, *Numerical inversion of the Laplace transform: a survey and comparison of methods*, Journal of Computational Physics, vol. 33, 1–32 (1979).
14. S. W Provencher, *CONTIN: a general purpose constrained regularization program for inverting noise linear and integral equations*, Computational Physics Communications, vol. 27, 229–242 (1982).
15. S. W. Provencher, *A constrained regularization method for inverting data represented by linear algebraic or integral equations*, Computational Physics Communications, vol. 27, 213–227 (1982).
16. A.P. Bak, J.P. Hornak and N.C. Schaller, *From impractical to practical: solving an MRI problem using parallelism*, RIT Digital Media Library, http://hdl.handle.net/1850/423 (2005).
17. R. Martín and M. Martín-Landrove, *A novel algorithm for tumor characterization by analysis of transversal relaxation rate distribution in MRI*, In P. Bluemler, B. Blumich, E. Robert, R.E. Botto and E. Fukushima, Spatially Resolved Magnetic Resonance: Methods and Applications in Materials Science, Agriculture and Biomedicine, Wiley-VCH Publishers, Weinheim (1998).
18. G. Golub and V. Pereyra, *The differentiation of pseudo-inverses and the nonlinear least squares problem whose variables separate*, SIAM Journal of Numerical Analisys, vol. 10, 413–432 (1973).
19. M. Martín-Landrove, G. Figueroa, M. Paluszny and W. Torres. *Boosting the inverse interpolation problem by a sum of decaying exponentials using an algebraic approach*, Electronic Transactions on Numerical Analysis, (in press).

20. M. Martín-Landrove, G. Figueroa, M. Paluszny and W. Torres. *A quasi-analytical method for relaxation rate distribution determination of T2 -weighted MRI in brain*, Proceedings of the 29th Annual International Conference of the IEEE EMBS, Lyon, France, 1318–1321 (2007).
21. *(http://www.bic.mni.mcgill.ca/brainweb/)*, Simulated Brain Data.
22. M. Pokric, N. Thacker, M.L.J.A. Scott *et al. The importance of partial voluming in multi-dimensional medical imaging segmentation*, MICCAI 2001 LNCS, 1293–1294 (2001).
23. K. Van Leemput, F. Maes, D. Vandermeulen *et al. A unifying framework for partial volume segmentation of brain MR images*, IEEE Transactions on Medical Imaging, 22: 105–119 (2003).
24. W. Torres, M. Paluszny, M. Martín-Landrove *et al. Tumor segmentation of multiecho MR T2-weighted images with morphological operators.* In: Proc. of SPIE Vol. 7259, 72594E, Medical Imaging 2009: Image Processing, edited by J.P.W. Pluim, B.M. Dawant (2009).
25. M. Martín-Landrove, M. Paluszny, G. Figueroa *et al. A multi-strategy method for MRI segmentation*, In: Proc. World Congress, 25/IV, IFMBE, edited by O. Doessel and C. Schlegel, 1222–1225 (2009).

CHAPTER 4

Exponential time series in lattice quantum field theory

Saul D. Cohen
Thomas Jefferson National Accelerator Facility
Newport News, VA 23606, USA
sdcohen@jlab.org

George T. Fleming
Department of Physics, Yale University
New Haven, CT 06520, USA
George.Fleming@yale.edu

Huey-Wen Lin
Department of Physics
University of Washington
Seattle, WA 98195
hwlin@phys.washington.edu

ABSTRACT. Exponential time series analysis has been an integral part of lattice quantum field theory calculations for three decades. Until recently, the level of sophistication has been relatively modest since the number of computable time samples was limited by available computational resources to at most a few dozen times, enabling the reliable estimation of only a few exponentials. Recent algorithmic advances, coupled with continued growth in high performance computing following Moore's Law, has enabled calculations of exponential time series with a hundred or more time samples and generated new interest in finding reliable analysis methods for estimating many exponentials. We review the methods currently used to analyze lattice quantum field theory calculations.

Keywords: Exponential time series; lattice quantum chromodynamics.

4.1. Introduction

In the early part of the last century, as protons and neutrons were discovered, physicists realized that the effective nuclear force that binds these constituent baryons to form atomic nuclei must be much stronger than electromagnetism in order to overcome the electrostatic repulsion. Finding the correct theoretical description of the strong interactions on the distance scale of atomic nuclei proved to be a formidable task, as the prevailing analytic methods at the time were only valid when interactions between particles led to small perturbations in their motions.

Victor Pereyra & Godela Scherer (Eds)

Throughout the 1960s mounting experimental and theoretical evidence indicated that all hadrons, including the baryons mentioned above plus a related class of particles called mesons, were not point-like particles but composites of other even smaller constituent particles. Phenomenology hinted that these constituents might be weakly interacting on distance scales much smaller than a proton [**17, 8**]. Then, quite dramatically, in the summer of 1973, Gross, Wilczek [**25**] and Politzer [**44**] (Nobel Prize in Physics 2004) found the correct description of the strong interactions at short distances in terms of weakly interacting quarks and gluons in a theory now called quantum chromodynamics (QCD). By the following summer, Wilson [**63**] (Nobel Prize in Physics 1982) reformulated the strong interactions of QCD on a discrete Euclidean spacetime lattice, called lattice QCD (LQCD), creating the theoretical framework that eventually led to confirmation of QCD as the correct microscopic theory of the strong interactions at all distance scales.

A final calculational breakthrough occurred in the summer of 1979 when Creutz, Jacobs and Rebbi [**11**] showed that Monte Carlo techniques developed to perform statistical mechanics calculations in lower-dimensional spin systems could also be used to perform nonperturbative calculations in relativistic quantum field theories. Within a few years, a wide variety of non-perturbative calculations had been attempted, including the low-energy spectrum of hadrons in QCD [**21, 27, 28, 29, 36, 61**], which is the subject at the heart of this chapter.

The numerical algorithms useful for lattice field theory calculations are in the general class known as Markov-chain Monte Carlo (MCMC) methods. Starting from some initial configuration of field variables defined on the spacetime lattice, a sequence configurations is generated by a Markov process that has the desired partition function as its equilibrium distribution. As with most MCMC methods, it is difficult to determine precisely how many steps in the Markov process are necessary before the resulting configuration can be considered a good sample of the equilibrium distribution. So, it is common practice in this field to start from some configuration which is known to have very little weight in the equilibrium distribution (totally ordered or disordered are common choices) and generate a single Markov chain of configurations while computing at regular intervals a small set of some interesting observables. When the distribution of these sampled observables appears to be stationary, the chain is considered thermalized and the Markov process is normally continued to accumulate statistics. This typically results in autocorrelations between samples that must be taken into account when computing expectation values and their uncertainties from the sample ensemble. While the determination of autocorrelations is another example of exponential time series analysis in lattice field theory calculations, it is not the focus of this chapter since it is merely a consequence of the chosen method of sampling.

The hadron spectrum can be calculated in LQCD using two-point hadronic correlation functions, often called a vacuum-to-vacuum transition amplitude in quantum field theory

$$C_{AB}\left(\vec{p},|t-t_0|\right) = \sum_{\vec{x}} \exp(i\vec{p}\cdot\vec{x}) \left\langle 0 \left| O_B(\vec{x},t)\; O_A^\dagger(\vec{x}_0,t_0) \right| 0 \right\rangle, \tag{4.1}$$

where we have made explicit use of the translation invariance symmetry of the ensemble average to state that the correlation function should be independent, on average, of the spatial location $\vec{x}_0$ and only depends on the temporal separation $|t-t_0|$. The correlator will be nonzero only if the quantum creation operator

$O_A^\dagger(\vec{x},t)$ and annihilation operator transform irreducibly under the same representation of the space group of lattice symmetries [**4, 5, 40, 41**]. In general, such operators will create (or annihilate) states which are a linear superposition of many hadronic eigenstates of the LQCD Hamiltonian that transform non-trivially under the same irreducible representation. After taking momentum (and spin for baryons) projection and inserting a complete set of hadronic eigenstates (ignoring for now the variety of boundary condition choices possible), this becomes

$$C_{AB}(\vec{p},t_n) = \sum_{m=1}^{M} Z_{Am}(\vec{p}) Z_{Bm}(\vec{p}) \exp\left[-naE_m(\vec{p})\right] \tag{4.2}$$

$$n \geq 0, \quad Z_{Am}, Z_{Bm},\ E_m \in \mathbb{R}, \quad 0 < E_1 \leq E_2 \leq \cdots \leq E_M,$$

where Z_{Am} and Z_{Bm} contain not only the overlap factor between the eigenstate and states created by the operators but also any kinetic factors that do not depend on the Euclidean time separation $|t-t_0|$. The number of states included in the model is usually small; calculations with as many as eight states are extremely rare.

The special algebraic structure of the model function is revealed if we make the following identifications:

$$\mathbf{y} \in \mathbb{R}^N \qquad y_n = C_{AB}\left(\vec{p}, t_n\right) \tag{4.3}$$

$$\boldsymbol{\alpha} \in \mathbb{R}^M \qquad \alpha_m = \exp\left[-aE_m(\vec{p})\right] \tag{4.4}$$

$$\mathbf{a} \in \mathbb{R}^M \qquad a_m = Z_{Am} Z_{Bm} \exp\left[-t_0 E_m(\vec{p})\right]. \tag{4.5}$$

Now, the model function can be written simply as $\mathbf{y}(\boldsymbol{\alpha}, \mathbf{a}) = \boldsymbol{\Phi}(\boldsymbol{\alpha})\,\mathbf{a}$ where $\boldsymbol{\Phi} \in \mathbb{R}^{N\times M}$. Furthermore, $\boldsymbol{\Phi}$ has the special structure of a Vandermonde matrix: $\phi_{nm} = \alpha_m^n$.

In a Monte Carlo calculation, the hadronic correlation function of interest is usually computed for all timeslices on each configuration considered to be part of the sample distribution. This also leads to correlations in the errors between nearby timeslices when computing the expectation values for the correlation function at each timeslice. Let us assume that S sample configurations were generated, and the sampling interval was chosen such that autocorrelations are not important. On each sample configuration $s \in \{1, \cdots, S\}$, the hadronic correlation function can be computed on N timeslices. We label these numbers $\mathbf{y}_s$ following Eq. (4.3). The sample mean and standard covariance of the sample mean are

$$\overline{\mathbf{y}} = \frac{1}{S}\sum_{s=1}^{S} \mathbf{y}_s\,, \quad \mathcal{C} = \frac{1}{S(S-1)} \sum_{s=1}^{S} \left(\mathbf{y}_s - \overline{\mathbf{y}}\right)\left(\mathbf{y}_s - \overline{\mathbf{y}}\right)^T\,, \quad \mathcal{C} \in \mathbb{R}^{N\times N}\,. \tag{4.6}$$

4.2. Least-squares methods

By far, the least-squares method is most commonly used to extract the model parameters $A_m = Z_{Am}Z_{Bm}$ and E_m of Eq. (4.2) from ensemble averages of computed hadronic correlation functions [**37, 38, 53**]. The functional to be minimized is the generalized least-squares estimator, also known as the Aitken estimator [**2**]

$$L = \left(\overline{\mathbf{y}} - \mathbf{y}(\boldsymbol{\alpha}, \mathbf{a})\right)^T \mathcal{C}^{-1} \left(\overline{\mathbf{y}} - \mathbf{y}(\boldsymbol{\alpha}, \mathbf{a})\right). \tag{4.7}$$

We can define a residual vector as the difference between the sample mean and the model $\mathbf{r}_1 = \overline{\mathbf{y}} - \mathbf{y}(\boldsymbol{\alpha}, \mathbf{a})$ so that the least-squares functional can be viewed as the 2-norm length of the residual vector $\|\mathbf{r}_1\|$ provided $\mathcal{C}^{-1}$ is used as the metric tensor. This length is sometimes called the Mahalanobis distance [**35**].

The argument in favor of using the generalized least-squares method is based on properties initially established by Gauss [**22**]. When the model contains only linear dependence on the fit parameters, then the parameters that minimize the least-squares estimator are (1) unique, (2) unbiased, (3) optimal and, if the sampling errors in $\mathbf{y}$ are normally distributed or the sample size is sufficiently large that the central limit theorem holds, (4) is a maximum-likelihood estimator given by the χ^2 distribution which can be used to compute the goodness-of-fit. Confidence limits on best-fit parameters can be computed by error propagation.

However, the model function $\mathbf{y}(\boldsymbol{\alpha}, \mathbf{a})$ has both linear $(\mathbf{a})$ and nonlinear $(\boldsymbol{\alpha})$ fit parameters. It has been widely established that most of the nice properties above are lost when the model function is no longer strictly linear. The fit parameter estimates may not be unique, meaning the least-squares estimator could have degenerate global minima. Also, the general solution is not directly computable, so the fit-parameter space must be searched to find the solution. The success of various search methods strongly depends on user-based input and is not guaranteed. Finally, the fit parameter estimates are generally biased and sub-optimal.

Fortunately, it is believed that if a sufficient number of samples are available, such that the covariance matrix may be reliably estimated and that the central limit theorem still holds, then the least squares is a maximum-likelihood estimator and the goodness-of-fit can be computed. Furthermore, it is believed that combining least squares with resampling methods like jackknife and bootstrap may lead to improved estimates of bias corrections and confidence limits.

4.2.1. Estimation of data covariance. There is still an expectation that if the covariance matrix $\boldsymbol{C}$ can be reliably estimated from the sample, then the goodness-of-fit property is not lost and confidence limits determined by propagation of error are reliable. However, it is the inverse of the covariance matrix which appears in the least-squares functional, which places particular importance on the accurate estimation of the smallest eigenvalues from the sample. Unfortunately, the standard estimator in Eq. (4.6) is not a particularly good estimator of the small eigenvalues. It may even produce nearly singular covariance-matrix estimates, which complicates the problem of finding minima of the least-squares functional.

This situation may be treated in various ways. For low-statistics samples, it is not uncommon to neglect the off-diagonal covariances and keep only the diagonal variances in the covariance matrix. This usually simplifies the problem of finding minima of the least-squares functional, but it clearly sacrifices the goodness-of-fit property. It is also expected that ignoring the off-diagonal covariances in the sample data will lead to underestimated errors for the best-fit parameters when computed by standard propagation of error. In such cases, it is observed that a resampling method such as jackknife or bootstrap, when applied to the whole fitting procedure, generally produce larger error estimates for fit parameters and these are hoped to be more reliable.

Various methods of improving the condition of the sample covariance have been suggested. One common method is to choose the nearest matrix of sufficiently lower rank using the singular-value decomposition (SVD), as indicated by the Eckart–Young–Mirsky theorem [**16, 39**], such that the covariance matrix is suitably conditioned. This is a somewhat subjective criteria since often the spectrum of singular values may appear rather smooth.

An alternative procedure was suggested by Michael and McKerrell [**38**] where the sample covariance matrix itself can be replaced by a model matrix with relatively few parameters. The particular model is well-justified because it reflects the underlying cause of the correlations due to the physical nature of the system. Several groups have reported good results using these methods, including the recent well publicized, and most accurate to date, calculation of the light-hadron spectrum of QCD [**15**].

Another common treatment of the covariance matrix is to consider just the diagonal part of the full covariance matrix estimate diag($\boldsymbol{\mathcal{C}}$) as itself being a relatively well determined but biased estimate of the true covariance matrix. By combining the two estimators with a continuous interpolating parameter δ

$$\boldsymbol{\mathcal{C}}_{\mathbf{s}} = \delta \ \mathrm{diag}(\boldsymbol{\mathcal{C}}) + (1-\delta) \ \boldsymbol{\mathcal{C}}, \tag{4.8}$$

it has been shown [**50**] that this shrinkage estimator for the covariance matrix is closest to the true covariance matrix (under the Frobenius norm) for some value of the shrinkage parameter in the range $0 < \delta < 1$ that does not include the endpoints for a finite number of samples. While several groups have reported some success with this method, it is clearly difficult to determine the optimal shrinkage value δ^* where error of the estimate is smallest, restoring goodness-of-fit. A discussion of the shrinkage estimator and some model estimates for δ^* were presented at the QCDNA IV workshop [**33**] and the The XXVII International Symposium on Lattice Field Theory [**12**]. There is also a comprehensive review of shrinkage estimators from the field of functional genomics [**48**], which discusses at least six different methods for estimating the optimal shrinkage parameter. Some initial tests by the authors on lattice QCD data are encouraging and suggest that more extensive testing of these methods are warranted.

Recently, a more sophisticated treatment has appeared [**54**] that attempts to correct the underestimation of the confidence limits of fit parameters due to a poorly estimated sample covariance matrix. While analytic expressions are derived for these corrections, their test results indicate the corrections are more reliably computed through either bootstrap or jackknife resampling methods.

4.2.2. Variable projection. In Sec. 4.1, we presented the basic exponential model in Eq. (4.2). In anticipation, we showed how this model could be written to separate the linear ($\mathbf{a}$) and nonlinear ($\boldsymbol{\alpha}$) parameters in the model: $\mathbf{y}(\boldsymbol{\alpha}, \mathbf{a}) = \boldsymbol{\Phi}(\boldsymbol{\alpha})\ \mathbf{a}$ where $\boldsymbol{\Phi} \in \mathbb{R}^{N\times M}$. $N > 2M$ is necessary for the problem to be overdetermined. The nonlinear parameter vector $\boldsymbol{\alpha}$ is used to determine the components of the nonlinear parameter matrix $\boldsymbol{\Phi}$ of the general form

$$\boldsymbol{\Phi} = \begin{pmatrix} \phi_1(t_1, \boldsymbol{\alpha}) & \cdots & \phi_M(t_1, \boldsymbol{\alpha}) \\ \vdots & \ddots & \vdots \\ \phi_1(t_N, \boldsymbol{\alpha}) & \cdots & \phi_M(t_N, \boldsymbol{\alpha}) \end{pmatrix}. \tag{4.9}$$

Problems of this type form a special class known as separable nonlinear least squares and have been well studied in the numerical analysis community for the past thirty years.

To see how this special structure can be exploited, recall the least-squares functional to be minimized is

$$r_1^2(\boldsymbol{\alpha}, \mathbf{a}) = \left\|\mathbf{y} - \boldsymbol{\Phi}(\boldsymbol{\alpha})\mathbf{a}\right\|^2. \tag{4.10}$$

Recall that the 2-norm is computed using the inverse covariance matrix $\mathcal{C}^{-1}$ as metric. Now, suppose we were given *a priori* the value of the nonlinear parameters $\boldsymbol{\alpha}$ at the minimum of Eq. (4.10) which we denote $\hat{\boldsymbol{\alpha}}$. We can easily determine *a posteriori* the linear parameters $\hat{\mathbf{a}}$ by solving the corresponding *linear* least-squares problem. The solution is simply

$$\hat{\mathbf{a}} = \boldsymbol{\Phi}^{+}(\hat{\boldsymbol{\alpha}})\mathbf{y}, \tag{4.11}$$

where $\boldsymbol{\Phi}^{+}(\hat{\boldsymbol{\alpha}})$ is the Moore–Penrose pseudoinverse of $\boldsymbol{\Phi}(\hat{\boldsymbol{\alpha}})$ **[62]**. Substituting Eq. (4.11) back into Eq. (4.10) we get a new least-squares functional that depends only on $\boldsymbol{\alpha}$

$$r_2^2(\boldsymbol{\alpha}) = \left\|\mathbf{y} - \boldsymbol{\Phi}(\boldsymbol{\alpha})\boldsymbol{\Phi}^{+}(\boldsymbol{\alpha})\mathbf{y}\right\|^2. \tag{4.12}$$

Again, we compute the 2-norm using $\mathcal{C}^{-1}$ as metric. $\mathbf{P}(\boldsymbol{\alpha}) \equiv \boldsymbol{\Phi}(\boldsymbol{\alpha})\boldsymbol{\Phi}^{+}(\boldsymbol{\alpha})$ is the orthogonal projector onto the linear space spanned by the column vectors of $\boldsymbol{\Phi}(\boldsymbol{\alpha})$, so $\mathbf{P}^{\perp}(\boldsymbol{\alpha}) \equiv \mathbf{1} - \mathbf{P}(\boldsymbol{\alpha})$ is the projector onto the orthogonal complement of the column space of $\boldsymbol{\Phi}(\boldsymbol{\alpha})$. Hence, we can rewrite Eq. (4.12) more compactly as

$$r_2^2(\boldsymbol{\alpha}) = \left\|\mathbf{P}^{\perp}(\boldsymbol{\alpha})\mathbf{y}\right\|^2. \tag{4.13}$$

This form makes it easier to see why $r_2^2(\boldsymbol{\alpha})$ is commonly called the *variable projection* (VARPRO) functional. It has been shown **[23]** that the minima of $r_2(\boldsymbol{\alpha})$ and the corresponding values of $\mathbf{a}$ from Eq. (4.11) are the same as the minima of $r_1^2(\boldsymbol{\alpha}, \mathbf{a})$.

One complication of the VARPRO method is computing the gradient $\partial\mathbf{r}_2/\partial\boldsymbol{\alpha}$ when the gradients $\partial\phi_k(t_n, \boldsymbol{\alpha})/\partial\boldsymbol{\alpha}$ are known. The solution is presented in some detail in **[23]** and an excellent `FORTRAN` implementation **[9]** is available in the Netlib Repository.

We see potentially significant benefits to minimizing the VARPRO functional instead of the usual least-squares functional, all related to the reduction of the dimensionality of the search space by postponing the determination of $\hat{\mathbf{a}}$ and the improved condition of the problem. In Sec. 4.2.3, we show that the cost of some search methods depends quite strongly on the dimensionality of the search space such that use of VARPRO might make a particular method viable. For those search methods that require good initial guesses, VARPRO offers the advantage of fewer initial guesses. For LQCD, this is a great benefit, since good guesses for $\boldsymbol{\alpha}$ are easily obtained from the black box methods of Sec. 4.4. When the incorporation of Bayesian prior knowledge is desired, described in Sec. 4.3, for LQCD it seems easier to develop reasonable priors for the energies E_m than the amplitudes A_m. When using the VARPRO method, only priors for the energies are needed. Of course, if reliable priors for the amplitudes are available, one should instead use the standard method.

4.2.3. Search strategies. As the least-squares method is well established in many fields, there is a wealth of literature, algorithms, implementations, *etc.* for finding minima for the nonlinear least-squares functional. A good starting place for the beginner would be the classic monograph by Dennis and Schnabel **[14]**. Minimization methods we know to be in common use within the LQCD community are MINPACK's `LMDER` Levenberg-Marquardt algorithm, the ACM TOMS algorithm 573 commonly called `NL2SOL`, and CERNLIB's `MINUIT` package, all of which are known to be globally convergent to some local minima. Many authors report success using the Levenberg-Marquardt algorithm described in Numerical Recipes [**45**], even though it is well known that this implementation is not globally convergent. It is likely the case that when black-box methods prove to be effective, the initial guesses provided are sufficiently near to a minimum that the Numerical Recipes implementation can succeed.

Even for globally convergent minimization methods, there is no guarantee that the located minimum is a global minimum, nor can they determine if there are degenerate global minima. One obvious method to enable sampling the various minima of the model is the method of simulated annealing [**30**]. However, this method does not seem to get much use in the LQCD community despite the fact that it is based on the same Monte Carlo methods used to generate the ensembles of configurations needed to compute the hadronic correlation functions. From our reading of the LQCD literature, it is clear that a demonstration of consistency between solutions found by least-squares and black-box methods are considered sufficient for publication without further proof that the solution is a global minima of the least-squares functional. Generally speaking, the vast majority of the past literature has been focused on determining only the leading exponential which dominates the correlation function at large times. Much more emphasis is now being placed on determining the sub-leading exponentials, where it is not obviously true that a method like simulated annealing won't be needed to locate global minima.

A new method for locating global minima was recently introduced to the LQCD community by Alexandrou *et al.* [**3**] based on a method called AMIAS [**51**]. In this approach, the user simply defines a bounded region in the parameter space and then covers the space uniformly with a sufficiently dense set of points as to essentially compute the least-squares functional everywhere in the region. In other words, it is like the high-temperature limit of a simulated annealing method. They have presented some nice results that were clearly computationally demanding in a relatively low-dimensional parameter space. It would be nice if they would compare the computational cost of their results with similar ones achieved using simulated annealing at some lower temperature. Finally, we note that the cost of the AMIAS method could be reduced by using the VARPRO functional described in Sec. 4.2.2 simply due to the reduction in the dimensionality of the search space. Moreover, an even more radical reduction could be obtained by using VARPRO as a local minimizer starting from a much coarser mesh and employing the techniques described in [**43**].

Another recent method introduced to the LQCD community is based on evolutionary algorithms [**57, 58**]. Here, the goodness-of-fit computed from the least-squares functional plays the role of the fitness function. Candidate solutions play the role of individuals in a population undergoing evolution by reproduction, mutation, recombination and selection. What appears particularly appealing about this method is that many discrete choices typically made by the user, such as the range of times to be included in the analysis or the number of exponentials to include in the model, can be incorporated into the analysis. Thus, while it is essentially a least-squares method, it frees the user from having to make expert choices about the analysis. It would seem that establishing the goodness-of-fit property for the least-squares functional over the sample would be crucial for this method since the goodness-of-fit for various candidate solutions that may have different degrees of freedom will be used, *e.g.*, in a selection process where all individuals with goodness-of-fit below some threshold are culled from the population. As before, we note that the use of the VARPRO functional may be an interesting variation for evolutionary algorithms as the complexity of the individuals (candidate solutions) is reduced to include only nonlinear parameters, but the fitness function (the VARPRO functional) may be substantially more complex. It would be interesting to learn which least-squares functional works more effectively in this setting.

4.3. Bayesian methods

Bayes's theorem describes how a conditional probability of some event X given the condition Y depends on its inverse (the probability of Y given X) and the corresponding unconditional probabilities of the two events

$$P[X|Y] = \frac{P[Y|X]P[X]}{P[Y]}. \tag{4.14}$$

We can apply the theorem to the case of extracting energies from lattice data D by asking the conditional probability that a particular model M is valid, given the lattice data and any prior knowledge p that can be applied to the particular physical system under consideration:

$$P[M|Dp] = \frac{P[D|Mp]P[M|p]}{P[D|p]}. \tag{4.15}$$

In other words, the probability that the model M correctly describes the data D can be related to the probability that the data D would result if the model M were true. This manipulation and the introduction of additional constraints via the priors p allow new avenues of attack on the problem of extracting exponentials. In this section, we discuss two such Bayesian methods in the context of lattice QCD: the Maximum-Entropy Method (MEM) (Sec. 4.3.1) and Constrained Curve Fitting (Sec. 4.3.2).

4.3.1. Maximum-entropy method. The maximum-entropy method is a technique for extracting results from data where the data do not have enough degrees of freedom to well constrain the desired extracted quantities. For example, in lattice QCD, one might want to extract the spectral function (related to the experimental cross-section) from lattice two-point functions. However, a reasonable spectral function might be sampled over hundreds of frequencies, while a typical lattice correlator is measured over only tens of times. This problem can be resolved by requiring the spectral function to resemble a so-called model function. By simultaneously requiring the fit form to match the lattice data and the spectral function to resemble the model, a reasonable spectral function may be obtained from accessible lattice volumes.

Consider the Euclidean two-point Green function of some operator O

$$C(t) = \int \langle O(t)O^\dagger(0)\rangle. \tag{4.16}$$

The correlator has a spectral decomposition into frequency space

$$C(t) = \int_0^\infty K(t,\omega)\rho(\omega)d\omega, \tag{4.17}$$

where ω is a real frequency, ρ is the spectral function and K is the kernel, which is the Laplace transform of a free propagator of mass ω. For the zero-temperature case, this kernel is $K(t,\omega) = e^{-\omega t}$, a simple exponential; however, the method will work equally well for other kernels, and is thus quite useful for high-temperature applications.

We wish to use Bayes's Theorem $P[\rho|CH] \propto P[C|\rho H]P[\rho|H]$, where C here represents the lattice estimation of the Green function including statistical noise, ρ represents the true value of the spectral function and H represents our prior knowledge about the parameters, such as the positivity condition $\rho(\omega) \geq 0$.

The probability $P[C|\rho H]$ can be found using a least-squares method described in Sec. 4.2, with due consideration of the conditions under which the least-squares solution may be interpreted as a maximum-likelihood estimator. It is the exponential of the least-squares functional, denoted here as L for likelihood:

$$P[C|\rho H] = \frac{1}{Z_L} e^{-L}, \tag{4.18}$$

$$L = \frac{1}{2} \sum_{a,b} (C(t_a) - \hat{C}(t_a)) \boldsymbol{C}_{ab}^{-1} (C(t_b) - \hat{C}(t_b)). \tag{4.19}$$

In this formula $Z_L = (2\pi)^{T/2}\sqrt{\det \boldsymbol{C}}$ is a normalizing factor with T being the time-length of the data, $\hat{C}$ is the correlator reconstructed from the spectral function as in Eq. 4.17, and $\boldsymbol{C}$ is the $T \times T$ covariance matrix.

The novel aspect of the maximum-entropy approach is the estimation of the other probability $P[\rho|H]$, which has a similar form, being the exponential of the Shannon-Jaynes entropy S:

$$P[\rho|H\alpha m] = \frac{1}{Z_S} e^{\alpha S} d\omega \tag{4.20}$$

$$S = \int_0^\infty \left(\rho(\omega) - m(\omega) - \rho(\omega) \log \left(\frac{\rho(\omega)}{m(\omega)} \right) \right), \tag{4.21}$$

where $Z_S = \int e^{\alpha S} D\rho$ is a normalization factor, and we introduce the weighting factor $\alpha > 0$ and the model function m. The arbitrary parameter α determines how much weight to give the entropy S with respect to the likelihood L. The former quantifies the discrepancy of the spectral function from the given model, while the latter quantifies the discrepancy of the reconstructed correlator from the measured lattice data. The model function should incorporate some knowledge of the system, and the stability of the results under variations should be checked. In the case where the spectral function ρ is exactly equal to the model m, the entropy reaches a maximum of zero; for all other spectral functions, it is negative. In the case of QCD, a model function proportional to ω^2 at large ω is well motivated by perturbative QCD.

The spectral function derived using this technique will be

$$\rho_{\text{out}}(\omega) = \int \rho(\omega) P[\rho|CH\alpha m] P[\alpha|CHm] D\rho \, d\alpha \tag{4.22}$$

$$\approx \int \rho_\alpha(\omega) P[\alpha|CHm] d\alpha, \tag{4.23}$$

where ρ_α is the functional form maximizing $\alpha S - L$. Any one of a number of algorithms may be employed to perform this maximization step. Some choices

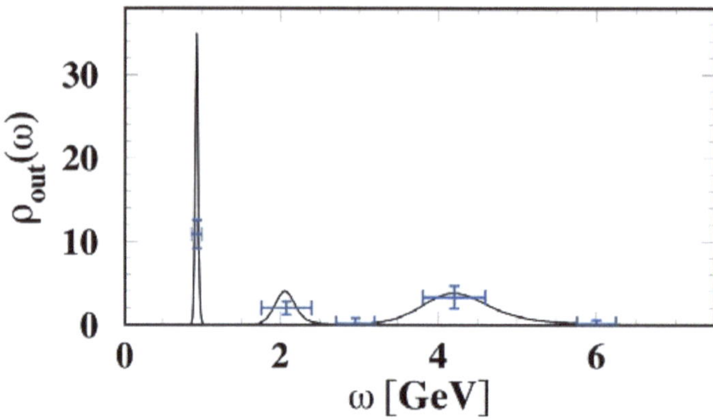

FIGURE 4.3.1. Spectral function of the light-quark vector meson taken from Ref. [**42**]

used in the literature include singular-value decomposition (SVD) and simulated annealing.

We show here an example of how one may obtain the spectral function for the light-quark vector meson using lattice data; see Ref. [**42**]. In this work, the authors assume that $P[A|DH\alpha m]$ is sharply peaked around its most-probable point and estimate the covariance by the diagonal statistical error, resulting in the vector-meson spectral function shown in Fig. 4.3.1. The height of each horizontal bar is $\langle\rho_{\text{out}}(\omega)\rangle$ in each ω interval with its statistical error. The lowest-energy peak in Fig. 4.3.1 is the ground state of vector meson, while second peak and third bump could indicate signals for higher excited states; however, in this case, their shapes are rather marginal. A similar method can be used to look at the excited nucleon spectrum, for example in Ref. [**47**].

4.3.2. Constrained-curve fitting methods. Constrained curve fitting is a simple modification of standard nonlinear least-squares techniques (see Sec. 4.2). Although widely used in other research areas, such fits were not used much by the lattice QCD community until Lepage *et al.* introduced it in 2001 [**32**]. Such a technique is built upon Bayesian statistics, similar to the maximum-entropy method. However, unlike the MEM, where the standard likelihood is modified by a term in the probability density which minimizes the information content or, equivalently, maximizes the entropy, here, a different Gaussian form is chosen:

$$P[\rho|CH] \propto e^{\chi'^2/2}. \tag{4.24}$$

The χ'^2 is a modified least-squares function

$$\chi'^2 = \chi^2 + \chi^2_{\text{prior}}, \tag{4.25}$$

where χ^2 corresponds to the least-squares function in Sec. 4.2 and χ^2_{prior} is a weighting factor put in by the analysts based on their knowledge about special properties of the data. (In the following section, we will give an example of how such a factor may be chosen in a lattice calculation.)

With the lattice hadron two-point correlator, we can extract energies (denoted E_m) and their corresponding overlap factors (Z_m) between the operators used and the QCD vacuum. From physics, we know that all physical masses (or energies) must be positive ($E_m > 0$) and that each excited state must be heavier than all the states preceding it ($E_m > E_{m-1}$). In certain cases, similar constraints can be applied to amplitudes if we know that the overlap factor is dominated by lowest-energy states, $A_m < A_{m+1}$. Another common tactic is to perform multi-exponential fits in an iterative fashion, where the results of each fit are used as priors for the next. Given a set of m masses and amplitudes, we can set χ^2_{prior} to

$$\chi^2_{\text{prior}} = \sum_m \left[\frac{(A_m - \tilde{A}_m)^2}{\tilde{\sigma}^2_{A_m}} + \frac{(E_m - \tilde{E}_m)^2}{\tilde{\sigma}^2_{E_m}} \right], \tag{4.26}$$

which makes the $\{A, E\}_m$ preferred when they fall in the parameter space around $\{A, E\}_m = \{\tilde{A}, \tilde{E}\}_m \pm \tilde{\sigma}_{\{A_m, E_m\}}$.

Constrained curve fitting has been adopted to analyze lattice QCD correlators. For example, in Ref. **[24]** the Υ spectrum was calculated using such a fitting strategy. In this work, the authors generated a 3×3 correlator matrix and fit to the form $C_{ij} = \sum_m^M A_{m,ij} e^{-E_m t}$, where $A_{m,ij}$ is Hermitian. They re-parameterize E_n in terms of $\ln(E_0)$ and $\ln(E_{m+1} - E_m)$; this choice enforces the prior knowledge that the energies are positive and ordered. They chose the $\tilde{\sigma}$ for the priors to be tight for the initial fits, and later relaxed the widths to 1 for their final fits. Fig. 4.3.2 shows the lowest three E_m with $M \in [4, 10]$ in the fitted formula; the large number of exponentials should keep systematic contamination from high-order states under control. Since the result with six exponentials gave the same result as seven, seven masses were chosen for their final results for the ground, first- and second-excited states of the Υ spectrum.

4.4. Black-box methods

Black-box methods, where the performance of the method does not depend upon initial guesses, are also useful for extracting particle energies from Euclidean-time correlation functions. In particular, it has been possible to extend the widely used effective-mass method to incorporate multiple correlation functions and produce effective-mass estimates for multiple excited states **[19, 20]**.

In lattice QCD, a two-point correlation function computed on $N = 2M$ time-slices t_n will admit an exact algebraic solution having the form of Eq. (4.2) with M energies E_m and amplitudes A_m. The problem to solve is the nonlinear system of equations $\mathbf{y} = \mathbf{V}(x)\ \mathbf{a}$

$$\begin{bmatrix} y_1 \\ y_2 \\ y_3 \\ y_4 \\ \vdots \\ y_{2M} \end{bmatrix} = \begin{bmatrix} 1 & 1 & \cdots & 1 \\ x_1 & x_2 & \cdots & x_M \\ x_1^2 & x_2^2 & \cdots & x_M^2 \\ x_1^3 & x_2^3 & \cdots & x_M^3 \\ \vdots & \vdots & \ddots & \vdots \\ x_1^{2M-1} & x_2^{2M-1} & \cdots & x_M^{2M-1} \end{bmatrix} \begin{bmatrix} a_1 \\ \vdots \\ a_M \end{bmatrix} \tag{4.27}$$

for $x_m = \exp\left[-aE_m(\vec{p})\right]$ and $a_m = A_m(\vec{p}) \exp\left[-t_0 E_m(\vec{p})\right]$ where $y_n = C(\vec{p}, t_n)$. $\mathbf{V}(x)$ is known as $2M \times M$ rectangular Vandermonde matrix.

By inspection, it appears the problem is of polynomial degree $2M$ and thus by the Abel-Ruffini theorem **[1, 46]** should not admit a general closed form solution in terms of radicals for $M > 2$. The $M = 1$ solution is simple to compute and is widely known in the lattice QCD literature as the *effective mass*. Note already that

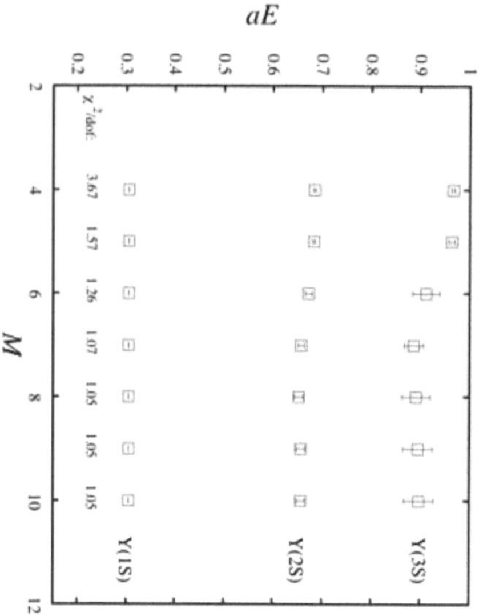

FIGURE 4.3.2. Υ energy (in lattice units) from Ref. [**24**] as a function of the number n of states included in the constrained curve fitting. The goodness of the fits is also listed in the plot.

the simple effective-mass problem is linear and has only one solution, suggesting that the polynomial degree is actually of order M.

The $M = 2$ solution was explicitly constructed by one of the authors [**18**] and was independently constructed some time later by others [**26**]. It was noted [**18**] that the problem, when reduced, required only the solution of a quadratic equation, and so it was conjectured that the general problem of size M could be reduced to a polynomial equation in one variable of degree M.

An efficient algorithm has been available for some time for solving square Vandermonde systems [**7**] by making them upper triangular. This approach works equally well for rectangular Vandermonde systems as in Eq. (4.27). Furthermore, this approach reveals why the solution for the energies E_m can be found without solving for the amplitudes A_m and why the problem is of polynomial degree M.

As a first step toward extracting the energies E from our data, we transform the system so that $V(x)$ is in upper triangular form [**7**] by pre-multiplying by the lower $2M \times 2M$ bi-diagonal matrices:

$$L_m(x) = \begin{bmatrix} 1 & & & & & & \\ 0 & \ddots & & & & & \\ & \ddots & 1 & & & & \\ & & 0 & 1 & & & \\ & & & x_m & -1 & & \\ & & & & \ddots & \ddots & \\ & & & & & x_m & -1 \end{bmatrix} \tag{4.28}$$

where the first -1 on the diagonal appears in the $m+1$ row and column. In the appendices of Refs. **[19, 20]**, we demonstrate in detail how the general solutions for $M = 2$, 3 and 4 work.

Finding a general approach for $M > 4$ would be a tough challenge. Although Abel's Impossibility Theorem proves there are no general solutions in radicals for polynomials higher than quartic order, there are numerical methods for finding the roots of polynomials of any order. The general form for the polynomial follows is:

$$|\mathcal{H}| = \left| \begin{array}{cccc:c} y_1 & y_2 & \cdots & y_M & 1 \\ y_2 & y_3 & \cdots & y_{M+1} & x_1 \\ \vdots & \vdots & \ddots & \vdots & \vdots \\ y_{M+1} & y_{M+2} & \cdots & y_{2M} & x_1^M \end{array} \right| = 0. \tag{4.29}$$

4.4.1. Prony method. Prony **[13]** showed that problems in the form of Eq. (4.2) implied the following system of equations $\mathbf{y} = \mathbf{H}(y)\,\mathbf{p}$

$$\begin{bmatrix} y_1 \\ y_2 \\ \vdots \\ y_M \end{bmatrix} = - \begin{bmatrix} y_2 & \cdots & y_{M+1} \\ y_3 & \cdots & y_{M+2} \\ \vdots & \ddots & \vdots \\ y_{M+1} & \cdots & y_{2M} \end{bmatrix} \begin{bmatrix} p_1 \\ p_2 \\ \vdots \\ p_M \end{bmatrix} \tag{4.30}$$

where the $M \times M$ matrix $\mathbf{H}(y)$ has the special structure of a Hankel matrix and the components p_m of $\mathbf{p}$ are the coefficients of a polynomial

$$P(x) = \prod_{m=1}^{M} (x - x_m) = 1 + \sum_{m=1}^{M} p_m x^m. \tag{4.31}$$

The Prony-Yule-Walker method (or just Prony's method, for short) **[13, ?]** solves Eq. (4.30) to find the coefficients and then finds the M roots of the polynomial in Eq. (4.31). The amplitudes are determined by substituting the roots into Eq. (4.27) and solving it. Note again that using $2M$ timeslices of correlation function data to determine M effective masses is a problem of polynomial order M.

The general conditions under which the solutions of the Hankel and Vandermonde systems coincide is presented in Ref. **[56]**. Here we provide a simple demonstration that both solutions are the same under the assumption that there are no complications like degeneracies in the energy spectrum of Eq. (4.2). Assuming $\mathbf{H}(y)$ is invertible, solving Eq. (4.30) gives

$$\mathbf{p} = \mathbf{H}^{-1}\mathbf{y}, \qquad P(x) = 1 + \mathbf{p}^T \mathbf{x} = 1 + \left(\mathbf{H}^{-1}\mathbf{y}\right)^T \mathbf{x} \tag{4.32}$$

for the polynomial of Eq. (4.31) and where $\mathbf{x}^T = (x, x^2, \cdots, x^M)$. Recall that the inverse can be written in terms of the adjoint, or matrix of cofactors, $\mathbf{H}^{-1} = \mathbf{C}/|\mathbf{H}|$, $C_{ij} = (-1)^{i+j}|\mathbf{H}(i;j)|$, where the notation $\mathbf{H}(i;j)$ means removing row i and column j. For Prony's method, we can rescale $P(x) \to |\mathbf{H}|\, P(x)$ and still find the roots x_m by solving

$$|\mathbf{H}| + (\mathbf{C}\,\mathbf{y})^T\,\mathbf{x} = 0 \tag{4.33}$$

for x.

In Refs. **[19, 20, 34]**, we demonstrate this approach using a single correlator. There are a few parameters in the Prony's method which we can tune: the number of desired states K, the number of time slices used to predict the later time point N, and the order of the polynomial M. In this work, we will show a selection of the better choices in these degrees of freedom. Figure 4.4.1 shows the effective mass plot for $L = 2, 3, 4$ from a single Gaussian smeared-point correlator with fixed parameters $N = 20$ and $M = 8$. The excited states are consistent with each other as one increases the value of L. Since we have used a large value of N to form the polynomial, each point uses information extracted from 20 time slices. Thus, one does not need a large plateau to determine the final mass. One also notes that since we only use a single correlator to extract multiple states, the multiple states will be correlated; that is, large errors on higher-excited states will make the ground state noisy as well. Similar attempts have been pursued by NPLQCD collaboration with high-statistics data on nucleon (and other) correlators **[6]**, where one can see very clean signal-to-noise ratios.

4.4.2. Vandermonde method. Returning to the Vandermonde method, the determinant of Eq. (4.29) can be expanded in terms of its cofactors $\mathcal{C}_{ij} = (-1)^{i+j}|\boldsymbol{\mathcal{H}}(i;j)|$

$$|\boldsymbol{\mathcal{H}}| = (-1)^M|\mathbf{H}| + \sum_{i=1}^{M}\mathcal{C}_{i+1,M+1}x^i = (-1)^M|\mathbf{H}| + \sum_{i=1}^{M}(-1)^{i+M}|\boldsymbol{\mathcal{H}}(i+1;M+1)|\,x^i. \tag{4.34}$$

As usual, each cofactor can be expanded in terms of further cofactors where additional rows and columns are removed:

$$|\boldsymbol{\mathcal{H}}(i+1;M+1)| = \sum_{j=1}^{M}(-1)^{j+1}|\boldsymbol{\mathcal{H}}(1,i+1;j,M+1)|\,y_j. \tag{4.35}$$

By eliminating the first row and last row of $\boldsymbol{\mathcal{H}}$ in Eq. (4.29) we recover $\mathbf{H} = \boldsymbol{\mathcal{H}}(1;M+1)$ and for the cofactors

$$(-1)^{j+1}|\boldsymbol{\mathcal{H}}(1,i+1;j,M+1)| = (-1)^j|\mathbf{H}(i;j)| \tag{4.36}$$

so the desired identity is recovered

$$|\boldsymbol{\mathcal{H}}| = (-1)^M|\mathbf{H}| + (-1)^M\sum_{i=1}^{M}\sum_{j=1}^{M}(-1)^{i+j}|\mathbf{H}(i;j)|\,y_j x^i, \tag{4.37}$$

up to a possible overall minus sign for odd M, which is irrelevant for finding roots. There is a unique set of solutions to the Vandermonde and Hankel systems (under the assumption of noise-free correlation functions with non-degenerate energy levels), so other considerations should determine which is the better method to construct the polynomial. It is our experience that computing coefficients from

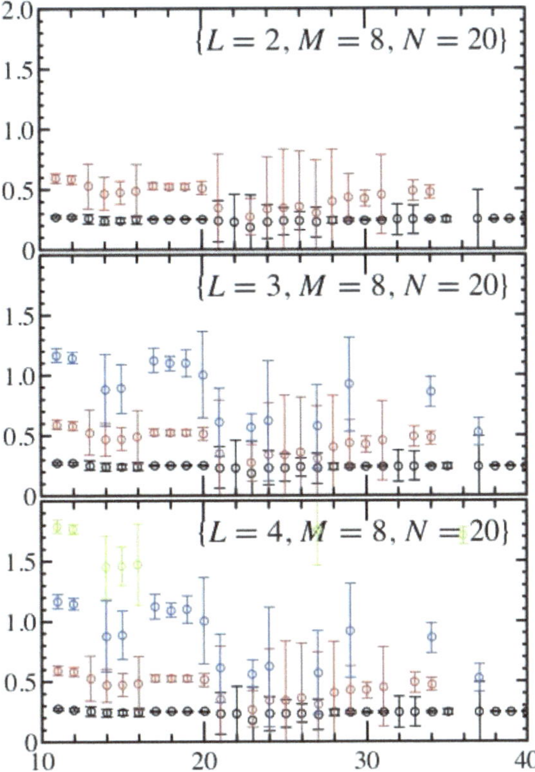

FIGURE 4.4.1. Effective-mass plots from Prony's method at fixed parameters $N = 20$ and $M = 8$ from Refs. [**34, 19, 20**]. The points are plotted at the midpoint of the data range used.

Eq. (4.29) is preferred to solving Eq. (4.30), as statistical noise in the correlation functions can lead to nearly singular Hankel matrices that are difficult to invert.

In an earlier work [**18**], one of the authors showed that Prony's method (also called *linear prediction*) could easily be extended to use more than $2M$ timeslices of a correlation function to extract only M masses by constructing an over-constrained system of equations analogous to Eq. (4.30). It is not obvious how to construct and solve a similar over-constrained system in the Vandermonde case. Thus, Prony's method has a potential advantage that more time samples of the correlation function can be used to extract the same number of energy levels leading to reduced statistical fluctuations.

When constructing correlation functions in LQCD, care is taken to ensure that the correlation function transforms irreducibly under the symmetries of the lattice space group [**4, 5, 40, 41**]. For the model function, as in Eq. (4.2), this implies that the amplitudes depend on the details of the specific correlation function but that the energies depend only on the irreducible representation. Since it is common in lattice QCD simulations to compute at least two distinct correlation functions for each irreducible representation, effective-mass solutions that combine data from multiple correlators are also possible.

Assume that there are K correlation functions available as in Eq. (4.2) that differ only in their amplitudes:

$$C_k(\vec{p}, t_n) = \sum_{m=1}^{M} A_{km}(\vec{p}) \exp\left[-(t_0 + na)E_m(\vec{p})\right] \tag{4.38}$$

$$n \geq 0, \quad A_{km},\ E_m \in \mathbb{R}, \quad 0 \leq E_1 \leq E_2 \leq \cdots \leq E_M.$$

Data from the same N time slices will be used in the following from each correlation function to construct M effective masses. Under this assumption the condition that there will be equal number of data points as unknowns is $KN = (K+1)M$.

The general form of the polynomial equation can be inferred by studying the solved examples in matrices of smaller rank. (See the appendices in Ref. **[19, 20]** for simpler examples.) Define K Hankel matrices $H_k^{N \times M_k}$ for each of the correlation functions with the constraints $\sum_{k=1}^{K} M_k = M$ and $N = M + 1$. Then the general form of the polynomial equation is

$$\left| \begin{array}{c:c:c:c:c} H_1^{N\times M_1} & H_2^{N\times M_2} & \cdots & H_M^{N\times M_K} & \begin{array}{c} 1 \\ x_1 \\ x_1^2 \\ \vdots \\ x_1^M \end{array} \end{array} \right| = 0. \tag{4.39}$$

As previously discussed, each Hankel matrix is generally of full column rank, and if the correlation functions are linearly independent, then the columns of different Hankel matrices are also linearly independent. So, Eq. (4.39) will only be satisfied for discrete values of x_1 corresponding to the roots of the polynomial.

In practical LQCD calculations, the temporal extent is finite, so the choice of temporal boundary conditions affects hadronic correlation functions near the boundary. For simplicity, starting from Eq. (4.2), set $t_0 = 0$ and identify the points $t_0 = 0$ and $t_N = Na$ that can be done using modular arithmetic, *i.e.*, $t_n = (n \bmod N)a$. For anti-periodic boundary conditions, the typical hadronic Euclidean time correlation function is described by the model function

$$\begin{aligned} C(\vec{p}, t_n) &= \sum_{m=1}^{M} \{A_m(\vec{p}) \exp\left[-(n \bmod N)aE_m(\vec{p})\right] \\ &+ (-1)^B A_m^*(\vec{p}) \exp\left[-(N - n \bmod N)aE_m^*(\vec{p})\right]\}, \end{aligned} \tag{4.40}$$

where $n \geq 0, \quad A_m,\ A_m^*,\ E_m,\ E_m^* \in \mathbb{R}, \quad 0 \leq E_1 \leq E_2 \leq \cdots \leq E_M\ , \quad 0 \leq E_1^* \leq E_2^* \leq \cdots \leq E_M^*$. For periodic boundary conditions, set $(-1)^B \to 1$. For mesons, $B = 0$ but more importantly $A_m = A_m^*$ and $E_m = E_m^*$, which is not true for baryons ($B = 1$). So, baryon correlation functions represent M states propagating to the left and M different states propagating to the right for a total of $2M$ states.

Meson correlation functions represent the same M states propagating to the right and left. However, time-reversal symmetry requires $C(\vec{P}, t_n) = C(\vec{P}, t_{N-n})$ up to noise terms, so that only half of the computed timeslices are truly independent. Thus, as was the case with baryons, information about only M states in any given quantum number channel can be extracted from a single correlation function computed on $2M$ timeslices in a finite box. As shown in Ref. **[18]**, this can be made explicit by writing the meson correlation function as

$$C(\tau_n) = \sum_{m=1}^{M} A_m \exp(-aNE_m/2)\cosh(anE_m), \quad \tau_n = (n - N/2)a. \tag{4.41}$$

To write this result in the Vandermonde form of Eq. (4.27), define the variables

$$\begin{aligned} a_m &= A_m \exp(-aNE_m/2), \quad x_m = \cosh(aE_m), \\ y_n &= \frac{1}{2^{n-1}} \sum_{j=0}^{n-1} \binom{n-1}{j} C(\tau_{n-2j-1}). \end{aligned} \tag{4.42}$$

When solving Eq. (4.27), the domain of the solutions x_m will be the real numbers or complex conjugate pairs since real-valued correlation functions are used as input. Complex-valued solutions are clearly unphysical and should be discarded as they are likely due to noise. Real solutions may also be unphysical if they cannot be used to extract a non-negative energy, and this will depend on the details of the model function and hence the boundary conditions. For example, for the basic model of Eq. (4.2), only the solutions $0 < x_m \leq 1$ will yield non-negative energies. For mesons in periodic boxes, $x_m = \cosh(aE_m)$, so only $x_m \geq 1$ will yield non-negative energies. Finally, for baryons in periodic boxes, the M states propagating to the right have $x_m = \exp(-aE_m)$ and the M states propagating to the left have $x_{M+m} = \exp(aE^*_m)$, so all solutions $x_m > 0$ are physical and $x_m > 1$ means the state is propagating to the left.

For some lattice fermion actions, *e.g.* staggered **[10, 49, 55]** or domain-wall fermions **[52, 60]**, a variation of Eq. (4.2) is needed as a starting point to account for states that oscillate in time. For example, an appropriate model for staggered mesons on an infinite lattice is

$$C(\vec{p}, t_n) = \sum_{m=1}^{M} \left\{ A_m(\vec{p}) \exp\left[-naE_m(\vec{p})\right] + (-1)^n A^*_m(\vec{p}) \exp\left[-naE^*_m(\vec{p})\right] \right\}, \tag{4.43}$$

where n, A, E and E^* have the same constraints as in Eq. 4.40. There are two independently ordered sets of states, half of which oscillate as $(-1)^n$. When solving Eq. (4.27), such oscillating solutions will have physical solutions if $-1 \leq x_m < 0$. Similarly, for staggered baryons with periodic boundary conditions, physical solutions with $x_m \leq -1$ are certainly expected as oscillating states moving to the left.

Generally speaking, model functions appropriate for the common lattice discretizations and choice of boundary conditions can be formulated and rewritten in the Vandermonde form of Eq. (4.27). The physical interpretation of the solutions x_m depends on the details of the discretization and boundary conditions. In some cases, all real solutions may have a physical interpretation and thus cannot be immediately discarded without further statistical analysis.

4.4.3. State-space method. The state-space method has much in common with Prony's method already described, but has its origin in systems-control theory

[**31**]. It begins with the usual Hankel matrix of the form

$$\mathbf{H} = \begin{bmatrix} y_0 & y_1 & \cdots & y_M \\ y_1 & y_2 & \cdots & y_{M+1} \\ \vdots & \vdots & \ddots & \vdots \\ y_{N-M-1} & y_{N-M} & \cdots & y_N \end{bmatrix}. \quad (4.44)$$

Recalling that $y_t = \sum_{k=0}^{K-1} c_k e^{-E_k t}$, we note that it should be possible to break up this matrix into the following form:

$$\begin{aligned} \mathbf{H} &= \mathbf{SAT}^T, \\ \mathbf{S} &= \begin{bmatrix} 1 & 1 & \cdots & 1 \\ e^{-E_0} & e^{-E_1} & \cdots & e^{-E_K} \\ \vdots & \vdots & \ddots & \vdots \\ e^{-(N-M-1)E_0} & e^{-(N-M-1)E_1} & \cdots & e^{-(N-M-1)E_K} \end{bmatrix}, \\ \mathbf{A} &= \begin{bmatrix} A_0 & 0 & \cdots & 0 \\ 0 & A_1 & \cdots & 0 \\ \vdots & \vdots & \ddots & \vdots \\ 0 & 0 & \cdots & A_K \end{bmatrix}, \\ \mathbf{T} &= \begin{bmatrix} 1 & 1 & \cdots & 1 \\ e^{-E_0} & e^{-E_1} & \cdots & e^{-E_K} \\ \vdots & \vdots & \ddots & \vdots \\ e^{-ME_0} & e^{-ME_1} & \cdots & e^{-ME_K} \end{bmatrix}, \end{aligned} \quad (4.45)$$

where we have truncated the expansion to the lowest K states, and we require that $M \geq K$ and $N > M + K$. Although there is no simple way to perform such a decomposition, we note that the structure of the first and last matrices is special; each row's ratio with the row above is a simple exponential:

$$\begin{aligned} \mathbf{S}^{\uparrow} &= \mathbf{S}^{\downarrow}\mathbf{E}, \\ \mathbf{E} &= \begin{bmatrix} e^{-E_0} & 0 & \cdots & 0 \\ 0 & e^{-E_1} & \ddots & 0 \\ \vdots & \ddots & \ddots & \vdots \\ 0 & 0 & \cdots & e^{-E_K} \end{bmatrix}, \end{aligned} \quad (4.46)$$

where the arrows denote deletion of the top or bottom rows of their respective matrices. This means that despite the large (vertical) size of the matrix, it only has rank K, and that the Hankel matrix will have a singular value decomposition with the structure

$$\mathbf{H} = \mathbf{U\Sigma V}^{\dagger} = \begin{bmatrix} \mathbf{U}_K & \mathbf{U}_{N-M} \end{bmatrix} \begin{bmatrix} \mathbf{\Sigma}_K & \mathbf{0} \\ \mathbf{0} & \mathbf{\Sigma}_N \end{bmatrix} \begin{bmatrix} \mathbf{V}_K & \mathbf{V}_{M+1} \end{bmatrix}^{\dagger}, \quad (4.47)$$

where the matrices subscripted K contain information about the lowest K states and the remaining matrices are hopefully negligible. As can be seen by examining Eqs. 4.45 and 4.47, the two matrices $\mathbf{S}$ and $\mathbf{U}_K$ (and $\mathbf{T}$ and $\mathbf{V}_K$) live in the same space and are related by a nonsingular matrix multiplication: $\mathbf{U}_K = \mathbf{SR}$. Plugging this into Eq. 4.46 then yields

$$\mathbf{U}_K^{\uparrow} = \mathbf{U}_K^{\downarrow}\mathbf{R}^{-1}\mathbf{ER}, \quad (4.48)$$

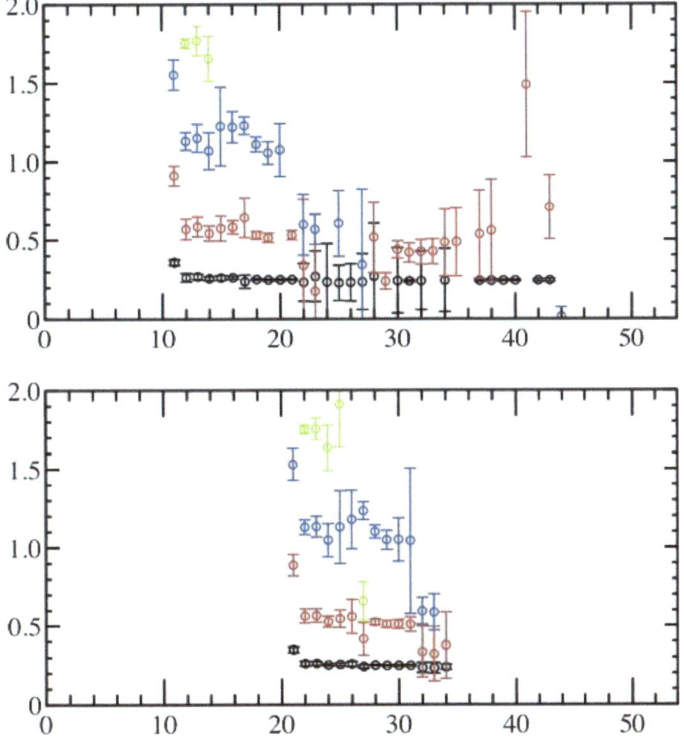

FIGURE 4.4.2. Nucleon spectrum (in lattice units) for two choices of parameters ($K = 5, M = 8, N = 20$ and $K = 5, M = 20, N = 40$) using the state-space method. The points are plotted at the midpoint of the data range used. The former choice may be compared with Fig. 4.4.1, in which Prony's method is used with the same M, N. The latter choice makes more sense for the state-space method.

and since the extra multiplications have no impact on the eigenvalues of $\mathbf{E}$, we can extract these by taking the eigenvalues of $(\mathbf{U}_K^{\downarrow})^{-1}\mathbf{U}_K^{\uparrow}$. Since $\mathbf{U}_K^{\downarrow}$ is not a square matrix, we must use pseudoinversion to determine this quantity. As in the previous section, there are a few parameters (K, M and N) which may be chosen arbitrarily. Experience shows that $M \approx N/2$ works well, and that N should be significantly larger than K. The number of model states K must be tuned; if too small, the extracted masses will be contaminated by higher modes; if too large, the eigenvalues will become noisy.

We show an example of energies extracted using the state-space method on the same data set as depicted in Fig. 4.4.2. We select $K = 5$ to account for enough excited states to eliminate contamination without introducing excessive noise. In the upper plot, we choose $N = 20$ to make a direct comparison against Fig. 4.4.1; $N = 40$ works somewhat better for the state-space method, as shown in the bottom plot.

4.5. Conclusion

For the last three decades when Markov-chain Monte Carlo (MCMC) methods have been regularly employed to perform calculations in quantum field theories, estimates of the energy eigenvalues of the Hamiltonian have been determined by analysis of computed exponential time series. Many of these eigenvalues represent the masses of physically observable particles and others can be related to physically observable scattering phenomena of two or more particles. In the past, the time series could be computed at $\mathcal{O}(10)$ times, limiting to one or two the number of exponentials that could be reliably estimated.

With the advent of ever more powerful high performance computing (HPC) systems and substantial algorithmic developments, exponential time series can now be computed at $\mathcal{O}(100)$ times. This should enable the estimation of many more exponentials and has led to a strong growth of interest within the lattice quantum field theory community in the general problem of exponential time series analysis. Accordingly, many groups worldwide are focused on learning the techniques already developed in other fields of study and testing their effectiveness for modeling LQCD time series. Some groups are working to develop novel techniques optimally suited for LQCD analysis. This review is a snapshot of the current state of the art, as well as future research directions, of exponential time series analysis as applied to hadronic correlation functions in the lattice quantum field theory community.

Bibliography

1. Niels H. Abel, *Beweis der Unmöglichkeit, algebraische Gleichungen von höheren Graden als dem vierten allgemein aufzulösen.*, J. reine angew. Math. **1** (1826), 65, See `http://mathworld.wolfram.com/AbelsImpossibilityTheorem.html` for more references.
2. Alexander Craig Aitken, *On least squares and linear combinations of observations*, Proc. Roy. Soc. Edinburgh **55** (1935), 42–48.
3. Constantia Alexandrou, C. N. Papanicolas, and E. Stiliaris, *A novel method for the determination of hadron excited states in Lattice QCD applied to the nucleon*, PoS **LATTICE 2008** (2008), 099.
4. S. Basak et al., *Group-theoretical construction of extended baryon operators in lattice QCD*, Phys. Rev. **D72** (2005), 094506.
5. Subhasish Basak et al., *Clebsch-Gordan construction of lattice interpolating fields for excited baryons*, Phys. Rev. **D72** (2005), 074501.
6. Silas R. Beane et al., *High Statistics Analysis using Anisotropic Clover Lattices: (I) Single Hadron Correlation Functions*, (2009).
7. Åke Björck and Victor Pereyra, *Solution of Vandermonde systems of equations*, Math. Comput. **24** (1970), 893–903.
8. James D. Bjorken and Emmanuel A. Paschos, *Inelastic Electron Proton and gamma Proton Scattering, and the Structure of the Nucleon*, Phys. Rev. **185** (1969), 1975–1982.
9. John Bolstad, *varpro.f*, Available at: `http://www.netlib.org/opt/index.html`, January 1977.
10. Michael Creutz, *Species Doubling and Transfer Matrices for Fermionic Fields*, Phys. Rev. **D35** (1987), 1460.
11. Michael Creutz, Laurence Jacobs, and Claudio Rebbi, *Experiments with a gauge-invariant Ising system*, Phys. Rev. Lett. **42** (1979), 1390–1393.
12. Chris Dawson, *Issues in fitting lattice data*, PoS **LAT2009** (2009), 072.
13. Gaspard Clair François Marie Riche de Prony, *Essai expérimental et analytique sur les lois de la dilatabilité et sur celles de la force expansive de la vapeur de l'eau et de la vapeur de l'alkool, à différentes températures*, J. Ecole Poly. **1** (1795), 24–76, Partial translation available in [**56**].
14. John E. Dennis, Jr. and Robert B. Schnabel, *Numerical methods for unconstrained optimization and nonlinear equations*, Classics in Applied Mathematics, no. 16, Soc for Industrial & Applied Math, 1996.
15. Stephan Dürr et al., *Ab Initio Determination of Light Hadron Masses*, Science **322** (2008), 1224–1227.
16. Carl H. Eckart and Gale Young, *The approximation of one matrix by another of lower rank*, Psychometrika **1** (1936), 211–218.
17. Richard P. Feynman, *Very high-energy collisions of hadrons*, Phys. Rev. Lett. **23** (1969), 1415–1417.
18. George T. Fleming, *What can lattice QCD theorists learn from NMR spectroscopists?*, QCD and Numerical Analysis III (A. Boriçi, A. Frommer, B. Joó, A. Kennedy, and B. Pendleton, eds.), Lecture Notes in Computational Science and Engineering, no. 47, Springer-Verlag, 2005, pp. 143–152.
19. George T. Fleming, Saul D. Cohen, Huey-Wen Lin, and Victor Pereyra, *Excited state effective masses*, PoS **LAT2007** (2007), 096.
20. George T. Fleming, Saul D. Cohen, Huey-Wen Lin, and Victor Pereyra, *Excited-State Effective Masses in Lattice QCD*, Phys. Rev. **D80** (2009), 074506.

21. Francesco Fucito, Guido Martinelli, C. Omero, Giorgio Parisi, Roberto Petronzio, and Federico Rapuano, *Hadron spectroscopy in lattice QCD*, Nucl. Phys. **B210** (1982), 407.
22. Karl F. Gauss, *Theoria combinationis observationum erroribus minimis obnoxiae*, Comment. Soc. Reg. Sci. Gotten. Recent. **5** (1823), 33.
23. Gene H. Golub and Victor Pereyra, *The differentiation of pseudoinverses and nonlinear least squares problems whose variables separate*, SIAM J. Numer. Anal. **10** (1973), 413–432.
24. A. Gray et al., *The Upsilon spectrum and m_b from full lattice QCD*, Phys. Rev. **D72** (2005), 094507.
25. David J. Gross and Frank Wilczek, *Ultraviolet behavior of non-Abelian gauge theories*, Phys. Rev. Lett. **30** (1973), 1343–1346.
26. D. Guadagnoli, M. Papinutto, and S. Simula, *Extracting excited states from lattice QCD: The Roper resonance*, Phys. Lett. **B604** (2004), 74–81.
27. Herbert W. Hamber, Enzo Marinari, Giorgio Parisi, and Claudio Rebbi, *Spectroscopy in a lattice gauge theory*, Phys. Lett. **B108** (1982), 314.
28. Herbert W. Hamber and Giorgio Parisi, *Numerical estimates of hadronic masses in a pure SU(3) gauge theory*, Phys. Rev. Lett. **47** (1981), 1792.
29. Anna Hasenfratz, Zoltan Kunszt, Peter Hasenfratz, and Christian B. Lang, *Hopping parameter expansion for the meson spectrum in SU(3) lattice QCD*, Phys. Lett. **B110** (1982), 289.
30. S. Kirkpatrick, C. D. Gelatt, and M. P. Vecchi, *Optimization by Simulated Annealing*, Science **220** (1983), 671–680.
31. S. Y. Kung, K. S. Arun, and D. V. Bhaskar Rao, *State-space and singular value decomposition-based approximation methods for the harmonic retrieval problem.*, J. Opt. Soc. Am. **73** (1983), 1799–1811.
32. G. P. Lepage et al., *Constrained curve fitting*, Nucl. Phys. Proc. Suppl. **106** (2002), 12–20.
33. Adam C. Lichtl, *Model optimization in the presence of correlations*, `http://www.yale.edu/qcdna/talks4/lichtl_07.pdf`, 2007, Presented at the Fourth International Workshop on Numerical Analysis and Lattice QCD, Yale University, 1–3 May 2007.
34. Huey-Wen Lin and Saul D. Cohen, *Lattice QCD Beyond Ground States*, (2007).
35. Prasanta Chandra Mahalanobis, *On the generalized distance in statistics*, Proc. Nat. Inst. Sci. India **2** (1936), 49–55.
36. Enzo Marinari, Giorgio Parisi, and Claudio Rebbi, *Computer estimates of meson masses in SU(2) lattice gauge theory*, Phys. Rev. Lett. **47** (1981), 1795.
37. Chris Michael, *Fitting correlated data*, Phys. Rev. **D49** (1994), 2616–2619.
38. Chris Michael and Archie McKerrell, *Fitting correlated hadron mass spectrum data*, Phys. Rev. **D51** (1995), 3745–3750.
39. Leon Mirsky, *Symmetric gauge functions and unitarily invariant norms*, Quart. J. Math. Oxford Ser. **11** (1960), 50–59.
40. David C. Moore and George T. Fleming, *Multiparticle states and the hadron spectrum on the lattice*, Phys. Rev. **D74** (2006), 054504.
41. David C. Moore and George Tamminga Fleming, *Angular momentum on the lattice: The case of non-zero linear momentum*, Phys. Rev. **D73** (2006), 014504.
42. Y. Nakahara, M. Asakawa, and T. Hatsuda, *Hadronic spectral functions in lattice QCD*, Phys. Rev. **D60** (1999), 091503.
43. V. Pereyra, M. Koshy, and J. Meza, *Asynchronous global optimization for medium and large inversion problems*, SEG 65 Anual Meeting Extended Abstracts **65** (1995), 1091–1094.
44. H. David Politzer, *Reliable perturbative results for strong interactions?*, Phys. Rev. Lett. **30** (1973), 1346–1349.
45. William H. Press, Saul A. Teukolsky, William T. Vetterling, and Brian P. Flannery, *Numerical recipes: The art of scientific computing*, third ed., Cambridge University Press, Cambridge (UK) and New York, 2007.
46. Paolo Ruffini, *Teoria generale delle equazioni, in cui si dimostra impossibile la soluzione algebraica delle equazioni generali di grad superiore al quarto, di Paolo Ruffini*, Nella stamperia di S. Tommaso d'Aquino, Bologna, 1799.
47. Kiyoshi Sasaki, Shoichi Sasaki, and Tetsuo Hatsuda, *Spectral analysis of excited nucleons in lattice QCD with maximum entropy method*, Phys. Lett. **B623** (2005), 208–217.
48. Juliane Schäfer and Korbinian Strimmer, *A shrinkage approach to large-scale covariance matrix estimation and implications for functional genomics*, Statist. Appl. Genet. Mol. Biol. **4** (2005), 32.

49. H. S. Sharatchandra, H. J. Thun, and P. Weisz, *Susskind Fermions on a Euclidean Lattice*, Nucl. Phys. **B192** (1981), 205.
50. Charles Stein, *Inadmissibility of the usual estimator for the mean of a multivariate normal distribution*, Proc. Third Berkeley Symp. on Math. Statist. and Prob. **1** (1956), 197–206.
51. E. Stiliaris and C. N. Papanicolas, *Multipole Extraction: A novel, model independent method*, AIP Conf. Proc. **904** (2007), 257–268.
52. Sergey Syritsyn and John W. Negele, *Oscillatory terms in the domain wall transfer matrix*, PoS **LAT2007** (2007), 078.
53. Doug Toussaint, *Error analysis of simulation results: A sample problem*, From Actions to Answers (Singapore) (T. DeGrand and D. Toussaint, eds.), World Scientific, 1990, Proceedings of Theoretical Advanced Study Institute in Elementary Particle Physics, Boulder, USA, June 5-30, 1989, p. 121.
54. Doug Toussaint and Walter Freeman, *Sample size effects in multivariate fitting of correlated data*, (2008).
55. Cees van den Doel and Jan Smit, *Dynamical symmetry breaking in two flavor $SU(N)$ and $SO(N)$ lattice gauge theories*, Nucl. Phys. **B228** (1983), 122.
56. David Vandevoorde, *A fast exponential decomposition algorithm and its applications to structured matrices*, Ph.D. thesis, Rensselaer Polytechnic Institute, Troy, New York, USA, October 1996, `http://wwwlib.umi.com/dissertations/fullcit/9806112`.
57. Georg M. von Hippel, Randy Lewis, and Robert G. Petry, *Using evolutionary algorithms to extract field theory mass spectra*, PoS **LAT2007** (2007), 043.
58. Georg M. von Hippel, Randy Lewis, and Robert G. Petry, *Evolutionary Fitting Methods for the Extraction of Mass Spectra in Lattice Field Theory*, Comput. Phys. Commun. **178** (2008), 713–723.
59. Gilbert Walker, *On periodicity in series of related terms*, Proc. Roy. Soc. Lond. **A131** (1931), 518–532.
60. A. Walker-Loud et al., *Light hadron spectroscopy using domain wall valence quarks on an Asqtad sea*, (2008).
61. Don Weingarten, *Monte Carlo evaluation of hadron masses in lattice gauge theories with fermions*, Phys. Lett. **B109** (1982), 57–62.
62. Eric W. Weisstein, *Moore-Penrose matrix inverse*, `http://mathworld.wolfram.com/Moore-PenroseMatrixInverse.html`, 2004, From MathWorld – A Wolfram Web Resource.
63. Kenneth G. Wilson, *Confinement of quarks*, Phys. Rev. **D10** (1974), 2445–2459.
64. G. Udny Yule, *On a method of investigating periodicities in disturbed series, with special reference to Wolfer's sunspot numbers*, Phil. Trans. Roy. Soc. Lond. **A226** (1927), 267–298.

CHAPTER 5

Solving separable nonlinear least squares problems with multiple datasets

Linda Kaufman
Coach House, Room 213, Computer Science Dept.
William Patterson University
Wayne, NJ 07470
kaufmanl@wpunj.edu

ABSTRACT. In 1978 Golub and LeVeque considered an exponential fitting problem with multiple datasets where the nonlinear variables, e.g., the decay rates, had to hold for all the datasets simultaneously, but the linear variables, e.g., the pre-exponentials, could vary from one dataset to the next. They showed that with the variable projection technique, one could reduce the problem to only the nonlinear variables. Golub and LeVeque also showed that the main matrix of the algorithm was block diagonal with the same matrix down the diagonal. This allowed them to compute a solution while storing only the main matrix associated with a single dataset, so that the memory requirements of the problem are independent of the number of datasets. Since then, papers using this observation have appeared in the biophysics literature, in the systems identification literature, in the medical literature for studying disease of the retina, in the spectroscopy literature, and in the numerical analysis literature for determining the knots in a 2 dimensional spline problem. In 2007 the TIMP package was created in the statistical language R by Mullen and van Stokkum to handle spectroscopy problems which might have as many as 1000 datasets. The TIMP package, which handles several models, uses finite differences to approximate derivatives. In this paper we show that by using a tensor product of orthogonal matrices, the number of rows for the Jacobian for the multiple dataset problem can be significantly reduced.

Keywords: Separable nonlinear least squares; multiple data sets; variable projections

5.1. Introduction

In [**2**] Golub and LeVeque consider one of the most common problems in data fitting: that of exponential fitting under the least squares criterion. They consider models of the form

$$y \approx a_1 e^{\alpha_1 t} + a_2 e^{\alpha_2 t} + a_3 e^{\alpha_3 t}, \tag{5.1}$$

that arise while analyzing measurements of the spectroscopic properties of the substance bacteriorhodopsin. The data measured the amount of light absorbed by the substance at $m = 175$ different times during the course of a chemical reaction. Moreover, at these same times they had measurements for $s = 5$ different wavelengths and according to kinetic theory, the rate constants, the α 's in (5.1) should

Victor Pereyra & Godela Scherer (Eds)

be the same for measurements at each wavelength. Thus for this problem, there are 15 linear parameters, 3 nonlinear parameters, and $5 \times 175 = 875$ data points.

We discuss several algorithms in this setting of 3 exponentials for clarity, but of course, the algorithms apply to any number n of exponentials.

Let G be the $m \times 3$ matrix

$$G(\alpha) = \begin{pmatrix} e^{\alpha_1 t_1} & e^{\alpha_2 t_1} & e^{\alpha_3 t_1} \\ e^{\alpha_1 t_2} & e^{\alpha_2 t_2} & e^{\alpha_3 t_2} \\ \cdot & \cdot & \cdot \\ e^{\alpha_1 t_m} & e^{\alpha_2 t_m} & e^{\alpha_3 t_m} \end{pmatrix}, \tag{5.2}$$

and let the a's in (5.1) for the kth dataset be represented as $\mathbf{a_k}= [a_{1k}, a_{2k}, a_{3k}]^T$ and $\mathbf{a}=(\mathbf{a_1}, \mathbf{a_2}, ..., \mathbf{a_s})^{\mathbf{T}}$. Similarly, let the $\alpha's$ in (5.1) for the kth dataset be represented as $\alpha_{\mathbf{k}}=[\alpha_{1k}, \alpha_{2k}, \alpha_{3k}]^T$ and $\alpha=(\alpha_{\mathbf{1}}, \alpha_{\mathbf{2}}, ..., \alpha_{\mathbf{s}})^T$ and let $\mathbf{y_k}$ represent the data in (5.1) for the kth dataset and $\mathbf{y}=(\mathbf{y_1}, \mathbf{y_2}, ..., \mathbf{y_s})^{\mathbf{T}}$.

One can write the least squares problem either as minimizing

$$||\Phi(\alpha)\mathbf{a} - \mathbf{y}||_{\mathbf{2}} \tag{5.3}$$

where

$$\Phi(\alpha) = \begin{pmatrix} G(\alpha) & 0 & 0 & 0 & 0 \\ 0 & G(\alpha) & 0 & 0 & 0 \\ 0 & 0 & G(\alpha) & 0 & 0 \\ 0 & 0 & 0 & G(\alpha) & 0 \\ 0 & 0 & 0 & 0 & G(\alpha) \end{pmatrix}, \tag{5.4}$$

or one can also write the least squares problem as minimizing

$$||G(\alpha)A - Y||_2, \tag{5.5}$$

where the s columns of the A matrix are the columns $(\mathbf{a_1}, \mathbf{a_2}, \mathbf{a_3}, \mathbf{a_4}, ..., \mathbf{a_s})$ and the s columns of the Y matrix are the columns $(\mathbf{y_1}, \mathbf{y_2}, \mathbf{y_3}, \mathbf{y_4}, ..., \mathbf{y_s})$. The formulation given in (5.5), like others considered in this book, is separable and amenable to the variable projection technique of Golub and Pereyra [**3**] and the simplification given by Kaufman [**5**].

One can see that the formulation in (5.5)

(1) Takes advantage of the zero structure in (5.4).
(2) Takes advantage of the fact that all the diagonal blocks are the same.
(3) Permits one to use matrix manipulations as in level 2 BLAS [**1**].
(4) Limits the scientist to handling complete datasets.

In the separable framework, the optimal A for any α is given by

$$A = G^+(\alpha)(Y) \tag{5.6}$$

where G^+ is the Moore-Penrose generalized inverse of G (see [**9**]). Golub and Pereyra [**3**] and Golub and LeVeque [**2**] show that the value of α that minimizes

$$||(G(\alpha)G^+(\alpha) - I)Y|| \tag{5.7}$$

also minimizes (5.5).

A numerically stable way to compute $(G(\alpha)G^+(\alpha) - I)Y$ involves the QR decomposition of $G(\alpha)$ given by

$$Q(\alpha)G(\alpha)Z(\alpha) = \begin{pmatrix} R(\alpha) & R_1(\alpha) \\ 0 & 0 \end{pmatrix}, \tag{5.8}$$

where Q is an orthogonal matrix, perhaps created as a sequence of Householder matrices (see [4]), Z is a permutation matrix that interchanges the columns of G if needed, and R is a $u \times u$ upper triangular matrix where u is the rank of G.

Of the stable techniques that one may use to solve a linear least squares problem, the QR decomposition approach tends to be the least expensive. The normal equation approach, which involves forming G^TG, can lead to a singular matrix when the underlying G matrix is not singular. The condition number of G^TG, which determines the sensitivity of the solution, is the square of the condition number of G, so that the normal equations approach is considered unstable. The SVD approach is reliable but may cost between 4 and 10 times the cost of the QR approach.(See [9] or [4] for a more complete comparison.)

With the QR decomposition of $G(\alpha)$, the matrix GG^+Y is given by

$$GG^+Y = Q^T\begin{pmatrix} R(\alpha) & R_1(\alpha) \\ 0 & 0 \end{pmatrix} Z^T Z \begin{pmatrix} R(\alpha) & R_1(\alpha) \\ 0 & 0 \end{pmatrix}^+ QY = Q^T\begin{pmatrix} I_u & 0 \\ 0 & 0 \end{pmatrix} QY \tag{5.9}$$

and that of $(G(\alpha)G^+(\alpha) - I)Y$ is given by

$$(G(\alpha)G^+(\alpha) - I)Y = Q^T\begin{pmatrix} 0 & 0 \\ 0 & I_{m-u} \end{pmatrix} QY. \tag{5.10}$$

If one partitions $Q(\alpha)$ as

$$Q(\alpha) = \begin{pmatrix} Q_1(\alpha) \\ Q_2(\alpha) \end{pmatrix}, \tag{5.11}$$

where $Q_2(\alpha)$ has $m - u$ rows, then finding α means minimizing $||Q_2(\alpha)Y||_2$.

Note that there is no reason to save either Z explicitly as an $n \times n$ matrix or Q explicitly as an $m \times m$ matrix. For Z all one needs is an integer array PIVOT of length n. The meaning of PIVOT(i)=j is that at the ith step, column i and column j have been interchanged. The Q matrix might be a sequence of Householder matrices $Q = P_u P_{u-1} ... P_2 P_1$ where P_i has the form $I - \beta_i v_i v_i^T$ with the first $i - 1$ elements of v_i are zero. The matrix R and the v vectors can overwrite the first u columns of G. One just needs an additional vector of length u to store the β's. To apply Q to a vector y, one could use the following algorithm that takes approximately $2um$ multiplications.

For i = 1 to u
  Set ξ to $v_i^T y \times \beta_i$
  Replace y with $y - \xi v_i$

If one were applying the matrix Q on the left to a matrix Y, one might use BLAS and proceed as follows:

For i = 1 to u
  Set x^T to $v_i^T Y$ using the BLAS function DGEMV
  Scale x by the scalar β using the BLAS function DSCAL
  Replace Y with $Y - v_i x^T$ using the BLAS function DGER

The formulation in (5.4) begs the question whether each dataset must be exactly the same. What happens if in the biology experiment with the model in (5.1) data for different wavelengths are not taken at the same times, perhaps some data is missing and some are added? For example, what happens if

$$\Phi(\alpha) = \begin{pmatrix} G(\alpha) & 0 & 0 & 0 & 0 \\ 0 & G(\alpha) & 0 & 0 & 0 \\ 0 & 0 & G_B(\alpha) & 0 & 0 \\ 0 & 0 & 0 & G_B(\alpha) & 0 \\ 0 & 0 & 0 & 0 & G_B(\alpha) \end{pmatrix}, \tag{5.12}$$

where G_B might be missing the data at t_1 and t_2? This problem can be reduced to minimizing

$$||G(\alpha)A_1 - Y_1||_2 + ||G_B(\alpha)A_B - Y_B||_2, \tag{5.13}$$

where A_1 and Y_1 correspond to the first 2 wavelengths and A_B and Y_B correspond to the last 3 wavelengths.

If one first computes the orthogonal decomposition for the smaller matrix $G_B(\alpha)$ given by

$$Q(\alpha)_B G_B(\alpha) Z_B(\alpha) = \begin{pmatrix} R_B(\alpha) & R_{B,1}(\alpha) \\ 0 & 0 \end{pmatrix}, \tag{5.14}$$

multiplies the last $m-2$ rows of $G(\alpha)$ on the left and applies $Z_B(\alpha)$ on the right, a matrix W results that has the shape

$$W = \begin{pmatrix} x & x & x \\ x & x & x \\ x & x & x \\ x & x & x \\ 0 & x & x \\ 0 & 0 & x \end{pmatrix}, \tag{5.15}$$

where x represents a scalar not known to be zero. By multiplying W by a sequence of Householder transformations in planes (1,2,3), (2,3,4), and (3,4,5), we can reduce W to triangular form. Thus from the orthogonal decomposition of $G_B(\alpha)$ we can recover the orthogonal decomposition of $G(\alpha)$ without much work.

5.2. Applications

Although the problem in **[2]** was presented in the 1970's, there is still interest in this type of problem. In January, 2007, Mullen and van Stokkum **[10]** described a package TIMP written in the open source language R **[14]** for modeling multi-way spectroscopic measurements. They not only look at models specified in the independent variable t representing time, pH, temperature, excitation wavelength or quencher concentration, in which spectra are resolved, but they also consider models specified in the spectral domain with independent parameter λ, which might represent wavelength, wave number, magnetic field strength, or location **[8]**. A model element in the spectral domain for a wave number λ could be a Gaussian with parameters μ, Δ, and a_l for the location, fullwidth at half maximum, and amplitude given by

$$a_l e^{-log(2)(2\frac{\lambda-\mu)}{\Delta})^2}. \tag{5.16}$$

The TIMP package also allows instrument response models (IRF) that might be applicable in multiway spectroscopy experiments when a short laser pulse excites the systems and the resulting spectra is measured in time. The IRF model could involve the convolution of the shape of the exciting pulse and the detector response, whose i^{th} term might look like

$$e^{-k_i t}/2e^{k_i(\mu+k_i\Delta^2/2)}(1+erf(\frac{t-(\mu+k_i\Delta^2)}{2^{1/2}\Delta})). \tag{5.17}$$

In TIMP, each dataset does not have to have the same number of measurements, and hence the basic matrix could resemble (5.12). Mullen and van Stokkum claim that their system can handle 1000 datasets, each with 1000 data points. Thus, with a model like (5.17,) with say 6 nonlinear parameters overall and 4 linear parameters for each dataset, one is reducing the problem using TIMP from say 4006 parameters to 6 parameters, a rather large reduction. Mullen, van Stokkum and Vengris discuss their experience in modeling time resolved spectra in [**12**].

Although TIMP was created for spectroscopic data, it has also been used in microscopy (see [**8**]), more specifically, in Fluorescent Lifetime Imaging Microscopy (FLIM). FLIM is used to detect interactions between various fluourescently labeled molecules such as protein, lipids, DNA and RNA. Data representing the number of photons detected is accumulated at many spatial locations and time points. Sometimes proteins are tagged with versions of the green fluourescent protein (see [**19**]), whose discovery, expression and development earned the Nobel prize in Chemistry in 2008 for Roger Tsien, Martin Chalfie, and Osamu Shimomura.

Before TIMP was created, van Stokkum had been solving problems in various fields using "multiway data", including biophysics [**18**], medicine, where he was studying chorodial circulation in the retina to determine its effect on diseases of the eye like glaucoma [**17**], and molecular photophysics, where he was studying a mixture of components whose concentrations change with time [**16**]. The topics are all reviewed in [**11**].

Nagle, Zimyani, and Lanyi [**13**] have been using the variable projection method with fitting three or four exponentials at multiple wavelengths and all times as in the early Golub and LeVeque paper [**2**]. They were trying to understand the mechanism of proton pumping in the membrane of Halobacterium salinarium and trying to find the number of chemical intermediates in the photocycle.

System identification is another field where the multiple dataset variable projection algorithm has been applied. system identification involves constructing mathematical models of dynamic systems based on experimental data. In [**20**] Vandersteen, Rolain and Schoukens of the Department of Electrical Engineering of Vrije University, Brussels, Belgium, identify the nonlinear distortion and the time base distortion of a a data acquisition channel using sine wave measurements using the variable projection technique. In [**7**] Kaufman, Sylvester and Wright consider frequency domain problems and estimate the modal parameters from multiple-driver, multiple-receiver transfer data. Their typical problem had $m = 500$ and $s = 200$, so the vector $\mathbf{y}$ in (5.3) had 100,000 rows.

Back in the field of scientific computing, Schütze and Schwetlick [**15**] have used the multiple dataset approach for determining the placement of knots in a tensor product spline approximation in 2 dimensions. It is based on ideas developed by them for one dimension and their algorithm takes advantage of the specially structured problem similar to the technique used in the next section.

5.3. The Jacobian

TIMP [10] computes derivatives numerically although in the 1970's Golub and Pereyra [3] and Kaufman [5] have given analytic formulae for the Jacobian if one can analtically differentiate the model with respect to the nonlinear parameters.

The formulation in (5.4) helps us when dealing with nonlinear least squares solvers. Let us assume we had only one dataset, so that we are minimizing $||\mathbf{r}||_2 = ||\mathbf{Q_2}(\alpha)\mathbf{y_1}||_2$. Most nonlinear equation solvers require Jacobians J where the kth column of J is given by the vector $\frac{\partial r}{\partial \alpha_k}$. In [5] it is shown that

$$\frac{\partial Q_2(\alpha)\mathbf{y_1}}{\partial \alpha_k} = \left(-Q_2(\alpha)\frac{\partial G}{\partial \alpha_k} Z_1 R^{-1} Q_1 + H\right)\mathbf{y_1}, \tag{5.18}$$

where Z_1 contains the first u columns of Z and H is dependent on the exact representation chosen for Q_2. In our original exponential problem $\frac{\partial G}{\partial \alpha_1}$ is a matrix that is zero except for its first column which is given by

$$\begin{pmatrix} t_1 e^{\alpha_1 t_1} \\ t_2 e^{\alpha_1 t_2} \\ . \\ . \\ t_m e^{\alpha_1 t_m} \end{pmatrix}. \tag{5.19}$$

Similarly $\frac{\partial G}{\partial \alpha_2}$ is a matrix which is zero except for its second column which looks like (5.19) with α_2 substituted for α_1.

For multiple datasets we want α which minimizes the 2 norm of

$$\begin{pmatrix} Q_2(\alpha)\mathbf{y_1} \\ Q_2(\alpha)\mathbf{y_2} \\ . \\ . \\ Q_2(\alpha)\mathbf{y_s} \end{pmatrix} \tag{5.20}$$

and neglecting H,

$$\frac{\partial Q_2(\alpha)}{\partial \alpha_k}\mathbf{y} = \begin{pmatrix} -Q_2(\alpha)\frac{\partial G}{\partial \alpha_k} Z_1 R^{-1} Q_1 \mathbf{y_1} \\ -Q_2(\alpha)\frac{\partial G}{\partial \alpha_k} Z_1 R^{-1} Q_1 \mathbf{y_2} \\ . \\ . \\ -Q_2(\alpha)\frac{\partial G}{\partial \alpha_k} Z_1 R^{-1} Q_1 \mathbf{y_s} \end{pmatrix}. \tag{5.21}$$

Setting $\hat{\mathbf{a}}_i = Z_1 R^{-1} Q_1 \mathbf{y_i}$ (the use of $\hat{\mathbf{a}}$ is not accidental, since these are approximations of the linear parameters), the kth column of the Jacobian can be then expressed as

$$\frac{\partial Q_2(\alpha)}{\partial \alpha_k}\mathbf{y} = \begin{pmatrix} -Q_2(\alpha)\frac{\partial G}{\partial \alpha_k}\hat{\mathbf{a}}_1 \\ -Q_2(\alpha)\frac{\partial G}{\partial \alpha_k}\hat{\mathbf{a}}_2 \\ . \\ . \\ -Q_2(\alpha)\frac{\partial G}{\partial \alpha_k}\hat{\mathbf{a}}_s \end{pmatrix}. \tag{5.22}$$

For our biology example the Jacobian will have 875 rows and 3 columns.

Two questions present themselves:

(1) Should one multiply $Q_2\frac{\partial G(\alpha)}{\partial \alpha_k}$ first or should one multiply $\frac{\partial G}{\partial \alpha_k}\mathbf{y}$ first?

(2) Can something be done to take advantage of the repetitious structure of (5.22)?

A clue to the first question lies in the fact that applying the Q matrix to $\frac{\partial G}{\partial \alpha_k}$ will not upset its zero columns. If a column of $\frac{\partial G}{\partial \alpha_k}$ is originally zero, then the same column of $Q_2 \frac{\partial G}{\partial \alpha_k}$ will be identically zero. Let $D(\alpha)$ contain all the nonzero columns of $\frac{\partial G}{\partial \alpha_k}$ and let d represent the number of columns of $D(\alpha)$. If α has p components each appearing once in the model, then $d = p$. If, on the other hand, we have variables like μ and Δ in (5.17), that appear in every term of the model, and if we had say 3 terms in the model, then p would be six and d would be twelve.

Applying D to $\hat{\mathbf{a}}_{\mathbf{k}}$ first for each dataset would require $d \times s \times m$ multiplications. Next applying Q_2 to $D\hat{\mathbf{a}}_{\mathbf{k}}$ requires $2m \times n^2 \times s$ multiplications for all datasets. On the other hand, if one applies the Householder transformations first to D, requiring $2m \times d \times n$ multiplications and then, for each dataset, applies $Q_2 D$ to $\hat{\mathbf{a}}_{\mathbf{k}}$, requiring $d \times s \times m$ multiplications, we see that the second approach is faster only if $d < n \times s$. For our sample problem in (5.1) $d = 3, n = 3$, and $s = 5$. Since $3 < 15$, one should first form $Q_2 D(\alpha)$ and then apply the result to each of the $\hat{\mathbf{a}}$'s in (5.22).

We thus arrive at the following algorithm for determining the residual vector and the Jacobian.

Algorithm Q_2

(1) Construct the G matrix
(2) Construct the nonzero columns of the D matrix as the derivatives of each column of G with respect to the nonlinear paramters as exemplified in (5.19)
(3) Construct the QR decomposition given in (5.8) using LAPACK's DGE-QRF
(4) Apply the Q matrix from (5.8) to Y using LAPACK's DORMQR.
(5) Apply the Q matrix from (5.8) to D using DORMQR and let W represent the last $m - u$ rows of the result.
(6) Determine $\hat{\mathbf{a}}_i$ for $i = 1, 2, \cdots, s$ by backsolving the first u elements of QY using R in (5.8) perhaps using LAPACK's DTRTRS.
(7) Concatenate the last $m - u$ rows of QY to make the residual vector in (5.20).
(8) For the kth column of the Jacobian form $-W_k \hat{\mathbf{a}}_i$ for $i = 1, 2, \cdots, s$ where W_k corresponds to the columns of D that represent the kth nonlinear variable and concatenate the results for each dataset as in (5.22).

A suggestion in **[6]** indicates how we can take advantage of the repetitious structure of (5.22). For our sample problem, where the Jacobian has 875 rows and 3 columns, it may not pay to take advantage of the algebraic structure of (5.22), but one can use such a problem as an instructional device. In **[5]** it is noted that if Q_2 is multiplied on the left by an orthogonal matrix, then the only term that would change would be the matrix H in (5.18), which is being ignored. Let Q_3 represent a sequence of Householder transformations such that

$$- Q_3 Q_2 D(\alpha) = \begin{pmatrix} R_3 \\ 0 \end{pmatrix}, \tag{5.23}$$

where R_3 is upper triangular. In general, R_3 will have at most d rows and its construction would require $O(m \times d \times (d+1))$ multiplications. Thus in the sample biology problem (5.1), R_3 would have 3 rows and 3 columns and the Jacobian for the 5 datasets would have 15 rows rather than 875. The cost of multiplying R_3 by the 5 $\hat{\mathbf{a}}$ vectors requires 30 multiplications rather than $15m$=2625 multiplications. Since the cost of forming R_3 is $12m$ multiplications, the saving is minimal here.

To elucidate the process for the biology problem. represent R_3 as

$$\begin{pmatrix} r_{11} & r_{12} & r_{13} \\ & r_{22} & r_{23} \\ & & r_{33} \end{pmatrix}. \tag{5.24}$$

The negative of the Jacobian will then have the form

$$\begin{pmatrix} r_{11}a_{11} & r_{12}a_{21} & r_{13}a_{31} \\ & r_{22}a_{21} & r_{23}a_{31} \\ & & r_{33}a_{31} \\ r_{11}a_{12} & r_{12}a_{22} & r_{13}a_{32} \\ & r_{22}a_{22} & r_{23}a_{32} \\ & & r_{33}a_{32} \\ r_{11}a_{13} & r_{12}a_{23} & r_{13}a_{33} \\ & r_{22}a_{23} & r_{23}a_{33} \\ & & r_{33}a_{33} \\ r_{11}a_{14} & r_{12}a_{24} & r_{13}a_{34} \\ & r_{22}a_{24} & r_{23}a_{34} \\ & & r_{33}a_{34} \\ r_{11}a_{15} & r_{12}a_{25} & r_{13}a_{35} \\ & r_{22}a_{25} & r_{23}a_{35} \\ & & r_{33}a_{35} \end{pmatrix}. \tag{5.25}$$

One difficulty with using Q_3 to help form the Jacobian is that the Jacobian must correspond to the residual vector given in (5.20). Thus if we are multiplying the Jacobian by $I \otimes Q_3$, we must multiply (5.20) by $I \otimes Q_3$. Applying Q_3 to each of the s subvectors in (5.20) requires in total about msd multiplications, which if $d > n$ is more than would be required to process the residual vector during a least squares computation with the whole Jacobian. If $s >> d$, processing the residual vector can dwarf the computation of forming the Jacobian and say using the Jacobian in a Gauss-Newton setting. Thus although using Q_3 might lead to a smaller Jacobian of $d \times s$ rows and decreases the cost of forming the Jacobian in (5.22) from $O(msd)$ to $O((m+s)d^2)$, because of the cost of applying the transformations to (5.20), the decrease in the operation count might not be as large as anticipated as our examples in the next section indicate.

Using (5.23) we come to the following algorithm for forming the Jacobian and the residual vector.

Algorithm Q_3

- (1)-(6) As in Algorithm Q_2.
- (7) Construct Q_3 and R_3 in the QR decomposition Q_2D in (5.23) using LAPACK's DGEQRF
- (8) Apply Q_3 to the last $m-u$ rows of QY to make the matrix F.
- (9) Concatenate the last d rows of F to make the residual vector.

- (10) For the kth column of the Jacobian form $R_{3,k}\hat{\mathbf{a}}_i$ for $i = 1, 2, \cdots, p$ where $R_{3,k}$ corresponds to the columns of D that represent the kth nonlinear variable and concatenate the results for each dataset as in (5.25).

If d is much larger than n, or if one does not have many data points per dataset, say $m < 3d$, using Q_3 to form the Jacobian would also not be beneficial. In this case or in any case where there are many datasets as suggested by [**12**], there is still something one can do to take advantage of the structure of (5.22). Denote the vector $\mathbf{v_{i,k}}$ as the ith row of $-Q_2(\alpha)\frac{\partial G}{\partial \alpha_k}$, so that the first element of the kth column of the Jacobian in (5.22) is $\mathbf{v_{1,k}^T}\hat{\mathbf{a}}_1 = \hat{\mathbf{a}}_1^T\mathbf{v_{1,k}}$. If one rearranges the rows of the Jacobian and the residual vector in (5.20), so that rows involving $\mathbf{v_{1,k}}$ are together followed by a block involving the rows of $\mathbf{v_{2,k}}$, we get a Jacobian of the form

$$\frac{\partial Q_2(\alpha)}{\partial \alpha_k}\mathbf{y} = \begin{pmatrix} \hat{A}\mathbf{v_{1,k}} \\ \hat{A}\mathbf{v_{2,k}} \\ \cdot \\ \cdot \\ \hat{A}\mathbf{v_{m-1,k}} \end{pmatrix}, \tag{5.26}$$

where $\hat{A}$ has s rows and n columns containing the row vectors $\hat{\mathbf{a}}_1^T$ through $\hat{\mathbf{a}}_s^T$.

The formulation in (5.26) is reminiscent of the formulation in (5.22) with the roles of Q_2D and $\hat{A}$ reversed. Hence let Q_4 represent a sequence of Householder transformations such that

$$-Q_4\hat{A} = \begin{pmatrix} R_4 \\ 0 \end{pmatrix}, \tag{5.27}$$

where R_4 is upper triangular. In general R_4 will have at most n rows and its construction would require $O(s \times n \times (n+1))$ multiplications.

This technique would not have benefitted the sample biological problem where 5 datasets would essentially be reduced to 3, but if one had initially 300 datasets then it would give us some mileage. Again we would have to apply Q_4 to the residual vector (5.20) at a cost of about $2msn$ multiplications. An advantage of this approach over using Q_3 is that we do not have to worry about a variable occurring more than once in the model. Using Q_3 means that we solve a problem with $m - n$ rows followed by one using $s \times d$ rows, while using Q_4 means that we solve a problem with s rows followed by one with $(m - n) \times n$ rows. If all the nonlinear variables appear just once in the model and if $m > s$, one should use Q_3 and otherwise one should use Q_4.

In practice, the method one uses to determine Q_4 from the QR decomposition in (5.27) depends on how the data Y is stored. If Y is an $m \times s$ matrix where the observations for each dataset form a column of the Y matrix, and after steps (4) through (6) of Algorithm Q_2 the matrix $\hat{A}^T$ is placed back in the first n rows of Y, less space is required if one forms Q_4 using the RQ decomposition of $\hat{A}^T$ given by

$$-\hat{A}^TQ_4 = \begin{pmatrix} 0 & R \end{pmatrix}, \tag{5.28}$$

where R is upper triangular. The matrix R will have at most n columns.

Thus if $d > n$, where n is the number of terms in the model, and d is the number of times the nonlinear variables appear in the model, or if there are more datasets than the number of data points per dataset, one might use Algorithm Q_4 given by

Algorithm Q_4

- (1)-(6) As in Algorithm Q_2.
- (7) Construct Q_4 and R_4 in the RQ decomposition of $\hat{A}$ in (5.28) perhaps using LAPACK's DGERQF
- (8) Apply Q_4 on the right to the last $m - n$ rows of QY to make the matrix F.
- (9) Concatenate the last $s - n$ columns of F to make the residual vector.
- (10) Using the matrix W from step (5) of Algorithm Q_2, for the kth column of the Jacobian form $-W_k R_{4i}$ for $i = 1, 2, \cdots, n$ where W_k corresponds to the columns of D that represent the kth nonlinear variable and concatenate the results for each of the n datasets as in (5.22).

The obvious question is: are there any benefit in marrying the techniques? A suggestion in [7] indicates that we should be slightly careful. Let us assume we have applied Q_3 to our biology problem. Ignoring the zero and algebraic structure of (5.25) is rather inconsequential considering we have only 5 datasets and 3 unknown α's. However, had we had 100 datasets and 20 unknowns, then our Jacobian would have 2000 rows with 20×20 triangles stacked on each other. We might wish to investigate the situation further.

First, let us permute the rows in (5.25) so that the first grouping has the first row for each dataset, the second grouping has the second row for each dataset as we did in (5.26). The Jacobian J_3 will then have the form

$$\begin{pmatrix} r_{11}a_{11} & r_{12}a_{21} & r_{13}a_{31} \\ r_{11}a_{12} & r_{12}a_{22} & r_{13}a_{32} \\ r_{11}a_{13} & r_{12}a_{23} & r_{13}a_{33} \\ r_{11}a_{14} & r_{12}a_{24} & r_{13}a_{34} \\ r_{11}a_{15} & r_{12}a_{25} & r_{13}a_{35} \\ & r_{22}a_{21} & r_{23}a_{31} \\ & r_{22}a_{22} & r_{23}a_{32} \\ & r_{22}a_{23} & r_{23}a_{33} \\ & r_{22}a_{24} & r_{23}a_{34} \\ & r_{22}a_{25} & r_{23}a_{35} \\ & & r_{33}a_{31} \\ & & r_{33}a_{32} \\ & & r_{33}a_{33} \\ & & r_{33}a_{34} \\ & & r_{33}a_{35} \end{pmatrix}. \tag{5.29}$$

Let Q_5 be an orthogonal matrix such that

$$Q_5 \begin{pmatrix} a_{11} & a_{21} & a_{31} \\ a_{12} & a_{22} & a_{32} \\ a_{13} & a_{23} & a_{33} \\ a_{14} & a_{24} & a_{34} \\ a_{15} & a_{25} & a_{35} \end{pmatrix} = \begin{pmatrix} 0 \\ L \end{pmatrix}, \tag{5.30}$$

where L is a lower triangular matrix. The matrix L will be the transpose of the matrix R in (5.28) and Q_5 is Q_4^T. If L has the form

$$\begin{pmatrix} l_{11} & & \\ l_{21} & l_{22} & \\ l_{31} & l_{32} & l_{33} \end{pmatrix}, \tag{5.31}$$

then the nonzero rows of $Q_5 \otimes J_3$ have the form

$$\begin{pmatrix} r_{11}l_{11} & & \\ r_{11}l_{21} & r_{12}l_{22} & \\ r_{11}l_{31} & r_{12}l_{32} & r_{13}l_{33} \\ & r_{22}l_{22} & \\ & r_{22}l_{32} & r_{23}l_{33} \\ & & r_{33}l_{33} \end{pmatrix}. \tag{5.32}$$

Thus by multiplying the Jacobian by $Q_5 \otimes Q_3$, where Q_5 comes from (5.30) and Q_3 comes from (5.23), we have reduced the Jacobian for our sample problem from 875 rows to 6 rows. If Q_5 had created an upper triangular matrix, as we did in (5.27) rather than a lower triangular matrix, we would have had 9 rows.

Assume we had a model that had $p = 4$ nonlinear unknowns with each appearing just once. If each dataset had $m = 1000$ points and there were $s = 500$ datasets, without premultiplying by $Q_5 \otimes Q_3$, the Jacobian would have had 500,000 rows and 4 columns. By premultiplying by $Q_5 \otimes Q_3$, we have reduced the Jacobian to 10 rows and 4 columns.

The cost of producing R_3 is the cost of reducing an 1000×4 array to upper triangular form, and the cost of forming L in (5.30) is the cost of reducing a 500×4 array to lower triangular form. If the optimizer takes the Jacobian and then reduces it to triangular form, we have reduced the work by about 97 percent. In general if each of the p nonlinear variables appears just once in the model and if there are m points per dataset and s datasets, we have reduced the work of handling a Jacobian of $m \times s$ rows to handling three problems: one with m rows, one with s rows and one with $p \times (p+1)/2$ rows. The situation is summarized in the first column of Table 1.

Consider now the situation in 4 terms with 4 nonlinear parameters appearing just once and two additional nonlinear parameters appearing in each term. Thus d would be 12. In this situation R_3 would have 12 rows and L would have 4 rows. The matrix $Q_5 \otimes Q_3 J$ would have 30 rows. The cost of constructing $Q_5 \otimes Q_3 J$ is the same as the cost of reducing an $m \times 12$ matrix to upper triangular form, $m \times 12 \times 13$ multiplications plus the cost of reducing an $s \times 4$ matrix to lower triangular form, $s \times 4 \times 5$ multiplications. If $m \times s > 9m + s$, then it is worth forming $Q_5 \otimes Q_3 J$ from a theoretical operation count point of view. This situation is summarized in the last column of Table 1. Moreover, if $m \times s$ is so large that J itself cannot fit in core or one has to be very careful manipulating J to avoid cache misses, then dealing with the smaller matrices and taking advantage of the tensor product nature of the Jacobian is certainly worthwhile.

Table 1: Characteristics of the Jacobian for 500 datasets with 1000 points each, and 4 terms in the model		
	4 nonlinear variables each appearing once	6 nonlinear variables 4 appearing once and 2 in each term
Number of columns in J	4	6
Number of rows in J	500,000	500,000
Number of rows in $Q_5 \otimes Q_3 J$	10	30
Size of matrices reduced to triangular form to produce $Q_5 \otimes Q_3 J$	1000×4 and 500×4	1000×12 and 500×4

Again depending on how Y is stored, one may either want to form Q_4 via an RQ decomposition, say with LAPACK's DGERQF, with the approximate linear parameters stored as an $n \times s$ matrix $\hat{A}$ or via QL say with LAPACK's DGEQLF, with the approximate linear parameters stored as an $s \times n$ matrix. It does not matter whether one finds Q_4 first or Q_3 first. However, which one is applied first to the Y matrix is problem dependent. Applying Q_4 first requires $2(n(m-n)s+n(m-n)d)$ multiplications, while applying Q_3 first requires $2(d(m-n)s+nsd) = 2dms$ multiplications. We thus have the following algorithm

Algorithm Q_5

- (1)-(6) As in Algorithm Q_2.
- (7) Construct Q_4 and R_4 in the RQ decomposition of $\hat{A}$ in (5.28) using LAPACK's DGERQF
- (8) Construct Q_3 and R_3 in the QR decomposition $Q_2 D$ in (5.23) using LAPACK's DGEQRF
- (9)If $n(m-n)(s+d) < dms$ then
  - Apply Q_4 on the right to the last $m-n$ rows of QY to make the matrix F
  - Apply Q_3 to the last $m-u$ rows of F to make the matrix $\hat{F}$

  else
  - Apply Q_3 to the last $m-u$ rows of QD to make the matrix F
  - Apply Q_4 on the right to the last $m-n$ rows of F to make the matrix $\hat{F}$
- Return the residual vector
- Construct the Jacobian which has at most $d \times n$ rows and n columns from U_3 from step (8) and L from step (7)

The ultimate question is whether marrying the two ideas from Algorithm Q_3 and Algorithm Q_4 is worthwhile. Usually, the operation count is lowered by Algorithm Q_5, but our operation counts in Table 2 suggest that only when p is sufficiently large that one will notice the decrease in practice. Indeed, in our first two examples in the next section, where we have $p = 4$ and $p = 6$, the difference in computation times between Algorithm Q_4 and Algorithm Q_5 is insignificant. The third column of Table 2 indicates that if $s = p^2$ and $m = p^2$ we should see a noticeable decrease in computation time.

Table 2: Higher order terms in operation count; $m=$ # observationsdataset, $s=$ number of datasets, $p=$ number of nonlinear variables, $d=$ # times nonlinear appear and $n =$ # terms in the model

Algorithm	op. count	op.count when $s = m = n^2, d = n = p$
Algorithm Q_2	$msd + msp^2 + 2msp$	$n^6 + 3n^5$
Algorithm Q_3	$md^2 + sdp^2 + dsp + 2ds(m + p)$	$3n^5 + 4n^4$
Algorithm Q_4	$sn^2 + mnp + mnp^2 + 2mn(s + p)$	$3n^5 + 3n^4$
Algorithm Q_5	$sn^2 + md^2 + dnp^2 + 2n(ms + md + dp)$	$2n^5 + 5n^4$

5.4. Computational evidence

In this section we compare the computational times of Algorithms Q_2, Q_3, Q_4 and Q_5 on various problems for determing the residual vector and the Jacobian. Recall that in a typical separable nonlinear least squares problem this operation is in the inner loop of a Gauss-Newton or Levenberg-Marquardt procedure, so that it might be done a number of times. We include the time of a final QR decomposition of the resulting Jacobian and its application to the residual vector, as if we were doing a Gauss-Newton step with the given Jacobian and residual vector. The primary reason for the inclusion of the final QR decomposition is because Algorithm Q_2 delivers a much larger Jacobian than the other algorithms but costs the least and we want to determine the total cost.

Our computations were done on an Sun T5220 UltraSparc-T2 1.6 GH 8 core in the Computer Science Department at William Paterson University. The QR decompositions were done using LAPACK subroutines in FORTRAN along with ATLAS BLAS.

We first considered a model of the form

$$y \approx a_1 e^{\alpha_1 t} + a_2 e^{\alpha_2 t} + a_3 e^{\alpha_3 t} + a_4 e^{\alpha_4 t}, \tag{5.33}$$

so that $p = n = d = 4$.

In Table 3 below we compare the algorithms for various values of m, the number of data points, and s, number of datasets. For algorithms Q_3,Q_4, and Q_5, the computation of the Jacobian is linear in m and s and it really does not matter which of these algorithms is chosen: they are all far superior for large m and s to the standard Algorithm Q_2. What is also intriguing is that the times for calculating the Jacobian and obtaining its QR decomposition through algorithms Q_3,Q_4, and Q_5 is about the same time required to compute the residual vector. Thus for this problem, the old story that calculating the Jacobian is too expensive is not true if one uses the separable form of the Jacobian.

Table 3: Time (sec.) for evaluation of the residual vector, Jacobian for (5.33)				
Algorithm	$m = 1000$ $s = 200$	$m = 1000$ $s = 400$	$m = 400$ $s = 1000$	$m = 200$ $s = 1000$
residual vector	.041	.074	.069	.036
Jacobian from Algorithm Q_2	.286	.678	.665	.272
Jacobian from Algorithm Q_3	.033	.064	.069	.032
Jacobian from Algorithm Q_4	.037	.068	.062	.031
Jacobian from Algorithm Q_5	.032	.063	.062	.036

In Table 4 we consider the model

$$y \approx a_1 e^{(\alpha_1 t - \alpha_5)^2/\alpha_6} + a_2 e^{(\alpha_2 t - \alpha_5)^2/\alpha_6} + a_3 e^{(\alpha_3 t - \alpha_5)^2/\alpha_6} + a_4 e^{(\alpha_4 t - \alpha_5)^2/\alpha_6}, \quad (5.34)$$

so that $p = 6$, $n = 4$, and $d = 12$ for various values of m and s. Again we included the times for doing a final QR decomposition on the Jacobian and applying the orthogonal transformation to the residual vector. The times for the standard algorithm Q_2 and Algorithm Q_3 suggests that they should be discarded for large values of m and s in favor of algorithms 4 and 5. The times for algorithms Q_3,Q_4, and Q_5 are linear in the variables s and m. The difference between algorithm Q_3 and algorithm Q_4 in this case is caused by the fact that d is $3n$, so that if $m = s$ the contribution of the decomposition in (5.23) to the total computation time of Algorithm Q_3 is nine times that of the contribution of the decomposition in (5.27) to the total computation time of Algorithm Q_4. Moreover the operation count for applying the transformations from the decompositions to the residual vector is three times the time in Algorithm Q_3 as it is in Algorithm Q_4. For algorithm Q_5, the transformation from (5.27) were applied first, so that the transformations from (5.27) would be applied to n rather than s vectors.

Table 4: Time (sec.) for evaluation of the residual vector, Jacobian for(5.34)				
Algorithm	$m = 1000$ $s = 200$	$m = 1000$ $s = 400$	$m = 400$ $s = 1000$	$m = 200$ $s = 1000$
residual vector	.056	.082	.069	.052
Jacobian from Algorithm Q_2	.560	1.30	1.27	.547
Jacobian from Algorithm Q_3	.102	.195	.205	.108
Jacobian from Algorithm Q_4	.041	.071	.063	.033
Jacobian from Algorithm Q_5	.039	.070	.064	.032

In order to obtain a problem where Algorithm Q_5 would be suitable, a toy problem was created with a model with 16 terms similar to (5.33). The times in Table 5 tend to corroborate the results in Table 2. The time for Algorithm Q_5 was about 2/3 that of Algorithm Q_3 and Algorithm Q_4

Table 5: Time(sec.) for evaluation of the residual vector, Jacobian (5.33) for a model with 16 terms and $m = s = 256$	
Algorithm	
residual vector	.047
Jacobian from Algorithm Q_2	.621
Jacobian from Algorithm Q_3	.073
Jacobian from Algorithm Q_4	.071
Jacobian from Algorithm Q_5	.048

Conclusion We have shown in a multiple dataset setting how to significantly reduce the number of rows in the Jacobian using its tensor structure. We have also shown that this results in a significant decrease in the computation time. It seems fitting that we have used a linear algebra technique involving separation of variables to reduce the cost in time and space for solving a separable nonlinear least squares problem with multiple datasets.

Acknowledgement I would like to thank Daniel Colaneri and Aubry Lu, undergraduates at William Paterson University, for their assistance.

Bibliography

1. J. J. Dongarra, J. Du Croz, S. Hammarling and R. J. Hanson, *An extended set of FORTRAN Basic Linear Algebra Subprograms*, ACM Trans. Math. Soft., **14**:1-17 (1988).
2. G.H. Golub and R. LeVeque, *Extensions and uses of the variable projection algorithm for solving nonlinear least squares problems*, Computer Science Report SU 326, Stanford University, Stanford, CA. (1978).
3. G.H. Golub and V. Pereyra, *The differentiation of pseudo-inverses and nonlinear least squares problems whose variables separate*, SIAM J. Numer. Anal. **10**:413-432 (1973).
4. G.H. Golub and C.F. Van Loan. *Matrix Computation* The Johns Hopkins University Press, Baltimore (1996).
5. L. Kaufman, *A variable projection algorithm for solving separable nonlinear least squares problems*, BIT **15**:49-57 (1973)
6. L. Kaufman and G. Sylvester, *Separable nonlinear least squares with multiple right hand sides*, SIAM J. Matrix Anal. A. **13** No. 1 68-89 (1992).
7. L. Kaufman, G. Sylvester and M. Wright, *Structured linear least squares problems in system identification and Separable Nonlinear Data Fitting* , SIAM J. Optimiz. **4**:847-871 (1994).
8. S. Laptenok, K.M. Mullen, J.W. Borst, I.H.M. van Stokkum, V.V. Apanasovich and A. Visser, *Flourescence lifetime imaging microscopy (FLIM) with TIMP*. J. Stat. Softw. **18** No.8 (2007).
9. C.L. Lawson and R.J. Hanson. *Solving Least Squares Problems*, Prentice Halls, Englewood Cliffs, NJ (1974).
10. K.M. Mullen and I.H.M. van Stokkum, *TIMP: An R package for modeling multi-way spectroscopic measurements*, J. Stat. Softw. **18**:1-46 (2007).
11. K.M. Mullen and I.H.M. van Stokkum, *The variable projection algorithm in time-resolved spectroscopy, microscopy and mass spectrometry applications*, Numer. Algorithms, **51** No.3, 319-340 (2009).
12. K.M. Mullen, M. Vengris and I.H.M. van Stokkum, *Algorithms for separable nonlinear least squares with application to modeling time-resolved spectra*, J. Glob, Optim., **38**:201-213 (2007).
13. J. F. Nagle, L. Zimanyi and J.K. Lanyi, *Testing BR photocycle kinetics*, Biophys. J. **68**:1490-1499 (1995).
14. R Development Core Team, *R: A language and environment for statistical computing*, R Foundation for Statistical Computing, Vienna, Austria (2009), http://www.R-project.org
15. T. Schütze and H. Schwetlick, *Bivariate free knot splines*, BIT Numerical Mathematics, **43** Number 1, 153-178 (2003).
16. I.H.M. van Stokkum, *Precision in global analysis of time resolved spectra*,Procedings of the IEEE Instrumentation and Measurement Technology Conference Brussels, Belgium, June 4-6, 1996.
17. I.H.M. van Stokkum, G. N. Lambrou and T.J.T.P. van den Berg, *Hemodynamic parameter estimation from ocular fluorescein angiograms*, Graefe's Arch Clin Exp **233** pp. 123-130 © Springer-Verlag (1995).
18. I.H.M. van Stokkum, D. S. Larsen and R. van Grondelle. *Global and target analysis of time-resolved spectra*, BBA-Bioenergetics, **1657**:82-104 (2004).
19. R.Y. Tsien, *The green fluorescent protein*. Ann. Rev. Biochem. **67**:509-544 (1998).
20. G. Vandersteen, Y. Rolain, J. Schoukens. *System identification for data acquisition characterization*, Instrumentation and Measurement Technology Conference, 1998. IMTC/98. Conference Proceedings. IEEE, **2**:1211-1216 (1998).

CHAPTER 6

Sum-of-exponentials models for time-resolved spectroscopy data

Katharine M. Mullen
Ceramics Division
National Institute of Standards and Technology (NIST)
100 Bureau Drive, M/S 8520
Gaithersburg, MD, 20899, USA
kmullen@nist.gov

Ivo H. M. van Stokkum
Department of Physics and Astronomy
Faculty of Sciences,
Vrije Universiteit Amsterdam
de Boelelaan 1081, 1081 HV Amsterdam,
The Netherlands; ivo@nat.vu.nl

ABSTRACT. A model consisting of a sum of exponential functions is very useful for the description of time-resolved spectroscopy data. Each exponential term in the sum can often be associated with a given state of the physical system underlying the measurement, such as a protein excited by laser light. Then the exponential decay rate associated with each state describes the time profile of the contribution of the state to the observed data. The linear coefficients of the sum represent the relative amplitudes of the contributions of each state. When time-resolved spectroscopy data represent more than one wavelength, a linear coefficient is associated with each exponential decay term at each wavelength. In this chapter sum-of-exponentials models for time-resolved spectroscopy applications are reviewed. The parameter estimation problem of fitting the decay rates and linear coefficients of the sum under the least squares criteria is also reviewed, with attention to implementation of algorithms for model fitting. Case studies in fitting models to picosecond time-scale spectroscopic data illustrate the reviewed topics.

Keywords: Sum of exponentials; time-resolved spectroscopy

6.1. Introduction

Many phenomena in nature can be described in terms of a first-order differential equation

$$\frac{df(t)}{dt} = -\lambda f(t), \qquad (6.1)$$

Victor Pereyra & Godela Scherer (Eds)

where f is a function descriptive of the phenomena, t is time and λ is a constant. Equation (6.1) has solution

$$f(t) = a\exp(-\lambda t) + b, \tag{6.2}$$

where a and b are constants, which is the basic reason that exponential models have such ubiquitous applications in physics and chemistry, as Istratov and Vyvenko **[14]** review.

Here we focus on the application of exponential models to time-resolved spectroscopy data. Time-resolved spectroscopy data monitors a spectroscopic property (such as absorption or emission of light) in time, and may be collected in a ragged matrix Ψ **[4]**, where each column represents a wavelength (or location or other variable of interest) j at which the spectroscopic property is measured, and each row represents a time i. Such data often consists of the linear superposition of the contributions of a number of states, each of which can be described in terms of an exponential decay model in time. Here the contribution of each state is referred to as a *component*. Then the data at time i associated with a given value j can be described in terms of the sum-of-exponentials model

$$\psi_{ij} = \sum_{l=1}^{n_{\text{comp}}} a_{j,l}\exp(-k_l t_i), \tag{6.3}$$

where n_{comp} is the number of components, $a_{j,l}$ is the linear coefficient associated with each component l at each value j, and k_l is an exponential decay rate. In matrix notation,

$$\psi_j = C(k)a_j, \tag{6.4}$$

where C is a matrix, the columns of which represent the time profiles of the components, so that at time t_i, $C[i,l] = \exp(-k_l t_i)$, and a_j is a column vector representing the n_{comp} linear coefficients.

In many time-resolved spectroscopy experiments, the decay rates k_l underlying the data for all values j are the same, whereas the linear coefficients $a_{j,l}$ vary. To fix ideas, consider the case where j represents a wavelength at which a time profile was measured and the data can be collected in an $m \times n$ matrix Ψ, where m is the number of time points comprising each time profile, and n is the number of wavelengths measured. Then in matrix notation,

$$\Psi = CE^T, \tag{6.5}$$

where E is a matrix, with $E[j,l] = a_{j,l}$ representing the linear coefficient associated with component l at wavelength j. The columns of E are then often interpreted as the optical spectra associated with each of the states underlying the data.

In order to obtain insight regarding the states underlying the measurements, it is often of interest to find the most likely values of the decay rates k_l and linear coefficients $a_{j,l}$ under the assumption that the stochastic element in the data (i.e., the noise) is an independent and identically distributed (i.i.d.) Gaussian random variable that contributes additively to each data point. This requires solution of the separable nonlinear least squares problem

$$\min_{k\in\mathbb{R}^{n_{\text{comp}}},\, a_j\in\mathbb{R}^{n_{\text{comp}}}} \| \psi_j - C(k)a_j \|^2, \tag{6.6}$$

in the case the exponential decays are associated with vector data at one value j and

$$\min_{k \in \mathbb{R}^{n_{\mathrm{comp}}}, E \in \mathbb{R}^{n \times l}} \| \Psi - C(k)E^T \|^2 \tag{6.7}$$

in the case the exponential decays underly each column of matrix data Ψ. These problems are *separable* since given some value for the decay rates $k = k_1, \ldots, k_{n_{\mathrm{comp}}}$, estimates for the linear coefficients that are optimal under the least squares criterion can be obtained as the solution of the linear least squares problems

$$\min_{a_j \in \mathbb{R}^{n_{\mathrm{comp}}}} \| \psi_j - C(k)a_j \|^2 \tag{6.8}$$

and

$$\min_{E \in \mathbb{R}^{n \times l}} \| \Psi - C(k)E^T \|^2 \tag{6.9}$$

which is to say, by calculation of $a_j = C(k)^\dagger \psi_j$ and $E^T = C(k)^\dagger \Psi$, respectively, where $\dagger$ is the Moore-Penrose pseudoinverse. Golub and Pereyra **[12]** review the solution of separable nonlinear least squares problems, and Mullen and van Stokkum **[26]** review these problems as they arise in time-resolved spectroscopy, microscopy and mass spectrometry in particular.

The remainder of this chapter is organized as follows. Section 6.2 discusses the extension of the basic sum-of-exponentials model to arbitrary compartmental models for the kinetics. Parameter estimation is discussed in Section 6.3. Implementation of the variable projection algorithm for parameter estimation is outlined in Section 6.3. An approach for estimation of the standard errors associated with parameter estimates is given in Section 6.5. Section 6.6 discusses constraints on the parameters. Lastly, two case studies in fitting models based on a sum of exponential decays to time-resolved spectroscopy data are presented in Sections 6.7 and 6.8.

6.2. Linear compartmental models

The basic exponential decay model described in Section 6.1 is useful for the description of systems in which all possible states are formed simultaneously and then decay, as in the left panel of Figure 6.2.1. In other systems, a single state may be formed initially, the decay of which results in the formation of a second state, and so on, for all possible states of the system, as in the right panel of Figure 6.2.1. Alternatively, the states may be related in some other, arbitrarily complicated, way.

A linear compartmental model is used to describe the relationship between states like those shown graphically in Figure 6.2.1. The behavior of the compartmental model is given as a matrix $C(z)$ in which the concentration of a single compartment in time is represented by a column $C[, l]$, with

$$C(z) = \exp(K(z)t) \star j(t) \tag{6.10}$$

where z are free parameters, K is a transfer matrix that encodes the allowable transitions between components, and uses microscopic decay rate parameters $k \in z$ and scaling parameters $b \in z$ to describe the rate at which a state is formed and decays, and t is the vector of times that the rows of $C(z)$ represent. The vector $j(t)$ represents the proportion of the system in each compartment at the initial time point, multiplied by the instrument response function (IRF) $i(t)$. The operator $\star$ stands for convolution. In the case that the IRF is described with a Gaussian distribution or other simple function, the convolution may be performed analytically.

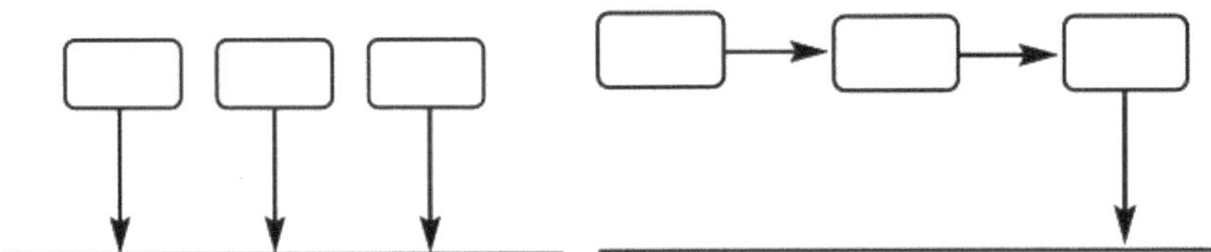

FIGURE 6.2.1. Two possible compartmental models for a system represented by three components. In the left model, the initial excitation populates all three components, which decay in parallel. In the right model, the initial excitation populates the leftmost compartment, the decay of which populates the middle compartment, and so on, so that the compartments are said to be arranged sequentially.

Compartmental models are often used for describing the kinetics of time-resolved spectroscopy data [**3, 13, 28, 29, 30, 43**]. More details on their application can be found in the reviews of van Stokkum *et al.* [**42, 44**] and in several textbooks [**7, 34**]. The public-domain software package **TIMP** [**24**] allows specification of the transfer matrix K and the initial inputs $j(t)$ for fitting arbitrary compartmental models to data. Section 6.7 describes an application in fitting a compartmental model to ultra-fast time-resolved spectroscopy data.

6.3. Parameter estimation

Golub and Pereyra [**8, 9**] developed an algorithm for separable nonlinear least squares termed *variable projection*, which eliminates the conditionally linear parameters a analytically from the problem, and assumes, as we do throughout, that the objective function is twice differentiable. Variable projection is applied in a wide variety of applications, as Golub and Pereyra [**12**] review. Lukeman [**20**] traces the history of developments of algorithms for Problem (6.6), and describes the connection to solving systems of n_{comp} nonlinear equations written as $C(z)a + \psi = 0$. Golub and LeVeque [**11**] provide an extension of the algorithm to problems in which the same nonlinear functions are used to describe each column of matrix data Ψ but the conditionally linear parameters a vary per-column j, which results in Problem (6.7). Golub and LeVeque [**11**] and Kaufman [**5**] refer to Problem (6.7) as a separable nonlinear least squares problem with multiple right-hand sides. In the time-resolved spectroscopy and microscopy literature, Problem (6.7) is termed the problem of *global analysis*, referring to the assumption that the same nonlinear functions underlie each column of matrix data [**3**]. Mullen and van Stokkum [**26**] have reviewed applications of variable projection to global analysis problems.

6.3.1. Variable projection. First consider the case that the observations ψ are in vector form. Given fixed nonlinear parameters z (which may be simply the exponential decay rates k) and a model for the kinetics $C(z)$ of full rank, the problem

$$\min_{a \in \mathbb{R}^{n_{\text{comp}}}} \| \psi - C(z)a \|^2 \tag{6.11}$$

is solved analytically as $a = C(z)^+\psi$, where $C(z)^+$ is the Moore-Penrose pseudoinverse $C(z)^+ = (C(z)^T C(z))^{-1} C(z)^T$. Using $a = C(z)^+\psi$, the objective function to minimize with respect to z for Problem (6.11) is

$$\begin{aligned} f(z) &= \frac{1}{2} \| \psi - C(z)a \|^2 \\ &= \frac{1}{2} \| (I - C(z)C(z)^+)\psi \|^2 \\ &= \frac{1}{2} \| Q_2 Q_2^T \psi \|^2, \end{aligned} \tag{6.12}$$

where the QR decomposition of $C(z) = QR = [Q_1 \ Q_2]R$ is used for numerical stability, so that Q_1 is $m \times n_{\text{comp}}$, Q_2 is $m \times (m - n_{\text{comp}})$, Q is orthogonal, and $R = \begin{bmatrix} R_{11} \\ 0 \end{bmatrix}$, with R_{11} being $n_{\text{comp}} \times n_{\text{comp}}$ and upper triangular **[10]**. $f(z)$ is the variable projection functional, so named because $I - C(z)C(z)^+$ is the projector on the orthogonal complement of the column space of $C(z)$. Some computational efficiency may be gained by dropping the factor Q_2, and formulating $f(z)$ as $f(z) = \frac{1}{2} \| Q_2^T \psi \|^2$ **[5]**.

Standard algorithms for nonlinear least squares problems, namely Gauss-Newton and Levenberg-Marquardt, can be used to estimate $\hat{z}$ that minimize $f(z)$. However, these algorithms require the Jacobian matrix $J = \frac{\partial r(z)}{\partial z}$ of the residual vector $r(z) = Q_2 Q_2^T \psi$, (or, dropping the Q_2 factor, $r(z) = Q_2^T \psi$). Two classes of approaches to obtain J may be distinguished: methods that use a finite difference approximation, and methods that rely on an analytical expression. Many widely applied implementations of nonlinear least squares allow J to be determined by either approach, as in, e.g., the modification of Levenberg-Marquardt found in MINPACK **[22]** or the Gauss-Newton method employed by the R function `nls` **[32]**.

If a finite difference approach is used to build up an approximation of J, $r(z)$ is repeatedly evaluated for different parameter vectors $\check{z}$ obtained by perturbing z by an amount h. Using a forward difference approximation, the ith parameter in z is incremented by h, yielding $\check{z}$, and the ith column of J is determined as $J[,i] = \frac{r(\check{z}) - r(z)}{h}$, requiring $length(z)$ evaluations of $r(\check{z})$ to calculate an update of J. The associated computational expense is often more than offset by the advantage of not having to derive and compute an analytic expression for J. In the applications described in Sections 6.7 and 6.8, the method of determining $C(z)$ is partially numerical, and there is no closed-form expression available for even $C(z)$. In these applications a finite difference approximation must be used. Minimization of the variable projection functional $f(z)$ with Levenberg-Marquardt using a finite difference approximation of J was described by Lawton and Sylvestre **[19]**.

If an analytical expression for $\frac{\partial C(z)}{\partial z}$ is available, then the method suggested by Golub and Pereyra [**9**] may be used to determine J per-column i as

$$J[,i] = -\left[\left(C(z)C(z)^{+}\frac{\partial C(z)}{\partial z[i]}C(z)^{+}\right) + \left(C(z)C(z)^{+}\frac{\partial C(z)}{\partial z[i]}C(z)^{+}\right)^{T}\right]\psi, \quad (6.13)$$

where we follow the presentation in [**12**]. Kaufman [**15**] suggested that this expression for J could be well-approximated by only using the first term, i.e.,

$$J[,i] = -\left(C(z)C(z)^{+}\frac{\partial C(z)}{\partial z[i]}C(z)^{+}\right)\psi, \quad (6.14)$$

thereby introducing only a negligible loss in accuracy and significant savings in the number of computations required. The Kaufman approximation is discussed in detail elsewhere [**1, 5, 27**].

Once J or an approximation of J has been determined, the standard algorithms for nonlinear least squares calculate the gradient $\bigtriangledown$ of $f(z)$ as

$$\bigtriangledown f(z) = J^{T}r(z) \quad (6.15)$$

and also calculate an approximation for the Hessian $\bigtriangledown^2 f(z)$. $\bigtriangledown f(z)$ and $\bigtriangledown^2 f(z)$ allow determination of a direction and step size to move the current estimates $\hat{z}$ in z-space so that $f(\hat{z})$ is reduced. From the new parameter estimates, the process of determining J and making a new step in z-space is iterated until stopping criteria are met. The details of the standard algorithms are found in e.g., [**2, 34**].

Several results justify and motivate the minimization of $f(z)$ as opposed to the unreduced objective function with parameters $x = (z, a)$. Golub and Pereyra [**9**] give a proof that the stationary points of $f(z)$ are the same as for the unseparated problem when the rank of $C(z)$ is constant over z-space. Therefore given $\hat{z}$ that determines either a local or global optimum in $f(z)$, we determine $\hat{a} = C(\hat{z})^{+}\psi$, and arrive at estimates $\hat{x} = (\hat{a}, \hat{z})$ that define a local or global optimum in the objective function of the unseparated problem. Asymptotic convergence analysis under the Gauss-Newton algorithm by Ruhe and Wedin [**33**] shows that variable projection has superlinear convergence whereas methods that alternate between solving the linear and nonlinear problems separately are only linearly convergent. This is because, as Sjöberg and Viberg [**37**] show, the separated problem is better-conditioned than the unseparated problem. Obtaining a better-conditioned problem is indeed a primary motivation for minimizing the variable projection functional as opposed to the objective function for the unseparated problem. Krogh [**16**] provides simple examples in which optimization of an unseparated nonlinear least squares problem results in divergence whereas optimization of the separated problem results in convergence in a small number of iterations. Osborne [**31**] points to the extraordinary effectiveness of variable projection in least squares problems involving fitting the parameters of a linear combination of real or complex exponential functions, which are ubiquitous in applications and notoriously difficult. Golub and Pereyra [**12**] suggest that this success is due to the fact that the unseparated exponential fitting problem becomes increasingly ill-conditioned as (and if) the optimal parameters are converged upon, whereas the variable projection functional does not suffer from this problem.

6.4. Implementation

Problem (6.7) can be reformulated as an instance of Problem (6.6) by letting $vec(\Psi) = (I_n \otimes C(z))vec(E^T)$, where $\otimes$ is used to denote the Kronecker product. Then variable projection as presented in Section 6.3 can be applied. However, as Golub and LeVeque **[11]** realized, this does not take advantage of the special structure of Problem (6.7), and requires storing and operating on the matrix $(I_n \otimes C(z))$, which is large for large n. Golub and LeVeque **[11]** thus suggested forming the residual vector associated with Problem (6.7) as

$$r(z) = \begin{bmatrix} Q_2^T \Psi[,1] \\ Q_2^T \Psi[,2] \\ \vdots \\ Q_2^T \Psi[,n] \end{bmatrix}, \qquad (6.16)$$

from which $f(z)$ and J can be determined without ever storing or operating on $(I_n \otimes C(z))$.

Mullen and van Stokkum **[24, 26]** expand on the idea of determining $r(z)$ in a partitioned manner for the description of (ragged) matrix data per-column j. They consider in particular the description of multiple datasets using separable nonlinear models, with some nonlinear or linear parameters shared between models for each dataset.

6.5. Standard error estimation

For the purpose of performing inference on the parameter estimates, an approximation of the covariance matrix based on linearization of the model may be derived. The degree to which this approximation provides insight into the true uncertainties for the parameter estimates depends on the model and the characteristics of the noise in the data **[2, 34]**. For models based on a sum of two exponentials fit to data in which the noise is described by an additive i.i.d. Gaussian term, it has been shown that confidence intervals based on the approximation of the covariance matrix describe the true likelihood-based confidence intervals well **[27]**.

The matrix of first derivatives of the model function with respect to both the nonlinear parameters z and the conditionally linear parameters a_j is

$$J_m = \begin{bmatrix} \frac{\partial C_j(z) a_j}{\partial x} \end{bmatrix} = \begin{bmatrix} \frac{\partial C_j(z)}{\partial z} a_j & C_j(z) \end{bmatrix}. \qquad (6.17)$$

Under the assumption that the noise vector ϵ added to the model $\psi_j = C_j(z)a_j$ is such that every element ϵ_i is $NID(0, \sigma^2)$, the covariance matrix associated with both z and a_j is

$$cov \begin{bmatrix} z \\ a_j \end{bmatrix} = \hat{\sigma}^2 (J_m^T J_m)^{-1}, \qquad (6.18)$$

where $\hat{\sigma}^2 = RSS(\hat{x})/df$, RSS is the residual sum of squares and the degrees of freedom $df = (\sum_{j=1}^n length(\psi_j)) - length(z) - (\sum_{j=1}^n length(a_j))$**[34]**.

After writing the residual function as outlined in Section 6.4 and using a standard nonlinear least squares implementation to minimize the sum of squares of the residual vector with respect to z, $cov(\hat{z})$ is often returned along with $\hat{z}$, whereas

$cov(\hat{a}_j)$ must be determined. Using

$$J_m^T J_m = \begin{bmatrix} (\frac{\partial C_j(z)}{\partial z} a_j)^T \frac{\partial C_j(z)}{\partial z} a_j & (\frac{\partial C_j(z)}{\partial z} a_j)^T C_j(z) \\ C_j^T(z) \frac{\partial C_j(z)}{\partial z} a_j & C_j(z)^T C_j(z) \end{bmatrix} \equiv \begin{bmatrix} A_{11} & A_{12} \\ A_{21} & A_{22} \end{bmatrix}, \quad (6.19)$$

we have, from the block matrix inversion theorem found in e.g., [**34**], Appendix A,

$$(J_m^T J_m)^{-1} = \begin{bmatrix} X_{11}^{-1} & X_{11}^{-1} X_{12} \\ -X_{21} X_{11}^{-1} & A_{22}^{-1} + X_{21} X_{11}^{-1} X_{12} \end{bmatrix}, \quad (6.20)$$

where $X_{11} = A_{11} - A_{12} A_{22}^{-1} A_{21}$, $X_{12} = A_{12} A_{22}^{-1}$, and $X_{21} = A_{22}^{-1} A_{21}$. Then $\sigma^2 X_{11}^{-1} = cov(\hat{z})$ and we are interested in determining the bottom right block. Since $A_{22}^{-1} = (C_j(z)^T C_j(z))^{-1}$, we have

$$X_{21} = A_{22}^{-1} A_{21} \quad (6.21)$$

$$= (C_j(z)^T C_j(z))^{-1} C_j^T(z) \frac{\partial C_j(z)}{\partial z} a_j \quad (6.22)$$

$$= C_j(z)^+ \frac{\partial C_j(z)}{\partial z} a_j \equiv G_j, \quad (6.23)$$

and $X_{12} = A_{12} A_{22}^{-1} \equiv G_j^T$, where G_j consists of columns $C_j^+ \frac{dC_j}{dz_i} a_j$, for each non-linear parameter z_i. Hence it is possible to write

$$cov(\hat{a_j}) \quad = \quad \sigma^2 (C_j^+ C_j^{+^T}) + G_j cov(\hat{z}) G_j^T. \quad (6.24)$$

This expression allows determination of $cov(\hat{a_j})$ for all $j = 1, 2, \ldots, n$ with modest memory resources even when n is large.

6.6. Constraints on the parameters

Constraints on the nonlinear parameters, e.g., to enforce non-negativity, may be accomplished via parameter transformation as for standard non-linear regression problems [**2, 34**].

For constraints on the linear parameters a and E in Problems 6.8 and 6.9, respectively, optimization of a modified variable projection functional is necessary. Consider the case that a is constrained to non-negative values. Then Problem (6.11) is replaced with the non-negative least squares (NNLS) problem

$$\begin{aligned} &\min_{a^* \in \mathbb{R}^{n_{\text{comp}}}} \parallel \psi - C(z) a^* \parallel^2 \\ &\text{subject to } 0 \leq a_i^* \text{ for } i = 1, 2, \ldots, n_{\text{comp}}. \end{aligned} \quad (6.25)$$

Problem (6.25) must be solved in place of $a = C^+(z)\psi$ in the expression $f(z)$, e.g., with the NNLS algorithm by Lawson and Hanson [**18**], so that Equation (6.12) becomes

$$f(z) = \frac{1}{2} \parallel \psi - C(z) a^* \parallel^2 \quad (6.26)$$

Non-negativity constraints on a arise when ψ represents count data. Then the noise statistics are often best represented using the Poisson distribution, but for data comprised of large counts may be well-approximated by additive i.i.d. Gaussian noise, so that parameter estimation may proceed by minimization of $f(z)$. When using a finite difference method to obtain J, a variable projection algorithm that adds non-negativity constraints to the conditionally linear parameters a is obtained by using the definition of $f(z)$ given in Equation (6.26) in place of that given in Equation

(6.12), as Mullen **[23]** discusses. van Stokkum *et al.* **[45]** have successfully applied this methodology in time-resolved mass spectrometry data analysis. When using an analytical expression for J, an approximate expression based on the Jacobian in the absence of constraints may be used, as Sima and Van Huffel **[36]** discuss.

In the case that the constraints applied to a do not ensure non-negativity, but rather some other property, the NNLS problem used to determine a^* must be replaced with the appropriate constrained optimization problem. The only restriction on the constraints applied is practical; the separated problem with constraints on a or E should remain easier to solve than the equivalent unseparated problem. Sima and Van Huffel **[35]** have described the imposition of regularization constraints on a by replacing the least squares problem $a = C(z)^+\psi$ in the variable projection functional with $a = (C(z)^T C(z) + m\lambda B)^{-1} C(z)^T \psi$, where the term $m\lambda B$ is used to impose a certain degree of smoothness on a.

Equality constraints that set $a_{j,l}$ to zero for component l, or set $a_{j,l} = a_{j,h}$ for components l and h are often incorporated to make the estimation problem better determined or account for a priori knowledge of the system underlying the observations. Such constraints are common in time-resolved spectroscopy applications where $a_{j,l}$ represents the spectrum of component l at wavelength j. In the case of equality constraints that set $a_{j,l}$ to zero, we remove column $C_{j,l}(z)$ and element $a_{j,l}$ from the model $\psi_j = C_j(z)a_j$. This results in a model with fewer free conditionally linear parameters.

For the case of equality constraints that set $a_{j,l}$ to be equal to $a_{j,h}$, possibly with a linear scaling factor α_i, we let column $C_j[,h](z)$ be equal to $C_j[,l](z) * \alpha_i + C_j[,h](z)$, and then remove column $C_j[,l](z)$ from the model $\psi_j = C_j(z)a_j$. This also results in a better determined model. Note that α_i may be optimized as a nonlinear parameter.

6.7. Case study I: Time-resolved fluorescence emission measurements of photosystem I

In order to give an idea of the use of sum-of-exponentials models in fitting time-resolved spectroscopy data in practice, we consider a case study in brief. Photosystem I (PS-I) is one of two photosystems in oxygenic photosynthesis, a process by which plants and green algae convert photons into chemical energy. The PS-I core is a distinct functional unit of PS-I, consisting of many proteins and attached chromophores. Gobets *et al.* **[6]** describe a system consisting of PS-I cores in a buffer excited by a short laser pulse of femtosecond duration. Measurements of the fluorescence of the system at many wavelengths and times after excitation are then collected with a synchroscan streak camera in combination with a spectrograph, a technique which has been reviewed elsewhere **[40, 41]**. The observations considered here represent 48 wavelengths equidistant in the interval 626-785 nanometer (nm), and 914 timepoints in the range 0-200 picosecond (ps) after laser excitation, stored as a 914×48 matrix of data Ψ. The goal of data analysis is to describe the kinetics in terms of a model that parameterizes the formation and decay of each distinct state of the underlying system, while solving for the spectra E as linear coefficients.

The compartmental model shown in Figure 6.7.1 was tested as a possible description for the kinetics of time-resolved spectroscopy data representing PS-I cores by fitting the free parameters of the model with variable projection. Where there is more than one allowable transition out of a compartment, parameters b_i are used to

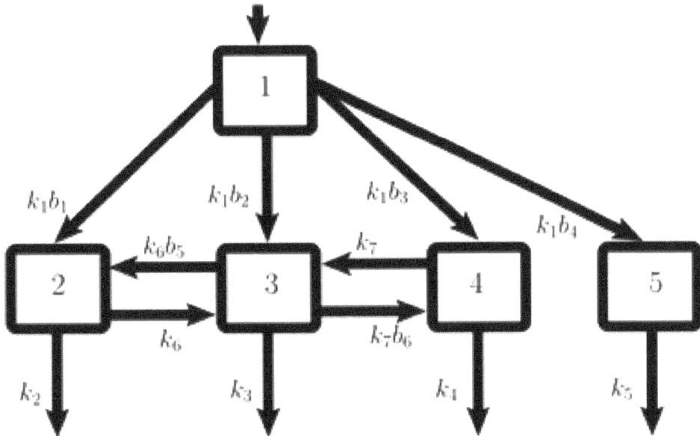

FIGURE 6.7.1. A compartmental model for the kinetics of PS-I core complexes. The decay rates of the components are parameterized by k_i. Where there is more than one allowable transition out of a compartment, parameters b_i are used to scale the decay rate k_i associated with the compartment. Here values of b_1, b_2, b_3, b_4 are fixed such that $b_1 + b_2 + b_3 + b_4 = 1$ and such that the spectra estimated for compartments 2 - 5 have approximately equal area, which is a physically motivated constraint.

scale the decay rate k_i associated with the compartment. Here values of b_1, b_2, b_3, b_4 are fixed such that $b_1 + b_2 + b_3 + b_4 = 1$ and such that the spectra estimated for compartments 2 - 5 have approximately equal area, which is expected from physical first principles. The parameters b_5 and b_6 describing the equilibrium between compartments 2 and 3 and compartments 3 and 4 can only be estimated by adding zero constraints (as described in Section 6.6) to some of the values in the matrix of spectra E. Here zero constraints are applied to all wavelengths of the spectrum for compartment 1, so that it is never emissive, to wavelengths of the spectrum of compartment 2 up to 690 nm, and to wavelengths of the spectrum of compartment 3 up to 697 nm.

The concentration profiles $C(z)$ and spectra E that result from application of this model are shown in Figure 6.7.2. Standard error estimates are shown on the spectra in Figure 6.7.2 as vertical bars, and are very small. In order to judge the quality of the fit, traces such as those in Figure 6.7.3 can be inspected, and the singular value decomposition of the residual matrix can be checked for evidence of systematic structure. The fit of the model described here was deemed satisfactory. The implementation of variable projection used is from the R package **TIMP** [**24**], and a script to reproduce these results is included as supplementary information, along with the package **TIMP** [**25**].

6.8. Case study II: Detection of protein-protein interactions

Applications of exponential models to the description of time-resolved microscopy data are becoming increasingly important as the technique of Fluorescent Lifetime Imaging Microscopy (FLIM) matures. FLIM is widely applied to detect interactions between fluorescently labeled biological molecules such as proteins, lipids, DNA and RNA, and results in a count of photons detected for many time points, at many spatial locations, often with 250 nanometer spatial resolution and sub-nanosecond temporal resolution. In many FLIM experiments, proteins of interest are genetically tagged with variants of the Green Fluorescent Protein (GFP) [**39**].

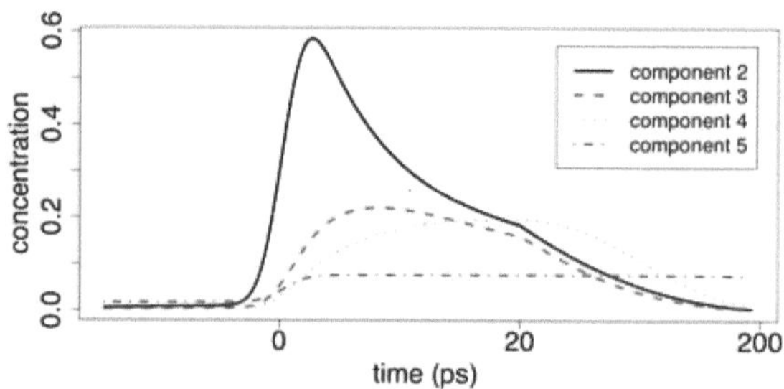

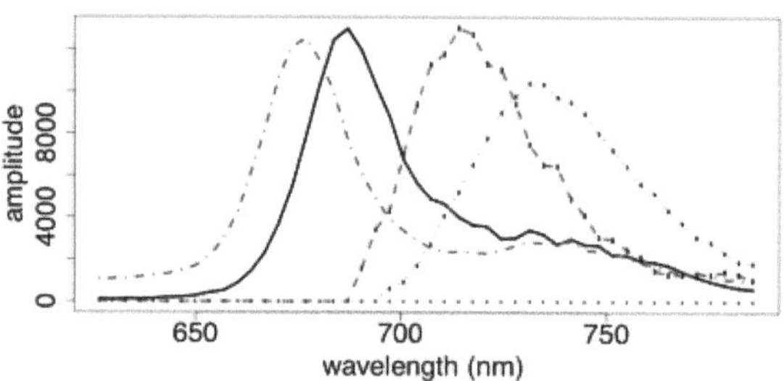

FIGURE 6.7.2. The concentration profiles (columns of the matrix $C(z)$, upper panel) and spectra (columns of the matrix E, lower panel) that result from using the compartmental model shown in Figure 6.7.1 to describe the kinetics of PS-I core complexes. The legend shown in the upper panel applies to the spectra as well. The concentration profile and spectrum of compartment 1 is not shown, since it is non-emissive. Standard error estimates are shown on the spectra as vertical bars, and are so small as to be barely visible. Note that the time axis is linear till 20 ps, and logarithmic thereafter.

FLIM experiments give rise to a global analysis problem when the same n_{comp} kinetic processes may be assumed to underlie the fluorescent decay at all locations. The decay of each kinetic process is exponential, but is complicated by the fact that it must be convolved with the time profile of the instrument response function (IRF). The IRF is often not described well by an analytical function with only a few parameters, and it is often necessary to make a measurement of the IRF time profile, and numerically convolve it with that of the exponential decay used to describe each kinetic process. Thus data analysis requires solution of an instance of Problem (6.7) where each kinetic process l is represented by a column of $C(z)$

$$C[,l] = \exp(-k_l t) \star i(t), \tag{6.27}$$

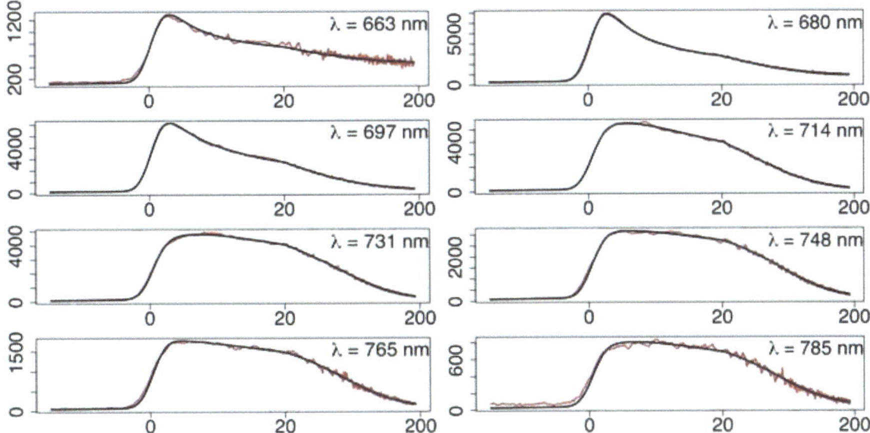

FIGURE 6.7.3. Columns of a matrix of time-resolved spectroscopy data (red), each representing the wavelength λ in nanometer (nm) shown in the upper right corner of each panel. The x-axis represents time in picoseconds. The model is shown in black. Free parameters were fit using variable projection. Note that the time axis is linear till 20 ps, and logarithmic thereafter.

where t is the vector of time points represented by the rows of $C(z)$, $k_l \in z$ is a parameter to be estimated, $\star$ indicates convolution and $i(t)$ is the measured time profile of the IRF. In many FLIM experiments, fluorescent dyes give rise to the observed fluorescence, which is measured at the maximum emission wavelength of the dye of interest, and can typically be described by two to four kinetic processes. The amplitude that each kinetic process contributes to the collected image at pixel j (that is, location j) is the row $E[j,]$ that appears in $\Psi = C(z)E^T$, where Ψ is the time-resolved image. The goal of data analysis is to estimate z and E.

Verveer *et al.* [**46**] recognized that variable projection could be applied to global analysis problems arising in FLIM data analysis, but did not implement the partitioned technique described in Section 6.4 and therefore were stymied by the large memory resources required. Laptenok *et al.* [**17**] studied the utility of variable projection for modeling FLIM data via a number of simulation studies and a control study in estimating the parameters describing the decay of Cyan Fluorescent Protein (CFP).

Note that FLIM data and fluorescence data in general represent a count of the number of photons detected at a given pixel and time. Poisson noise statistics apply to such non-negative count data. For datasets in which the counts are large, the assumption of additive i.i.d. Gaussian noise is acceptable. However, for datasets in which most counts are not large, optimal estimates under least squares criteria do not well-approximate the true underlying parameter values, an issue that has been studied previously [**21**]. This issue can be addressed to some extent by weighting each data point $\Psi[i,j]$ by $\frac{1}{\sqrt{\Psi[i,j]}}$, but in order to obtain fully correct estimates it would be necessary to develop an analogue of variable projection for the Poisson noise case.

In this case study we consider the simultaneous analysis of multiple FLIM images. Each pixel j in each image $1, 2, \ldots, K$ is modeled using Equation (6.3). The nonlinear parameters $k_l \in z$ used to describe the fluorescent decay are estimated using all data included in the simultaneous analysis. To allow a physical interpretation, the vectors $a_{j_1}, a_{j_2}, \ldots, a_{j_K}$, describing the amplitudes of the kinetic processes at pixel j in each dataset are constrained to non-negative values by the NNLS method, and the fluorescence decay rate parameters $k_l \in z$ are also constrained to non-negative values by a simple logarithmic transformation ($z_l = log(k_l)$).

The experiments giving rise to the data involve two proteins known to be homogeneously distributed in the cell nucleus. In one set of experiments, the first protein is tagged with CFP. In the second set of experiments, the first protein is tagged with CFP, and the second protein of interest is tagged with yellow fluorescent protein (YFP). When intracellular dynamics bring the proteins within 1-10 nm of each other, the CFP molecule transfers energy to the YFP molecule. This results in an increase in the decay rate of CFP, which can be observed. The general process in which excited-state energy of a donor fluorophore, like CFP, is non-radiatively transferred to a ground-state acceptor molecule, like YFP, is termed Förster Resonance Energy Transfer (FRET). FRET as measured by FLIM is extensively used to detect protein-protein interactions **[38]**.

Since CFP acts as a donor in the CFP-YFP FRET pair, we can use the FLIM set-up to measure only the wavelength at which CFP fluoresces, and examine whether the decay rate of CFP increases in the experiment with CFP and YFP tags as compared to in the experiment with only CFP tags. Such a decrease would be interpreted as evidence of FRET, which would imply that the proteins are often expressed in close proximity.

For the analysis, we select those pixels that represent the nucleus. The two CFP-only datasets whose intensity images are shown in Figure 6.8.1 (left) are used in a simultaneous analysis to estimate the associated decay rates. The two CFP-YFP datasets shown in Figure 6.8.1 (right) are analyzed together in the same way. The decay of CFP is described by a bi-exponential decay in both pairs of datasets.

The estimated decay rates for CFP in the first pair of datasets are $\hat{k} = \{1.53, 0.34\}$, whereas in the second pair of datasets these decay rates are estimated to be $\hat{k} = \{2.13, 0.44\}$. The average decay rate for pixel j is given as

$$\langle k_j \rangle = \frac{\sum_{l=1}^{n_{\text{comp}}} k_l a_{j,l}}{\sum_{l=1}^{n_{\text{comp}}} a_{j,l}}. \tag{6.28}$$

Figure 6.8.2 shows the estimated average decay rate per-pixel for CFP in the CFP-only datasets (left panels) and in the CFP-YFP datasets (right panels). Clearly, the bi-exponential decay of CFP is significantly faster in the CFP-YFP datasets as compared to in the CFP-only datasets. We conclude that there is evidence of significant FRET, and that the two tagged proteins are often expressed simultaneously in close proximity. As for the previous case study, a script to reproduce these results is included as supplementary information.

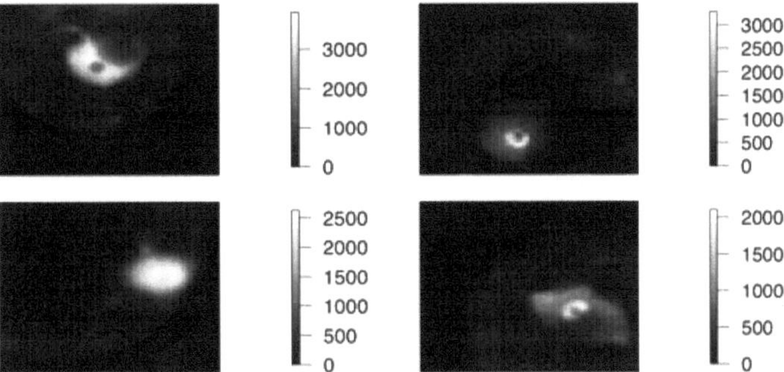

FIGURE 6.8.1. Intensity images resulting from FLIM experiments that measure fluorescence from cells at the wavelength at which CFP emission is maximum. Each pixel represents the sum of the data at that pixel over the 206 time-points in the entire time-resolved FLIM dataset. The left plots represent CFP tagged cells; the right plots represent cells tagged with both CFP and YFP. Only pixels representing the cell nucleus are subject to analysis.

6.9. Summary

Sum-of-exponentials models for time-resolved spectroscopy data have been reviewed, with pointers to the literature to supplement the discussion here. The utility of compartmental models for the kinetics has been described. The variable projection algorithm for parameter estimation has been presented, along with description of its implementation. Its extension for constraints on the parameters has also been discussed. Two case studies have been presented to illustrate the topics under consideration. Software and scripts to reproduce these case studies are included in the supplementary information for this chapter.

Acknowledgments

The authors are grateful for funding from Computational Science grant #635.000.014 from the Netherlands Organization for Scientific Research (NWO). Bas Gobets and Rienk van Grondelle provided the data in Section 6.7. Sergey Laptenok and Jan Willem Borst provided the data in Section 6.8.

Appendix

R scripts and data to reproduce the analysis and plots described in Sections 6.7 and 6.8 have been included as supplementary information in the directory `Mullen_etal/Mullen_van_StokkumFINAL/code`. R can be downloaded and installed from

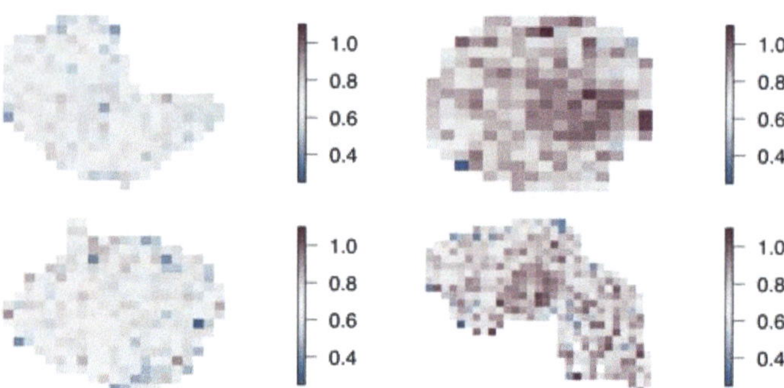

FIGURE 6.8.2. Average decay rate per pixel for the cells shown in Figure 6.8.1 after parameter estimation via global analysis. The higher decay rates in the datasets at right indicate protein-protein interactions.

`http://cran.r-project.org`; R version 2.9.0 was used here. The scripts utilize on the R package **TIMP**. Version 1.8 of **TIMP** is included as

`TIMP_1.8.tar.gz`	source code
`TIMP_1.8.tgz`	Mac OS X binary
`TIMP_1.8.zip`	Windows binary

The **TIMP** reference manual is included as `TIMP.pdf`. **TIMP** can also be downloaded and installed from `http://cran.r-project.org/web/packages/TIMP` but note that future versions may not be backward compatible.

Bibliography

1. Douglas M. Bates and Mary J. Lindstrom, *Nonlinear least squares with conditionally linear parameters*, Proceedings of the Statistical Computing Section (New York), American Statistical Association, 1986, pp. 152–157.
2. Douglas M. Bates and Donald G. Watts, *Nonlinear regression analysis and its applications*, John Wiley & Sons, New York, 1988.
3. J.M. Beechem, M. Ameloot, and L. Brand, *Global and target analysis of complex decay phenomena*, Analytical Instrumentation **14** (1985), 379–402.
4. Paul E. Black, *Dictionary of algorithms and data structures*, Tech. report, U.S. National Institute of Standards and Technology, 2004.
5. D. Gay and L. Kaufman, *Tradeoffs in algorithms for separable and block separable nonlinear least squares*, IMACS '91, Proceedings of the 13th World Congress on Computational and Applied Mathematics (Dublin) (R. Vichnevetsky and J. J. H. Miller, eds.), Criterion Press, 1991, pp. 157–158.
6. Bas Gobets, Ivo H. M. van Stokkum, Matthias Rogner, Jochen Kruip, Eberhard Schlodder, Navassard V. Karapetyan, Jan P. Dekker, and Rienk van Grondelle, *Time-Resolved Fluorescence Emission Measurements of Photosystem I Particles of Various Cyanobacteria: A Unified Compartmental Model*, Biophysical Journal **81** (2001), no. 1, 407–424.
7. Keith Godfrey, *Compartmental models and their application*, Academic Press, London, 1983.
8. G. H. Golub and V. Pereyra, *The differentiation of pseudo-inverses and nonlinear least squares problems whose variables separate*, Tech. report, Stanford University, Department of Computer Science, 1972.
9. G. H. Golub and V. Pereyra, *The differentiation of pseudoinverses and nonlinear least squares problems whose variables separate*, SIAM Journal on Numerical Analysis **10** (1973), 413–432.
10. G. H. Golub and C. F. van Loan, *Matrix computations* (3rd edn), The Johns Hopkins University Press, Baltimore, MD, USA, 1996.
11. Gene H. Golub and Randall J. LeVeque, *Extensions and uses of the variable projection algorithm for solving nonlinear least squares problems*, Proceedings of the 1979 Army Numerical Analysis and Computers Conference, 1979, pp. 1–12.
12. Gene H. Golub and Victor Pereyra, *Separable nonlinear least squares: the variable projection method and its applications*, Inverse Problems **19** (2003), R1–R26.
13. Alfred R. Holzwarth, *Data analysis of time-resolved measurements*, Biophysical Techniques in Photosynthesis (J. Amesz and A.J. Hoff, eds.), vol. I, Kluwer Academic Publishers, 1996, pp. 75–92.
14. Andrei A. Istratov and Oleg F. Vyvenko, *Exponential analysis in physical phenomena*, Review of Scientific Instruments **70** (1999), no. 2, 1233–1257.
15. Linda Kaufman, *A variable projection method for solving separable nonlinear least squares problems*, BIT **15** (1975), 49–57.
16. Fred T. Krogh, *Efficient implementation of a variable projection algorithm for nonlinear least squares problems*, Communications for the Association for Computing Machinery **17** (1974), no. 3, 167–169.
17. Sergey Laptenok, Katharine M. Mullen, Jan Willem Borst, Ivo H. M. van Stokkum, Vladimir V. Apanasovich, and Antonie J. W. G. Visser, *Fluorescence lifetime imaging microscopy (FLIM) data analysis with* **TIMP**, Journal of Statistical Software **18** (2007), no. 8, 1–20.
18. C. L. Lawson and R. J. Hanson, *Solving least squares problems*, Prentice Hall, Englewood Cliffs, NJ, 1974.

19. William H. Lawton and Edward A. Sylvestre, *Elimination of linear parameters in nonlinear regression*, Technometrics **13** (1971), 461–467.
20. G. G. Lukeman, *Application of the Shen-Ypma Algorithm for Separable Overdetermined Nonlinear Systems*, Master's thesis, Department of Mathematics and Statistics, Dalhousie University, Canada, 1999.
21. Michael Maus, Mircea Cotlet, Johan Hofkens, Thomas Gensch, Frans C. de Schryver, J. Schaffer, and C. A. M. Seidel, *An experimental comparison of the maximum likelihood estimation and nonlinear least-squares fluorescence lifetime analysis of single molecules*, Analytical Chemistry **73** (2001), no. 9, 2078–2086.
22. Jorge J. Moré, *The Levenberg-Marquardt algorithm, implementation and theory*, Numerical Analysis (G. A. Watson, ed.), Lecture Notes in Mathematics, vol. 630, Springer-Verlag, 1978, pp. 105–116.
23. Katharine M. Mullen, *Separable Nonlinear Models: Theory, Implementation and Applications in Physics and Chemistry*, Ph.D. thesis, Department of Physics and Astronomy, Vrije Universiteit Amsterdam, The Netherlands, 2008.
24. Katharine M. Mullen and Ivo H. M. van Stokkum, **TIMP***: an R package for modeling multiway spectroscopic measurements*, Journal of Statistical Software **18** (2007), no. 3, 1–46.
25. Katharine M. Mullen and Ivo H. M. van Stokkum, **TIMP***: a problem solving environment for fitting separable nonlinear models in physics and chemistry applications*, 2008, R package version 1.8.
26. Katharine M. Mullen and Ivo H. M. van Stokkum, *The variable projection algorithm in time-resolved spectroscopy, microscopy and mass spectrometry applications*, Numerical Algorithms **51** (2009), 319–340.
27. Katharine M. Mullen, Mikas Vengris, and Ivo H. M. van Stokkum, *Algorithms for separable nonlinear least squares with application to modelling time-resolved spectra*, Journal of Global Optimization **38** (2007), no. 2, 201–213.
28. J. F. Nagle, L. Zimanyi, and J. K. Lanyi, *Testing BR photocycle kinetics.*, Biophysical Journal **68** (1995), no. 4, 1490–1499.
29. John F. Nagle, *Photocycle kinetics: analysis of Raman data from bacteriorhodopsin*, Photochemistry and Photobiology **54** (1991), 897–903.
30. John F. Nagle, *Solving complex photocycle kinetics - theory and direct method*, Biophysical Journal **59** (1991), 476–487.
31. M. R. Osborne, *Separable least squares, variable projection, and the Gauss-Newton algorithm*, Electronic Transactions on Numerical Analysis **28** (2007), 1–15.
32. R Development Core Team, *R: A language and environment for statistical computing*, R Foundation for Statistical Computing, Vienna, Austria, 2009, ISBN 3-900051-07-0.
33. Axel Ruhe and Per Ake Wedin, *Algorithms for separable nonlinear least squares problems*, SIAM Review **22** (1980), no. 3, 318–337.
34. G. A. F. Seber and C. J. Wild, *Nonlinear Regression*, John Wiley & Sons, New Jersey, 2003.
35. Diana M. Sima and Sabine Van Huffel, *Regularized semiparametric model identification with application to nuclear magnetic resonance signal quantification with unknown macromolecular base-line*, Journal of the Royal Statistical Society: Series B **68** (2006), no. 3, 383–409.
36. Diana M. Sima and Sabine Van Huffel, *Separable nonlinear least squares fitting with linear bound constraints and its application in magnetic resonance spectroscopy data quantification*, Journal of Computational and Applied Mathematics **203** (2007), 264–278.
37. Jonas Sjöberg and Matts Viberg, *Separable non-linear least-squares minimization-possible improvements for neural net fitting*, Proceedings of the IEEE Workshop Neural Networks for Signal Processing VII (Amelia Island, FL, USA), 1997, pp. 345–354.
38. Klaus Suhling, Paul M. W. French, and David Phillips, *Time-resolved fluorescence microscopy*, Photochemical and Photobiological Sciences **4** (2005), 13–22.
39. Roger Y. Tsien, *The green fluorescent protein*, Annual Review of Biochemistry **67** (1998), 509–544.
40. I. H. M. van Stokkum, B. Gobets, T. Gensch, F. van Mourik, K. J. Hellingwerf, R. van Grondelle, and J. T. M. Kennis, *(Sub)-picosecond spectral evolution of fluorescence in photoactive proteins studied with a synchroscan streak camera system*, Photochemistry and Photobiology **82** (2006), 380–388.
41. I. H. M. van Stokkum, B. van Oort, F. van Mourik, B. Gobets, and H. van Amerongen, *(Sub)-Picosecond spectral evolution of fluorescence studied with a synchroscan streak-camera system*

and target analysis, Biophysical Techniques in Photosynthesis, Volume II, Series Advances in Photosynthesis and Respiration (Thijs J. Aartsma and Jörg Matysik, eds.), vol. 26, Springer, Dordrecht, 2008, pp. 223–240.

42. Ivo H. M. van Stokkum, *Global and target analysis of time-resolved spectra, Lecture notes for the Troisième Cycle de la Physique en Suisse Romande*, Tech. report, Department of Physics and Astronomy, Faculty of Sciences, Vrije Universiteit, Amsterdam, The Netherlands, 2005.
43. Ivo H. M. van Stokkum, A. M. Brouwer, H.J. van Ramesdonk, and T. Scherer, *Multiresponse parameter estimation and compartmental analysis of time resolved fluorescence spectra: Application to conformational dynamics of charge-separated species in solution*, Proceedings of the Koninklijke Nederlandse Akademie van Wetenschappen **96** (1993), 43–68.
44. Ivo H. M. van Stokkum, Delmar S. Larsen, and Rienk van Grondelle, *Global and target analysis of time-resolved spectra*, Biochimica et Biophysica Acta **1657** (2004), 82–104, and erratum, 1658, 262.
45. Ivo H. M. van Stokkum, Katharine M. Mullen, and Velitchka V. Mihaleva, *Global analysis of multiple gas chromatography-mass spectrometry (GC/MS) data sets: a method for resolution of co-eluting components with comparison to MCR-ALS*, Chemometrics and Intelligent Laboratory Systems **95** (2009), 150–163.
46. Peter J. Verveer, Anthony Squire, and Philippe I. H. Bastiaens, *Global analysis of fluorescence lifetime imaging microscopy data*, Biophysical Journal **78** (2000), no. 4, 2127–2137.

CHAPTER 7

Two exponential models for optically stimulated luminescence

Per Christian Hansen, Hans Bruun Nielsen,
Department of Informatics and Mathematical Modelling,
Technical University of Denmark, 2800 Kas. Lyngby, Denmark.
Email: pch,hbn@imm.dtu.dk.

Christina Ankjærgaard and *Mayank Jain*
Radiation Research Division
Risø National Laboratory for Sustainable Energy
Technical University of Denmark
DK-4000 Roskilde, Denmark
Email: cank,majarisoe.dtu.dk.

ABSTRACT. Optically Stimulated Luminescence (OSL) from quartz is used, e.g., for geological and archeological dating, and involves the measurement of light from a sample, followed by fitting a sum of exponentials to these data. We consider two different forms of exponential models for this purpose – one without weighting and another with a certain weighting of the data. In this work we compare the two models with regards to their ability to estimate the correct model parameters, including the unknown number of exponential components.

Keywords Stimulated Luminiscense; Geological Dating; Exponential Sum

7.1. Introduction

Optically stimulated luminescence (OSL) is extensively used to determine absorbed radiation doses (measured in J/kg) in crystals, caused by exposure to ionizing radiation. We start by giving a brief explanation of the physics underlying OSL, and refer to **[1]** and **[9]** for more details for readers not familiar with solid state physics.

The materials used to measure dose (dosimeters) are usually natural crystals, e.g., quartz and feldspars, or impurity-doped artificially grown crystals, such as lithium fluoride, aluminium oxide, etc. The irradiation of these crystals results in creation of free electrons and holes which are subsequently trapped in localized states (lattice defects) known as *traps* and *centers* within the atomic structure of the crystal. These trapping states, thus, store information about the absorbed dose, and the information can be read out in the form of luminescence by exposing

Victor Pereyra & Godela Scherer (Eds)

the crystal to visible or infrared photons having sufficient energy to cause photo-ionization of the occupied defects.

Electron-hole recombination following photo-ionization is the critical light generating step, and the resulting signal carrying dosimetric information is known as OSL; a dose estimate can be obtained from an appropriate sample by specific calibration of the signal. Since the OSL signal intensity is proportional to the concentration of trapped charge (electrons and holes), the light (e.g., the OSL intensity per incident photon) gradually decays with measurement time.

Traditionally, OSL measurements use a constant, continuous flux of incident photons. This is called continuous-wave OSL (CW-OSL), and it results in a signal that shows monotonous decay in time. The OSL technique is used for estimation of absorbed dose from ionizing radiation in a wide range of applications related to nuclear accidents, cosmic radiation in space, radiation facilities in health and power sectors, and in geochronology (dating sediments during the last half million years or so); see **[9]** for an overview.

In addition to being of use for dosimetry, the OSL signal contains information about the distribution of traps and recombination centers in the crystal, and this can provide insight into the charge excitation, movement, and recombination in crystals. Such insight is vital to our understanding of the luminescence mechanism.

In the case of natural quartz (the most commonly used material in accident dosimetry and sediment dating), it is generally argued that the monotonously decaying OSL emitted during exposure to blue light of constant intensity (i.e., CW-OSL) consists of several transients having exponential form **[34]**. The lifetimes of these transients are related to the physics of the luminescence process **[5]**. In natural quartz from around the world, up to seven electron trapping states have been identified as participating in the OSL process **[20]**, **[33]**.

An alternative method to stimulate the crystal is by keeping the light intensity constant and pulsing the light to obtain pulsed OSL. By measuring only the light emitted between the light pulses, resulting from the recombination process in the centers, and resolving this on a μs timescale, it is possible to measure time-resolved OSL (TR-OSL). The TR-OSL shape can also be described as a sum of decaying exponentials, but these now characterize the behavior of the recombination centers **[3]**, **[11]**. The TR-OSL signal from quartz acquired during pulsed optical stimulation can be described by a dominant exponential transient having a lifetime of approximately 35 microseconds and two relatively minor transients having relatively shorter and longer lifetimes than the main transient **[11]**.

Given measured OSL data (light intensity as a function of time) one can use a number of data fitting techniques to determine the parameters of the exponential-form model: the number of terms, the amplitudes, and the decay parameters. See **[17]** for a survey of such methods.

It was shown by Bulur **[7]** that CW-OSL data in the form of a sum of decaying exponentials can be transformed into a sum of functions that have a "peaked" appearance. There are advantages and disadvantages of this transformation, and the goal of this work is to compare the two approaches with simulated data, with respect to robustness of finding the parameters and fitting the data.

Our analysis primarily uses artificially generated multi-exponential data. These data are investigated using two fundamentally different protocols: a multi-exponential analysis using a nonlinear least squares formulation solved by a Levenberg-Marquardt approach [**20**], and a spectroscopic analysis using a first-kind Fredholm integral equation formulation [**4**], [**17**], [**36**]. More details about OSL measurements and the associated data processing can be found in [**2**].

The chapter is organized as follows. Section 7.2 gives a brief introduction to the OSL model as a sum of exponentials or peak functions, and in Section 7.3 we introduce the corresponding separable nonlinear least squares problem associated with estimating the parameters of the OSL model. Next, in Section 7.4 we introduce an alternative model in the form of a first-kind Fredholm integral equation, and we discuss how this problem leads to a constrained linear least squares problem. Section 7.5 gives a brief summary of the numerical methods used to solve the two problems, while Section 7.6 describes how we generate realistic artificial test data. Our simulation results are presented in Section 7.7, where we conclude that the nonlinear modulation using peak-form data is superior, and in Section 7.8 we apply this approach to a set of real data. Section 7.9 concludes our findings.

7.2. The OSL model

Experimental data acquired during either continuous (CW-OSL) or pulsed stimulation (TR-OSL) with superimposition of several first-order transients can be described by the sum-of-exponentials model

$$f_{\mathrm{D}}(t) = \sum_{j=1}^{p} \alpha_j \exp(-\lambda_j t), \qquad 0 \le t \le T. \tag{7.1}$$

We refer to this model as the *decay form.* Here, t denotes time, T is the total measurement time, λ_j are positive decay constants for the p discrete components in the signal, and α_j are positive amplitudes which are proportional to the initial population undergoing decay. Typically p is small, e.g., in the range 2–7.

The purpose of multi-component analysis of OSL data is to determine the number p of components and the model parameters α_j and λ_j, $j = 1, \ldots, p$. These quantities give information on the physical characteristic of the traps or centers, such as photo-ionization cross-section or recombination/relaxation lifetime.

Both for understanding the OSL processes as well as for higher accuracy in retrospective dosimetry, it is highly desirable that we can examine the individual transients in the OSL [**21**], obtained by fitting the model (7.1) to the OSL data. Unfortunately, fitting multiple exponential functions is a non-trivial and ill-posed problem (see, e.g., the review by Istratov and Vyvenko [**17**] and the analysis by Varah [**35**]). For numerical aspects, see also [**12**], [**28**], [**29**], [**31**].

For continuous stimulation Bulur [**6**] suggested that fitting of multi-exponential OSL data could be made more robust if the data had a peak form rather than a monotonous decay form. He also showed that peak shaped OSL signals could be obtained experimentally by linearly increasing the stimulation light intensity during the OSL measurement. This technique, called linearly modulated OSL (LM-OSL), results in a signal that can be described using a linear combination of single trap/centre models

$$f(t) = \sum_{j=1}^{p} \alpha_j \frac{t}{T} \exp\left(-\frac{\lambda_j t^2}{2T}\right), \qquad 0 \le t \le T. \tag{7.2}$$

in which all parameters are as described above.

Although the shape of the LM-OSL peak-form curve is fundamentally different from that of the CW-OSL curve, the physical process causing them and the information contained in the two types of data is identical; the apparent differences arise because we view data in the time domain rather than the event domain [**18**].

Bulur [**7**] and Poolton *et al.* [**26**] further showed that a similar peak-shaped signal (pseudo LM-OSL) can be achieved by transformation of the monotonously decaying multi-exponential data (assuming first order kinetics). This data-transformation approach can be applied to both CW-OSL and TR-OSL with one important difference: for CW-OSL there exists a corresponding "true" LM-OSL that can be measured instrumentally, but for TR-OSL there does not exist a "true" peak shaped signal. The latter is fundamentally a decaying signal in the time domain, irrespectively of how the pulses are delivered.

As opposed to true instrumental peak measurement (e.g., LM-OSL) the peak transformation approach has the disadvantage that a potential constant background in the decay-form data becomes a time-varying background in the peak-form data. This problem can partly be circumvented by subtracting the background before the transformation. Similarly, there occurs an undesirable transformation of the Poisson distributed noise in the signal. Nonetheless, for TR-OSL the transformation technique is the only means for obtaining a peak shaped signal.

Since the nature of multi-exponential and multi-peak data are fundamentally identical, it has been extensively discussed whether peak-form data has in fact any advantage over the decay-form data, see [**15**], [**16**], [**18**], [**19**]. It still remains to be carefully investigated whether the peak form is superior to the decay form for computing the parameters α_j and λ_j from noisy data via a least squares formulation. The aim of this chapter is to carry out a comparative analysis of the performances of the two approaches for estimating the "true" parameters for simulated TR-OSL signals and their corresponding peak transformed signals.

The mathematical form of the peak transformation used here is not exactly equivalent to pseudo LM-OSL. We use the substitution $t \to \sqrt{2Tt}$ to obtain the sum-of-peaks model

$$f_{\mathrm{P}}(t) = \sum_{j=1}^{p} \alpha_j \sqrt{t/T} \exp(-\lambda_j t), \qquad 0 \le t \le T \tag{7.3}$$

(we have omitted a redundant factor $\sqrt{2}$ in the expression). We refer to this model as the *peak form*, and we note that we can obtain data for this form simply by multiplying the decay-form data with the factor $\sqrt{t/T}$.

7.3. The least squares solution and its sensitivity

While our main contribution is a thorough simulation study, it is worthwhile to start with some theoretical insight into the two models (7.1) and (7.3) used here.

Let $\mathbf{t} = (t_1, t_2, \ldots, t_m)^T$ denote the vector of measurement times $t_i \ge 0$, and let (t_i, y_i), $i = 1, \ldots, m$ denote the data measured in a CW-OSL measurement setup.

Then, for the decay-form model, the least squares estimates of the parameters

$$\boldsymbol{\alpha} = (\alpha_1, \ldots, \alpha_p)^T \qquad \text{and} \qquad \boldsymbol{\lambda} = (\lambda_1, \ldots, \lambda_p)^T$$

are the solutions to the separable nonlinear least squares problem with criterion function

$$F_{\rm D}(\boldsymbol{\alpha}, \boldsymbol{\lambda}, t) = \sum_{i=1}^{m} (y_i - f_{\rm D}(t_i))^2 = \sum_{i=1}^{m} \Big(y_i - \textstyle\sum_{j=1}^{p} \alpha_j \exp(-\lambda_j\, t_i) \Big)^2. \qquad (7.4)$$

The term "separable" comes from the fact that the amplitude parameters α_j appear linearly in the nonlinear least squares problem, see **[12]** and also the first chapter of this book for details. For the peak-form problem – where we use the transformed decay-form data, i.e., $\big(\sqrt{t_i/T}\, y_i, t_i\big)$ – the criterion function takes the form

$$F_{\rm P}(\boldsymbol{\alpha}, \boldsymbol{\lambda}, t) = \sum_{i=1}^{m} \big(\sqrt{t_i/T}\, y_i - f_{\rm P}(t_i) \big)^2 = \sum_{i=1}^{m} w_i^2 \, \big(y_i - f_{\rm D}(t_i) \big)^2. \qquad (7.5)$$

We see that the peak-form least squares problem is simply a weighted version of the decay-form problem, with weights $w_i^2 = t_i/T$, $i = 1, \ldots, m$.

The sensitivity of the solution $(\boldsymbol{\alpha}, \boldsymbol{\lambda})$ to data errors can be analyzed as follows. First note that at the solution, the nonlinear least squares problem associated with (7.5) can be approximated by a quadratic problem. Thus small perturbations $\delta\boldsymbol{\alpha}$ and $\delta\boldsymbol{\lambda}$ of the solution satisfy – to first order – the equation

$$\mathbf{H} \begin{pmatrix} \delta\boldsymbol{\alpha} \\ \delta\boldsymbol{\lambda} \end{pmatrix} = \mathbf{J}^T \mathbf{e}.$$

Here $\mathbf{e}$ is the perturbation of the data vector, while $\mathbf{J} \in \mathbb{R}^{m\times(2p)}$ and $\mathbf{H} \in \mathbb{R}^{(2p)\times(2p)}$ are the Jacobian and Hessian matrices at the solution:

$$\begin{aligned} \mathbf{J} &= \mathbf{W} \big(-\mathbf{A} ,\, \mathrm{diag}(\mathbf{t})\, \mathbf{A}\, \mathrm{diag}(\boldsymbol{\alpha}) \big) \\ \mathbf{H} &= \mathbf{J}^T \mathbf{J} + \sum_{i=1}^{m} w_i \, (y_i - f_{\rm D}(t_i)) \begin{pmatrix} 0 & t_i\, \mathrm{diag}(\mathbf{a}_i) \\ t_i\, \mathrm{diag}(\mathbf{a}_i) & -t_i^2\, \mathrm{diag}(\mathbf{a}_i)\, \mathrm{diag}(\boldsymbol{\alpha}) \end{pmatrix} \end{aligned}$$

in which $\mathbf{W} = \mathrm{diag}(w_1, \ldots, w_m)$, and $\mathbf{a}_i$ is the ith row of $\mathbf{A} \in \mathbb{R}^{m\times p}$:

$$\mathbf{a}_i = \big(\exp(-\lambda_1 t_i), \ldots, \exp(-\lambda_p t_i) \big), \qquad i = 1, \ldots, m.$$

The choices $w_i = 1$ and $w_i = \sqrt{t_i/T}$ correspond to the decay- and peak-form problems, respectively. Thus, we have the first-order perturbation result

$$\delta\boldsymbol{\alpha} = \mathbf{M}_{\boldsymbol{\alpha}}\, \mathbf{e}, \qquad \delta\boldsymbol{\lambda} = \mathbf{M}_{\boldsymbol{\lambda}}\, \mathbf{e}, \qquad \begin{pmatrix} \mathbf{M}_{\boldsymbol{\alpha}} \\ \mathbf{M}_{\boldsymbol{\lambda}} \end{pmatrix} = \mathbf{H}^{-1} \mathbf{J}^T,$$

showing that the relative errors in λ_j and α_j (to first order) are bounded by

$$\frac{|\delta\alpha_j|}{\alpha_j} \le \frac{\|\mathbf{M}_{\boldsymbol{\alpha}}(j,:)\|_2}{\alpha_j} \|\mathbf{e}\|_2, \qquad \frac{|\delta\lambda_j|}{\lambda_j} \le \frac{\|\mathbf{M}_{\boldsymbol{\lambda}}(j,:)\|_2}{\lambda_j} \|\mathbf{e}\|_2, \qquad j = 1, \ldots, p.$$

The quantities $\|\mathbf{M}_{\boldsymbol{\alpha}}(i,:)\|_2/\alpha_j$ and $\|\mathbf{M}_{\boldsymbol{\lambda}}(i,:)\|_2/\lambda_j$ can be considered as the worst-case amplification factors for the propagation of the data noise to the solution. Once a solution has been found, it is easy to compute these quantities in order to evaluate the sensitivity of the amplitude and decay parameters of the solution.

7.4. An alternative integral-equation approach

As an alternative to solving the separable nonlinear least squares problems from the previous section, it has been suggested (see, e.g., **[4]**, **[17]**, **[36]**) to recast the parameter-identification problem as a linear Fredholm integral equation of the first kind

$$\int_{\lambda_{\min}}^{\lambda_{\max}} \exp(-\lambda\, t)\, a(\lambda)\, d\lambda = g(t), \tag{7.6}$$

where $\lambda \in [\lambda_{\min}, \lambda_{\max}]$ is a continuous variable, $a(\lambda) \geq 0$ is an unknown "amplitude density function," and the right-hand side $g(t)$ is the measured signal (modeled by $f_{\mathrm{D}}(t)$ in the decay-form model). This formulation clearly takes its basis in the separability of the nonlinear problem, in which the amplitudes appear linearly. We note that (7.6) is an ill-posed problem – the ill-posedness of the original problem does not vanish by a reformulation.

If the data indeed adheres to the sum-of-exponentials model in the decay-form model (7.1), then we can expect that the nonnegative function $a(\lambda)$ has narrow spikes for $\lambda \approx \lambda_j$. Moreover, if this is the case then we can also expect that the amplitudes are approximately equal to the area under each of the spikes, i.e., $\alpha_j \approx \int_{\Omega_j} a(\lambda)\, d\lambda$ where Ω_j denotes a small interval around λ_j.

We discretize the integral equation (7.6) by means of a simple quadrature method. This means that we replace (7.6) by a system of equations

$$\sum_{j=1}^{n} \Delta\lambda_j\, \exp(-\lambda_j\, t_i)\, x_j \approx y_i, \qquad i = 1, \ldots, m$$

where $\lambda_1, \ldots, \lambda_n$ are the quadrature points, $\Delta\lambda_j$ denotes the width of the interval that contains the jth quadrature point, and x_j is an approximation to $a(\lambda)$ at this quadrature point, i.e.,

$$x_j \approx a(\lambda_j), \qquad j = 1, \ldots, n.$$

Due to the large range of λ-values that are needed in OSL problems, the quadrature points λ_j are distributed logarithmically between some values $\lambda_{\min}$ and $\lambda_{\max}$.

Allowing both decay- and peak-form data, we obtain a weighted linear least squares problem with nonnegativity constraints:

$$\min_{\mathbf{x}} \|\mathbf{W}\,(\mathbf{K}\,\mathbf{x} - \mathbf{y})\|_2 \qquad \text{subject to} \quad \mathbf{x} \geq \mathbf{0}. \tag{7.7}$$

As before $\mathbf{W} = \mathrm{diag}(w_1, \ldots, w_m)$ with $w_i = 1$ or $w_i = \sqrt{t_i/T}$, and $\mathbf{K} \in \mathbb{R}^{m \times n}$ is a matrix whose elements are given by

$$k_{ij} = \Delta\lambda_j \exp(-\lambda_j t_i), \qquad i = 1, \ldots, m, \quad j = 1, \ldots, n.$$

Moreover, $\mathbf{y} \in \mathbb{R}^m$ is the vector consisting of the data and the vector $\mathbf{x} \in \mathbb{R}^n$ contains the approximations to $a(\lambda_j)$. For each of the spikes in the solution we compute the corresponding amplitude by means of

$$\alpha_j = \sum_{k \in \mathrm{spike}_j} \Delta\lambda_k\, x_k.$$

7.5. The numerical methods

Before the data are used in the least squares parameter identification problems, an unavoidable constant background is removed by subtracting an estimate found from averaging over the last 10 data points (which is standard procedure for analysis of measured TR-OSL data). This is important because our models do not include a constant term, and because a non-negligible constant background in the decay-form data becomes a time-varying (increasing) background when transformed to the peak-form data.

The separable nonlinear least squares problems associated with (7.5) are solved by means of the curve fitting feature included in the software package SIGMAPLOT, which is one of the standard packages for treating OSL data. The user must specify the number p of components, and we impose the positivity constraints $\lambda_j > 0$, $j = 1, \ldots, p$. The underlying numerical method is based on the Levenberg-Marquardt algorithm, tailored to the separable nonlinear least squares problem as described in [**12**], [**22**], [**29**]. Negative amplitudes α_j were never encountered; if this happens then one should use the approach described in [**25**], [**32**].

To solve the nonnegatively constrained linear least squares problem (7.7) associated with the Fredholm integral equation formulation, it is well known that regularization is needed to stabilize the solution [**13**]. Fortunately, the nonnegativity constraint $\mathbf{x} > \mathbf{0}$ enforces a great deal of regularization in our OSL problem. However, the matrix $\mathbf{K}$ is numerically rank deficient and therefore we replace the original problem (7.7) with the regularized version

$$\min_{\mathbf{x}} \left\| \begin{pmatrix} \mathbf{W}\,\mathbf{K} \\ \gamma \mathbf{I} \end{pmatrix} \mathbf{x} - \begin{pmatrix} \mathbf{W}\,\mathbf{y} \\ \mathbf{0} \end{pmatrix} \right\|_2 \qquad \text{subject to} \quad \mathbf{x} \geq \mathbf{0}, \tag{7.8}$$

in which $\mathbf{I}$ denotes the identity matrix, and γ is a small parameter of the order 10^{-6} (we found that the computed solutions are not sensitive to the choice of γ). This problem is solved by means of MATLAB's built-in function `lsqnonneg`, which implements the active-set algorithm from Lawson and Hanson [**24**, Chapter 23].

Clearly, there is no guarantee that this method will compute the correct number of components in the OSL data. Indeed, the vector $\mathbf{x}$ occasionally has more than p spikes – while we did not encounter a situation where it had less than p spikes – and thus we need a "rejection criterion" that can remove spurious spikes in $\mathbf{x}$. The contribution to the total signal from each component in (7.3) can be measured by the integral

$$\int_0^T \alpha_j \exp(-\lambda_j t)\, dt = \frac{\alpha_j}{\lambda_j}\left(1 - \exp(-\lambda_j T)\right) \approx \frac{\alpha_j}{\lambda_j},$$

and therefore we reject a spike if the corresponding ratio α_j/λ_j is smaller than a threshold determined by the area under the data and the noise level in the data.

In order to evaluate the computed fit, given by (7.1) or (7.3), we perform a simple statistical test of the residuals

$$r_i = w_i\,(y_i - f_{\mathrm{D}}(t_i)), \qquad i = 1, \ldots, m.$$

If the noise is not very small then, to a good approximation, it can be considered white and we can check whether the residuals r_i can also be considered as white noise (in which case we have extracted all available signal from the data).

The statistical tool for this check is the normalized cumulative periodogram (NCP) [**27**] (which has been used recently for determining regularization parameters

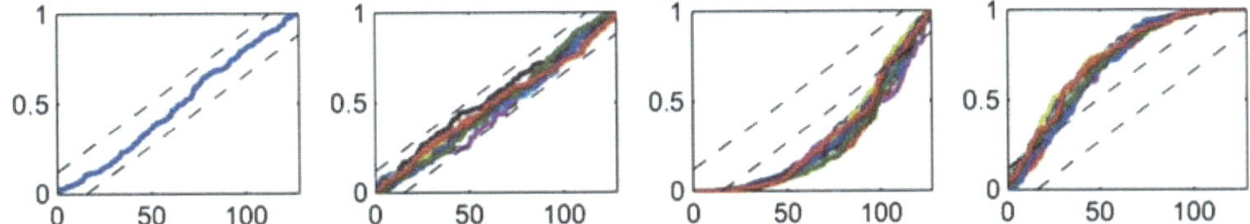

FIGURE 7.5.1. Left to right: a single instance of the NCP for a white-noise residual, 10 instances of white-noise residuals, 10 instances of residuals dominated by high-frequency components, and 10 instances of residuals dominated by low-frequency components. The dashed lines show the Kolmogorov-Smirnoff limits for a 5% significance level.

in inverse problems [**14**], [**30**]). Let $\hat{r}_i$, $i = 1, \ldots, m$ denote the discrete Fourier transform of the residuals, and define the vector $\mathbf{c}$ with elements

$$c_k = \|(\hat{r}_2, \ldots, \hat{r}_{k+1})\|_2^2 / \|(\hat{r}_2, \ldots, \hat{r}_{q+1})\|_2^2, \qquad k = 1, \ldots, q$$

with $q = \lfloor m/2 \rfloor$ (these elements are cumulated values of the power spectrum of the residual). If r_i are white noise then the expected values of c_k lie on a straight line from (0,0) to $(q, 1)$. Also, with a 5% significance level the NCP curve must lie within the Kolmogorov-Smirnoff limit $\pm 1.35\, q^{-1/2}$ of the straight line, see the example in Fig. 7.5.1. This means that we can use the the ratio

$$\rho = \max_k |c_k - k/q| \,/\, 1.35\, q^{-1/2} \tag{7.9}$$

as a measure of how well the NCP criterion is satisfied (the smaller ρ the better, and $\rho > 1$ means that the residual cannot be considered white noise).

7.6. Creating artificial data

For our performance evaluation we generate artificial data analogous to the TR-OSL of quartz for the 380 nm emission. The lifetimes, noise, and background levels modeled from real data are used in order to make our data as realistic as possible, and in the subsequent analysis these values are treated as unknown.

Following [**11**] the artificial data is chosen to contain $p = 3$ exponential transients following (7.1) with amplitudes α_j (measured in counts per 0.408 μs) and decay constants λ_j (measure in μs^{-1}) given by

$$\alpha_1 = 7\,000,\ \lambda_1 = 0.500, \quad \alpha_2 = 20\,000,\ \lambda_2 = 0.0300, \quad \alpha_3 = 3\,000,\ \lambda_3 = 0.0125.$$

These decay constants correspond to lifetimes of 2, 33, and 80 μs, respectively. We generate data sets containing $m = 2000$ points with a bin width of 0.408 μs giving a length between the light pulses of 816 μs. Following (7.1) we can express the artificial data as a sum of three exponentials plus an additive background resulting from "dark counts" of the system.

Real measurements of both the signal and the background show that these data are Poisson distributed [**2**]. The simulated measurement data y_i for the discrete time t_i can therefore be written as

$$y_i = Y_i + b_i, \qquad Y_i \sim \mathcal{P}(f_D(t_i)), \qquad B_i \sim \mathcal{P}(b), \qquad i = 1, \ldots, m \tag{7.10}$$

meaning that the "pure signal" Y_i and the background noise b_i are both Poisson distributions with mean values $f_D(t_i)$ and b, respectively. The variance in the data

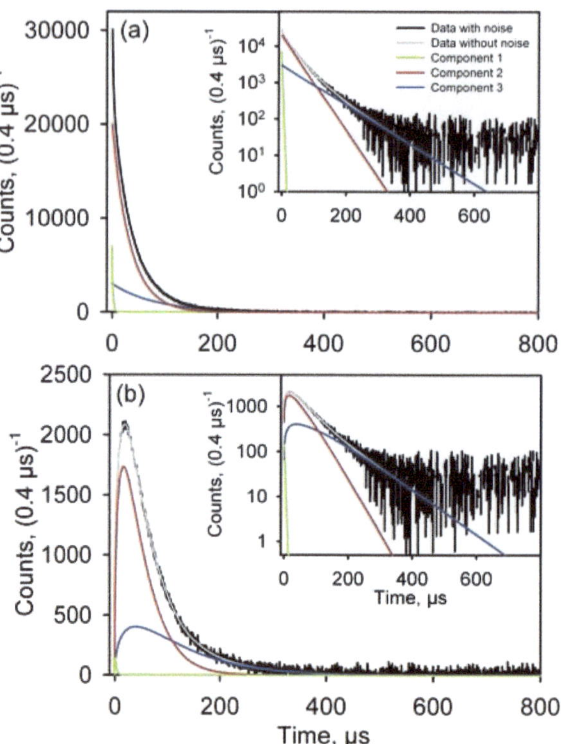

FIGURE 7.6.1. (a) The TR-OSL decay-form model $f_{\mathrm{D}}(t)$ (grey curve), together with the individual components shown by the green, red, and blue curves. The black curve shows the artificial data with added Poisson noise as well as background noise; in this example the initial-signal to noise ratio (ISNR) is 15. The insert shows all curves on a semi-logarithmic axis. (b) The data from (a) transformed into peak form; same legend as in (a).

y_i is thus given by

$$\sigma_i^2 = Y(t_i) + b.$$

The level of background noise is measured by the *initial-signal to noise ratio* (ISNR) defined as the ratio between the maximum signal amplitude at $t = 0$ and the background constant b.

Following [7] we also create a peak-shaped signal from the TR-OSL signal by simply multiplying the data by a factor $\sqrt{t_i/T}$. The artificial decay and peak data will therefore correspond to the same time interval and have the same number of data points. Furthermore, the amplitudes α_j and the decay constants λ_j of the three components are unchanged during the transformation, such that the fitted peak parameters can easily be compared to those of the decay data. Figure 7.6.1 shows an example of these data. We used 10 different ISNR in the range 6–6000, and for each ratio we generated five instances of the noisy signal, leading to a total of 50 different decay-form and peak-form signals.

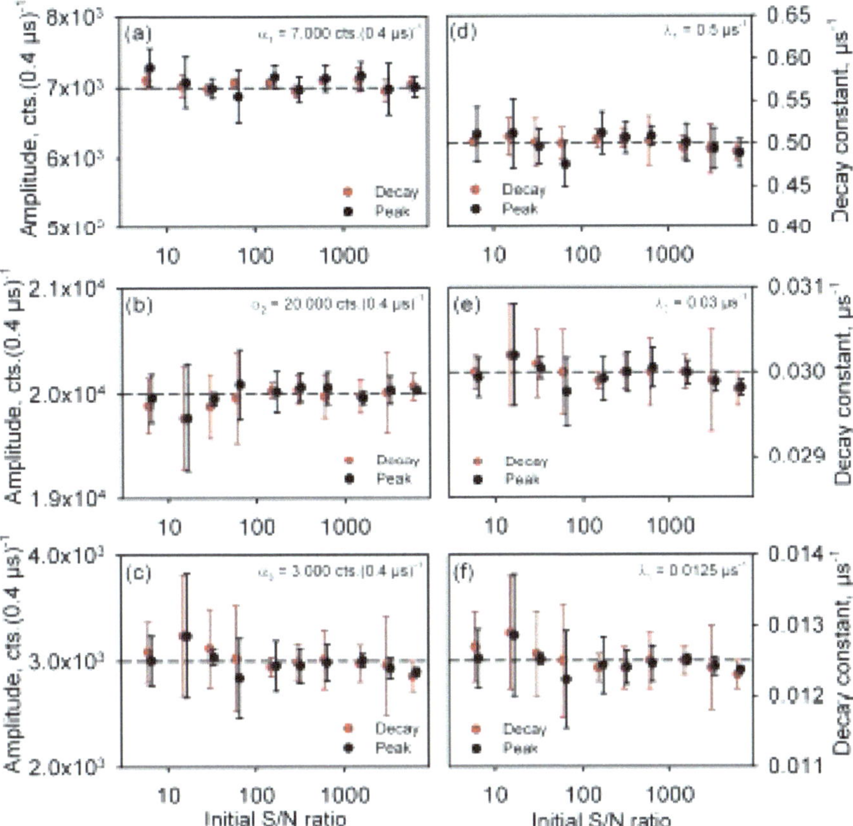

FIGURE 7.7.1. Results from fitting both peak-form data (black symbols) and decay-form data (red symbols) using SIGMAPLOT. In each plot the dashed line is the "true" parameter value, and each point is the average over five parameter values for the same ISNR. The left column shows the results for the amplitudes (a) $\alpha_1 = 7\,000$ cts.$(0.4\ \mu\text{s})^{-1}$, (b) $\alpha_2 = 20\,000$ cts.$(0.4\ \mu\text{s})^{-1}$, and (c) $\alpha_3 = 3\,000$ cts.$(0.4\ \mu\text{s})^{-1}$. The right column shows the results for the decay parameters (d) $\lambda_1 = 0.5\ \mu\text{s}^{-1}$, (e) $\lambda_2 = 0.03\ \mu\text{s}^{-1}$, and (f) $\lambda_1 = 0.0125\ \mu\text{s}^{-1}$.

7.7. Simulation results

Using the built-in nonlinear least squares method in SIGMAPLOT, we fitted the 50 decay-form and peak-form data sets. The procedure was to fit each data set with first two components, then three components, and finally with four components to identify the right number of components present in the data set. Fitting with too few components caused a systematic behavior in the residuals, and the NCP ratio ρ (7.9) was always greater than one. On the other hand, too many components were reflected in either more than one component with the same decay constant or another component with a very similar decay constant; both possibilities resulted in no further improvement of the residuals or the NCP ratio.

TABLE 1. Number of data sets with either one, two, or three components overestimated in the fit, when using the Fredholm integral equation model (7.6), (7.8). The numbers are given before and after the use of the rejection criterion.

	Before RC		After RC	
No. of extra components	Decay	Peak	Decay	Peak
1	24	24	5	3
2	11	17	0	0
3	3	1	0	0

The results from fitting the data with the nonlinear models (7.1) and (7.3) using SIGMAPLOT are shown in Fig. 7.7.1. The computed amplitudes α_1, α_2, and α_3 are compared in (a)—(c) for the different ISNR. Likewise, the decay constants λ_1, λ_2, and λ_3 are compared in Fig. 7.7.1 (d)–(f). The dashed lines in each plot represent the "true" value. All points are the average from the five noisy realizations of the same ISNR, and the corresponding error bar is the standard deviation of these five results. All amplitudes and decay constants are consistent, within the error, of the "true" value, although there is a slight tendency for very high ISNR that the parameters from the peak-form data are underestimated (see Fig. 7.7.1 (c), (e), (f)).

When fitting with the Fredholm integral equation model (7.6) and (7.8), the number of components ($p = 3$) present in a data set is often overestimated by one to three components – but using our rejection criterion described in Section 7.5 almost all of these extra components are omitted. This is shown in Table 1, which lists the number of extra components found in the 50 data sets before and after the rejection criterion has been used. Out of the 50 decay-form data sets, 38 had too many components and this number was reduced to 5 after using the rejection criterion. Similarly, from the 50 peak-form data sets, 42 had too many components and this number was reduced to 3.

Figure 7.7.2 shows the results from fitting with the Fredholm integral equation model, and again the amplitudes are compared in (a)–(c) while the decay constants are compared in (d)–(f). Similar to Fig. 7.7.1, the points in Fig. 7.7.2 are averages over the parameters from five data sets with the same ISNR. We note, however, that results from five decay-form data sets and three peak-form data sets were rejected due to overestimation of the number of components (see Table 1). The estimates generally have larger uncertainties compared to those using SIGMAPLOT, and again it is seen that there is a tendency to underestimate the parameters (Fig. 7.7.2 (c), (e), and (f)) and to overestimate (Fig. 7.7.2 (b)) for high ISNR. Furthermore, in all the plots several of the parameters for both the decay- and peak-form data are not consistent with the "true" values.

Let us now consider the sensitivity of the parameters computed by means of the decay- and peak-form data. Figure 7.7.3 shows the quantities $\|\mathbf{M}_{\boldsymbol{\alpha}}(i,:)\|/\alpha_j$ and $\|\mathbf{M}_{\boldsymbol{\lambda}}(i,:)\|/\lambda_j$ ($j = 1, 2, 3$) introduced in Section 7.3, for both the decay-form and peak-form problems (7.1) and (7.3). We note that the results are independent of the numerical method used to solve the problem, and hence the sensitivities are valid for both numerical methods studied here. We see that all sensitivities are less

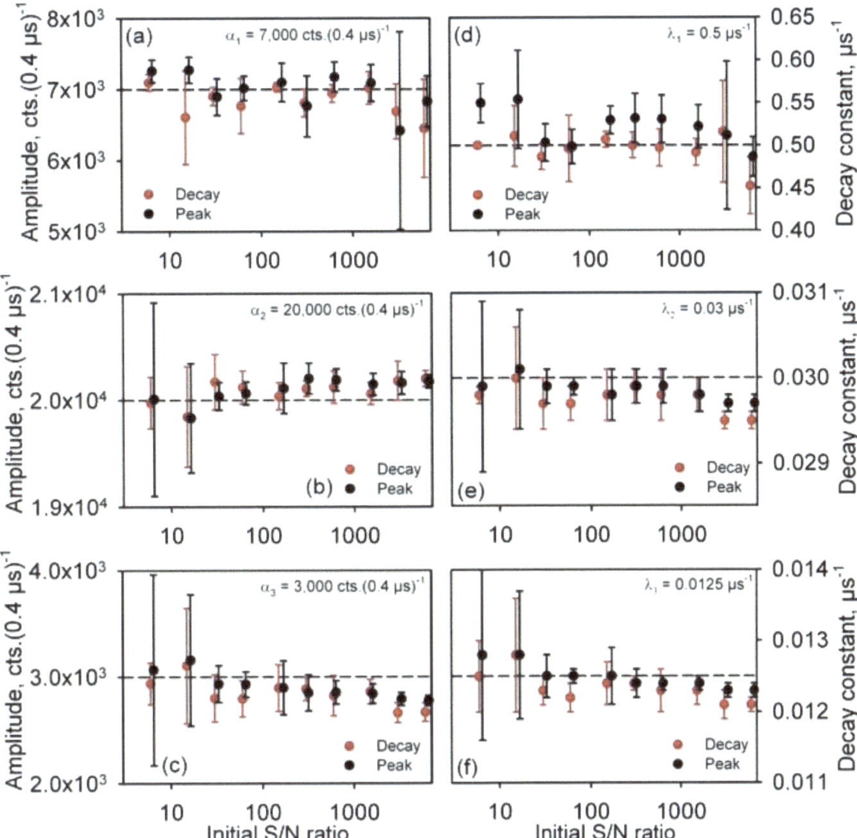

FIGURE 7.7.2. Results from fitting both peak-form data (black symbols) and decay-form data (red symbols) using the Fredholm integral equation model. See Fig. 7.7.1 for figure description. The results from eight data sets were discarded (five for decay-form and three for peak-form) as a result of inadequate removal of false components by the rejection criterion.

than 0.01, and that the parameters for the peak-form problem are always greater than those for the decay-form problem. Since smaller sensitivities are preferable, this suggests a preference for the decay form if we use this characteristic only; but what is more important is the overall robustness of the method.

To make an overall assessment of the performance of the two fitting methods and the two types of data, the residuals from all the fitted decay- and peak-form data were analyzed by means of the NCP method. In particular, we computed the NCP ratio ρ in order to evaluate whether the residual can be considered equivalent to white noise (for $\rho < 1$). Figure 7.7.4 shows histograms of the NCP ratio for both methods and both data sets. The red bars represent NCP ratios which are less than 1, representing white noise, and all NCP ratios above 5 are collected in the last bin for better visualization of the histograms.

It is clearly seen from Fig. 7.7.4 that the best results are obtained using the peak form, since the tail of the distribution for peak-form data is much smaller

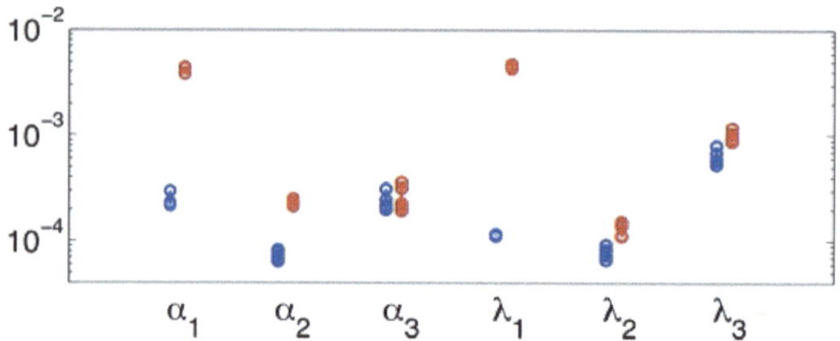

FIGURE 7.7.3. The quantities $\|\mathbf{M}_\alpha(i,:)\|_2/\alpha_j$ and $\|\mathbf{M}_\lambda(i,:)\|_2/\lambda_j$ (defined in Section 7.3), which measure the parameters' relative sensitivity to perturbations of the data. For each parameter, we show the computed sensitivities for five noise realizations, and for both the peak form (blue) and the decay form (red). The decay form has the smaller sensitivities and therefore an advantage if we use this characteristic only.

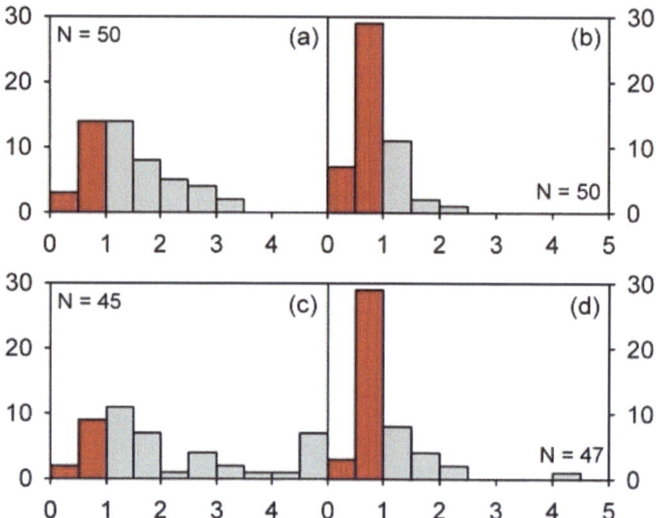

FIGURE 7.7.4. Distributions of NCP ratios ρ for (a) decay-form data fitted using SIGMAPLOT, (b) peak-form data fitted using SIGMAPLOT, (c) decay-form data fitted using the Fredholm integral equation model, and (d) peak-form data fitted using the same model. For NCP ratios less than 1 (red bars), the residuals from the fit can be considered white noise, and the fit is satisfactory. For NCP ratios larger than 1 (grey bars), the residuals exhibit a trend that is inconsistent with white noise. Note that while the complete 50 data sets were used in (a) and (b), only 45 and 47 data sets were used in (c) and (d), respectively.

than that for the decay-form data. We also see from the figure that this conclusion is independent of the numerical method used to compute the parameters, since the top right and bottom right subplots are essentially identical.

From Fig. 7.7.4 we concluded that for the type of data considered in our study, it is advantageous to use the transformation to peak form, and fit the data using

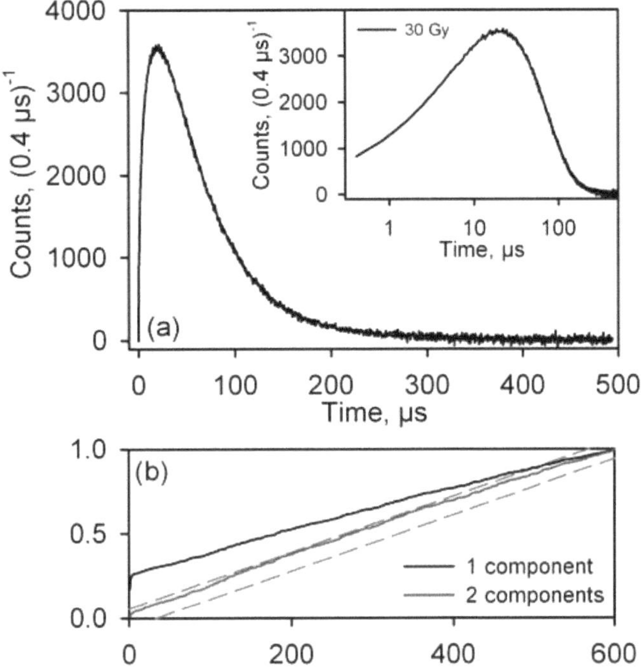

FIGURE 7.8.1. (a) TR-OSL data measured from a colluvium quartz sample from Tanzania. The sample contains a dose of 30 Gy and was heated to 260°C for 10 s prior to blue LED stimulation at 125°C. After data collection, the data was transformed to peak-form data. The insert shows the data in log-scale. (b) NCP curves for a one-parameter fit (black curve) and a two-parameter fit (red curve) using SIGMAPLOT. The KS limits are shown as grey dashed lines.

the nonlinear model (7.3) via a numerical method such as Levenberg-Marquardt. Although the parameters found by the peak-form data seem to be potentially more sensitive to perturbations, the peak-form model is much better at fitting the data (in the sense that the residuals are much more likely to appear like white noise).

7.8. Analysis of real data

TR-OSL data was measured using an automated reader at Risø DTU by stimulating a colluvium quartz sample from Tanzania with blue light. The Risø reader is an automated measurement facility with a built-in beta irradiation facility ($^{90}Sr/^{90}Y$ beta emitting source), blue light emitting diodes (LED) stimulation, a heater facility and photo-multiplier tube detection [**8**]. Even with no light present, there are detected counts often known as 'dark counts' or background, which are generated by thermal excitation of electrons in the photocathode, system electronics, and/or interaction of the detector with cosmic radiation. The TR-OSL data is recorded by pulsing the LEDs and time-stamping photons emitted from the samples between the stimulation light pulses **[23]**. The net signal is then derived by summing several hundred thousand of these light pulses emitted from the sample.

The transformed peak-form TR-OSL data from the Tanzanian quartz sample is shown in Fig. 7.8.1 (a) for an irradiation dose of 30 Gy. The insert shows the curve on a log scale. The ISNR for the decay-form data prior to the transformation was approximately 40. The data was initially fitted with SIGMAPLOT using one component, and the corresponding NCP curve calculated from the residuals is shown as the black curve in Fig. 7.8.1 (b); it clearly falls outside the KS-limits (black line) with a NCP ratio $d = 4.57$. If instead the data is fitted with two components, the NCP curve (red line) now fall within the KS-limits, and the NCP ratio is $d = 0.95$.

The decay constants found from the two-component fit are $\lambda_1 = 0.0259\ \mu s^{-1}$ and $\lambda_2 = 0.0097\ \mu s^{-1}$, giving approximate lifetimes 39 μs and 103 μs, respectively. This result is in good agreement with the components observed in **[10]** and **[11]**. The two amplitudes are $\alpha_1 = 36\,959$ cts.$(0.4\ \mu s)^{-1}$ and $\alpha_2 = 685$ cts.$(0.4\ \mu s)^{-1}$, which gives component amplitude to noise ratios of 49 and 0.9, respectively. It is therefore possible to determine a second component (α_2, λ_2) with an initial amplitude very close to the background level.

7.9. Conclusion

We compared two different exponential models for OSL commonly used in the literature, the decay form and the peak form; the latter is equivalent to the former with weights that depend on the measurement time. Two different numerical methods were used to compute the model parameters, one based on solving the nonlinear data-fitting problem by a Levenberg-Marquardt algorithm, and the other based on solving a linear first-kind Fredholm integral equation by means of a nonnegatively constrained linear least squares problem.

Our experimental results in Figs. 7.7.2 and 7.7.4 suggest that the formulation based on the nonlinear model can handle higher levels of noise than the integral equation model. Moreover, the results in Fig. 7.8.1 (based on the NCP analysis) suggest that among the two formulations, the peak-form model performs better in the sense that it fits the data better.

Based on evaluation of residuals using the NCP approach for the two models we conclude that fitting of the peak-form data is the better way of handling the OSL data-fitting problem. We also conclude that both numerical methods and both data models considered here lead to essentially the same estimated parameters.

Bibliography

1. M. J. Aitken, *An Introduction to Optical Dating*, Oxford University Press (1998).
2. C. Ankjærgaard, M. Jain, P. C. Hansen, and H. B. Nielsen, *Towards multi-xxponential analysis in optically stimulated luminescence: A comparison of data collection and analytical methods*, submitted to J. Appl. Phys. D.
3. C. Ankjærgaard, M. Jain, R. Kalchgruber, T. Lapp, D. Klein, S. W. S.McKeever, A. S. Murray, and P. Morthekai, *Further investigations into pulsed optically stimulated luminescence from feldspars using blue and green light*, Radiation Measurements, in press (2009).
4. N. Agersnap, *Dosimetry based on thermally and optically stimulated luminescence*, unpublished Ph.D. Thesis, Niels Bohr Institute, University of Copenhagen (2007).
5. R. M. Bailey, B. W. Smith, and E. J. Rhodes, *Partial bleaching and the decay form characteristics of quartz OSL*, Radiation Measurements, **27**:123–136 (1997).
6. E. Bulur, *An alternative technique for optically stimulated luminescence (OSL) experiment*, Radiation Measurements, **26**:701–709 (1996).
7. E. Bulur, *A simple transformation for converting CW-OSL curves to LM-OSL curves*, Radiation Measurements, **32**:141–145 (2000).
8. L. Bøtter-Jensen, C. E. Andersen, G. A. T. Duller, and A. S Murray, *Developments in radiaton, stimulation and observation facilities in luminescence measurements*, Radiaton Measurements, **37**:535–541 (2003).
9. L. Bøtter-Jensen, S. W. S. McKeever, and A. G. Wintle, *Optically Stimulated Luminescence Dosimetry*, Elsevier, Amsterdam, The Netherlands (2003).
10. M. L. Chithambo and R. B. Galloway, *A pulsed light-emitting-diode system for stimulation of luminescence*, Measurement Science and Technology, **11**:418–424 (2000).
11. M. L. Chithambo, F. Preusser, K. Ramseyer, and F. O. Ogundare, *Time-resolved luminescence of low sensitivity quartz from crystalline rocks*, Radiation Measurements, **42**:205–212 (2007).
12. G. H. Golub and V. Pereyra, *Separable nonlinear least squares: the variable projection method and its applications*, Inverse Problems, **19**:R1–R26 (2003).
13. P. C. Hansen, *Rank-Deficient and Discrete Ill-Posed Problems: Numerical Aspects of Linear Inversion*, SIAM, Philadelphia (1998).
14. P. C. Hansen, M. E. Kilmer, and R. H. Kjeldsen, *Exploiting residual information in the parameter choice for discrete ill-posed problems*, BIT **46**:41–59 (2006).
15. D. J. Huntley, *Thoughts arising from "Choi, Duller and Wintle: Analysis of quartz LM-OSL curves. Ancient TL 24, 9-20 (2006)"*, Ancient TL, **24**:69–70 (2006).
16. D. J. Huntley, *Response to Jain and Lindvold*, Ancient TL, **25**:76–80 (2007).
17. A. A. Istratov and O. F. Vyvenko, *Exponential analysis in physical phenomena*, Review of Scientific Instruments, **70**:1233–1257 (1999).
18. M. Jain and L. R. Lindvold, *Blue light stimulation and linearly modulated optically stimulated luminescence.* Ancient TL, **25**:69–75 (2007).
19. M. Jain and L. R. Lindvold, *Response to Huntley*, Ancient TL, **25**:80 (2007).
20. M. Jain, A. S. Murray, and L. Bøtter-Jensen, L., *Characterisation of blue-light stimulated luminescence components in different quartz samples: implications for dose measurement*, Radiation Measurements, **37**:441–449 (2003).
21. M. Jain, A. S. Murray, L. Bøtter-Jensen, and A. G. Wintle, *A single-aliquot regenerative-dose method based on IR (1.49 eV) bleaching of the fast OSL component in quartz*, Radiation Measurements, **39**:309–318 (2005).
22. L. Kaufman, *A variable projection method for solving separable nonlinear least squares problems*, BIT, **15**:49–57 (1975).

23. T. Lapp, M. Jain, C. Ankjærgaard, and L. Pirzel, *Development of pulsed stimulation and photon timer attachments to the Risø TL/OSL reader*, Radiation Measurements, **44**:571-575 (2009).
24. C. L. Lawson and R. J. Hanson, *Solving Least Squares Problems*, Classics in Applied Mathematics **15**, SIAM, Philadelphia (1995).
25. K. M. Mullen and I. H. M. van Stokkum, *The variable projection algorithm in time-resolved spectroscopy, microscopy and mass spectrometry applications*, Numerical Algorithms **51**:319–340 (2009).
26. N. R. J. Poolton, L. Bøtter-Jensen, C. E. Andersen, M. Jain, A. S. Murray, A. E. R. Malins, and F. M. Quinn, *Measuring modulated luminescence using non-modulated stimulation: ramping the sample period*, Radiation Measurements, **37**:639–645 (2003).
27. B. W. Rust, *Parameter selection for constrained solutions to ill-posed problems;* in "Computing Science and Statistics," Interface Foundation of North America, Inc., Fairfax Station, VA, 333–347 (2000); www.galaxy.gmu.edu/interface/I00/HTMLProceedings/BRust.htm.
28. B. W. Rust, *Fitting nature's basic functions part III: Exponentials, sinusoids, and nonlinear least squares*, Computing in Science and Engineering, **4**:72–77 (2002).
29. B. W. Rust, *Fitting nature's basic functions part IV: The variable projection algorithm*, Computing in Science and Engineering, **5**:74–79 (2003).
30. B. W. Rust and D. P. O'Leary, *Residual periodograms for choosing regularization parameters for ill-posed problems*, Inverse Problems, **24**:034005 (30pp) (2008).
31. R. I. Shrager and R. W. Hendler, *Some pitfalls in curve-fitting and how to avoid them: A case in point*, Journal of Biochemical and Biophysical Methods, **36**:157–173 (1998).
32. D. M. Sima and S. Van Huffel, *Separable nonlinear least squares fitting with linear bound constraints and its application in magnetic resonance spectroscopy data quantification*, Journal of Computational and Applied Mathematics, **203**:264–278 (2007).
33. J. S. Singarayer and R. M. Bailey, *Further investigations of the quartz optically stimulated luminescence components using linear modulation*, Radiation Measurements, **37**:451–458 (2003).
34. B. W. Smith and E. J. Rhodes, *Charge movement in quartz and their relevance to optical dating*, Radiation Measurements, **23**:329–333 (1994).
35. J. M. Varah, *On fitting exponentials by nonlinear least squares*, SIAM Journal of Scientific and Statistical Compututing, **6**:30–44 (1985).
36. V. H. Whitley and S. W. S. McKeever, *Linearly modulated photoconductivity and linearly modulated optically stimulated luminescence measurements on Al2O3:C*, Journal of Applied Physics, **90**:6073–6083 (2001).

CHAPTER 8

Modelling type Ia supernova light curves

Bert W. Rust
Mathematical and Computational Sciences Division
National Institute of Standards and Technology (NIST)
100 Bureau Drive, MS 8910
Gaithersburg, MD 20899-8910, USA
bert.rust@nist.gov

Dianne P. O'Leary
Computer Science Department and Institute for Advanced Computer Studies
University of Maryland
College Park, MD 20742; and
National Institute of Standards and Technology
Gaithersburg, MD 20899-8910
oleary@cs.umd.edu

Katharine M. Mullen
Ceramics Division
National Institute of Standards and Technology (NIST)
100 Bureau Drive, M/S 8520
Gaithersburg, MD, 20899, USA
kmullen@nist.gov

ABSTRACT. Type Ia supernova light curves are characterized by a rapid rise from zero luminosity to a peak value, followed by a slower quasi-exponential decline. The rise and peak last for a few days, while the decline persists for many months. It is widely believed that the decline is powered by the radioactive decay chain $^{56}\text{Ni} \rightarrow {}^{56}\text{Co} \rightarrow {}^{56}\text{Fe}$, but the rates of decline in luminosity do not exactly match the decay rates of Ni and Co. In 1976, Rust, Leventhal, and McCall [**19**] presented evidence that the declining part of the light curve is well modelled by a linear combination of two exponentials whose decay rates were proportional to, but not exactly equal to, the decay rates for Ni and Co. The proposed reason for the lack of agreement between the rates was that the radioactive decays take place in the interior of a white dwarf star, at densities much higher than any encountered in a terrestrial environment, and that these higher densities accelerate the two decays by the same factor. This paper revisits this model, demonstrating that a variant of it provides excellent fits to observed luminosity data from 6 supernovae.

Keywords: Supernova light curves; exponential modelling; radioactive decays; luminosity data

Victor Pereyra & Godela Scherer (Eds)

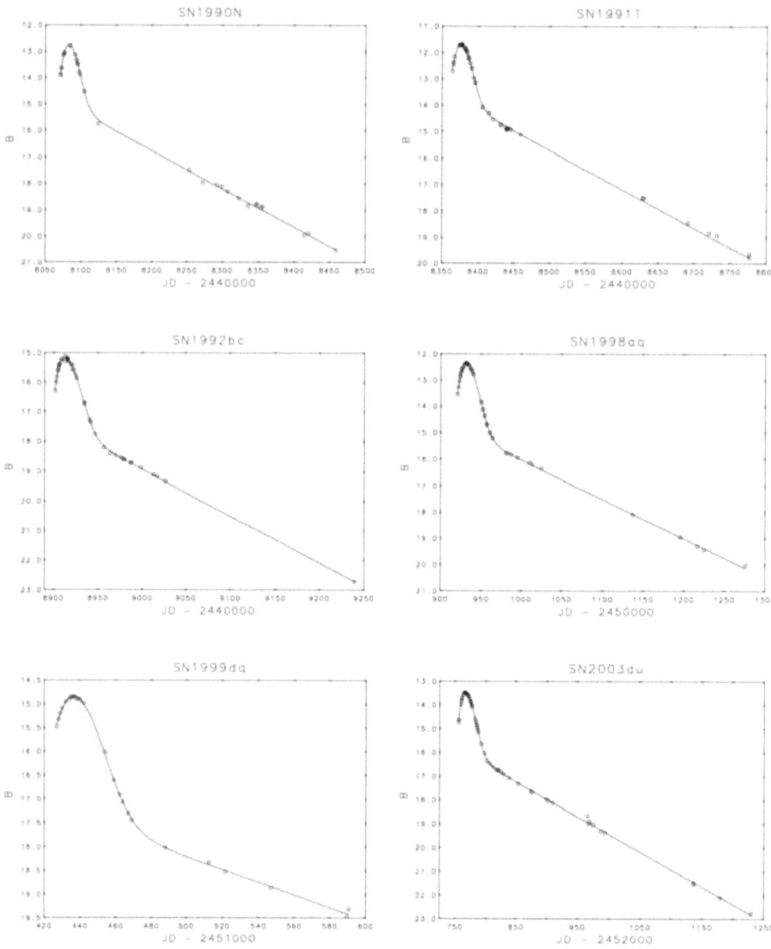

FIGURE 8.1.1. B-magnitude light curves for 6 Type Ia supernovae. The label on each plot is the name assigned to the supernova, specifying the year of the explosion and the order of discovery in that year. The time unit for the measurements is *Julian Days* (JD), the number of days since Greenwich noon on January 1, 4713 BC. The brightness units are astronomical magnitudes measured in the B (blue) wavelength passband.

8.1. Introduction

Supernovae are exploding stars that, for a few weeks, can be as bright as or even brighter than their parent galaxies. Most types of supernovae have irregular light curves, but for one class, Type Ia, the light curves display a very uniform and regular behavior. The light curves of 6 such supernovae are given in Figure 8.1.1, where the discrete data points are measurements of the apparent brightness of the supernova and the smooth curves are fits of a 6-parameter model that will be described in Section 8.2. The similarity of the 6 plots attests to the uniformity of the phenomenon.

This uniformity makes Type Ia supernovae excellent standard candles for estimating distances to their parent galaxies. In 1974 Rust [**18**, Chapt. 11] demonstrated a linear dependence of estimates of the peak absolute magnitude on the post-maximum rate of decline of the light curve. The absolute magnitude is a measure of the intrinsic luminosity that can be combined with the apparent (observed) magnitude to get an estimate of the distance. If the relationship is calibrated by observations of supernovae in nearby galaxies whose distances can be reliably estimated by other means, then the observed rate of decline of the light curve of a distant supernova leads to an estimate of its absolute magnitude and thence its distance. Rust's sample of light curves was limited and not completely homogeneous, so the linear dependence that he pointed out was scarcely noted by the astronomical community. Fortunately the correlation was rediscovered in 1993 by Phillips [**16**] who established it as a foundation for Type Ia standard candles. The light curve model that we describe in this paper has potential use in refining this tool for distance estimation.

The uniformity of the linear long time decays in the light curves, together with theoretical considerations, has led to the belief that the light curve is powered by the radioactive decay chain $^{56}\mathrm{Ni} \rightarrow {}^{56}\mathrm{Co} \rightarrow {}^{56}\mathrm{Fe}$, where the ^{56}Ni is deposited by fusion reactions in a carbon-oxygen white dwarf star [**2**]. A white dwarf star contains a mass comparable to that of our sun, collapsed into a volume smaller than that of the earth, so the interior densities are extraordinarily high. All atoms in the star are totally stripped of their electrons, which circulate through the interior in a Fermi sea, providing the pressure that keeps the star from collapsing further. The cause of the collapse is thought to be the exhaustion of the hydrogen fuel that provided the fusion energy powering the star before the collapse. According to this theory, the star is part of a binary system in which the other star expands and sheds its outer layers. Some of this lost material falls onto the white dwarf to ignite a new round of fusion reactions that burn the carbon and oxygen to produce ^{56}Ni. One problem for this scenario is the fact that the supernova light curve decay rates are always faster than the terrestrial decay rates of ^{56}Ni and ^{56}Co.

In 1974 Van Hise [**22**] analyzed the light curve of SN1937c. He found two decay rates, faster than those of (terrestrial) ^{56}Ni and ^{56}Co, but having approximately the same ratio as these rates. Thus the decays in the star seemed to be accelerated by the same factor. In a terrestrial environment, ^{56}Ni beta decays to ^{56}Co entirely by electron capture, and ^{56}Co beta decays to ^{56}Fe by electron capture 80 % of the time. In 1975, Leventhal and McCall [**12**] suggested that the decays occur in the high-density interior of the white dwarf, where the electron capture rates are enhanced. In 1976, Rust, Leventhal and McCall [**19**] fit a model consisting of a sum of two exponentials to the post-maximum light curves for 15 supernovae. This work was one of the first real-world applications of the renowned *VARPRO* [**5, 6**] program for solving separable non-linear least squares problems, and the first of many subsequent applications of the variable projection algorithm in spectroscopy [**14**]. They found a statistically significant correlation between the two exponential decay rates, with average lifetime values $\tau_1 = (6.46 \pm 1.98)$ d and $\tau_2 = (81.2 \pm 25.7)$ d [1]. The ratio of these two values, $81.2/6.46 = 12.6$ is approximately the same as the ratio $111.42/8.764 = 12.71$ of the terrestrial average lifetimes of ^{56}Co and

[1]The abbreviation "d" denotes "days", and we have specified standard uncertainties for the quantities.

^{56}Ni. In spite of this evidence, the astronomical community [**1, 3**] rejected the Leventhal and McCall hypothesis, and concluded that even though the light curve is powered by the radioactive decay chain, the observed decay rates were not related to the radioactive decay rates, but rather depended on the physical conditions of the expanding atmosphere of the supernova, and that the apparent exponential decay in the late-time light curve was not even necessarily a true exponential. Placing a straight edge along the long tails in the light curves in Figure 8.1.1 provides a sufficient rebuttal to this last idea.

In this paper we revisit this data-fitting problem, using higher-quality data that have become available since the 1970s. We describe our model in Section 8.2 and the computational tools and results in Sections 8.3 and 8.4. Our basic hypothesis is that radioactive β-decay rates increase in high density environments by an amount proportional to the density. While as far as we know this result is not predicted by theory, other explanations of the apparent observed increase in decay rates are not forthcoming. We show that under this hypothesis, the B-passband light curve is well explained, and that combining those results with a light echo effect allows the luminosity evolution in the other passbands to be explained also.

8.2. The basic model

We present a model consistent with the assumption that the fusion reactions that deposit the ^{56}Ni and the subsequent decays to ^{56}Co and ^{56}Fe all occur in the interior of a white dwarf that is not totally disrupted by the outburst. The atmosphere of the star may be exploded outward, but the central engine powering the whole outburst remains intact, providing a very stable energy source that maintains a constant, enhanced decay rate even at very late times in the light curve. The energy is generated in the form of gamma ray photons that are degraded to visible light by interactions with the expanding atmosphere and possibly also with a pre-existing planetary nebula surrounding the white dwarf.

The model can be represented schematically as follows:

$$W(t;\alpha_1,\alpha_2,\alpha_3) \longrightarrow \boxed{^{56}\text{Ni}} \xrightarrow{k_1} \boxed{^{56}\text{Co}} \xrightarrow{k_2} \boxed{^{56}\text{Fe}}\ ,$$

where $W(t;\alpha_1,\alpha_2,\alpha_3)$ is a pulse of ^{56}Ni deposition and k_1 and k_2 are the nuclear decay rates of ^{56}Ni and ^{56}Co. The initial pulse is modelled by a Weibull probability density function

$$W(t;\alpha_1,\alpha_2,\alpha_3) = \frac{\alpha_2}{\alpha_3}\left(\frac{t-\alpha_1}{\alpha_3}\right)^{(\alpha_2-1)} \exp\left[-\left(\frac{t-\alpha_1}{\alpha_3}\right)^{\alpha_2}\right], \tag{8.1}$$

where α_1 is a location parameter, α_2 is a shape parameter, and α_3 is a scale parameter. These three adjustable parameters give the Weibull function great flexibility in modelling the Ni deposition process. Note that the parameter α_1 is the starting time for the fusion pulse.

In a terrestrial setting, the decay rates k_1 and k_2 would be the inverses of the average lifetimes 8.764 d and 111.42 d, but in the high density interior of the star, the model allows these two rates to be accelerated by a common factor α_4, so

$$k_1 = \frac{1}{8.764\,\alpha_4}\ , \qquad k_2 = \frac{1}{111.42\,\alpha_4}\ , \tag{8.2}$$

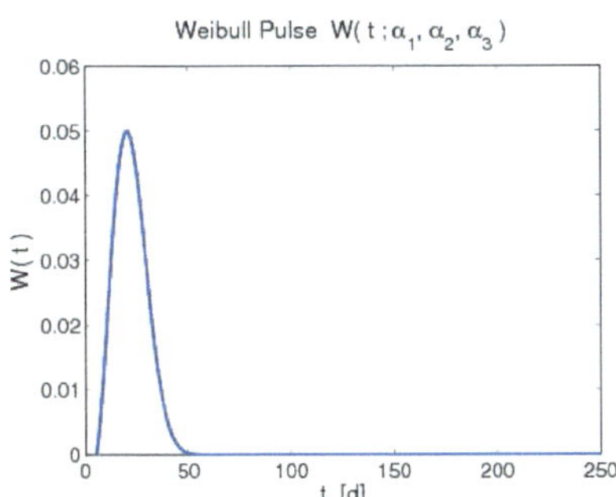

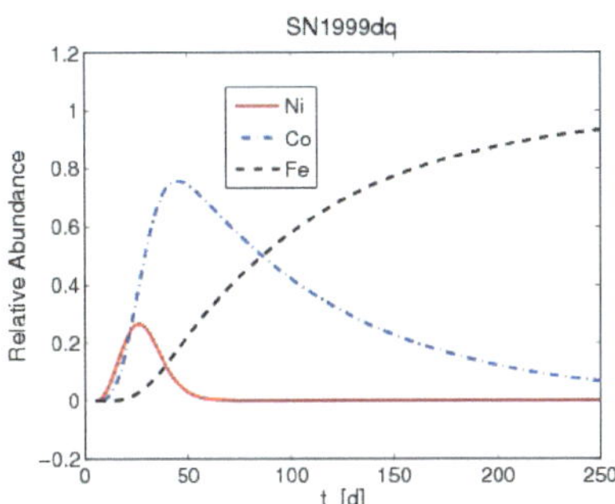

FIGURE 8.2.1. The Weibull pulse for SN1999dq and the relative abundances of Ni, Co and Fe that it generates.

and α_4 becomes a fourth parameter for the model. If $N_1(t)$, $N_2(t)$, and $N_3(t)$ represent the abundances of ^{56}Ni, ^{56}Co, and ^{56}Fe, respectively, then the ordinary differential equations (ODEs) for the ^{56}Ni deposition and subsequent decay processes can be written

$$\begin{aligned} \frac{dN_1}{dt} &= W(t;\alpha_1,\alpha_2,\alpha_3) - \frac{1}{8.764\,\alpha_4} N_1 \,, & N_1(\alpha_1) = 0 \,, \\ \frac{dN_2}{dt} &= \frac{1}{8.764\,\alpha_4} N_1 - \frac{1}{111.42\,\alpha_4} N_2 \,, & N_2(\alpha_1) = 0 \,, \\ \frac{dN_3}{dt} &= \frac{1}{111.42\,\alpha_4} N_2 \,, & N_3(\alpha_1) = 0 \,. \end{aligned} \tag{8.3}$$

Since the Weibull pulse is a probability density function, it has unit area, which means that it produces a unit amount of ^{56}Ni, so $N_1(t)$, $N_2(t)$ and $N_3(t)$ are relative abundances that are scaled up in the fit of the model to the observed data. Plots of the Weibull pulse and the relative abundances that it produces for the supernova SN1999dq are given in Figure 8.2.1.

It is luminosity generated by the nuclear decays, rather than relative abundance, that is actually observed. We can write our model for luminosity in the standard *VARPRO* notation by defining

$$\Phi_1(t;\boldsymbol{\alpha}) = \frac{1}{8.764\,\alpha_4} N_1(t) \,, \qquad \Phi_2(t;\boldsymbol{\alpha}) = \frac{1}{111.42\,\alpha_4} N_2(t) \,, \tag{8.4}$$

where Φ_1 and Φ_2 are the relative contributions to the total luminosity by the decays of ^{56}Ni and ^{56}Co, respectively. The total observed luminosity can then be written

$$L(t,\boldsymbol{\alpha}) = C_1\Phi_1(t;\boldsymbol{\alpha}) + C_2\Phi_2(t;\boldsymbol{\alpha}) \,, \tag{8.5}$$

where C_1 and C_2 are linear adjustable parameters that convert the relative luminosities to observed luminosities. So our model has 6 free parameters: 4 nonlinear parameters α_1, α_2, α_3, and α_4 that specify the properties of the central engine generating the gamma rays that power the luminosity, and 2 linear parameters C_1 and C_2 that specify how the gamma rays interact with the expanding atmosphere and/or the surrounding planetary nebula to generate the observed luminosity. It is easy to get initial estimates for α_1 and α_4 from the observed light curves. It is somewhat more difficult to get initial estimates of α_2 and α_3. Since we used *VARPRO* to do the fits, no initial estimates for C_1 and C_2 were needed.

8.3. Fitting the model to the B-passband observations

Substituting Eqs. (8.4) into (8.5) allows us to write the model in the form

$$L(t, \boldsymbol{\alpha}) = C_1 \frac{1}{8.764\,\alpha_4} N_1(t) + C_2 \frac{1}{111.42\,\alpha_4} N_2(t)\,, \tag{8.6}$$

where $N_1(t)$ and $N_2(t)$ depend on α_1, α_2, and α_3 and are obtained by solving the system of ODEs (8.3). It is possible to find closed form solutions for $N_1(t)$ and $N_2(t)$, but the formulas obtained are complicated, involving an integral of the Weibull pulse (8.1). The formulas for the partial derivatives $\partial\Phi_1/\partial\boldsymbol{\alpha}$ and $\partial\Phi_2/\partial\boldsymbol{\alpha}$ are even more complicated, so we instead compute $N_1(t)$ and $N_2(t)$ by numerically integrating the system (8.3) using the Runge-Kutta code DERKF [**20**].

8.3.1. Choice of units.

In the light curves in Figure 8.1.1, astronomical magnitudes are plotted versus Julian Days, but this is not the space in which the fits were computed.

Julian Day would be a very unwieldy time variable, so for each supernova, the zero point for the time t was reset to be a few days before the first observed magnitude. Row 5 in Tables 1 and 2 gives, for each of the 6 supernovae, the Julian Day chosen to define the zero point for t.

Astronomical magnitude would also be an unwieldy variable for fitting. The magnitude scale is logarithmic, with a difference of five magnitudes corresponding to a change by a factor of 100 in apparent brightness. The scale runs backward, with smaller magnitudes corresponding to brighter objects. To produce a more convenient variable for fitting, a reference magnitude B_{ref} was chosen for each supernova, and the measured magnitudes B_i were converted to *relative luminosities* L_i by the formula

$$L_i = 10^{-0.4\,(B_i - B_{ref})}\,. \tag{8.7}$$

The reference magnitudes chosen for each of the supernovae are given in row 6 of Tables 1 and 2. So the fits were calculated in the $\{t, L\}$ space, and the light curves obtained were transformed back to the $\{JD, B\}$ space, using the inverse relation

$$B(t) = B_{ref} - 2.5\log_{10}[\,L(t)\,]\,, \tag{8.8}$$

to get the light curves plotted in Figure 8.1.1.

8.3.2. The variational equations for the partial derivatives.

The model (8.6) is nonlinear in the four parameters $\boldsymbol{\alpha}$, so it was necessary for *VARPRO* to iterate in the 4-dimensional $\boldsymbol{\alpha}$-space. That required the 8 partial derivatives

$$\frac{\partial\Phi_1}{\partial\boldsymbol{\alpha}} = \frac{\partial}{\partial\boldsymbol{\alpha}}\left[\frac{1}{8.764\,\alpha_4} N_1(t)\right]\,, \qquad \frac{\partial\Phi_2}{\partial\boldsymbol{\alpha}} = \frac{\partial}{\partial\boldsymbol{\alpha}}\left[\frac{1}{111.42\,\alpha_4} N_2(t)\right]\,. \tag{8.9}$$

All attempts to use finite difference approximations to these derivatives met with complete failure. *VARPRO* was never able to improve on any given set of initial estimates when it was using numerical derivatives. The fact that noisy derivatives cause difficulty in optimization settings has been previously documented; see, e.g., [**11**].

Analytic derivatives can be obtained by noting that

$$\frac{\partial \Phi_1}{\partial \alpha_j} = \frac{1}{8.764\,\alpha_4}\frac{\partial N_1}{\partial \alpha_j}\,, \qquad j=1,2,3\,, \tag{8.10}$$

$$\frac{\partial \Phi_1}{\partial \alpha_4} = \frac{1}{8.764\,\alpha_4}\frac{\partial N_1}{\partial \alpha_4} - \frac{1}{8.764\,\alpha_4^2}N_1\,, \tag{8.11}$$

$$\frac{\partial \Phi_2}{\partial \alpha_j} = \frac{1}{111.42\,\alpha_4}\frac{\partial N_2}{\partial \alpha_j}\,, \qquad j=1,2,3\,, \tag{8.12}$$

$$\frac{\partial \Phi_2}{\partial \alpha_4} = \frac{1}{111.42\,\alpha_4}\frac{\partial N_2}{\partial \alpha_4} - \frac{1}{111.42\,\alpha_4^2}N_2\,. \tag{8.13}$$

Thus the problem is reduced to one of computing the 8 partial derivatives

$$\frac{\partial N_1}{\partial \boldsymbol{\alpha}} \quad \text{and} \quad \frac{\partial N_2}{\partial \boldsymbol{\alpha}}\,,$$

where N_1 and N_2 are defined by the ODEs (8.3). Since we did not want to solve that system in closed form, we instead used the identities

$$\frac{d}{dt}\left(\frac{\partial N_1}{\partial \alpha_j}\right) = \frac{\partial}{\partial \alpha_j}\left(\frac{dN_1}{dt}\right), \qquad j=1,2,3,4\,, \tag{8.14}$$

$$\frac{d}{dt}\left(\frac{\partial N_2}{\partial \alpha_j}\right) = \frac{\partial}{\partial \alpha_j}\left(\frac{dN_2}{dt}\right), \qquad j=1,2,3,4\,, \tag{8.15}$$

to extend the system to include 8 more ODEs defining the required partial derivatives. Substituting the derivative expressions from (8.3) into the two expressions above gives

$$\frac{d}{dt}\left(\frac{\partial N_1}{\partial \alpha_j}\right) = \frac{\partial}{\partial \alpha_j}W(t;\alpha_1,\alpha_2,\alpha_3) - \frac{1}{8.764\,\alpha_4}\left(\frac{\partial N_1}{\partial \alpha_j}\right), \quad j=1,2,3\,, \tag{8.16}$$

$$\frac{d}{dt}\left(\frac{\partial N_1}{\partial \alpha_4}\right) = \frac{1}{8.764\,\alpha_4^2}N_1 - \frac{1}{8.764\,\alpha_4}\left(\frac{\partial N_1}{\partial \alpha_4}\right), \tag{8.17}$$

$$\frac{d}{dt}\left(\frac{\partial N_2}{\partial \alpha_j}\right) = \frac{1}{8.764\,\alpha_4}\left(\frac{\partial N_1}{\partial \alpha_j}\right) - \frac{1}{111.42\,\alpha_4}\left(\frac{\partial N_2}{\partial \alpha_j}\right), \quad j=1,2,3\,, \tag{8.18}$$

$$\begin{aligned}\frac{d}{dt}\left(\frac{\partial N_2}{\partial \alpha_4}\right) &= -\frac{1}{8.764\,\alpha_4^2}N_1 + \frac{1}{111.42\,\alpha_4^2}N_2 \\ &\quad + \frac{1}{8.764\,\alpha_4}\left(\frac{\partial N_1}{\partial \alpha_4}\right) - \frac{1}{111.42\,\alpha_4}\left(\frac{\partial N_2}{\partial \alpha_4}\right),\end{aligned} \tag{8.19}$$

which, using the initial conditions

$$\frac{\partial N_1}{\partial \alpha_j} = 0\,, \quad \frac{\partial N_2}{\partial \alpha_j} = 0\,, \quad j=1,2,3,4\,, \tag{8.20}$$

can be integrated numerically along with the ODEs in (8.3). But to do so, it is necessary to find expressions for the 3 partial derivatives of $W(t;\alpha_1,\alpha_2,\alpha_3)$ defined by (8.1). We used Matlab's *Symbolic Math Toolbox* with the program

```
syms a1 a2 a3 t

w = a2/a3*(t-a1)^(a2-1)/a3^(a2-1) * exp(-((t-a1)/a3)^a2)

dw_da1 = diff(w,a1)
dw_da2 = diff(w,a2)
dw_da3 = diff(w,a3)

fortran(dw_da1)
fortran(dw_da2)
fortran(dw_da3)
```

to generate not only the symbolic derivatives, but also Fortran statements to be inserted into a Fortran subroutine for computing them numerically.

8.3.3. The fits. We fit the model (8.6) to the relative luminosity data for the 6 supernovae whose relative luminosity light curves are plotted in Figure 8.3.1. These particular 6 examples were chosen for this study because they have modern photometric observations, in several wavelength passbands, with observations beginning well before maximum luminosity, and with B-passband light curve data extending at least 150 days past that maximum. The shortest light curve (SN1999dq) contains 25 data points spanning 163.66 days, and the longest (SN2003du) contains 51 data points spanning 474.04 days.

In computing the fits, we weighted each observation inversely with the observed luminosity so that all of the observations contributed equally to determining the parameter estimates. This was absolutely necessary to assure that the long tails were fitted as well as the peaks. The good fits in the tails in Figure 8.1.1 demonstrate the effectiveness of this weighting strategy. Even very small misfits in the tails in Figure 8.3.1 would have transformed into large misfits in the tails in Figure 8.1.1.

We have already noted that *VARPRO* was unable to improve on our initial estimates when we used numerical approximations for the partial derivatives (8.9). Programming the analytic derivatives by the method outlined in Section 8.3.2 was an intricate and complicated task, but using them enabled *VARPRO* to always converge to a good fit, even if the initial estimates were poor. However, a surprisingly large number of iterations was required for convergence. If the initial estimates were not very close to the final converged values, then 20 000 - 40 000 iterations might be required. Apparently this simple model produces a very difficult fitting problem, even though we were iterating in a 4-dimensional space rather than the 6-dimensional space required by conventional nonlinear least squares programs that do not take advantage of the conditional linearity of C_1 and C_2.

We checked to see if any of the observed luminosity could have come from the fusion reactions in the Weibull pulse. We did this by appending an additional term

$$C_3\Phi_3(t;\boldsymbol{\alpha}) = C_3W(t;\alpha_1,\alpha_2,\alpha_3) \tag{8.21}$$

to the model and fitting it to several light curves. In every case the modified model failed to yield a significant improvement in the fit. The fits often gave physically meaningless estimates for C_3, e.g., $\hat{C}_3 = -15 \pm 124$ for SN1992bc, and always gave covariance matrices exhibiting extremely high correlations, e.g., $\pm 0.999\cdots$ between some of the parameters. This is a sure indication of a model with too many free

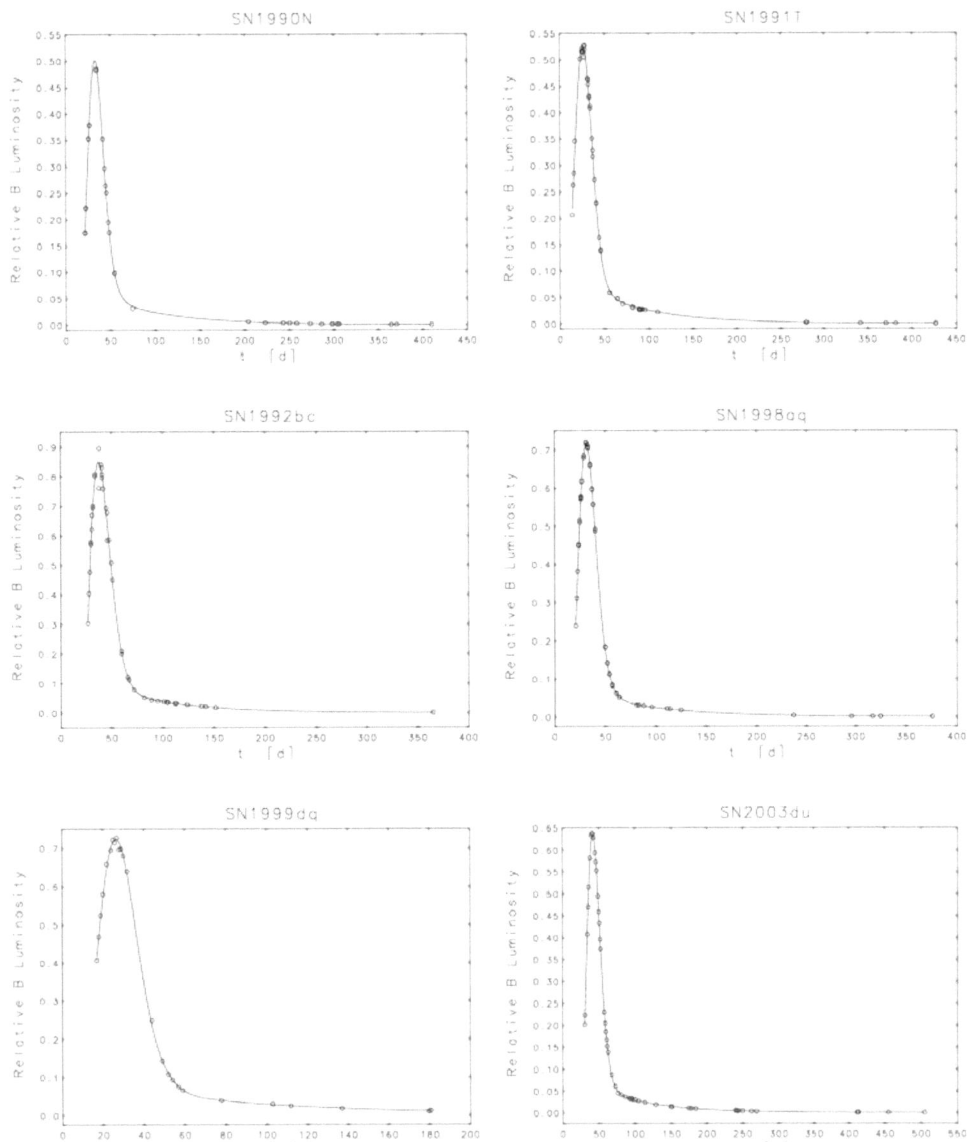

FIGURE 8.3.1. B-luminosity light curves for the 6 supernovae whose B-magnitude light curves are plotted in Figure 8.1.1. The observed luminosities here were computed by applying the transform (8.7) to the observed magnitudes plotted in Figure 8.1.1. The curves shown here were obtained by fitting the model (8.6) to these observed luminosities. The curves shown in Figure 8.1.1 were calculated by applying the inverse transform (8.8) to the curves shown here.

parameters. Thus it appears that all of the observed luminosity from a Type Ia supernova comes from the radioactive decay chain.

The parameter estimates and their uncertainties for the 6 supernovae are given, together with some other pertinent data, in Tables 1 and 2. The key to these tables follows:

row 1: Source for the measured magnitudes.
row 2: Name of the parent galaxy.
row 3: Galactocentric velocity of recession implied by measured redshift of the galaxy. These data, together with those in row 4, were taken from the NASA/IPAC Extragalactic Database (NED) [**10**] which is operated by JPL under contract with NASA.
row 4: Galactocentric distance to the galaxy estimated from the Hubble law $V_r = H_0 D$ using $H_0 = (73.0 \pm 5.0)$ km/s/Mpc, where the units are kilometers per second per 10^6 parsecs.
row 5: Julian Day chosen for zero point in time.
row 6: Reference magnitude used in Eqs. (8.7) and (8.8) for transforming between magnitudes and relative luminosities.
row 7: Estimate of Weibull location parameter (gives time of initial eruption of Weibull pulse).
row 8: Estimate of Weibull shape parameter.
row 9: Estimate of Weibull scale parameter.
row 10: Estimate of acceleration parameter speeding up Ni and Co decay rates.
row 11: Estimate of linear parameter which determines how supernova's atmosphere transforms energy from Ni decays into observed luminosity.
row 12: Estimate of linear parameter which determines how supernova's atmosphere transforms energy from the Co decays into observed luminosity.
row 13: Percentage of total variance explained by fit. R^2 is from Eq. (8.22).
row 14: Time of maximum luminosity.
row 15: Julian Day of maximum luminosity.
row 16: B magnitude at maximum luminosity.

Since the fits were nonlinear, the uncertainties for the parameter estimates were derived from an estimate of the covariance matrix based on a local quadratic approximation to the sum-of-squared-residuals (SSR) surface at the point where the SSR was minimized. Therefore those uncertainties should be treated with caution. The value R^2 in row 13 of the table is the coefficient of determination,

$$R^2 = 1 - \frac{SSR}{CTSS} , \tag{8.22}$$

where SSR is the weighted residual sum of squares and $CTSS$ is the corrected total sum of squares. The latter quantity is computed by

$$CTSS = \sum_{i=1}^{N} w_i^2 (L_i - \bar{L})^2 , \tag{8.23}$$

where the L_i , $i = 1, \ldots, N$, are the observed relative luminosities, $\bar{L}$ is the weighted average luminosity, and the $w_i = 1/L_i$ are the weights used in the fits. Thus R^2 is a normalized residual sum of squares which will always have a value between 0 and 1. We express it as a percentage, indicating the percentage of the total variance.

TABLE 1. Results for SN1990N, SN1991T, and SN1992bc for the B passband.

	SN	1990N	1991T	1992bc
1	Reference	**[13]**	**[13]**	[8]
2	Galaxy	NGC 4639	NGC 4527	ESO 300-9
3	V_r [km/s]	974 ± 6	1654 ± 3	5881 ± 600
4	D [Mpc]	13.3 ± 0.9	22.7 ± 1.6	80.6 ± 10.0
5	JD ($t = 0$)	2 448 050.0	2 448 350.0	2 448 875.0
6	B_{ref}	12.0	11.0	15.0
7	$\hat{\alpha}_1$	13.7 ± 1.6	2.1 ± 2.8	$22.08 \pm .40$
8	$\hat{\alpha}_2$	$2.32 \pm .25$	$2.66 \pm .34$	$1.730 \pm .052$
9	$\hat{\alpha}_3$	17.5 ± 1.6	22.0 ± 2.9	$15.56 \pm .43$
10	$\hat{\alpha}_4$	0.676 078 5 $\pm$ .000 006 8	0.662 474 7 $\pm$ .000 003 0	0.618 920 3 $\pm$ .000 004 3
11	$\hat{C}_1$	$10.63 \pm .22$	$12.02 \pm .16$	$19.21 \pm .17$
12	$\hat{C}_2$	$4.24 \pm .10$	$5.004 \pm .080$	$6.104 \pm .073$
13	R^2	99.57 %	99.67 %	99.88 %
14	$t_{\max}$ [d]	32.83	25.91	37.36
15	$JD_{\max}$	2 448 082.83	2 448 375.91	2 448 912.36
16	$B_{\max}$	12.75	11.70	15.18

8.4. Extending the model to U-, V-, R- and I-passband observations

The B passband light curves in Figures 8.1.1 and 8.3.1 are quite extraordinary. But the model is not so successful when it is fit to observations in other wavelength passbands. Astronomers often measure apparent brightness in 5 different passbands, U, B, V, R, and I which represent ultraviolet, blue, visual, red, and infrared, respectively. The U, B, V, R, and I light curves for SN2003du are shown in Figure 8.4.1. The departures of the measurements from the simple model used to fit the B light curve (upper right hand plot) are apparent in the V, R, and I light curves.

8.4.1. A light echo model for the I-passband observations. The most striking departures are in the I light curve, where it appears that a secondary peak occurs about 30 days after the maximum luminosity. This suggests that it may have been caused by a light echo from the back side of a pre-existing shell of dust surrounding the supernova. White dwarfs are often surrounded by planetary nebula which were presumably formed when the parent star ejected its outer layers before

TABLE 2. Results for SN1998aq, SN1999dq, and SN2003du for the B passband.

	SN	1998aq	1999dq	2003du
1	Reference	[17]	[9]	[21]
2	Galaxy	NGC 3982	NGC 976	UGC 9391
3	V_r [km/s]	1187 ± 7	4370 ± 6	2055 ± 7
4	D [Mpc]	16.3 ± 1.1	59.9 ± 4.2	28.1 ± 2
5	JD ($t = 0$)	2 450 900.0	2 451 410.0	2 452 725.0
6	B_{ref}	12.0	14.5	13.0
7	$\hat{\alpha}_1$	$14.72 \pm .40$	5.4 ± 2.6	$25.07 \pm .60$
8	$\hat{\alpha}_2$	$2.085 \pm .058$	$2.37 \pm .29$	$1.966 \pm .095$
9	$\hat{\alpha}_3$	$15.33 \pm .42$	19.3 ± 2.6	$15.40 \pm .66$
10	$\hat{\alpha}_4$	0.655 925 3 $\pm$ .000 003 1	0.729 83 $\pm$ .000 11	0.662 263 8 $\pm$ .00000 11
11	$\hat{C}_1$	$14.752 \pm .090$	$16.76 \pm .37$	$13.54 \pm .14$
12	$\hat{C}_2$	$4.355 \pm .043$	$5.59 \pm .18$	$4.395 \pm .048$
13	R^2	99.93 %	99.87 %	99.79 %
14	$t_{\max}$ [d]	31.19	26.45	41.35
15	$JD_{\max}$	2 450 931.19	2 451 436.45	2 452 766.35
16	$B_{\max}$	12.36	14.85	13.49

collapsing into a white dwarf. If we make the crude assumption that the echo comes almost entirely from material very close to our line of sight to the star, then we can approximate the observed relative luminosity with a model of the form

$$L(t;\boldsymbol{\beta}) = D_1\Psi_1(t) + D_2\Psi_2(t) + D_3\Psi_3(t;\boldsymbol{\beta}) + D_4\Psi_4(t;\boldsymbol{\beta}) \,, \tag{8.24}$$

where the D_i are linear parameters to be determined by fitting, and the functions $\Psi_i(t;\boldsymbol{\beta})$ are defined by

$$\Psi_1(t) = \frac{1}{8.764\,\hat{\alpha}_4}\hat{N}_1(t) \,, \tag{8.25}$$

$$\Psi_2(t) = \frac{1}{111.42\,\hat{\alpha}_4}\hat{N}_2(t) \,, \tag{8.26}$$

$$\Psi_3(t;\boldsymbol{\beta}) = \begin{cases} 0 \,, & t \le \hat{\alpha}_1 + \beta_1 \\ \left[\frac{1}{8.764\,\hat{\alpha}_4}\hat{N}_1(t-\beta_1)\right] Q(t;\beta_2,\beta_3) \,, & t > \hat{\alpha}_1 + \beta_1 \end{cases} \,, \tag{8.27}$$

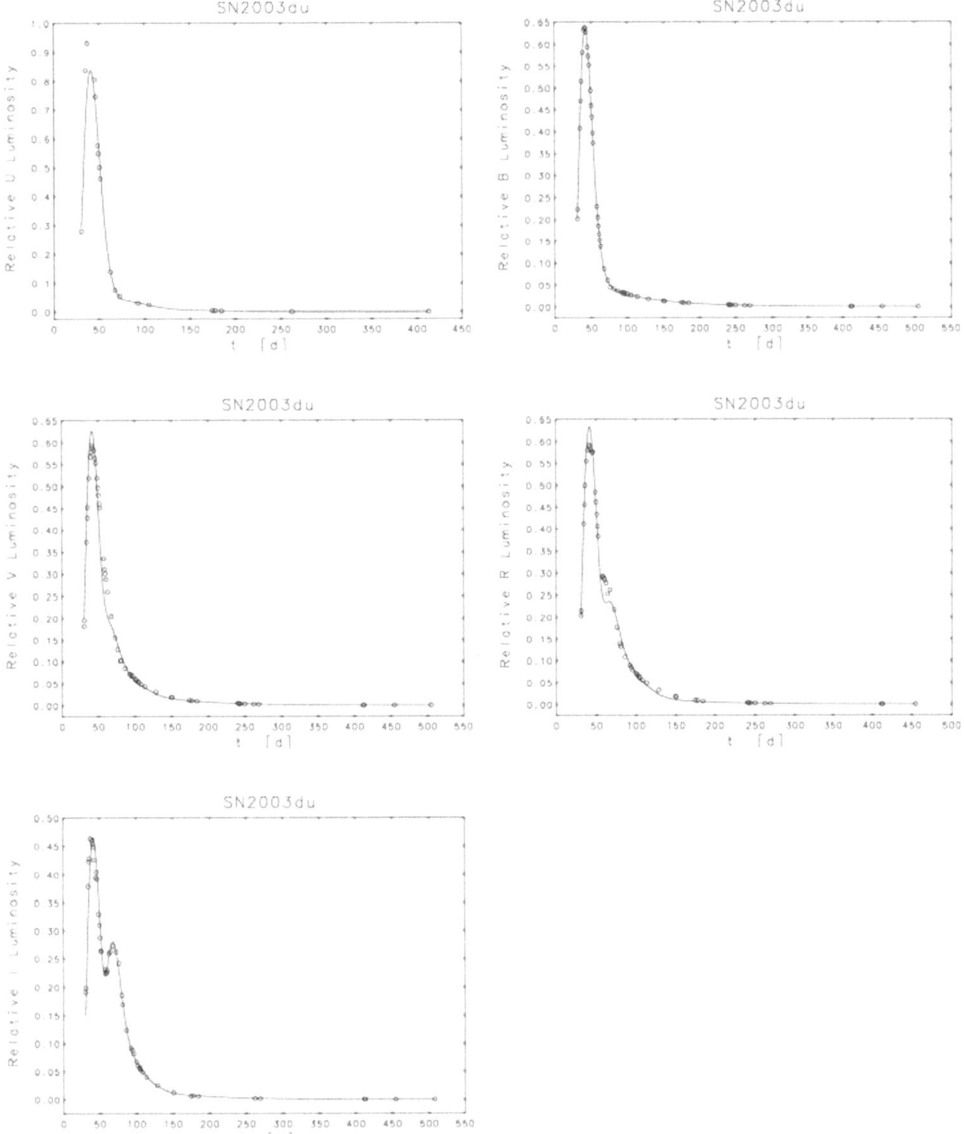

FIGURE 8.4.1. UBVRI light curves, in relative luminosity space, for SN2003du. The discrete points represent the measurements and the smooth curves are model fits. The fit for the B passband is the same as the one in Figure 8.3.1. The other fits are for the model described in section 8.4.

$$\Psi_4(t;\boldsymbol{\beta}) = \begin{cases} 0\,, & t \leq \hat{\alpha}_1 + \beta_1 \\ \left[\frac{1}{111.42\,\hat{\alpha}_4}\hat{N}_2(t-\beta_1)\right] Q(t;\beta_2,\beta_3)\,, & t > \hat{\alpha}_1 + \beta_1 \end{cases} . \tag{8.28}$$

In Eqs. (8.25) and (8.26) the $\hat{\alpha}_4$ is not a parameter to be determined by fitting, but rather the estimate of α_4 that was obtained in fitting the B light curve. Similarly, the functions $\hat{N}_1(t)$ and $\hat{N}_2(t)$ are the estimates of $N_1(t)$ and $N_2(t)$ that were obtained in the B-curve fit. They depend only on the estimates $\hat{\boldsymbol{\alpha}}$ and do not involve any free parameters to be determined by the fit. The functions $\Psi_3(t;\boldsymbol{\beta})$ and $\Psi_4(t;\boldsymbol{\beta})$ are essentially lagged versions of $\hat{N}_1(t)$ and $\hat{N}_2(t)$, with the nonlinear free parameter β_1 being the lag. They are multiplied by a quenching function

$$Q(t;\beta_2,\beta_3) = \frac{1}{2}\mathrm{erfc}[\beta_3(t-\beta_2)], \tag{8.29}$$

which is included to model the vaporization of the reflecting dust as the shell surrounding the supernova is heated to ever higher temperatures. When all of the dust is vaporized, the shell will cease to reflect. We used the complementary error function

$$\mathrm{erfc}(z) = 1 - \mathrm{erf}(z) = 1 - \frac{2}{\sqrt{\pi}}\int_{-\infty}^{z} \exp\left(-u^2\right) du \tag{8.30}$$

to model the quenching because it has the appropriate general shape, and the two free parameters β_2 and β_3 give it the flexibility to model a wide range of possible shapes and extents. The quenching function for SN2003du is shown in Figure 8.4.2.

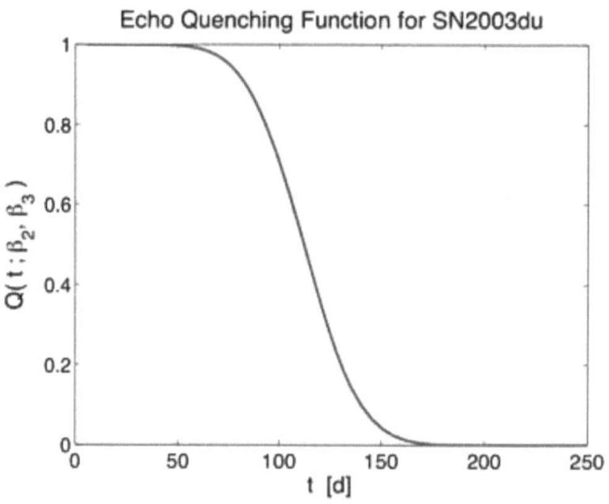

FIGURE 8.4.2. The light echo quenching function for SN2003du

The model (8.24) has 4 linear and 3 nonlinear parameters, which again makes it a candidate for *VARPRO*. It was stable enough to permit the use of numerical derivatives. The fitted I-luminosity light curve for SN2003du is shown in the lower left panel in Figure 8.4.1, and the corresponding parameter estimates are given in column 4 of Table 3. The fit is good, but not as close as the B passband fit. This deterioration in quality is also reflected in the decrease in the R^2 value. The I-magnitude light curve is shown in the lower left panel of Figure 8.4.3. It too is not nearly so close as the B-magnitude light curve in the upper right panel. The decline in the quality of the fit is probably due to the use of a very crude model for the light echo. A proper model would take the spherical geometry of the shell into account, and the light observed at any give time would be a mixture of many different lags. If our light curve model is correct, then the estimate $\hat{\beta}_1 = 27.86$ implies that the inner radius of the reflecting shell is 13.93 light days.

8.4.2. Extending the light echo model to the V, R, and I observations. Since the I-light curve gave by far the best representation of the light echo, we decided to keep the estimates $\hat{\beta}_1$, $\hat{\beta}_2$, and $\hat{\beta}_3$ fixed in fitting the model to the R, V,

TABLE 3. The parameter estimates for the B, I, R, V, and U light curve fits for SN2003du. The ordering of the columns reflects the order in which the fits were done. A ← entry means that the value was not a free parameter but rather an estimate obtained in a preceding fit. A blank entry means that neither the corresponding parameter not its estimate was used in the fit. Row 14 gives the percentage of the total variance explained by the fit, and Row 15 gives the total number of free parameters in the fit.

	Color	B	I	R	V	U
1	$\hat{\alpha}_1$	25.07 ± .60	←	←	←	←
2	$\hat{\alpha}_2$	1.966 ± .095	←	←	←	←
3	$\hat{\alpha}_3$	15.40 ± .66	←	←	←	←
4	$\hat{\alpha}_4$	0.662 263 8 ± .000 001 1	←	←	←	←
5	$\hat{C}_1$	13.54 ± .14				
6	$\hat{C}_2$	4.395 ± .048				
7	$\hat{\beta}_1$		27.86 ± .90	←	←	←
8	$\hat{\beta}_2$		112 ± 34	←	←	←
9	$\hat{\beta}_3$		0.032 ± .029	←	←	←
10	$\hat{D}_1$		9.95 ± .42	13.72 ± .57	13.34 ± .38	18.37 ± 0.94
11	$\hat{D}_2$		3.34 ± .21	2.81 ± .14	4.75 ± .15	1.54 ± .11
12	$\hat{D}_3$		4.38 ± .58	3.07 ± .43	1.80 ± .25	-0.12 ± .19
13	$\hat{D}_4$		6.2 ± 7.1	7.52 ± .66	3.97 ± .41	2.59 ± .48
14	R^2	99.79 %	97.32 %	96.94 %	98.55 %	97.95 %
15	N_{fp}	6	7	4	4	4

and U light curves. This means that each of those fits was a linear least squares problem with only 4 free parameters. The results, shown in Figures 8.4.1 and 8.4.3, are reasonably good fits. It is not obvious why the light echo would appear in the U but not in the B observations. Perhaps the departures from regularity in the U light curve are due to limb brightening rather than a light echo.

Row 15 of Table 3 gives the number of free parameters in each fit. It is remarkable that we were able to get good fits to five different light curves using an average of only 5 free parameters per fit.

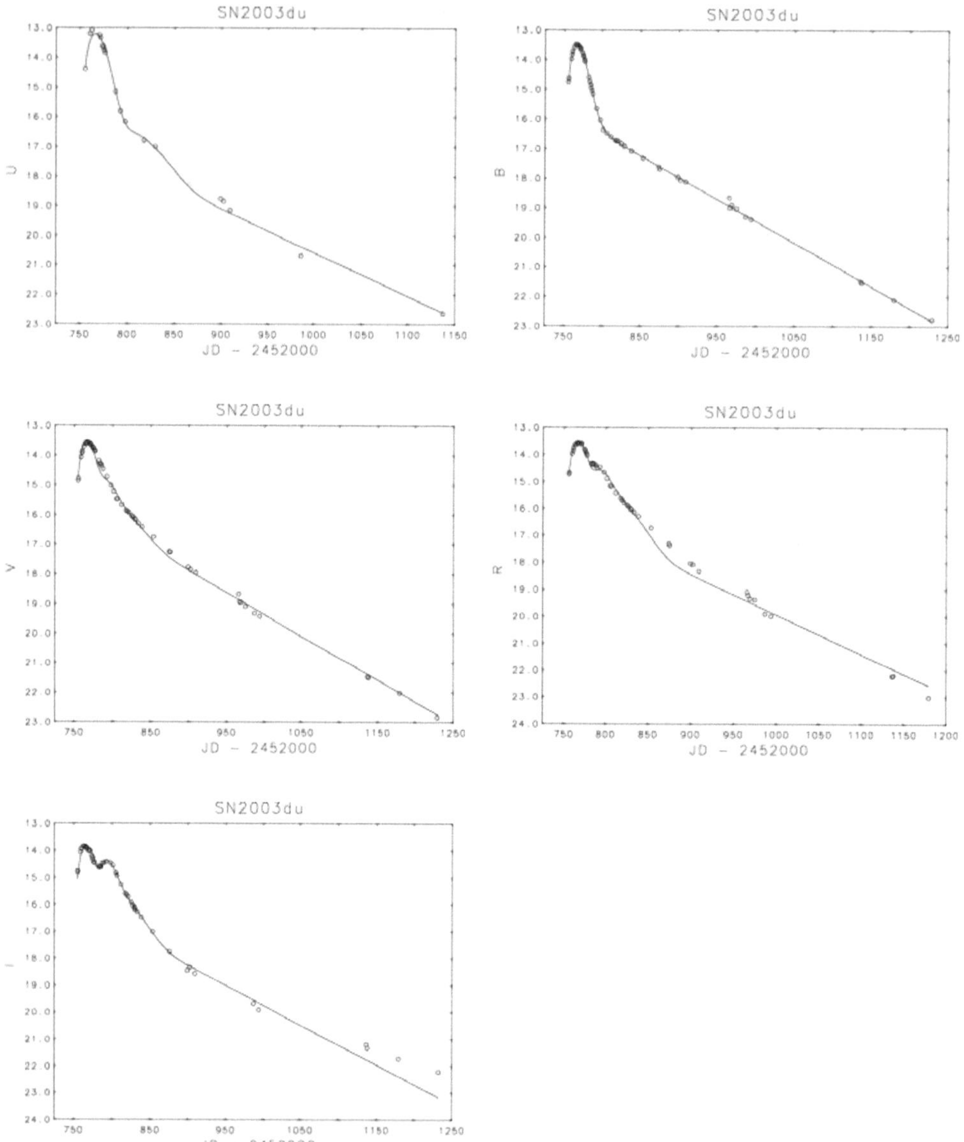

FIGURE 8.4.3. UBVRI magnitude light curves for SN2003du, calculated by applying the inverse transform (8.8) to the relative luminosity curves in Figure 8.4.1.

8.5. Conclusion

We have proposed a model for Type Ia supernova light curves and validated it using observed luminosity data from 6 supernovae. Our results support the hypothesis that decay rates for Ni and Co are proportional to, but not exactly equal to, their terrestrial values, perhaps because higher densities accelerate the two decays by the same factor.

Our model was fit using the *VARPRO* algorithm. *VARPRO*'s reduction of the parameter space is essential for the efficiency and even the feasibility of studying such models.

In future work we will examine differences in transmission curves as a source of error in comparing fits from one supernovae to another, and we will compare the UVRI fits for these supernovae. We will also investigate the idea of fitting multiple passbands simultaneously; see, for example, [**4, 7, 14**].

Acknowledgments

The authors would like to thank Drs. David Gilsinn, Stefan Leigh, and Daniel Lozier for their advice and encouragement. The light curve data were found using two very helpful websites [**10, 15**].

Disclaimer

Certain commercial software products are identified in this paper in order to adequately specify the computational procedures. Such identification does not imply recommendation or endorsement by the National Institute of Standards and Technology nor does it imply that the software products are necessarily the best available for the purpose.

Bibliography

1. R. Barbon, E. Cappellaro, and M. Turatto, *Radioactive decays and supernova light curves*, Astronomy and Astrophysics **135** (1984), 27–31.
2. D. Branch and G. A. Tammann, *Type IA supernovae as standard candles*, Annual Reviews of Astronomy and Astrophysics **30** (1992), 359–389.
3. S. A. Colgate, A. G. Petschek, and J. T. Kriese, *The luminosity of type I supernovae*, Astrophysical Journal Letters **237** (1980), L81–L85.
4. D. Gay and L. Kaufman, *Tradeoffs in algorithms for separable and block separable nonlinear least squares*, IMACS '91, Proceedings of the 13th World Congress on Computational and Applied Mathematics (Dublin) (R. Vichnevetsky and J. J. H. Miller, eds.), Criterion Press, 1991, pp. 157–158.
5. G. H. Golub and V. Pereyra, *The differentiation of pseudo-inverses and nonlinear least squares problems whose variables separate*, Tech. report, Stanford University, Department of Computer Science, 1972.
6. G. H. Golub and V. Pereyra, *The differentiation of pseudoinverses and nonlinear least squares problems whose variables separate*, SIAM Journal on Numerical Analysis **10** (1973), 413–432.
7. G. H. Golub and R. J. LeVeque, *Extensions and uses of the variable projection algorithm for solving nonlinear least squares problems*, Proceedings of the 1979 Army Numerical Analysis and Computers Conference, 1979, pp. 1–12.
8. M. Hamuy, M. M. Phillips, N. B. Suntzeff, R. A. Schommer, J. Maza, A. R. Antezan, M. Wischnjewsky, G. Valladares, C. Muena, L. E. Gonzales, R. Aviles, L. A. Wells, R. C. Smith, M. Navarrete, R. Covarrubias, G. M. Williger, A. R. Walker, A. C. Layden, J. H. Elias, J. A. Baldwin, M. Hernandez, H. Tirado, P. Ugarte, R. Elston, N. Saavedra, F. Barrientos, E. Costa, P. Lira, M. T. Ruiz, C. Anguita, X. Gomez, P. Ortiz, M. della Valle, J. Danziger, J. Storm, Y.-C. Kim, C. Bailyn, E. P. Rubenstein, D. Tucker, S. Cersosimo, R. A. Mendez, L. Siciliano, W. Sherry, B. Chaboyer, R. A. Koopmann, D. Geisler, A. Sarajedini, A. Dey, N. Tyson, R. M. Rich, R. Gal, R. Lamontagne, N. Caldwell, P. Guhathakurta, A. C. Phillips, P. Szkody, C. Prosser, L. C. Ho, R. McMahan, G. Baggley, K.-P. Cheng, R. Havlen, K. Wakamatsu, K. Janes, M. Malkan, F. Baganoff, P. Seitzer, M. Shara, C. Sturch, J. Hesser, A. N. P. Hartig, J. Hughes, D. Welch, T. B. Williams, H. Ferguson, P. J. Francis, L. French, M. Bolte, J. Roth, S. Odewahn, S. Howell, and W. Krzeminski, *BVRI light curves for 29 type IA supernovae*, Astronomical Journal **112** (1996), 2408–2437.
9. S. Jha, R. P. Kirshner, P. Challis, P. M. Garnavich, T. Matheson, A. M. Soderberg, G. J. M. Graves, M. Hicken, J. F. Alves, H. G. Arce, Z. Balog, P. Barmby, E. J. Barton, P. Berlind, A. E. Bragg, C. Briceño, W. R. Brown, J. H. Buckley, N. Caldwell, M. L. Calkins, B. J. Carter, K. D. Concannon, R. H. Donnelly, K. A. Eriksen, D. G. Fabricant, E. E. Falco, F. Fiore, M. R. Garcia, M. Gómez, N. A. Grogin, T. Groner, P. J. Groot, K. E. Haisch, Jr., L. Hartmann, C. W. Hergenrother, M. J. Holman, J. P. Huchra, R. Jayawardhana, D. Jerius, S. J. Kannappan, D.-W. Kim, J. T. Kleyna, C. S. Kochanek, D. M. Koranyi, M. Krockenberger, C. J. Lada, K. L. Luhman, J. X. Luu, L. M. Macri, J. A. Mader, A. Mahdavi, M. Marengo, B. G. Marsden, B. A. McLeod, B. R. McNamara, S. T. Megeath, D. Moraru, A. E. Mossman, A. A. Muench, J. A. Muñoz, J. Muzerolle, O. Naranjo, K. Nelson-Patel, M. A. Pahre, B. M. Patten, J. Peters, W. Peters, J. C. Raymond, K. Rines, R. E. Schild, G. J. Sobczak, T. B. Spahr, J. R. Stauffer, R. P. Stefanik, A. H. Szentgyorgyi, E. V. Tollestrup, P. Väisänen, A. Vikhlinin, Z. Wang, S. P. Willner, S. J. Wolk, J. M. Zajac, P. Zhao, and K. Z. Stanek, *UBVRI light curves of 44 type Ia supernovae*, Astronomical Journal **131** (2006), 527–554.
10. J. P. Laboratory, *NASA/IPAC extragalactic database (NED)*, `http://nedwww.ipac.caltech.edu/`, accessed June 2009.

11. R. Leidenberger and K. Urban, *Automatic differentiation for the optimization of a ship propulsion and steering system*, Tech. report, University of Ulm, Germany, 2008.
12. M. Leventhal and S. L. McCall, *Hypothesis for the type I supernova light curve*, Nature **255** (1975), 690–692.
13. P. Lira, N. B. Suntzeff, M. M. Phillips, M. Hamuy, J. Maza, R. A. Schommer, R. C. Smith, L. A. Wells, R. Avilés, J. A. Baldwin, J. H. Elias, L. González, A. Layden, M. Navarrete, P. Ugarte, A. R. Walker, G. M. Williger, F. K. Baganoff, A. P. S. Crotts, R. M. Rich, N. D. Tyson, A. Dey, P. Guhathakurta, J. Hibbard, Y.-C. Kim, D. M. Rehner, E. Siciliano, J. Roth, P. Seitzer, and T. B. Williams, *Optical light curves of the Type IA supernovae SN 1990N and 1991T*, Astronomical Journal **115** (1998), 234–246.
14. K. M. Mullen and I. H. M. van Stokkum, *The variable projection algorithm in time-resolved spectroscopy, microscopy and mass spectrometry applications*, Numerical Algorithms **51** (2009), 1017–1398.
15. N. Pavlyuk and the SAI Supernovae Research Group, *SAI supernova light curve online*, `http://virtual.sai.msu.ru/~pavlyuk/snlcurve/`, accessed June 2009.
16. M. M. Phillips, *The absolute magnitudes of Type IA supernovae*, Astrophysical Journal Letters **413** (1993), L105–L108.
17. A. G. Riess, W. Li, P. B. Stetson, A. V. Filippenko, S. Jha, R. P. Kirshner, P. M. Challis, P. M. Garnavich, and R. Chornock, *Cepheid calibrations from the Hubble space telescope of the luminosity of two recent type Ia supernovae and a redetermination of the Hubble constant*, Astrophysical Journal **627** (2005), 579–607.
18. B. W. Rust, *Use of Supernovae Light Curves for Testing the Expansion Hypothesis and Other Cosmological Relations*, Univ. of Illinois, ORNL-4953, Ph.D. thesis, Oak Ridge National Lab., TN., December 1974.
19. B. W. Rust, M. Leventhal, and S. L. McCall, *Evidence for a radioactive decay hypothesis for supernova luminosity*, Nature **262** (1976), 118–120.
20. L. F. Shampine and H. A. Watts, *DEPAC – design of a user oriented package of ODE solvers*, Tech. Report SAND79-2374, Sandia National Laboratories, Albuquerque, NM, September 1980.
21. V. Stanishev, A. Goobar, S. Benetti, R. Kotak, G. Pignata, H. Navasardyan, P. Mazzali, R. Amanullah, G. Garavini, S. Nobili, Y. Qiu, N. Elias-Rosa, P. Ruiz-Lapuente, J. Mendez, P. Meikle, F. Patat, A. Pastorello, G. Altavilla, M. Gustafsson, A. Harutyunyan, T. Iijima, P. Jakobsson, M. V. Kichizhieva, P. Lundqvist, S. Mattila, J. Melinder, E. P. Pavlenko, N. N. Pavlyuk, J. Sollerman, D. Y. Tsvetkov, M. Turatto, and W. Hillebrandt, *SN 2003du: 480 days in the life of a normal type Ia supernova*, Astronomy and Astrophysics **469** (2007), 645–661.
22. J. R. van Hise, *Light-decay curve of the supernova in IC 4182*, Astrophysical Journal **192** (1974), 657–659.

CHAPTER 9

Accurate calculations of the high-frequency impedance matrix for VLSI interconnects and inductors above a multi-layer substrate: A VARPRO success story

Navin Srivastava
Mentor Graphics Corporation
Wilsonville, OR, USA
navin_srivastava@mentor.com

Roberto Suaya
Mentor Graphics Corporation
Grenoble, France
roberto_suaya@mentor.com

Victor Pereyra
CSRC
San Diego State University, CA
vpereyra@yahoo.com

Kaustav Banerjee
Department of Electrical and Computer Engineering
University of California. Santa Barbara, CA 93106, USA
kaustav@ece.ucsb.edu

Victor Pereyra & Godela Scherer (Eds)

Abstract. Impedance characterization of Interconnects and intentional Inductors in the broad frequency domain that extends from near DC to 100's of GHz in integrated circuits is full of unachieved goals. Existing computational methods are near the end of their usefulness, since accurate characterization of the Impedance matrix $Z(\omega)$ at high-frequencies with existing methods can only be applied to small structures. We present a computationally inexpensive approach that extends the ability for accurate characterization to problem sizes that are between one and two orders of magnitude larger, opening the door to the validation of high frequency wireless circuits in terms of real time simulation, rather than the less desirable alter-native of validation by manufacturing and testing. The starting point in our approach is an integral representation of the Green's function for the magnetic vector potential in classical Electromagnetic theory. The intermediate computation involves a least-square fit to refection coefficients in terms of linear combinations of complex exponentials, so as to render integrable the coordinate space representation of the Green's function. The end result is an analytical description of derivative quantities, including the matrix elements of the serial Impedance matrix of the interconnect configuration, for all frequencies of interest. We study the problem in two and three dimensions. Among the alternative least square fits, we found that those utilizing VARPRO in the complex domain – an extension of VARPRO created specifically to attack this problem – give the best results. The levels of accuracy (errors less than 3%) and efficiency (better than an order of magnitude lower computational cost than existing methods) have a major impact on nano-electronic circuit design.

Keywords: High-frequency impedance matrix; VLSI interconnects; VLSI inductors; multi-layer substrate; high-frequency wireless circuits; real time simulation; complex exponentials

9.1. Introduction

Very large-scale integrated circuit (VLSI) chips form a complex network of wires (typically Copper) laid out over several metal layers (10 to 14 layers in modern technologies), stacked to a thickness of about 5 to 10 micrometers (μm). The wires lie above the transistors which are themselves implanted on top of a substrate (Silicon) several hundred μm thick. Billions of these wires, called interconnects, provide connectivity between the transistors and ensure circuit functionality at all levels. The lower metal layers are occupied by wires with small cross-sectional area and are used for short connections spanning μm distances between nearby transistors - called "local" interconnects. The delay of these wires is dominated by resistance, R, and capacitance, C (forming R-C diffusion networks) - while dynamic electromagnetic effects are negligible. The top metal layers are used to connect distant components on the chip with "global" interconnects, often spanning mm distances. Since they incur comparatively large delays, these interconnects have larger cross-sections to ensure lower resistance. However, the appreciable inductance (L) makes the impedance (Z) a function of frequency (ω): $Z = R + j\omega L$, where both R and L are functions of frequency beyond a certain threshold. Hence, as the frequency grows, electromagnetic effects become important for computing the propagation delay and noise of these interconnects, and a single complex scalar for each wire segment must be replaced by a complex impedance matrix for an entire chip.

Unprecedented levels of integration in semiconductor technology have enabled complex digital circuits containing billions of transistors to co-exist on the same chip with sensitive analog circuits operating at mm-wavelengths [**2**]. In the early days of integrated circuit (IC) technology, the physics of interconnects could be ignored, since their influence on circuit timing (delay) was negligible compared to transistor delay (which itself was orders of magnitude larger than that of today's transistors). Coupling noise due to signals on other wires was also a negligible concern. Since then, while transistor delay has shrunk due to the benefits of progressively decreasing feature sizes (from several micrometers to a few 10s of nanometers), interconnects have come to play a much more significant role in determining overall circuit timing and functionality **[15]**. Today, with 20 nm feature sizes on a chip, the propagation time of signals over 1 mm distances is significantly slower than the transition time of a logical switch **[2]**, while noise propagation among nearby wires can lead to chip failures. As a result, the physics of signal propagation on interconnects in a complex semiconductor chip has become a subject of deep concern. The most important application domains sensitive to signal propagation on interconnects are those of inductor design with applications in radio receivers and communications chips, as well as timing-critical signal lines in high-performance digital microprocessors. In the frequency domain, the region of interest extends from near zero up to hundreds of GHz for both analog wireless and high-performance microprocessor design.[1]

The physics of signal propagation on wires falls within the combined domain of electromagnetism and the constitutive equations of electron propagation on metals (Ohm's law in the frequency domain) and dielectrics (wave propagation in lossy media). The fundamental equations are well understood. The complexity and associated computational cost, on the other hand, is prohibitively large for chip-level solutions due to three underlying reasons: (i) the large number of wires and inductors, (ii) the multi-layered nature of both the dielectric media and the substrate profile where these phenomena take place, and (iii) the interval of wavelengths where these phenomena are to be accounted for includes (at the lower end) wavelengths of the same order as the longitudinal dimensions of the wires. This is the domain in which most approximations (short or long wave) fail. In this frequency domain, several physical phenomena are manifest - the conductor skin effect, proximity effects between conductors, and substrate eddy current effects. Together they impact the current distribution and, through Ohm's law, the macroscopic Impedance and Admittance matrices that are used to represent the interconnect.

In the regime where signal propagation wavelengths are larger than chip dimensions, electromagnetic effects have no measurable consequences and simple treatments of interconnect as distributed resistance-capacitance (R-C) networks suffice. There is a body of work **[11]**, **[22]**, **[18]**, that discusses appropriate numerical methods for wavelengths between $1 - 10cm$ where currents are uniform inside the wires. For wavelengths between $1 - 10mm$, currents cease to be uniform due to a limited penetration of the magnetic field $\vec{B}$ inside the conductors. Under these conditions, the computational expense of these numerical methods increases rapidly with decreasing wavelength, and new approaches have been developed **[9]**, eventually leading to efficient analytical methods **[21]**. As the wavelengths become smaller than

[1] The maximum frequency of signal propagation on interconnects is much larger than the more familiar "clock" frequency. It is inversely proportional to the rise time of the signal driven by the fastest transistor feeding the interconnect.

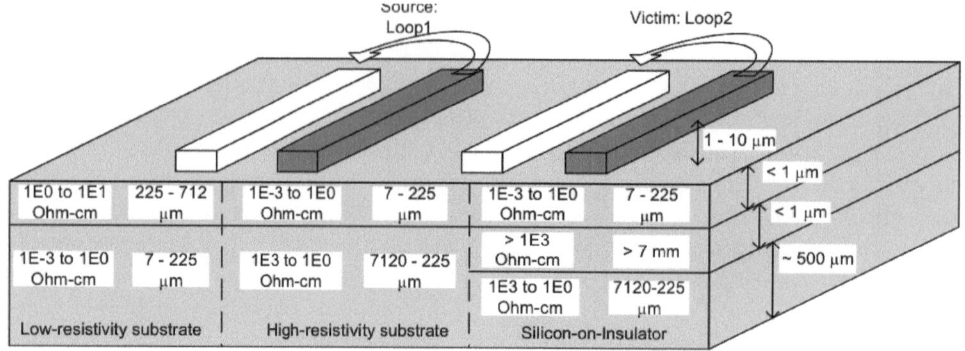

FIGURE 9.1.1. Schematic showing interconnect current loops over a layered substrate. Three typical substrate profiles in VLSI are shown with the range of resistivity ($\rho = \frac{1}{\sigma}$ Ohm-cm) values, and the corresponding skin depth - the depth of penetration of electromagnetic fields in the medium, given by $\delta = \sqrt{2/(\omega\mu\sigma)}$ - at 50 GHz.

$2mm$, the Silicon substrate media presents a path for current circulation that cannot be ignored, further exacerbating the challenge of computing the Impedance and Admittance matrices.

In this work, we discuss the consequences of including the substrate effects in the computation of the impedance matrix while still maintaining analytical solutions [**25**], [**23**]. The overall result is a uniform treatment from infinite wavelengths down to wavelengths comparable to the longitudinal dimensions of the interconnects. Due to lack of space, we give only a brief background of the physics in our approach, concentrating instead on the approximations to the Green's function formulation for the Magnetic Vector Potential of the magnetic field, in the presence of a multi-layered substrate. In particular, we show that the ability to use a linear combination of complex exponentials to approximate the reflection coefficients appearing in the spectral representation of the Green's function, leads to analytical expressions for the Green's function in coordinate space. Furthermore, we find that subsequent manipulations involving multi-dimensional (four to six) integrals involving the Green's function to extract the Impedance matrices can also be carried out analytically by using the initial approximation. The resulting Impedance matrices have less than 3% error when the complex exponential approximations are obtained using a complex extension of VARPRO (discussed in Chapter 1). Alternative methods do not lead to the same level of accuracy [**25**], especially for 3D problems [**23**]. Specialized 3D full electromagnetic field solvers [**1**] at the same level of accuracy are computationally expensive and do not permit us to scale the problem space beyond very simple structures. The computability and accuracy of our approximation method is made possible in part by the presence of accurate and smooth fits with VARPRO using complex coefficients.

9.2. Green's function computations

In digital integrated circuits, the interconnects are laid out along Cartesian directions ($\hat{x} - \hat{y}$) on the different metal layers. Each metal layer has interconnects running along one direction only ($\hat{x}$ or $\hat{y}$), with those on adjacent layers being orthogonal to each other (called Manhattan geometry), and vertical links (called vias) connecting them where needed. The number of wires in a modern high-performance microprocessor chip can be as large as 10^{10}, and the space of possible routes in three dimensions for these wires is quite large. It is necessary to identify the much smaller set of wires whose propagation delay and voltage noise can impair the functionality of the chip as a whole, and to do so we accurately compute their impedance parameters. On-chip interconnects in analog circuits do not always conform to Manhattan geometry and may have arbitrary orientation. This complicates the electromagnetic interaction at the lowest level, since it is computationally a much simpler problem to compute the capacitance and inductance of wires constrained along Cartesian directions. Moreover, while the number of circuit components (and hence, the number of wires) in analog designs is several orders of magnitude smaller than that in digital designs, the desired level of accuracy for impedance calculation of these wires is an order of magnitude higher. As much as 10% error in the electromagnetic parameters for critical wires may be acceptable in digital applications, while an order of magnitude better precision is demanded for passive inductors and transformers used in wireless analog designs. Increasingly common "mixed-signal" designs - digital circuits with several analog components included on the same chip - represent the most demanding scenario in terms of computational complexity, combining the large size of digital designs with the need for high accuracy in sensitive analog circuits.

We are interested in divergence free electromagnetic currents in the interconnects, such that:

$$\begin{aligned} \nabla \cdot \vec{J} &= 0 && \text{in the conductor volume} \\ \nabla \cdot \vec{J} &= -j\omega q && \text{on each conductor surface} \end{aligned} \tag{9.1}$$

where J is the current density, $\omega = 2\pi f$ is the signal frequency, and q is the charge density on the conductor surface. The relaxation time (τ) for free charges in Copper **[6]**:

$$\tau = \epsilon/\sigma \doteq O(10^{-18})\text{seconds}, \tag{9.2}$$

is much smaller than the time constants at the maximum signal frequency $f < 200GHz$, allowing us to neglect the effect of displacement currents inside the conductors.

A signal wire segment carrying rectilinear one-dimensional currents, and one or more nearby parallel power/ground wire segments capacitively coupled to the signal wire, together form our basic representation for a closed current loop. The power/ground wire segments share the current flowing through the signal wire among themselves in a direction opposite to that of the signal current, and are referred to as carriers of the return current, or simply return paths. In terms of the electric circuit for the closed current loop, the signal wire is represented by an impedance in series with the parallel combination of the impedances of all its return paths. The capacitors that couple the return paths to the signal wire can be computed separately with a field solver from the geometric data representing the wires. The collection of an interconnect and its return paths is partitioned along

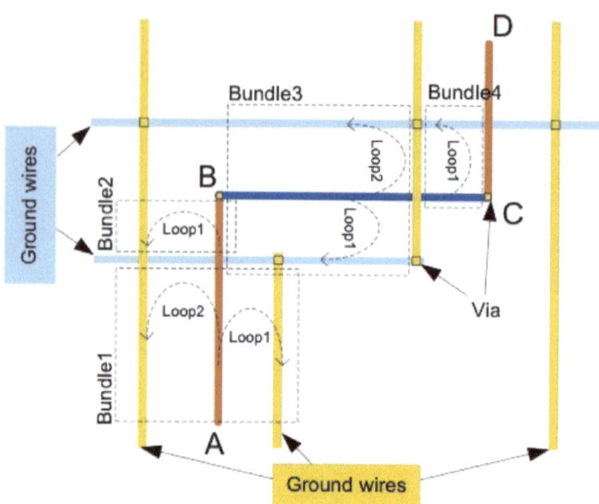

FIGURE 9.2.1. A VLSI interconnect with linear segments *AB*-*BC*-*CD* flanked by ground wires which offer return paths. Segmentation of the interconnect configuration into *bundles*, along with the constituent *loops*, are shown with dashed boxes and curves, respectively.

their length to form "bundles" **[11]** such that all wires in a bundle have the same length. Thus, per-unit-length quantities can be computed for each bundle using a 2D approach. Fig. 9.2.1 illustrates the partition of an interconnect configuration into bundles, and the constituent current loops.

9.2.1. Two-dimensional (2D) interconnect. The previous paragraph described the physical picture of the "current loops" for interconnect impedance computation in digital chips. An alternative to the "loop impedance" computed using this approach **[11]** is the "partial impedance" computed using the Partial Elements Equivalent Circuit (PEEC) approach **[22]**. Under PEEC, every segment of wire is considered independent from all other wire segments, and signal and return paths are not distinguished while building the impedance matrix. The closed path of physical currents is imposed a posteriori during circuit simulation, via the application of Kirchhoff's laws, making all possible paths available when solving the large linear system. Since the long distance behavior of the partial impedance decreases logarithmically with the separation between wire segments, as opposed to the inverse power law behavior of the physical loop impedance **[11]**, the impedance matrix in the PEEC is dense and not diagonally dominant. In the loop impedance formalism, mutual impedances between interconnect loops are appreciable only for separations smaller than ten times their transverse dimensions **[11]** resulting in diagonally dominant sparse impedance matrices. In terms of interconnect length, inductance effects are important when the time of flight for a signal along the interconnect length is comparable to the transition time of the logic driving the signal **[10]**. This requirement translates into wire lengths longer than $100\mu m$ for on-chip interconnects in the nanometer regime. Since the interconnect widths are seldom larger than a few microns, and the transverse separations where mutual impedance is important are equally bounded, it follows that for a substantial number of global

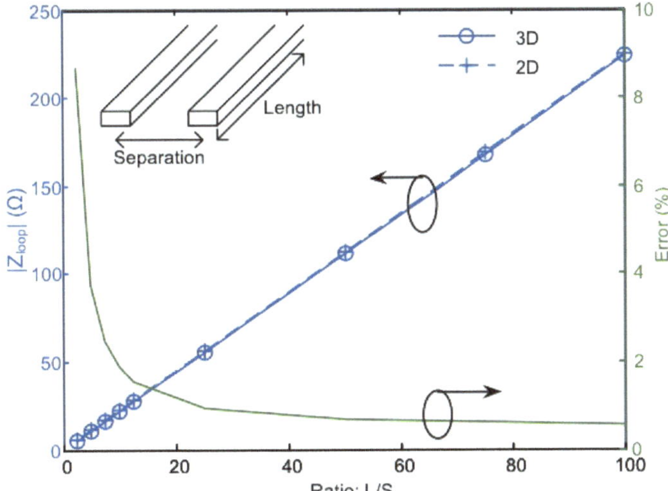

FIGURE 9.2.2. Comparison of 2D loop impedance computation with 3D computation (left y-axis) as a function of the ratio of conductor lengths to transverse separation (L/S), in presence of a 3-layer substrate, at 100 GHz. Error (%) due to the 2D approximation is shown on the right y-axis.

on-chip interconnects a two-dimensional (2D) analysis of electromagnetic effects will suffice.

Fig. 9.2.2 shows that the error in loop impedance when using the 2D approximation is quite small when the conductor lengths exceed 10 times the transverse separations between them.

A physically equivalent representation of a planar current loop is a magnetic dipole [**17**], as shown in Fig. 9.2.3. Since on-chip conductors are confined to discrete metal layers in the x-y plane (neglecting vias which have small dimensions), the current loops they form are planar, although they may have arbitrary orientations (ϕ). For a planar loop carrying current I, its magnetic dipole moment $\vec{p}$ is perpendicular to the plane containing the loop, and its magnitude is given by [**17**]:

$$|\vec{p}| = I \times LoopArea \tag{9.3}$$

Rotational symmetry allows us to choose the y-axis along the length of the wires forming the current loop, and this dimension is omitted in the 2D treatment. $\vec{p}$ has horizontal and vertical components:

$$\vec{p} = p_x\hat{x} + p_z\hat{z} = |\vec{p}|[sin(\phi)\hat{x} + cos(\phi)\hat{z}] \tag{9.4}$$

9.2.2. Integral representation of the 2D Green's function. Consider two opposite currents $I\hat{y}$ and $-I\hat{y}$, centered at (x',z') and separated by an infinitesimal distance a, lying above a multi-layered substrate. The two currents constitute a $\hat{z}$-directed 2D magnetic dipole.

In the region R_0 above the substrate, the corresponding $\hat{y}$-directed vector potential Green's function G_{ver}^{d,R_0} for a $\hat{z}$-directed unitary magnetic dipole source, with

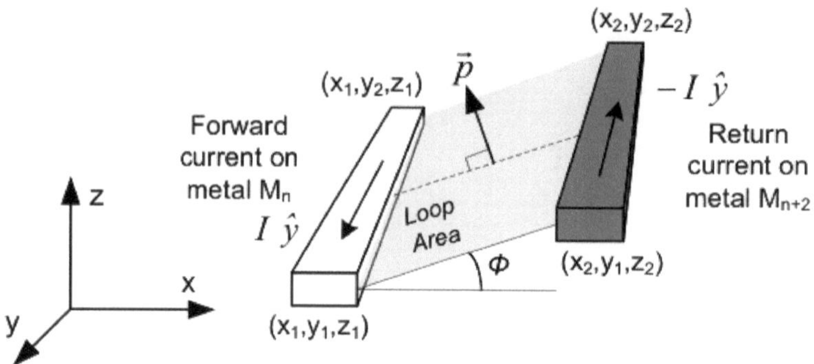

FIGURE 9.2.3. Current loop formed by two parallel current filaments carrying current in opposite directions constitutes a planar magnetic dipole source.

$I \to \infty$ and $a \to 0$ such that the dipole moment $|\vec{p}| = \frac{\mu}{2\pi}(Ia) = 1$, satisfies:

$$\nabla^2 G^{d,R_0}_{ver}(x,z,x',z') = \lim_{a\to 0} \frac{-2\pi}{a}\left[\delta(x-x'+\frac{a}{2})\delta(z-z') - \delta(x-x'-\frac{a}{2})\delta(z-z')\right];z,z'>0 \tag{9.5}$$

Since there are no sources inside the substrate, the Green's function in region R_i satisfies:

$$(\nabla^2 - \gamma_i^2)G^{R_i}(x,z) = 0; z<0 \tag{9.6}$$

where $\gamma_i^2 = j\omega\mu(\sigma_i + j\omega\epsilon_i)$ for the ith substrate layer.

Using the Fourier transform in x and continuity of the magnetic field at the interface boundaries between different regions, we obtain for an N-layer substrate:

$$\begin{aligned} &G^{d,R_0}_{ver}(x,z,x',z') \\ &= -\int_0^\infty \left(e^{-k_x|z-z'|} - \chi_N(k_x)e^{-k_x(z+z')}\right) sin(k_x(x-x'))dk_x; \\ &k_z = jk_x \end{aligned} \tag{9.7}$$

The above dipole Green's function expression is a sum of two terms: a *primary* term corresponding to the magnetic dipole in free space, and a *secondary* term which is nearly identical in form (except for the coefficient χ_N) arising due to reflections at the interfaces in the substrate. While the expressions for the primary and secondary field terms above may vary depending on the source (such as electric or magnetic dipoles), the coefficient χ_N always remains unaltered **[7]**, **[16]**, **[24]**. The Green's function for a horizontal magnetic dipole under the same boundary conditions is:

$$G^{d,R_0}_{hor}(x,z,x',z') = \begin{cases} -\int_0^\infty \left(e^{-k_x|z-z'|} + \chi_N(k_x)e^{-k_x(z+z')}\right) cos(k_x(x-x'))dk_x, & z>z' \\ -\int_0^\infty \left(-e^{-k_x|z-z'|} + \chi_N(k_x)e^{-k_x(z+z')}\right) cos(k_x(x-x'))dk_x, & z<z' \end{cases} \tag{9.8}$$

In general, $\chi_N(k_x)$, the term characterizing the substrate contribution for an N-layer substrate, can be cast into the form:

$$\chi_N(k_x) = \frac{Q_N(k_x) - k_x}{Q_N(k_x) + k_x} \tag{9.9}$$

where the terms $Q_N(k_x)$ depend only on the substrate properties: conductivity σ, permittivity ϵ, permeability μ) of each substrate layer. For the simplest case of a 1-layer substrate (N=*1*) extending to $z = -\infty$ (occupying a half-space),

$$Q_1(k_x) = \sqrt{k_x^2 + \gamma_1^2} \tag{9.10}$$

The quantity $\gamma_1^2 = j\omega\mu(\sigma_1 + j\omega\epsilon_1)$ is determined by the frequency (ω) and substrate properties.

The expressions for $Q_N(k_x)$ become increasingly cumbersome as the number of layers increases. The corresponding expressions for two- and three- layer substrates (the cases most often encountered) are:

$$Q_2(k_x) = m_1 \times \frac{(m_1 + m_2)e^{2m_1 z_1} - (m_1 - m_2)}{(m_1 + m_2)e^{2m_1 z_1} + (m_1 - m_2)} \tag{9.11}$$

$$Q_3(k_x) = m_1 \times \frac{1 - e^{-2m_1 z_1} q(k_x)}{1 + e^{-2m_1 z_1} q(k_x)}, \text{with} \tag{9.12}$$

$$q(k_x) = \frac{\begin{bmatrix} (m_1 + m_2)(m_2 - m_3) + \\ \qquad (m_1 - m_2)(m_2 + m_3)e^{2m_2 z_2} \end{bmatrix}}{\begin{bmatrix} (m_1 - m_2)(m_2 - m_3) + \\ \qquad (m_1 + m_2)(m_2 + m_3)e^{2m_2 z_2} \end{bmatrix}}$$

In (9.11) and (9.12), z_1 refers to the thickness of the top substrate layer and z_2 the thickness of the second substrate layer (in the case of 3-layer substrate) while the last substrate layer extends to $-\infty$. The coefficients m_i, corresponding to the ith substrate layer, are given by:

$$m_i(k_x) = \sqrt{k_x^2 + \gamma_i^2} = \sqrt{k_x^2 + j\omega\mu(\sigma_i + j\omega\epsilon_i)} \tag{9.13}$$

9.2.3. Discrete complex images. As described in the previous sub-section, the dipole Green's function expression is the sum of a *primary* term corresponding to the magnetic dipole source and a *secondary* term arising due to reflections at the interfaces in the substrate. While the primary term by itself is integrable and gives rise to the field of a static magnetic dipole, analytical computation of the entire integral is hampered by the coefficient χ_N. The key for computing the substrate Green's function lies in finding a suitable approximation to χ_N that transforms the secondary term into an analytically integrable form. The Discrete Complex Images Method (DCIM) [**4**], [**16**] is used to approximate χ_N with a linear combination of complex exponentials - an often favored approach for 3D problems:

$$\chi_N(k_x) \approx \sum_{j=1}^{M} b_j e^{c_j k_x} \tag{9.14}$$

Since the exponentials in (9.14) above readily combine with those in the secondary term in (9.7), (9.8), the substrate contribution to the Green's function takes a form identical to that of the source term. The sum of exponentials in (9.14) is interpreted

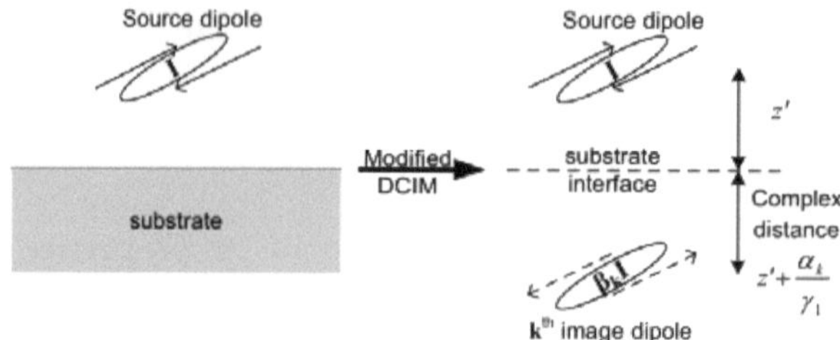

FIGURE 9.2.4. Physical interpretation of Modified Discrete Complex Images Method.

as a series of images of the source magnetic dipole. A challenge in this approach is to find a suitable set of 'complex images', c_j, that gives a sufficiently accurate Green's function in coordinate space. The accuracy requirements are determined a posteriori, with the computation of impedance parameters based on the Green's function. In 2D, the complete integrand of the term containing χ_N is a smooth function of the integration variable, which simplifies the demands for high accuracy in a parameterization of the form (9.14).

We use a simpler search that we motivate here with a new look at the form of the dipole Green's function (G) in the presence of a substrate. For a single-layer substrate, with $Q_1(k_x)$ given by (9.10), we can perform the following algebraic replacement:

$$\begin{aligned}\chi_1(k_x) &= e^{-2\tanh^{-1}\left(k_x/\sqrt{k_x^2+\gamma_1^2}\right)} \\ &= e^{-2\tanh^{-1}\left((k_x/\gamma_1)/\sqrt{1+(k_x/\gamma_1)^2}\right)} = e^{-2\sinh^{-1}\left(\frac{k_x}{\gamma_1}\right)}\end{aligned} \tag{9.15}$$

This alternative functional representation of $\chi_1(k_x)$ naturally leads us to a separation of the coefficient $1/\gamma_1$ in the complex exponent. We preserve this coefficient and search for $\alpha_k \in \mathbb{R}$, and $\alpha_k > 0$ for convergence, while we allow the coefficients β_k to remain complex, thus:

$$\chi_1(k_x) \approx \sum_{k=1}^{K} \beta_k e^{-\alpha_k (k_x/\gamma_1)} \tag{9.16}$$

Pictorially, in (9.16) the kth term represents an image of the dipole current source whose z-coordinate depends on α_k, as shown in Fig. 9.2.4, while the coefficient β_k emulates the fraction of the incident current carried by the kth image. This interpretation results from $\sum_k \beta_k = 1$ - a consequence of $\chi_1(0) = 1$. The analogy for β_k would be exact with the added constraints $\beta_k \in \mathbb{R}$ and $\beta_k \in (0,1)$. However, we do not impose these constraints to get higher accuracy. The detailed results and implications on accuracy of impedance extraction are addressed in more detail in the following section.

Inserting (9.16) into (9.7) and (9.8), results in:

$$
\begin{aligned}
&G_{ver}^{d,R_0}(x,z,z') \\
&\approx -\int_0^\infty \left(\begin{array}{l} e^{-|z-z'|k_x} \\ -\sum_{k=1}^{K} \beta_k e^{-\alpha_k \frac{k_x}{\gamma_1}} e^{-(z+z')k_x} \end{array} \right) \sin(k_x x) dk_x \\
&= -\left[\frac{x}{|z-z'|^2+x^2} - \sum_{k=1}^{K} \left(\beta_k \frac{x}{(z+z'+\frac{\alpha_k}{\gamma_1})^2+x^2} \right) \right]
\end{aligned}
\tag{9.17}
$$

$$
\begin{aligned}
&G_{hor}^{d,R_0}(x,z,z') \\
&\approx -\int_0^\infty \left(\begin{array}{l} e^{-|z-z'|k_x} \\ +\sum_{k=1}^{K} \beta_k e^{-\alpha_k \frac{k_x}{\gamma_1}} e^{-(z+z')k_x} \end{array} \right) \cos(k_x x) dk_x \\
&= -\left[\frac{|z-z'|}{|z-z'|^2+x^2} + \sum_{k=1}^{K} \left(\beta_k \frac{z+z'+\frac{\alpha_k}{\gamma_1}}{(z+z'+\frac{\alpha_k}{\gamma_1})^2+x^2} \right) \right]
\end{aligned}
\tag{9.18}
$$

We extend this restricted search for parameters (α_k, β_k) using (9.16) to 2-layer and 3-layer substrate configurations. Hence, for the general N-layer substrate:

$$
\chi_N(k_x) \approx \sum_{k=1}^{K} \beta_k e^{-\alpha_k (k_x/\gamma_1)} \tag{9.19}
$$

and the expressions (9.17), (9.18) remain valid. The set (α_k, β_k) of parameters only depend on the substrate profile (resistivity, dielectric constant and thickness of each layer) and the frequency of interest. The computation of these parameters constitutes a *one-time cost* for a given technology, at each frequency. We can use alternative fitting strategies, including Matlab's built-in 'fminsearch' and VARPRO, to compute the approximation (9.19).

9.2.4. Three-dimensional (3D) interconnect. When the conditions for a 2D treatment are not satisfied a 3D alternative is required. This is the case for the highly sensitive on-chip inductors which are typically designed as concentric spirals on a single or multiple metal layers. Each inductor forms a single current loop composed of an arrangement of segments electrically composed of several turns in series, with the segments being quite short compared to the wavelength, λ. In addition, the transverse separation between the segments of a loop are of the same order as the length of the segments, while the entire object can be of the order of λ. Such structures necessitate a 3D impedance computation.

9.2.5. Integral representation of the 3D Green's function. In 3D layered media, the Green's function for the vector potential can be written as a second rank tensor. Consider $\bar{\bar{G}}$, whose components are $G_{u,v}$, where u denotes the direction of the dipole source and v the direction of the resultant magnetic vector potential $\vec{A}$. For the three dimensional magnetic dipole formed by two opposite currents $I\hat{y}$ and $-I\hat{y}$, centered at (x',y',z') and separated by an infinitesimal distance a, the magnetic dipole moment is along $\hat{z}$. The $\hat{y}$-directed magnetic vector potential at (x,y,z) in the region above the substrate ($\vec{A}^{d,R_0}_{z,y}$) due to this magnetic dipole, satisfies:

$$\nabla^2 \vec{A}^{d,R_0}_{z,y}(x,y,z,x',y',z') = -\hat{y}\frac{\mu}{2\pi}(Ia)\times\frac{2\pi}{a}\begin{bmatrix}\delta(x-x'+\frac{a}{2})\delta(y-y')\delta(z-z')- \\ \delta(x-x'-\frac{a}{2})\delta(y-y')\delta(z-z')\end{bmatrix}; \quad z,z'>0 \tag{9.20}$$

In the region R_0 above the substrate, the corresponding $\hat{y}$-directed vector potential Green's function $G^{d,R_0}_{z,y}$ for a $\hat{z}$-directed unitary magnetic dipole source, with $I \to \infty$ and $a \to 0$ such that the dipole moment $|\vec{p}| = \frac{\mu}{2\pi}(Ia) = 1$, is:

$$G^{d,R_0}_{z,y}(x,y,z,x',y',z') = \frac{-\mu}{2(2\pi)^2}\times \int_{-\infty}^{\infty}\int_{-\infty}^{\infty}\left(\frac{k_x}{k_z}e^{jk_x(x-x')+jk_y(y-y')}\left(e^{jk_z|z-z'|}+\chi_N(|k_z|)e^{jk_z(z+z')}\right)\right)dk_x dk_y; \quad k_z = j\sqrt{k_x^2+k_y^2} \tag{9.21}$$

9.2.6. 3D Green's function with complex images. While several techniques have been proposed to implement DCIM to approximate the 3D substrate Green's function [4],[8], [12],[19], [27], it has been considered a challenging task [4], [26]. Two features have been widely mentioned in the literature as limitations of the DCIM [4], [5]. The first is the use of uniform sampling rate in the spectral variables k_x, k_y requiring either very fine sampling in k_x, k_y or different DCIM parameterizations, to capture steep variations in the fitted function χ_N for typical multi-layer substrates. The second is its sensitivity to the signal frequency interval.

We found that with the constraint $\alpha_k \in \mathbb{R}$ the impedance computation did not yield accurate results. On relaxing this constraint to allow $\alpha_k \in \mathbb{C}$, we found that the 'fminsearch' algorithm in Matlab did not yield an accurate set of 'complex images'. However, the VARPRO method once extended to the complex domain, yields the desired level of accuracy as shown in Sections 9.4 and 9.5.

The analytical expressions for the 3D vector potential Green's function with complex images are simple to obtain. For example, the y-directed component of the Green's function for a z-directed 3D magnetic dipole in free space is known in closed form [17]:

$$G^{d,free}_{z,y} = \frac{\mu}{4\pi}\frac{(x-x')}{[(x-x')^2+(y-y')^2+(z-z')^2]^{3/2}} \tag{9.22}$$

and the equivalent expression for a 3D magnetic dipole lying above a multi-layer substrate is:

$$\bar{\bar{G}}^{d,sub}(x,y,z,x',y',z') = \bar{\bar{G}}^{d,free}(x,y,z,x',y',z') + \sum_{k=1}^{K}\beta_k \bar{\bar{G}}^{d,free}(x,y,z,x',y',-z'-\frac{\alpha_k}{\gamma_1}) \tag{9.23}$$

9.3. Impedance computations

The Green's functions discussed in the previous section are solutions to the vector potential due to a unit magnitude dipole source located at a point $\vec{r'} = (x', y', z')$. To compute the vector potential at any point $\vec{r} = (x, y, z)$ due to a finite size current loop, we can consider the finite loop as a superposition of infinitesimally small point sources in the area occupied by the current loop, each having a loop area $\frac{1}{2}(dx' \times dy')$ and carrying current I. The co-ordinates of the source (x', y', z') span the rectangular (shaded) area shown in Fig. 9.2.3, whose extremities are defined by (x_1, y_1, z_1), (x_1, y_2, z_1), (x_2, y_1, z_2) and (x_2, y_2, z_2). Expressing the z-coordinate of the source in terms of x' and ϕ: $z_{x'} = z_1 + (x' - x_1)tan(\phi)$, the vector potential at $\vec{r} = (x, y, z)$ due to the finite current loop in free space is given by:

$$\begin{aligned}\vec{A}^{d,free}(x, y, z) \\ = \hat{y}\left(A^{d,free}_{G_{x,y}}(x, y, z) + A^{d,free}_{G_{z,y}}(x, y, z)\right) + \hat{x}A^{d,free}_{G_{z,x}}(x, y, z)\end{aligned} \tag{9.24}$$

where each $A^{d,free}_{G_{u,v}}$ is given by:

$$A^{d,free}_{G_{u,v}}(x, y, z) = \int_{y_1}^{y_2}\int_{x_1}^{x_2} G^{d,free}_{u,v}(x, y, z, x', y', z_{x'})Idx'dy' \tag{9.25}$$

For the particular choice of co-ordinates used here (currents along $\hat{y}$), the term $A^{d,free}_{G_{z,x}} = 0$. As expected, the resultant magnetic vector potential is directed along $\hat{y}$, just as the currents in the source loop. In the presence of a multi-layer substrate, $\bar{\bar{G}}^{d,free}$ in (9.24) must be replaced by $\bar{\bar{G}}^{d,sub}$ from (9.23), which gives:

$$\begin{aligned}\vec{A}^{d,sub}(x, y, z) = \int_{y_1}^{y_2}\int_{x_1}^{x_2} \bar{\bar{G}}^{d,free}(x, y, z, x', y', z_{x'}) \cdot \vec{p}(\vec{r'})dr' \\ + \sum_{k=1}^{K} \beta_k \int_{y_1}^{y_2}\int_{x_1}^{x_2} \bar{\bar{G}}^{d,free}(x, y, z, x', y', z^k_{x'}) \cdot \vec{p}(\vec{r'})dr'\end{aligned} \tag{9.26}$$

where $z^k_{x'} = -(z_1 + \alpha_k/\gamma_1) + (x' - x_1)tan(\phi)$ is the z-coordinate of the kth image dipole, and the angle ϕ is shown in Fig. 9.2.3.

For filament currents, or finite cross-sections with uniform current density, the mutual inductance between the source current loop and a victim conductor is given by:

$$M = \psi/I = \oint_l \vec{A}(\vec{r}) \cdot d\vec{l}/I \tag{9.27}$$

where $d\vec{l}$ is the length vector for an infinitesimal element of the victim conductor, $\vec{r}$ is the position vector for this element, ψ is the magnetic flux generated by the source current integrated over the surface of the victim current. The Stokes theorem is used to express the flux of the magnetic field $\vec{B}$ as the circulation of $\vec{A}$ along the boundary of the victim current and $\vec{l}$ is the contour along the conductor length. For a victim conductor oriented along $\hat{y}$ extending from (x_3, y_3, z_3) to (x_3, y_4, z_3), (9.27) becomes:

$$M^{d,sub}_y = \int_{y_3}^{y_4} \vec{A}^{d,sub}(x_3, y, z_3) \cdot d\hat{y}/I \tag{9.28}$$

All the integrals shown above can be evaluated in closed form.

The exact expressions for $M_{G_{x,y}}^{d,free}$ and $M_{G_{z,y}}^{d,free}$ are:

$$M_{G_{x,y}}^{d,free} = \frac{\mu}{4\pi}\left[\left[\left[M_{G_{z,y}}^{d,free} tan^2(\phi) + q\right]_{y'=y_1}^{y'=y_2}\right]_{x'=x_1}^{x'=x_2}\right]_{y=y_3}^{y=y_4};$$

$$M_{G_{z,y}}^{d,free} = \frac{\mu}{4\pi} cos^2(\phi)$$

$$\times\left[\left[\left[\frac{cos(\phi)}{2}\left(vln|\frac{\sqrt{m^2+v^2}-v}{\sqrt{m^2+v^2}+v}| + 2\sqrt{m^2+v^2}\right) - q\right]_{y'=y_1}^{y'=y_2}\right]_{x'=x_1}^{x'=x_2}\right]_{y=y_3}^{y=y_4};$$

$$q = sin(\phi)\left(z_k cos(\phi) tanh^{-1}\left(\frac{t}{\sqrt{m^2+v^2}}\right) + vtan^{-1}\left(\frac{t}{z_k cos(\phi)}\frac{v}{\sqrt{m^2+v^2}}\right)\right);$$

$$u = x_3 - x'; v = y - y'; z_k = (z_3 - z_1) - (x_3 - x_1)tan(\phi);$$

$$t = usec(\phi) + z_k sin(\phi); m^2 = t^2 + z_k^2 cos^2(\phi) \tag{9.29}$$

In the presence of a multi-layer substrate, the mutual impedance $M_y^{d,sub}$ for a filament (the corresponding procedure for an interconnect comprising multiple filaments is explained in **[25]**) can be reduced to a closed form quadrature when using a linear combination of exponentials on the integrand as in 2D, thus:

$$M_y^{d,sub} = M_{G_{x,y}}^{d,free} + M_{G_{z,y}}^{d,free} + \sum_{k=1}^{K}\beta_k(M_{G_{x,y}}^{d,img} + M_{G_{z,y}}^{d,img}) \tag{9.30}$$

where $M_{G_{x,y}}^{d,img}$ and $M_{G_{z,y}}^{d,img}$ are given by the same expressions as those for $M_{G_{x,y}}^{d,free}$ and $M_{G_{z,y}}^{d,free}$, respectively, with the following modification to (9.29):

$$z_k = (z_3 + z_1 + \alpha_k/\gamma_1) - (x_3 - x_1)tan(\phi) \tag{9.31}$$

The results presented here are sufficient to compute the *mutual* impedance of Manhattan interconnects of filament loops by orienting the co-ordinate axes such that relevant conductors are parallel to $\hat{y}$. We now discuss the changes needed to compute diagonal elements of the impedance matrix, as in computing the *self* inductance of a loop, in which case the victim loop coincides with the source. Since the center-to-center distance between the source and destination points $u = x_3 - x'$ in (9.29) is zero, the self-inductance is computed by replacing the distance $u = x_3 - x' = 0$ with the geometric mean distance (GMD) **[14]** of the conductors. The GMD of a rectangular cross-section conductor with respect to itself is given by $e^{log(w+t)-3/2}$ **[14]**. The self impedance is then given by $Z_{self} = R_{self} + j\omega M_{self}$, where $R_{self} = \rho L(\frac{1}{w_{s_1}t_{s_1}} + \frac{1}{w_{s_2}t_{s_2}})$ is the static resistance of the signal line (s_1) and return path (s_2) of the loop (w_{s_1}, w_{s_2} are widths and t_{s_1}, t_{s_2} are the thicknesses of the conductors).

9.3.1. Non-Manhattan interconnects. Besides Manhattan interconnects, it is of primary interest to compute the impedance of inductors, which may comprise conductor segments inclined at arbitrary angle θ. In this case, we choose a co-ordinate system that aligns the source current loop with $\hat{y}$. For the victim conductor extending from (x_3, y_3, z_3) to (x_4, y_4, z_3), the x-coordinate can be expressed in terms of its y-coordinate as: $x_y = x_3 + (y - y_3)tan(\theta)$. The mutual impedance is then given by (9.32). For conductor loops in the $\hat{x}-\hat{y}$ plane ($\phi = 0$), the integral in (9.32) also leads to closed form quadratures, albeit the resulting expression is too long to be included in this chapter.

$$\begin{aligned}
M_\theta^{d,free} &= \frac{\mu}{4\pi}\int_{y_3}^{y_4} I_y dy; \\
I_y &= cos(\phi)\left[\left[-sinh^{-1}\left(\frac{y-y'}{\sqrt{(x_y-x')^2+(z_3-z_{x'})^2}}\right)\right]_{x'=x_1}^{x'=x_2}\right]_{y'=y_1}^{y'=y_2} \\
&+ sin(\phi)\left[\left[tan^{-1}\left(\frac{(x_y-x')(y-y')(z_3-z_{x'})^{-1}}{\sqrt{(x_y-x')^2+(y-y')^2+(z_3-z_{x'})^2}}\right)\right]_{x'=x_1}^{x'=x_2}\right]_{y'=y_1}^{y'=y_2}; \\
x_y &= x_3+(y-y_3)tan(\theta)
\end{aligned} \tag{9.32}$$

9.4. Least square fits for multi-layer substrates

The modified discrete complex images approximation **[25]**, shown in (9.16), allows us to represent the effect of the substrate as the combined effect of a series of images of the source magnetic dipole. The advantage of this representation is evident from the convenient analytical expressions for mutual impedance shown in the previous section. The accuracy of this approximation is the key element for computing the effect of substrate eddy current effects on interconnect impedance. For simpler 2D interconnect configurations we compute the discrete complex images with $\alpha_k \in \mathbb{R}, \beta_k \in \mathbb{C}$, using Matlab's built-in function 'fminsearch' with reasonable accuracy. In the general 3D case, when the current loops are wide, and the transverse separation of a signal line from its return path is much larger than the height of the interconnects above the substrate, the effect of the substrate is much more pronounced. The need for higher accuracy in such cases dictates that $\alpha_k \in \mathbb{C}$, resulting in a larger set of unknown parameters. In this case, the 'fminsearch' algorithm does not yield good results. The Variable Projections algorithm **[13]**, on the other hand, inherently reduces the number of unknowns in the least square fit and provides a much better approximation with reasonable computation time. The VARPRO algorithm combined with the modified DCIM, which provides a good initial guess for the non-linear parameters in the exponents, extends several desirable properties to the exponential fits as shown below. In the following paragraphs we first describe the basic principle of the VP algorithm and then outline the procedure for obtaining accurate complex image approximations for multi-layer substrates employing this algorithm.

9.4.1. Variable Projection method for non-linear least squares fitting. The search for an accurate set of images (α_k, β_k) for a particular substrate configuration at frequency ω constitutes a non-linear least squares problem - we seek values for α_k and β_k so as to minimize the sum of the squares of the discrepancies between the right and left hand sides of (9.16), for all values of the Fourier transform variable $k_x \in (0, \infty)$. Exact expressions for $\chi_N(k_x)$ (subsequently referred to simply as χ, for conciseness) are known **[25]**, in terms of k_x, for each frequency. Hence, for a set of J observation points in $(0, \infty)$, we have a vector of observations $\{k_{xj}, \chi_j; k_{xj} \in (0, \infty)\}$ as the input data set to the following non-linear least squares problem:

$$min_{\beta,\alpha} \sum_{j=1}^{J} \left[\sum_{k=1}^{K} \left(\beta_k \phi(\alpha_k, k_{xj}) - \chi_j \right)^2 \right] \tag{9.33}$$

α_k and β_k are the parameters to be determined such that the discrepancy of the model $\beta_k\phi(\alpha_k, k_{xj})$ with respect to the complex observations χ_j is minimized.

Since this is a non-linear non-convex problem in general, it can have multiple solutions. Writing the $J \times K$ matrix $\{\phi(\alpha_k, k_{xj}\}$ as $\mathbf{\Phi}$ and the vector of observations $\{\chi_j\}$ as $\mathbf{x}$, the vector residual in (9.33) is concisely represented as:

$$\mathbf{r_2}(\alpha) = \mathbf{\Phi}(\alpha)\beta - \mathbf{x} \tag{9.34}$$

Now, for each fixed value of α, (9.34) is a linear least squares problem, whose solution can be explicitly written as:

$$\beta = \mathbf{\Phi}^{+}(\alpha)\mathbf{x}, \tag{9.35}$$

where $\mathbf{\Phi}^{+}(\alpha)$ is the pseudo-inverse of $\mathbf{\Phi}$. Replacing this expression in (9.33), the original non-linear least squares problem becomes:

$$min_{\alpha} \| \left[\mathbf{I} - \mathbf{\Phi}(\alpha)\mathbf{\Phi}^{+}(\alpha) \right] \mathbf{x} \| \tag{9.36}$$

Since $I - \Phi(\alpha)\Phi^{+}(\alpha) = P^{\dagger}_{\Phi(\alpha)}$ is the projector on the subspace orthogonal to the column space of Φ, (9.36) has been called the Variable Projection (VP) functional. An obvious gain by this procedure, as opposed to the initial problem, is a reduction in the number of variables, since the linear parameters (β_k) have been eliminated from the problem.

9.4.2. Complex images using Variable Projection algorithm. The VP algorithm described above is applied to solve the non-linear least squares problem to determine the complex images in terms of the best fit parameters α_k and β_k. We allow values $(\alpha_k, \beta_k) \in \mathbb{C}$. To ensure a good fit, the VP algorithm naturally satisfies the requirements that $Re(\alpha_k) > 0$ (for convergence) and $\sum_k \beta_k = 1$ (which is a property of the input data, χ). Fig. 9.4.1 shows the fits for a single layer $(N = 1)$ substrate. Before the VP algorithm is applied to solve the non-linear least squares problem, two choices must be made: the number of exponentials (K) in the model (the number of complex images), and the initial values for the non-linear parameters α_k.

In general, increasing the number of images improves the accuracy of the approximation, while simultaneously increasing the cost of computation. However, we find that the choice of initial values for the parameters α_k has a much greater bearing on the accuracy of the approximation than the number of images. As explained in the previous sub-section, the Variable Projection method eliminates the need to guess initial values for the linear parameters β_k. We are interested in complex image representations of the substrate over a wide range of frequencies (20-100 GHz). Since we expect from the modified DCIM that the exponential parameters lie in the vicinity of the complex number $1/\gamma_1$ **[25]**, we start at one end of the frequency spectrum (say 100 GHz) using random values between 0 and 1 as initial guesses for α_k. The best fit values for α_k obtained from the VP algorithm at this frequency are used as the initial guess for an adjacent frequency point. Since

χ is a smooth function of ω, the best fit values for α_k obtained from the VP algorithm at this frequency provide a good initial guess for the parameters at the next adjacent frequency, as long as the next frequency point is close enough to the first. This strategy of "continuation" in frequency is applied progressively over the entire frequency range of interest. If the desired level of accuracy is not achieved for all frequency points, this process should be repeated across the frequency range by choosing as initial values the parameters at the frequency point with minimum residual error. This procedure is summarized in Figure 9.4.2.

The residual errors and the computation time to perform the fit (9.19) is shown in Fig. 9.4.3, as a function of the number of complex images. Our algorithm results in a fit that is smooth as a function of frequency, in terms of the residual error of the fit (Fig. 9.4.4). Finally, Fig. 9.4.5 shows the error in the Green's function computation using the simplified discrete complex images approximation, for a large number of randomly generated technology parameters.

9.5. Impedance computation results

In this section, we show results of the impedance extraction method that incorporates the discrete complex images for a multi-layer substrate computed using the VARPRO algorithm. Through comparisons with electromagnetic field solvers, we demonstrate the accuracy as well as computational efficiency of the proposed method.

9.5.1. 2D interconnect structures. Fig. 9.5.1(a) plots the self-impedance and the mutual impedance of two conductor loops on different metal layers with a vertical separation of $1\mu m$, while Fig. 9.5.1(b) plots the error in the computation with respect to the magneto-quasi-static (MQS) electromagnetic field solver FastHenry [**18**]. The dashed lines in Fig. 9.5.1(b) show the significant error in impedance if the substrate were to be neglected - as much as 20% at 100 GHz. It is found that the proposed method captures the effect of the substrate on interconnect impedance with high accuracy (solid lines show errors less than 2%) in the entire frequency range of interest for digital circuits. Note that in this and

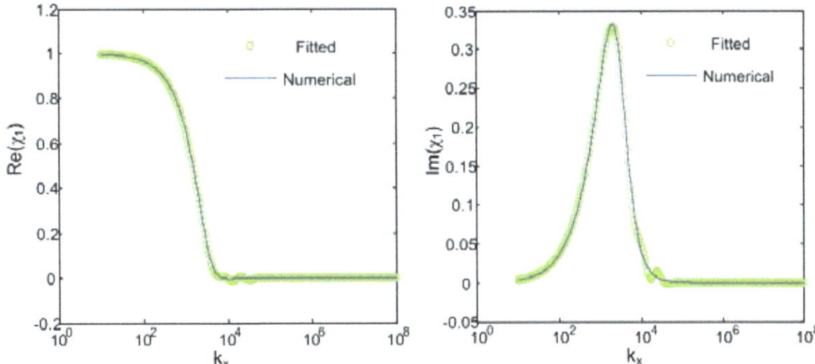

FIGURE 9.4.1. Approximation of the Real and Imaginary parts of χ_1 using our exponential fits with $K = 20$, for a single-layer substrate $\rho = 1 Ohm - cm$, in comparison with numerical computation.

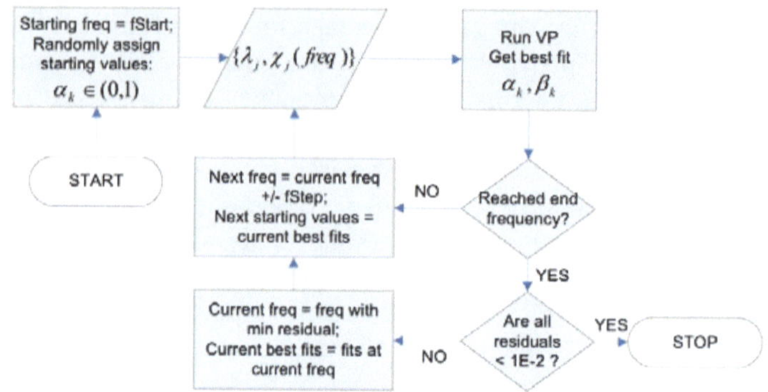

FIGURE 9.4.2. Algorithm flowchart for computing complex images approximation using Variable Projections.

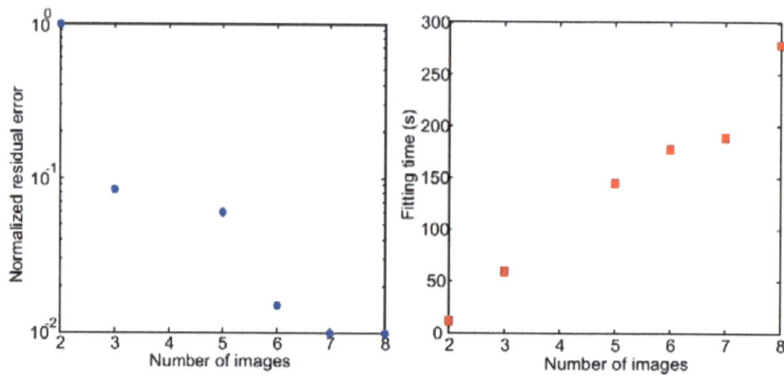

FIGURE 9.4.3. (a) Residual error (normalized to the error using 2 images), and (b) computation time, as a function of the number of complex images, for a 1-layer substrate at one frequency point (90 GHz).

all subsequent experiments, the conductors are always discretized into filaments to capture non-uniform current distribution within the conductors.

We now compare the network Z-parameter (Z_{in}) for a conductor loop, to that obtained from the commercial full-wave field solver, HFSS [**1**]. The Z_{in} parameter is computed by using a Spice distributed transmission line model, wherein the resistance and inductance per unit length are computed by using our method, and the capacitance is obtained from FastCap [**20**]. The geometry simulated with HFSS is shown in Fig. 9.5.2 (inset).[2] The results of the comparison are shown in Fig. 9.5.2. The maximum error observed in the magnitude of Z_{in} for this configuration is less than 2%. Note that for frequencies beyond 60 GHz the results from HFSS become unstable for the configuration shown.

---

[2] The conductor loop is closed by including additional metal strips at the far and near ends of the loop. The effect of the additional metal is insignificant since the length of the conductors is much larger than the transverse separation between them. A small gap ($0.2\mu m$) is left at the near end where a lumped port excites the conductor loop.

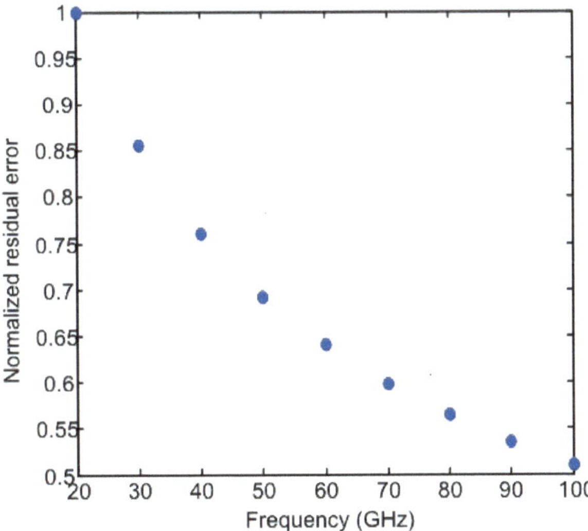

FIGURE 9.4.4. Residual error (normalized to the error at 20 GHz) in the sum of complex exponentials fit for a 3-layer substrate with 5 complex images, as a function of frequency.

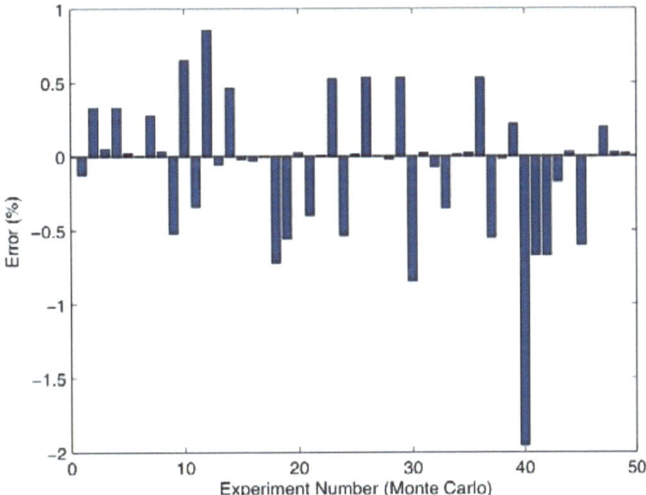

FIGURE 9.4.5. Error in the co-ordinate space representation of the dipole Green's function computation using 5 images, with respect to numerical computation for a 3-layer substrate. Monte Carlo simulations are done for: frequency 20 to 100 GHz, z-separation 0.5 to 1.0 μm, x-separation 0.5 to 10 μm.

Fig. 9.5.3 shows a long Manhattan wire with orthogonal segments running on adjacent metal layers M10 and M11, along with a regular grid of ground wires. Each segment of the signal line is routed in close proximity to a segment of the ground

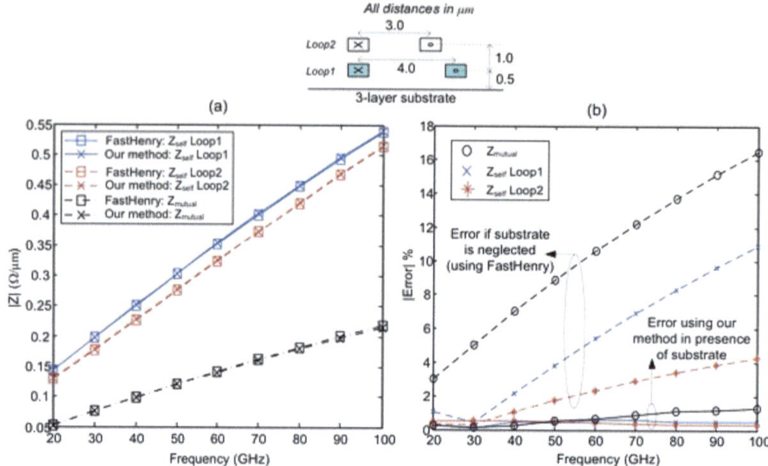

FIGURE 9.5.1. (a) Self and mutual impedance for two conductor loops lying on different metal layers above the three-layer substrate, as a function of frequency. (b) % error in magnitude of impedance using our method in comparison with FastHenry (solid lines), and the error in impedance if the substrate was to be neglected (dashed lines).

grid on the corresponding metal layer - a common design for timing-critical global interconnects to control inductive effects. The mutually perpendicular segments of the Manhattan wire are decoupled (for example, segments AB and BC). On the other hand, the mutual impedance between far apart parallel segments AB-CD (or between BC-DE) can be neglected because of the large separation ($100\mu m - 200\mu m$) between them. Hence, we can separately apply our approach to each linear segment (AB, BC, CD and DE, respectively) to obtain the impedance of the Manhattan wire. As shown in Fig. 9.5.3 our results have a maximum error about 2% over the entire frequency range of interest.

Further experiments using Monte-Carlo simulations for a large number of randomly generated interconnect geometries for global wires at the 45 nm node **[2]** over a wide range of frequencies show a maximum error of 2.3% (Fig. 9.5.4).

With prevalent methods for interconnect impedance computation that are based on the free space Green's function, for example FastHenry, the substrate layers must be included as explicit conductors. At relevant high frequencies, these layers must also be discretized into a large number of filaments (in addition to the interconnects) to capture the substrate eddy currents for a general interconnect configuration. The use of such methods is thus limited to relatively small structures such that the size of the resulting linear system including the multi-layer substrate does not overwhelm available memory. Our method for impedance computation is based on analytical expressions for the substrate Green's function, wherein the substrate boundary conditions are implicit. The only filaments that need to be considered in the solution are those corresponding to the interconnects themselves.

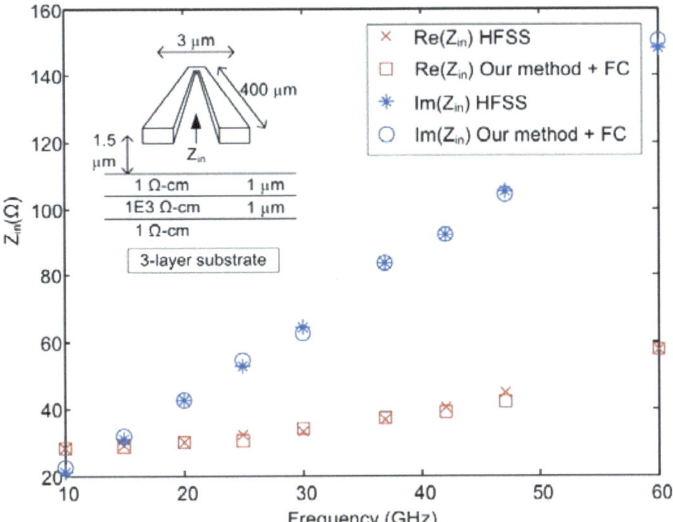

FIGURE 9.5.2. Impedance (Z_{in}) of the one-port network formed by a closed conductor loop (shown in inset) above a 3-layer substrate, compared with HFSS [**1**]. The indexmagneto-quasi-static magneto-quasi-static impedance obtained using our method is combined with capacitance from FastCap (FC) [**20**] using a transmission line model in Spice to obtain the Z_{in} parameter. Conductor width $1\mu m$, thickness $0.5\mu m$, each sub-divided into 15 filaments for impedance computation.

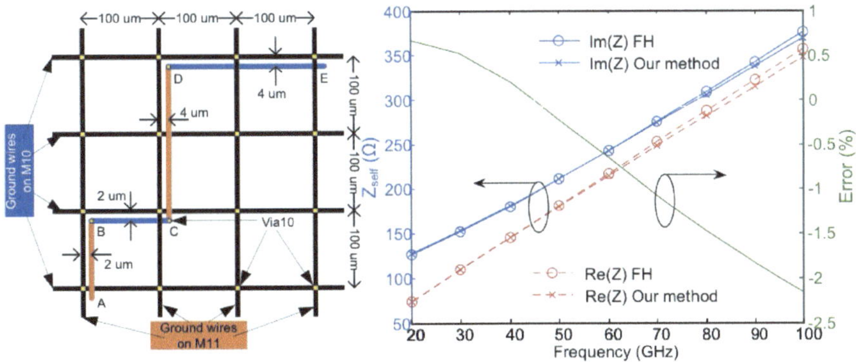

FIGURE 9.5.3. Impedance of a Manhattan interconnect laid out on metal layers M10 (blue) and M11 (orange) above a 3-layer substrate. A grid of ground wires provides nearby return paths to each wire segment. Interconnect geometry parameters are as per global wires at the 45 nm node [**2**].

Fig. 9.5.4(b) shows the speedup in self-impedance computation using our method with respect to a standard MQS computation where the substrate is represented using 2D filaments, as observed from Monte-Carlo simulations on a large

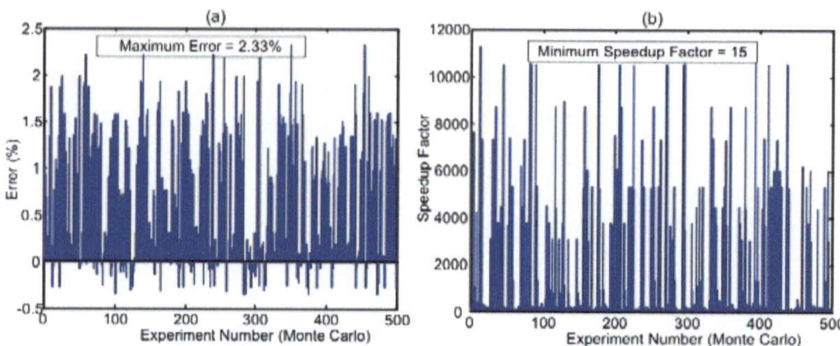

FIGURE 9.5.4. (a) Error in loop self impedance computation with respect to FastHenry, and (b) speedup in runtime with respect to a MQS computation with the substrate represented as 2D filaments, during Monte Carlo simulation of several randomly generated conductor configurations according to the following parameters: Frequency 20-100 GHz, pitch 2-8 μm, wire width 1-2 μm, height above substrate 1.5-2.2 μm (corresponding to metal layers M10 through M12). Interconnect geometry parameters correspond to global wires at the 45 nm node [**2**].

number of randomly selected interconnect geometries. In these experiments, our method is found to be at least 15 times faster. In the 2D MQS computation, the substrate must be discretized into a sufficient number of thin filaments so as to ensure that the filament cross-sections are smaller than the skin depth at the specified frequency. As a result, when the thickness of the low-resistivity top layer of the substrate increases to a few μm [**3**], the computation cost increases substantially due to the larger number of filaments required. On the other hand, with our method a change in the substrate layer thickness only demands evaluation of a new set of substrate images while the impedance computation cost remains constant. As a result, Table 1 shows orders of magnitude improvement in computational efficiency by using the analytical Green's functions.

9.5.2. 3D interconnect structures. Fig. 9.5.5(a) shows the computation for a single-turn square inductor configuration composed of two orthogonal loops ($loop-x$ and $loop-y$, shaded with different colors). In this case, the net impedance Z of the square is given by a series combination of the two loops. Note that orthogonal loops have no mutual impedance. The results are plotted separately for the real and imaginary parts of Z. As frequency increases, the deviation in the plots with and without the substrate shows the significance of the substrate eddy current effects. Our computation agrees well with FastHenry over the entire frequency range, with a maximum error in $|Z|$ of less than 2%.

To compare our results with the input impedance for the interconnect structure obtained from the full-wave field solver HFSS [**1**], the capacitance (frequency independent) is extracted separately using FastCap [**20**]. Fig. 9.5.5(b) shows the network input impedance (Z_{in}) for the single-turn square inductor (found by simulating the circuit shown using HSPICE®), in comparison with the result obtained

TABLE 1. Computation cost for self impedance extraction of a 2-conductor loop over a 500μm wide 3-layer substrate, each conductor 1μm wide and 0.5μm thick, at 100 GHz. Substrate profile is shown in Fig. 9.5.2. z_1: thickness of top substrate layer; F_{cond}: number of filaments per conductor; F_{sub}: number of filaments for substrate; T_i: time to compute images (one time cost); T_Z: time to compute impedance.

z_1	Substrate representation	F_{cond}	F_{sub}	T_i (s)	T_Z (s)
1μm	2D filaments	15	1323	-	110.2
	Analytical Green's function	15	0	90.6	$<$ 1 sec
2μm	2D filaments	15	1952	-	313.7
	Analytical Green's function	15	0	107.1	$<$ 1 sec
3μm	2D filaments	15	2581	-	821.5
	Analytical Green's function	15	0	166.9	$<$ 1 sec
4μm	2D filaments	15	3829	-	2816
	Analytical Green's function	15	0	75.2	$<$ 1 sec
5μm	2D filaments	15	4468	-	4522
	Analytical Green's function	15	0	146.8	$<$ 1 sec

from HFSS. In this case, the maximum error in $|Z|$ is less than 3%, with some discrepancy in the real part of Z beyond 60 GHz due to corner effects not incorporated in our method, and the MQS approximation.

The time taken for relevant parts of the impedance computation are shown in Fig. 9.5.6. Evidently, our code takes a fraction of the time taken by FastHenry for the MQS computation, This is despite the fact that FastHenry uses an accelerated method with $O(NlogN)$ complexity for solving the linear system, while we use a direct method with $O(N^3)$ complexity. This leaves significant room for further improvement in runtime by the use of accelerated methods to solve the linear system, although these are not discussed here. In comparison with the full-wave field solver, our method gives almost an order of improvement in runtime for impedance computation at each frequency point (not including the runtime for calculating the complex images corresponding to the substrate profile once per technology generation, capacitance extraction once per interconnect geometry, and for HSPICE® simulation to compute Z_{in}).

Fig. 9.5.7 shows the impedance computation for a 3-turn spiral inductor, where each turn is a square. In this case, the self impedance of each turn is computed as explained in Fig. 9.5.5(a). In addition, the mutual impedance between all the turns need also be considered. The mutual impedance computation between parallel two-conductor loops has been derived in Section 9.3, while the mutual impedance between perpendicular loops is zero.

Finally, Fig. 9.5.8 shows the impedance of a 3-turn spiral inductor where each turn is an octagon. In this case, each octagon is composed of four loops: one each oriented along $\hat{x}$ and $\hat{y}$, and two others inclined at 45° angles to each of these. While the mutual inductance between mutually orthogonal loops is zero, that between inclined loops must be computed as per (9.32). The maximum error in computing the magnitude of impedance $|Z|$ for this inductor using our method is 3% with respect to FastHenry.

9.6. Conclusions

In this chapter we have analyzed a computational problem of significant relevance to the analog integrated circuit design community. For wireless chips used in automotive sensors, digital radios and other high frequency devices, great care is needed to design accurate multiple inductor structures that show up in low noise amplifiers and other design components. The palette of tools available to the designer are three-dimensional Finite Element (time domain or frequency domain) electromagnetic solvers, whose capacity and CPU cost limit the broadband simulations of critical passive components. We have presented a system level approach based on analytical expressions for filling up the impedance matrix of the system for a broadband spectrum extending from near DC to 100 GHz. In doing so, we have restricted our attention to the most significant and computationally most expensive phenomena - those associated with the multi-layer substrate in the upper part of the frequency spectrum. We have demonstrated that the extension of VARPRO to complex non-linear parameters permits accurate fits of the reflexion coefficients for complex layered substrate configurations that are common in Silicon-based nanometer integrated circuit technologies. The fits involve a linear combination of complex exponentials with a small number of non-linear parameters. The fits at different frequencies involve solving separate non-linear optimization problems.

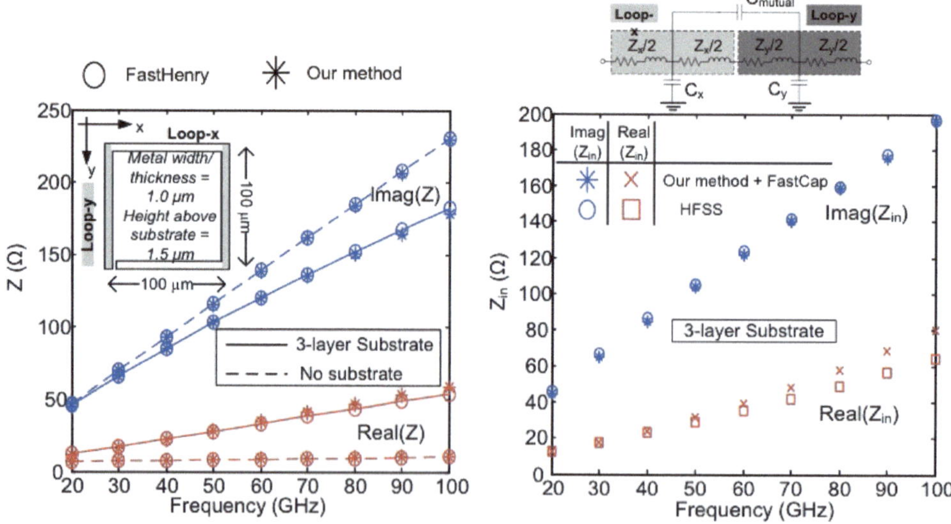

FIGURE 9.5.5. (a) Impedance of a single-turn square inductor as a function of frequency, with (solid lines) and without (dashed lines) the substrate, in comparison with FastHenry. (b) Input impedance network parameter Z_{in} for a square interconnect loop above a 3-layer substrate, as a function frequency, in comparison with HFSS **[1]**. Z_{in} is computed from the equivalent circuit shown above, using Spice, where the impedance (R, L parameters) are computed using our method and the capacitance elements are obtained from FastCap **[20]**. Substrate profile is the same as in Fig. 9.5.2.

	Full wave	MQS: R/L			
	HFSS	FH	Our method	Populating [Z]	Solving linear system
Time (s)	1230	927	146	8 s	138 s

FIGURE 9.5.6. Time taken for MQS impedance computation using FastHenry and our method, and full-wave computation using HFSS, at 100 GHz, for the example shown in Fig. 9.5.5. For our method, the time taken for the two steps - populating the impedance matrix and solving the corresponding linear system - is also shown separately.

The smoothness of the solution space, as indicated in Figures 9.4.3(a) and 9.4.4, guarantees the robustness of the approach. The chosen functional form ensures a

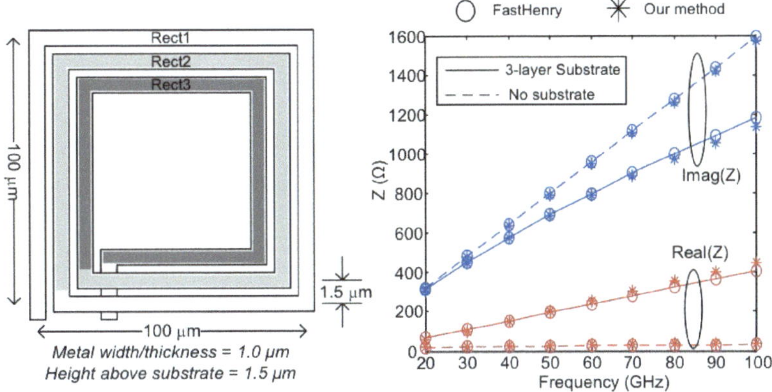

FIGURE 9.5.7. Impedance of a three-turn square inductor as a function of frequency, with and without substrate, in comparison with FastHenry. Substrate profile is the same as in Fig. 9.5.2.

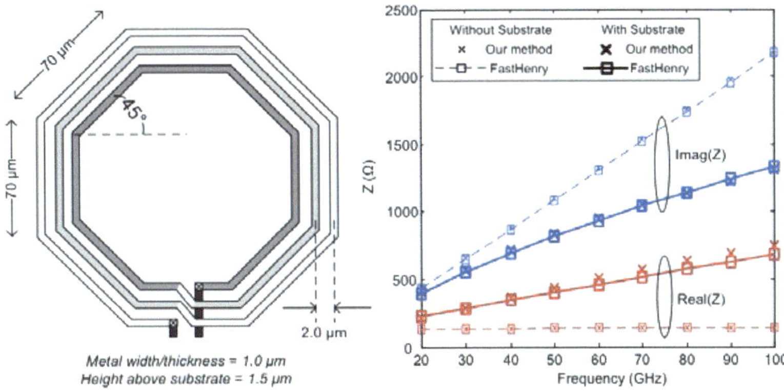

FIGURE 9.5.8. Impedance of a three-turn octagonal inductor as a function of frequency, with and without substrate, in comparison with FastHenry. Substrate profile is the same as in Fig. 9.5.2.

closed-form solution for the impedance matrix, which is related to the initial fit through a two-dimensional Fourier transform followed by a three dimensional integral over the coordinates of the conductors. It is altogether remarkable that for the physical conductors with rectangular cross sections and otherwise complex geometrical paths, as in for example in the case of general planar inductors, one can reduce the overall result to tractable analytical computations. The computational advantage of this analytical method over an electromagnetic field solver is evident from the analysis of Manhattan and non-Manhattan interconnects and inductors. From an accuracy perspective, the relatively lower sensitivity of impedance of two-dimensional structures to the accuracy of the fits for the reflection coefficient allows the use of simpler fitting algorithms than VARPRO. However, for three-dimensional structures where the sensitivity of the impedance to the accuracy of the reflection coefficient fits is large, VARPRO plays an important role in achieving the requisite levels of accuracy that cannot be achieved using alternative methods. With the increasing demand for complex wireless applications beyond 60 GHz frequency based on Silicon technologies, our efficient and accurate method offers a valuable solution for enabling designs in this frequency domain.

Bibliography

1. *User's Guide: HFSS v10.0*, Ansoft Corporation, 2005.
2. *http://www.itrs.net/reports.html*, ITRS, 2007.
3. *http://www.soitec.com/en/products/*, SOITEC, 2008.
4. M.I. Aksun, *A robust approach for the derivation of closed-form Green's functions*, IEEE Transactions on Microwave Theory and Techniques **44** (1996), no. 5, 651–658.
5. M.I. Aksun and G. Dural, *Clarification of issues on the closed-form Green's function in stratified media*, IEEE Transactions on Antennas and Propagation **53** (2005), no. 11, 3644–3653.
6. M. Born and E. Wolf, *Principles of Optics: Electromagnetic Theory of Propagation, Interference and Diffraction of Light*, Cambridge University Press, 1999.
7. W.C. Chew, *Waves and Fields in Inhomogeneous Media*, IEEE Press, New York, 1995.
8. Y.L. Chow, J.J. Yang, and G.E. Howard, *Complex images for electrostatic field computation in multilayered media*, IEEE Transactions on Microwave Theory and Techniques **39** (1991), no. 3, 1120–1125.
9. L. Daniel, *Simulation and Modeling Techniques for Signal Integrity and Electromagnetic Interference on High Frequency Electronic Systems*, Ph.D. thesis, University of California, Berkeley, CA, 2003.
10. A. Deutsch, G. Kopcsay, P. Restle, H. Smith, G. Katopis, W. Becker, P. Coteus, C. Surovic, B. Rubin, R.P.Jr Dunne, T. Gallo, K. Jenkins, L. Terman, R. Dennard, G. Sai-Halasz, B. Krauter, and D. Knebel, *When are transmission-line effects important for on-chip interconnections?*, IEEE Transactions on Microwave Theory and Techniques **45** (1997), no. 10, 1836–1846.
11. R. Escovar, S. Ortiz, and R. Suaya, *An improved long distance treatment for mutual inductance*, IEEE Transactions on Computer-Aided Design of Integrated Circuits and Systems **24** (2005), no. 5, 783–793.
12. D.G. Fang, J.J. Yang, and G.Y. Delisle, *Discrete image theory for horizontal electric dipoles in a multilayered medium*, IEE Proceedings H **135** (1988), no. 5, 297–303.
13. G. Golub and V. Pereyra, *The differentiation of pseudo-inverses and nonlinear least squares problems whose variables separate*, SIAM Journal on Numerical Analysis **10** (1973), no. 2, 413–432.
14. F.W. Grover, *Inductance Calculations: Working Formulas and Tables*, Dover, New York, U.S.A., 1962.
15. R. Ho, K.W. Mai, and M.A. Horowitz, *The future of wires*, Proceedings of the IEEE **89** (2001), no. 4, 490–504.
16. Xin Hu, *Full Wave Analysis of Large Conductor Systems Over Substrates*, Ph.D. thesis, MIT, Cambridge, MA, 2006.
17. J.D. Jackson, *Classical Electrodynamics*, Wiley, New York, U.S.A., 1975.
18. M. Kamon, M.J. Tsuk, and J.K. White, *FastHenry: A multi-pole accelerated 3-D inductance extraction program*, IEEE Transactions on Microwave Theory and Techniques **42** (1994), no. 9, 1750–1758.
19. F. Ling and J.-M. Jin, *Discrete complex image method for Green's functions of general multilayered media*, IEEE Microwave and Guided Wave Letters **10** (2000), no. 10, 400–402.
20. K. Nabors and J. White, *FastCap: A multipole accelerated 3-D capacitance extraction program*, IEEE Transactions on Computer-Aided Design of Integrated Circuits and Systems **10** (1991), no. 11, 1447–1459.
21. S. Ortiz, , Ph.D. thesis, Universite Joseph Fourier, Grenoble, France, 2007.

22. A.E. Ruehli, *Inductance calculations in a complex integrated circuit environment*, IBM Journal of Research and Development **16** (1972), no. 5, 470–481.
23. N. Srivastava, R. Suaya, and K. Banerjee, *Efficient 3D high-frequency impedance extraction for general interconnects and inductors above a layered substrate*, Design Automation and Test in Europe (DATE), 2010 (in press).
24. N. Srivastava, R. Suaya, and K. Banerjee, *High-frequency mutual impedance extraction of VLSI interconnects in the presence of a multi-layer conducting substrate*, Design Automation and Test in Europe (DATE), 2008, 426–431.
25. N. Srivastava, R. Suaya, and K. Banerjee, *Analytical expressions for high-frequency VLSI interconnect impedance extraction in the presence of a multilayer conductive substrate*, IEEE Transactions on Computer-Aided Design of Integrated Circuits and Systems **28** (2009), no. 7, 1047–1060.
26. M.E. Yavuz, M.I. Aksun, and G. Dural, *Critical study of the problems in discrete complex image method*, IEEE International Symposium on Electromagnetic Compatibility, 2003, 1281–1284.
27. M. Yuan, T.K. Sarkar, and M. Salazar-Palma, *A direct discrete complex image method from the closed-form Green's functions in multilayered media*, IEEE Transactions on Microwave Theory and Techniques **54** (2006), no. 3, 1025–1032.

INDEX

www.ingramcontent.com/pod-product-compliance
Lightning Source LLC
LaVergne TN
LVHW070118110826
845147LV00002B/149

* 9 7 8 1 6 0 8 0 5 3 4 5 2 *